THE THEOLOGIES
OF THE EUCHARIST
IN THE EARLY
SCHOLASTIC PERIOD

THE THEOLOGIES OF THE EUCHARIST IN THE EARLY SCHOLASTIC PERIOD

A Study of the Salvific Function of the Sacrament according to the Theologians *c.*1080–*c.*1220

GARY MACY

To Keith, the inspiration behind my interest in the Middle Age, a great scholar, a great human being. I can never thank you enough. Gary

CLARENDON PRESS · OXFORD
1984

Oxford University Press, Walton Street, Oxford OX2 6DP

London New York Toronto
Delhi Bombay Calcutta Madras Karachi
Kuala Lumpur Singapore Hong Kong Tokyo
Nairobi Dar es Salaam Cape Town
Melbourne Auckland

and associated companies in
Beirut Berlin Ibadan Mexico City Nicosia

Oxford is a trade mark of Oxford University Press

Published in the United States
by Oxford University Press, New York

British Library Cataloguing in Publication Data
Macy, Gary
The theologies of the Eucharist in the
early scholastic period.
1. Lord's Supper—History
I. Title
264'.36'09   BV823
ISBN 0-19-826669-3

Library of Congress Cataloging in Publication Data
Macy, Gary.
The theologies of the Eucharist in the early
scholastic period.
Bibliography: p.
Includes index.
1. Lord's Supper—History—Middle Ages, 600-1500.
I. Title.
BV823.M36 1984   234'.163'09021   83-22015
ISBN 0-19-826669-3

Set by DMB (Typesetting), Oxford
and printed in Great Britain
at the Alden Press, Oxford

To
my Mother
and Father

PREFACE

WHILE taking full credit for its substance, I am obliged to many people for the help and support provided me during the research and writing of this work. First and foremost, I wish to thank Professor David Luscombe who supervised the doctoral thesis from which this present work has evolved. His calm and scholarly approval and reproval provided the constant focus to this work in all its many stages.

I would also like to thank Professor Christopher Brooke, who along with Professor Luscombe, provided invaluable comment and correction to the first draft of the present volume. Of the many other scholars who offered guidance and suggestions during the development of this book, I should particularly like to acknowledge my indebtedness to Miss Beryl Smalley, Dr Margaret Gibson, Professor Nicholas Lash, Dr Keith Egan, Professor Walter Principe, and Mr Joseph Gallen.

Of the many libraries used in the course of this work, I would like to thank the librarians of the Cambridge University Library, the Biblioteca Gregoriana, and the libraries of Gonville and Caius, Jesus, and Sidney Sussex Colleges of the University of Cambridge for often going out of their way to provide me with manuscripts or other rare material. The Copley Library of the University of San Diego deserves special thanks for their unfailing ability to fulfil the obscure requests I put to its staff for inter-library loan materials.

I also wish to thank the University of San Diego for a faculty research grant which greatly aided in the gathering of research materials.

Finally I would like to thank Ms Susan McGill and Ms Mary Nuesca who aided me in the final preparation of the manuscript, and Mr Paul DiPietro who helped prepare the indexes.

CONTENTS

ABBREVIATIONS

BGPTMA Beiträge zur Geschichte der Philosophie und Theologie des Mittelalters. Texte und Untersuchungen.

DHGE *Dictionnaire d'histoire et de géographie ecclésiastique.* A. Baudrillart *et al.* (eds.), Paris, 1912-

DSAM *Dictionnaire de spiritualité ascétique et mystique. Doctrine et histoire.* M. Viller *et al.* (eds.), Paris, 1932-

DTC *Dictionnaire de théologie catholique contenant l'exposé des doctrines de la théologie catholique. Leurs preuves et leur histoire.* A. Vacant *et al.* (eds.), 15 vols., Paris, 1909-50.

LThK *Lexikon für Theologie und Kirche.* Michael Buchberger (ed.), 10 vols. plus index, Freiburg, 1957-65.

Mansi Giovanni Domenico Mansi. *Sacrorum conciliorum nova, et amplissima collectio.* 31 vols., Florence and Venice, 1757-98. Reprinted and continued by L. Petit and J. B. Martin. 53 vols. in 60, Paris, 1889-1927.

MGH *Monumenta Germaniae historica*, Berlin, 1826-

NCE *New Catholic Encyclopedia.* William J. McDonald *et al.* (eds.), 14 vols. plus index, New York, St. Louis, San Francisco, Toronto, London, and Sydney, 1967.

PL *Patrologiae cursus completus . . . Series latina.* Jacques Paul Migne (ed.), 217 vols. plus indices, Paris, 1878-90.

RThAM *Recherches de théologie ancienne et médiévale.* Louvain, 1929-

INTRODUCTION

OVER fifty years have passed since Joseph de Ghellinck provided a guide to the wealth of the twelfth-century literature dealing with the early scholastic theology of the Eucharist.[1] Yet this same article, itself essentially a propaedeutic to further study, remains the only general introduction to the early scholastic theology of the sacrament.[2] Although articles regularly appear dealing with the eucharistic theology of individual early scholastic theologians, only a very few scholars have attempted to deal with this material as a whole.

One of the main reasons why the abundance of materials dealing with the Eucharist during this period remains largely ignored by modern scholarship may well be the rather dismal place to which the more general modern studies on the sacrament have condemned the early scholastic period. These studies, beginning with the de Ghellinck article, refer to the early scholastic theology of the Eucharist as fumbling attempts to anticipate the teaching of Lateran IV and of Thomas Aquinas in the thirteenth century, by means of a logical and mechanical refinement of the teaching of Lanfranc in the eleventh century.

Dr Ghellinck certainly viewed the period in these terms. The introduction to his discussion of the eucharistic theology of the twelfth century begins:

For the history of the theology of the Eucharist, the twelfth century constitutes a period of transition during which the intrinsic value of the works cannot be measured by the interest which they arouse in our own time. They wrote much, they discussed no less. But the writings and discussion scarcely rise above the level of trial studies or tentative advances: imprecision of language, inexactitude of expression, tentativeness of research, vacillation of thought; all of these things place their achievements well short of the perfection of the following century.[3]

For de Ghellinck, the twelfth-century study of the Eucharist had value only in the light of its contribution to the terminology of the Fourth Lateran Council and later thirteenth-century writers, and he leaves little doubt that the particular terminology to which he refers centres on the question of 'transubstantiation'.[4]

A. J. MacDonald, in his study of the Berengarian controversy, reiterates the approach of de Ghellinck when he treats of the twelfth-century writers:

The idea of 'the thing of the sacrament' as a real presence, and the doctrine of Transubstantiation as the mode of the sacramental change, were admitted to be the orthodox interpretations of the Eucharist before the end of the eleventh century.... The eleventh century was occupied with the philosophic or scientific definition of the doctrine. The twelfth century conducted its theological grounding or foundation.[5]

MacDonald, like de Ghellinck, sees Lateran IV as the climax of twelfth-century eucharistic theology.[6] Both give the impression in their works that the twelfth century was a kind of incubation period between the Berengarian controversy and the statement on 'transubstantiation' made by Lateran IV in which scholars painstakingly worked toward an orthodox interpretation of the eucharistic change. De Ghellinck, as a Roman Catholic, saw the conciliar statement as a significant advance in dogma, while the Anglican MacDonald decried the same statement as the outcome of the mistaken identification of the body of Christ born of Mary and the body present on the altar made by most eleventh- and twelfth-century theologians.

The general attitude of de Ghellinck remains the most common stance adopted by contemporary authors who speak of the early scholastic theology of the Eucharist. Jean de Montclos, in his recent study of Berengar and Lanfranc, describes the early scholastic period precisely as the bridge between Lanfranc and Thomas:

It seems to us that with Lanfranc, Guitmund and Alger the sense of the evolution which will find its completion in the thomistic synthesis clearly manifests itself. One is able to trace a continuous line from Lanfranc to Saint Thomas, passing through Guitmund, Alger, and those who, during the course of the twelfth and thirteenth centuries, will continue the work accomplished by the antiberengarian polemicists with a view to discovering a better formulation of the real presence.[7]

Similar sentiments may be found in B. Neunheuser's discussion of medieval eucharistic theology,[8] and one finds echoes of it in other modern authors who speak of the early scholastic theology of the Eucharist incidentally in their works.[9]

Of the authors who treat of the theology of this period as part of a more general discussion, two authors deserve particular mention. Darwell Stone's monumental *A History of the Doctrine of the Holy Eucharist*, although now quite dated, presents the medieval teaching of the writers in a synoptic form, refraining as the author claims 'to enter into controversial arguments or theological reasonings to any extent beyond that which the intelligible treatment of facts necessarily involves'.[10] Jaroslav Pelikan includes a section entitled 'The Real Presence' in the third volume of his history of doctrines, *The Growth of Medieval Theology (600-1300)*. The section is necessarily brief, and concentrates on the Berengarian controversy presenting Lateran IV as the settlement of the issues raised therein. Within these limits, however, Pelikan offers what is probably the most complete and accessible presentation of early scholastic theology of the Eucharist.[11] These works, in so far as they refrain from denigrating the early scholastic writers in favour of their successors, offer exceptions to what appears to be a more common stance.

The understanding of the early scholastic period as peripheral to the later scholastic era focuses particularly on the question of the real presence and the use of the term *transsubstantiatio*. In the most important study in recent years on the theology of the Eucharist during the early scholastic period, Hans Jorisson has demonstrated the variety of interpretations which the term *substantia* had during this period and the consequent variety of interpretations of the eucharistic change.[12] Important as this study has been in helping to dissipate the notion of a monolithic evolution of eucharistic thought during this period, the basic approach which Jorisson adopts is similar in many ways to that of de Ghellinck, MacDonald, Montclos, and Neunheuser. Again, he concentrates on the development of the terminology of transubstantiation, particularly investigating the dogmatic value which the twelfth-century theologians placed on such terms.[13] Jorisson's work, while offering a real appreciation of the diversity of early scholastic eucharistic

thought, still positions that diversity within a movement
towards Lateran IV and Thomas Aquinas.

Another book which attempts to deal with the twelfth-
century theologians' approach to the Eucharist is the 1927
monograph of Wilhelm Auer. In what Auer himself has called
a 'kurzer und nicht wissenschaftlicher Form', the book argues
that the development of eucharistic theology during this period
found its impetus and locus for discussion in the problems surrounding the continued existence of the 'accidents' of the bread
and wine after the consecration.[14] The author makes no attempt to relate his thesis to developments in early scholastic
philosophy, and the result is more piety than scholarship. The
pious Auer, like the scholarly Jorisson, sees the early scholastic
period as important especially as it contributed to the terminology used by later theologians to describe the Lord's presence
in the Eucharist, or to use Auer's own phrase, the early scholastic theologians were 'direct heralds preparing for the golden
age of the great Aquinas'.[15]

The underlying premisses upon which these studies are
based will be examined at greater length below. For the moment, let it suffice to say that the early scholastic period has
been, and still is, largely seen in terms of the accomplishments
of the thirteenth century and continues to be ultimately discerned through the great prism of the Reformation. To under-
play the value of using the Reformation as a vantage point for
investigating the eucharistic theology of the early scholastic
period in these works would be both unrealistic and unfair.
Unrealistic, because only three of the works cited above even
purport to deal with the early scholastic period as such, and of
those, de Ghellinck's article is meant to be merely introductory
while Jorisson's research specifically deals with transubstantiation. The others present a more sweeping overview of the
period, and the Reformation provides an obvious landmark
from which to describe the larger panorama of theological
development. Further, the insights gained from such an approach are valuable, if somewhat limited. The development of
the terminology surrounding the eucharistic change is important precisely because of the light it sheds on later theological
controversy. The difficulty with such an approach is that it
tends to say more about the Reformation controversies and

what they saw as central than what the early scholastic period may have felt to be the importance of the Eucharist.

Before proceeding to detail the particular vantage point from which this thesis will proceed, a word should be said about three authors who have described the early scholastic theology of the Eucharist from viewpoints slightly different than those discussed above. One of the most important figures in the study of medieval eucharistic theology has been Joseph Geiselmann. Centring his research mainly on the early medieval period, especially the theology of Isidore of Seville, Geiselmann treats of the early scholastic period only in passing.[16] The few suggestions which Geiselmann offers concerning research into that period, however, are worth mentioning. In general, he describes the eucharistic theology of the early Middle Ages as a gradual rise in emphasis of an 'Ambrosian' or corporeal understanding of the Eucharist over against an 'Augustinian' or more spiritual understanding. The first of these approaches focused on the presence of Christ on the altar, while the second centred rather on a form of neo-platonic participation in the presence of Christ in the Eucharist. With the Berengarian controversy, Geiselmann sees the most blatant example of the ascendancy of the 'Ambrosian' over the 'Augustinian' approach to the sacrament.[17] In describing the aftermath of the controversy, however, he points out the continuing use of Augustine's terminology among the early scholastic theologians, particularly Anselm of Laon. Geiselmann suggests perhaps a new balance between the two general trends of 'Augustinian' and 'Ambrosian' elements came to exist during this period.[18] In a short article discussing the need for further research into the eucharistic theology of the early scholastics, Geiselmann repeats his views, adding that the rise of popular devotion during this period might provide an important key to its theology.[19] Geiselmann's studies do not deal directly with the early scholastic period, but like Jorisson's later study, they provide an indication that greater diversity existed during that period than is usually accredited to it.

Another scholar who treats of the early scholastic period in terms of a larger historical context is Henri de Lubac in his book *Corpus mysticum*. Treating specifically of the phrase which makes up the title of his book, de Lubac shows that *corpus mysticum* was originally used to differentiate the body of Christ present on the altar from the body of Christ born of Mary and present in heaven. Under the influence of medieval theology, the meaning of the phrase changed and gradually came rather to describe the Church as the Body of Christ symbolized in the Eucharist.

Like Geiselmann, de Lubac describes the closer and closer identification of the body of Christ present in heaven and the body of Christ present on the altar culminating in the complete identification of these two forms of Christ's presence by the opponents of Berengar.[20] De Lubac describes how this identification and the resultant insistent defence of the identification causes the term *corpus mysticum* to be transferred to the effect of the sacrament, the Body of Christ which is the Church.[21] Central to this change in terminology stands the figure of Peter Lombard, whom de Lubac sees as the chief advocate in promoting the change.[22] De Lubac has little but scorn for the Lombard and the early scholastic theologians, whose use of dialectic he holds as responsible for the loss of the patristic sense of balance in treating of the sacrament. By over-emphasizing the real presence and the logical questions raised by that presence, de Lubac feels that the early scholastics lost the notion of symbol essential to the understanding of the Eucharist.[23]

De Lubac's work, while dealing with a different idea from that of de Ghellinck, MacDonald, or Montclos, constitutes a similar approach. The Berengarian controversy marks a kind of watershed after which theologians, for better or worse, emphasized the real presence in speaking of the Eucharist. De Lubac's great contribution lies in his delineation of one of the other important concerns of the early scholastic theologians: the relationship of the Eucharist and the Church.[24]

Corpus mysticum remains essentially a textual study and as such has the strengths and weaknesses of a textual study. It demonstrates in a lucid and scholarly manner the change in terminology from the patristic to the medieval periods of the phrase in question. It necessarily does not treat of any particular shorter period of time, nor of other possible changes and problems. De Lubac, however, goes beyond the limits of this textual study in the conclusions he draws. To demonstrate that the early scholastic theologians modified patristic terminology in one area, however unfortunately, cannot serve as a demonstration of the inadequacy of the whole range of early scholastic thought on the Eucharist. Perhaps, because of what *Corpus mysticum* does not treat, de Lubac's sweeping condemnation of the early scholastic period goes beyond the evidence his study provides. The concern to describe the relationship between the Eucharist and the Church was, this study will hope to show, only one of the governing concerns of the early scholastics; a concern which *Corpus mysticum*, because of its focus on the problem of the real presence, perhaps overstresses.

Another work, also dealing with the relationship between the Eucharist and the Church as the mystical Body of Christ, is the doctoral dissertation of Ferdinand Holböck, *Der eucharistische und der mystiche Leib Christi in ihren Beziehungen zueinander nach der Lehre der Frühscholastik*. Holböck, unlike de Lubac, concentrated specifically on the early scholastic period. His work, mainly a compendium of the teaching of the early scholastic theologians on the mystical body, draws far more cautious conclusions than de Lubac. Holböck acknowledges the growing interest which the early scholastic theologians showed in the relationship between the Eucharist and the Church[25] and recognizes that the initial organization of sources by these theologians formed a base for later inquiry.[26] The importance of Holböck's work consists mainly in his thoroughness. He treats of nearly every important theologian from the early scholastic period, and manages to include references to several less well-known authors and works. One of the important results of this attention to detail lies in Holböck's recognition of the diversity of the authors whom he treats. In speaking of Durand of Troarn, he points out that this author, unlike later authors, understands the Church to be made up of those individuals united first of all to Christ.[27] He recognizes in the writings of the School of Laon and in Hugh of St. Victor the teaching that the union of the mystical body is made up of individuals first joined to God in faith and love.[28] Again Holböck notes that the School of Abelard saw the Eucharist as a sign of the union of the Church formed in baptism, but not as effecting that union.[29] Holböck does no more than point out these variations. His thesis does not demand any over-all synthesis nor does he attempt one.

Like Geiselmann before him and Jorisson after him, he merely
alludes to the richness of thought which might be found in the
eucharistic theology of the early scholastics.

Of all the works discussed here, only two, those of Jorisson
and Holböck, have attempted to deal exclusively with specific
questions raised in the early scholastic theology of the
Eucharist. Both studies have indicated an unsuspected richness
and diversity. The purpose of this book will be to present, in a
schematic fashion, the different understandings of the Eucharist which underlie the variety of teaching on the sacrament
during this period.

To suggest such a purpose, however, immediately raises a
host of problems which might best be subsumed under the
general heading of method. The two most obvious questions to
be raised would seem to be: (1) if a schematic presentation is
envisaged, what sort of schema will be used, and (2) how can
the use of such a method be justified?

To raise large questions of method in the introduction to a
book which purports to deal with one of many theological issues
dealt with in the relatively short time-span of the early scholastic period is in a sense to open a Pandora's box of debates
involving historiography, theological methodology, and episto-
mology in what might seem entirely inappropriate surround-
ings. The only justification for such unwarranted temerity
would be that a particular approach will be employed here,
somewhat different from that of earlier scholars who have dealt
with the question, and therefore some explanation and justification for that approach seem to be demanded. Yet to say that
is not to say that any attempt will be made, or indeed, ought to
be made here to resolve or even present in any kind of depth
the complexity of questions involved in the area of historical
and theological method. All that will be attempted will be a
very basic and perhaps simplistic sketch of the problems involved in choosing and justifying a method for discerning and
describing what is after all the real focus of this book, the early
scholastic teaching about the Eucharist.

Different assumptions used in handling the medieval sources
seem to yield different descriptions of the period in question.
To assume, for instance, that bread and wine cannot change
into flesh and blood would immediately discredit any literal

acceptance of the accounts of the miracle Host at Arras, despite the good historical evidence of several independent and reliable eye-witnesses. That *something* happened at Arras seems indisputable; the description which a historian gives that event (mass hysteria, red fungus, fraud, or miracle) will partially depend on his or her own assumptions about the physical universe. To take a less trivial example, historians differ considerably over their descriptions of the twelfth century and the effect (or lack thereof) of the intellectual and social foment during that century on the development of the recognition of the individual, and the relationship of this development to an interest in 'humanism'.[30] Part of this divergence is due to choice of subject-matter, but it may also in large part be due to the different historians' assumptions about what constitutes humanism and what determines recognitions of individuality and the social status of the individual. Was the twelfth century an ephemeral humanistic 'renaissance' or a propaedeutic for the thirteenth or even fifteenth centuries? It seems reasonable to suggest that the answer to this question lies not only, or even mainly, in a closer investigation of the sources, but in a more careful delineation of the assumptions and methods brought to the sources.

The problem compounds itself, or at least becomes more acutely evident, when one enters the area of historical theology. A. J. MacDonald and Jean de Montclos present almost mirror-image reflections in their descriptions of the culmination of the Berengarian controversy, despite their considerable concern for historical sources and detail. MacDonald, an Anglican in the Protestant tradition, describes Gregory VII's condemnation of Berengar as a disastrous error, a chance missed to effect the reformation of the Church which would only come more painfully in the sixteenth century. The theology of Lanfranc, Berengar's opponent, would lead inevitably to Lateran IV, Thomas Aquinas, and Trent, with the understanding that Trent was the embodiment of medieval error. De Montclos sees the theology of Lanfranc as a brilliant contribution to the theology of the Eucharist because it led inexorably to Lateran IV, Thomas Aquinas, and Trent, but Trent here is understood as the definitive enunciation of truth.

There is a particular method at work here, based on a set of

historical and theological presuppositions. The major historical
presupposition is that the theology and philosophy of Thomas
Aquinas were the pinnacle of medieval thought (for good or
evil), towards which all earlier thought was groping. This presupposition lies behind, for instance, de Ghellinck's description
of the theology of the twelfth century as imprecise, inexact, and
tentative. Although this presupposition is shared with some
historians of, say, philosophy or culture, and so might be designated a 'historical' presupposition, in this particular case, at
least, the presupposition is part of a larger theological position.
Leaving aside the rather knotty question of the role of Aquinas
in the history of medieval thought, it was to Aquinas's theology
that the fathers of Trent referred as support for their condemnation of reformed teaching on the Eucharist. If earlier theologians prefigured Thomas, and Trent promulgated Thomas's
teaching, then rejection or defence of twelfth- (not to mention
thirteenth-) century theology becomes, in a not so subtle way, a
rejection or defence of Trent. Thus to see the history of medieval theology is to judge the importance of this history in terms
of its relationship to the Reformation.

The approach to Christian history assumed here might be
described in more general terms as developmental. Based on
the analogy of organic growth, the history of theological
thought according to this line of thought, would be described as
a movement toward a certain more or less definitive and normative ('mature') expression. For de Montclos, de Ghellinck,
and Auer, for instance, such an expression would be Trent, the
decrees of which would be normative for understanding the
Eucharist. For MacDonald, on the other hand, the normative
expression would seem to be the Thirty-nine Articles as presented in the final chapter of his book.[31]

Two further characteristics ought to be delineated in the
general theological stance taken by these authors. First, the
authors are not explicitly aware of adopting any particular
theological stance. What they intend to present is what was
taught in the past, simply and directly. Without delving into
the thorny problems involved in the interpretations of historical
texts, it might at least be noted that such an unstated, and
therefore uncritical, adoption of a theological stance would
suggest that the authors are unaware of the way in which their

presuppositions might affect not only their selections of materials, but also the way in which these presuppositions might predetermine their conclusions.

Secondly, certain dogmatic assumptions tend further to enhance the possibility of a prejudicial presentation of the early scholastic teaching on the Eucharist. The authors discussed here assume that the 'mature' expression of the Christian teaching on the Eucharist is normative and hence irreformable at least in the negative sense of proscribing certain theological positions. The implication is that certain normative and usually credal expressions are revelatory in the sense of an immediate and self-validating disclosure of God in history. The pre-history of that disclosure, the unfolding of revelation as it were, then shares in the normative and revelatory nature of the final definitive expression. Since this final expression of revelation is definitive and irreformable, events leading up to that moment are of historical importance only in so far as they can be seen to contribute toward it. Theology, in both its historical and dogmatic functions, tends to be understood in this approach as attempts directly to describe the Divine in his relationship to humanity in order to provide norms for human belief and action. Dogmatic theologians are seen to strive for even more accurate descriptions of all aspects of divine-human relations. Historical theologians relate the success or failure of such attempts in the past by using those expressions of belief which have become canonized as revelatory by a particular Christian community as the criteria by which past events are to be judged.

As already stated, this particular method for doing historical theology should not be underestimated, and the insights gained from such a method are valuable. However, this approach does entail certain drawbacks which suggest that more adequate methods are needed. First of all, areas for research are too easily limited by this model to questions relevant to Reformation disputes. Of the works in question, for instance, nearly all have limited their research to medieval and patristic teaching about the presence of the Lord in the Eucharist. Surely a history of the theology of the Eucharist shaped by this one question offers a very narrow view of the richness of Eucharistic thought and practice. Secondly, the expressions of Christian teaching accepted as normative by the authors in question tend to be applied retrospectively to earlier periods and teaching. Those periods in which the discussions of the presence of the Lord in the sacrament received special attention tend to assume major historical importance for this approach. Thus, the works of Paschasius and Ratramnus are deemed to have comprised the first eucharistic controversy, rather than the earlier dispute between Amalarius and Florus. The Berengarian affair receives central attention rather than the ongoing dispute with the Cathars in the twelfth century or the hotly disputed question of the validity of the sacrament contemporaneous with the Berengarian dispute. Medieval teaching, too, becomes subject to the normative expressions accepted by the author. Works which differ from the norm are either heterodox, or 'imprecise, inexact, tentative and vacillating'. For Geiselmann, for instance, Ratramnus was clearly heterodox, despite the fact that the orthodoxy of his work was never questioned during his lifetime, and MacDonald upholds Berengar's teaching as a courageous proclamation of truth despite its multiple condemnations in the eleventh century. Finally terms stemming from the Reformation disputes tend to be used to describe positions held by medieval and patristic authors. Geiselmann, for instance, prefers to classify authors as espousing some form of either 'spiritualist' or 'realist' theology.

By simplifying the theological stance which appears to underlie much of the research done on the Eucharistic theology of the early scholastic period, and in the process perhaps overstressing its weaknesses, there is no intention to vilify the work done by these men, but merely to point out its limits. Certain unconscious, or at least, inexplicit, dogmatic presuppositions appear to have both limited the areas of research explored in the studies described above, and prejudiced some of the conclusions reached by them. By adopting a somewhat different set of theological assumptions, and by adopting them explicitly, this present study will attempt to broaden the areas of interest for a study of early scholastic Eucharistic theology and suggest a different method for schematizing the results of that study.

The major theological premiss that this work assumes understands the history of Christianity as the ongoing attempt to live out the Christian message differing social contexts. The history of

Christian thought, then, might be described as the continual attempt to mediate between the lived Christian message and the cultural matrix in which it exists.[32] What is envisaged in abandoning the theological stance of earlier writers is that shift in the understanding of the history of Christianity described by Yves Congar:

> ... history (is) understood less as continual process of 'development', that is as progress achieved through a gradual unfolding of what was already implicit, and more as a series of formulations of the one content of faith diversifying and finding expression in different cultural contexts.[33]

To adopt such a theological stance entails the abandonment of the assumption that particular expressions of Christian witness are definitive and irreformable criteria for evaluating the history of Christianity (apart from the quite problematic sense in which Scripture is witness to such an expression in the life and death of Jesus). The normative nature of say Trent or the Thirty-nine Articles would rest in their authoritative proscription of certain forms of religious language in specific historical situations because these usages are felt to misrepresent the relationship between God and humanity embodied in the Christian message. These proscriptions ought not to be applied retrospectively, nor should they be viewed as revelatory in the sense of an immediate and self-validating description of God's actions. They remain revelatory, however, in so far as they fulfil the Christian hope that such proscriptions are signs of God's continued care.

The stance described here raises serious theological questions. How does one know that historically conditioned and therefore changing language remains faithful to the Christian message, or even more basically, how can one know that it is the message of God's love which such historically conditioned language carries? Without attempting to resolve these very important questions, one might at least note that the language of faith has provided a series of metaphors for God by which Christians have lived and died in the hope that these metaphors have a referent, and that this hope comprises a necessary condition for such a life and death. Nicholas Lash appears to be referring to a similar idea in the conclusion of his discussion of the conditions under which theology might be done:

> It is not, I think, simply predictable academic caution that has in-
> hibited me from attempting the further task of specifying the suf-
> ficient conditions for such an enterprise (critical theology). It is,
> rather, the conviction that, in so far as any such further specification
> were to be possible at all within the limits of historical existence, its
> grammar would be closer to that of the language of prayer than of
> theoretical argument.[34]

Without resolving the question of how one judges past (or
present) language about God to be truly about *God*, the historian as theologian is faced with the task of recovering and
presenting for modern readers earlier attempts to appropriate
the Christian message in a particular cultural context. One inevitably faces choices here. What method will be used to uncover and disclose language and actions of the past? Which
language and/or actions of the past will be investigated and
why? No historian would be capable of investigating or even
selecting for investigation any particular period or problem in
the past without, implicitly or explicitly, making such deci-
sions. By making explicit, as far as possible, the particular
method used in this study, it is hoped that the method and the
premises behind it might be more open to correction, revision,
or even abandonment.

To mention these options suggests that straightforward
criteria exist for choosing and revising the methods used for
historical research. Once again, a realistic appraisal of the
literature available on methodology suggest at least that the
selection of criteria for choosing between methods remains
problematic. Without becoming involved in the much discussed
problems of what is termed by Bernard Lonergan as dialectic,[35]
the criteria employed here might be described as twofold. First,
the theological assumptions supporting the method ought to
meet the standards demanded of reasonable discourse, and
secondly, the method used ought to be suitable for appropriating information from historical sources without contradicting,
distorting, or arbitrarily dismissing those sources. What is
envisaged here might be described as an appeal to Rudolf Bultmann's distinction between the role of presuppositions and
prejudice in historical research.[36] What is desired, without

denying the problems inherent in such an attempt, is research based on reasonable presuppositions to the exclusion, as far as possible, of prejudice. The success or failure of that attempt remains more to be judged in the argument of the book than in that of the introduction.

Assuming, as this study does, that the language of faith is a constant attempt to provide metaphors for the inexpressible God in his relationship to humanity, the method used here will be that of searching out dominant metaphors used in the past, whether reflectively or unreflectively, to describe some aspect of the divine/human relationship. These metaphors would then be used as models to order and interpret the theological endeavours of the past. On this level, the model need not have been used consciously by the theologians under investigation, but need only provide an indication of how their thought might be identified and described in a schematic fashion. The period under investigation may be found to produce one particularly dominant metaphor to describe some particular aspect of religious life, or it may produce several different metaphors, which may themselves be irreconcilable on the level of theoretical models. Particular theologians in the past may display one or more models in their work; even if these models are divergent or conflicting. Certainly in this regard, theologians in the past ought to be accorded the same capacities for confusion, inconsistency, and stupidity as their modern descendants.

The models used here are not meant as descriptions of reality, but only as useful means of appropriating the past in a schematic fashion.[37] A description of each model as well as an explanation of its application to medieval theology occurs in the respective chapters dealing with that model.

The book intends to deal mainly with the work of professional academics rather than with more popular preaching or devotional practices. This is not to say that some attempt will not be made to place the work of the early scholastic theologians within the context of the more popular religious understandings of their time. A presentation of the early scholastic theology of the Eucharist which ignores the cultural setting in which that theology was written inevitably misleads. The *questiones* which appear in the *sententie* and *summe* of this period when presented on their own can frequently give the appearance of recounting opinions solely of academic interest. The authors assumed a whole cultural and social milieu with which they expected their readers to be familiar, and the poor modern reader is often left with the dry skeleton of what was once a vibrant debate. The theology of this period had not yet reached the state of purely academic discussion. It developed in response and sometimes in opposition to the social and cultural movements of the time, answering what were felt to be, not only theological, but also religious and pastoral problems. The discussions of the theologians, then, make sense only in terms of those movements and those problems. Yet, what this study hopes to present is the works of the theologians in their cultural setting rather than a study of popular religious movements.

Further, this study intends to investigate only one of many possible themes in eucharistic theology, that of the salvific function of the sacrament. To put the question under investigation in its simplest form: What use or uses did the educated Christian community in the early scholastic period see in the inherited ceremony of ritual offering and communal eating known as the Eucharist? The question, of course, can be asked of any period in the history of Christianity. It was during this period that, for the first time, the question became of central interest to a great number of professional scholars. The question will, it is hoped, uncover what purpose the theologians of that period themselves saw in the Eucharist and, hence, disclose the major metaphors used by those theologians in speaking of the Eucharist.

Yet, in so narrowing the question under investigation, other important and related questions inevitably suffer short shrift. Certainly, a thorough study of the soteriology of the period would aid in understanding how the early scholastics approached the theology of the Eucharist. Equally, if not more important, would be an investigation of the influence of the developing Christology of the medieval thinkers on the understanding of the ritual in which they held Christ to be present. Again, as Henri de Lubac has shown, a theology of the Eucharist nearly always presupposes some particular understanding of the Church. Surely a more thorough investigation of this area would aid in ascertaining the early scholastic theology of the Eucharist. Given the terminology used to describe the mode of the presence of the Lord in the sacrament, the rediscovery of Aristotelian metaphysics could not help but affect the teaching on the Eucharist. Finally, a study of the diversity of liturgical rites used during the period in question would help enflesh a study of a theology ultimately dependent upon those rituals. All these further areas for research will be touched on briefly in this work, but adequately to meet all these demands would require not one, but many studies. One can only hope that by pursuing one study well, one will raise other unanswered questions to entice other and better scholars to pick up where this work leaves off.[38]

The book deals, then, with a particular theological question, and with the answer given that question during the early scholastic period. In doing so, one hopes, it will bring into sharp focus the diversity of the theological thought on the Eucharist. Yet the celebration of the Lord's Supper, then as now, is a living ritual, enacted in community; a mystery which cannot be exhausted by any one theological discussion or question. Ritual, piety, and theology of the Eucharist were, in many ways, seen as more of a unity by the early scholastic writers than by present theologians, and this must be kept in mind when treating of one aspect of the whole complex of relationships present here.

I

BACKGROUND: THE TRADITION OF DIVERSITY

FOR I received from the Lord what I also delivered to you, that the Lord Jesus on the night when he was betrayed took bread, and when he had given thanks, he broke it and said, 'This is my body which is for you. Do this in remembrance of me.' In the same way also the cup, after supper, saying, 'This cup is the new covenant in my blood. Do this, as often as you drink it in remembrance of me.' For as often as you eat this bread and drink the cup, you proclaim the Lord's death until he comes.[1]

On the night before he died, Jesus shared bread and wine with his disciples, and identified this sharing with his life and death. In this first account of that event, St. Paul provides the first interpretation of the ritual enacted by Jesus on the night before his death. The three intertwined actions of narrating the account of Jesus' last night with his followers, of ritually re-enacting that supper, and of interpreting the historical event and living ritual for the Christian community have coexisted from its inception. From its inception, also, these three activities have been open to different understandings and different interpretations. Thus Paul himself wrote because the Corinthian community, it seems, celebrated the Lord's Supper as a type of enthusiast mystery rite.[2]

The famous 'bread of life' passage in the Gospel of John (6: 22-59)—itself the centre of much scholarly debate—may well have been written to clarify certain controversies over the understanding of how one might 'eat the flesh of the Son of Man, and drink his blood'. Certainly by the end of the first century different understandings of the event and the ritual were causing dissension in the Christian community in Antioch.[3]

Despite diversity from the very beginning, the early Christian community shared the belief that the ritual re-enactment of the Lord's Supper was a participation in the Mystery of Christ, and a sharing in the glorious salvation won for humans through the death and resurrection of the Lord. The earliest Christian writers seemed to have understood the 'Eucharist' as precisely that, a 'giving thanks'; a community celebration of thanksgiving. To celebrate the Lord's Supper was to offer thanksgiving, to 'eucharistize'. This 'sacrifice of praise' thanked God for the community's sharing in the salvation already achieved by the risen Lord who himself called the community to his exalted state.[4]

From at least the fourth century, and especially in the East, the union of the Christian with the risen Christ was understood to be effected by participation in the eucharistic ritual. Cyril of Alexandria particularly stressed the importance of this union for affecting salvation in his attacks on Nestorius. His theology may reflect a growing popular understanding of the Eucharist as a ritual mediating the presence of the now risen Christ to his followers awaiting his final return.[5] Such a view of the sacrament necessarily stressed the reality and power of the Lord's presence in the ritual actions. A slow but perceptible shift took place in Eastern estimations of the Eucharist. The sacrament became less a cause for celebration and more an occasion for adoration.[6]

In the West, this tendency to view the Eucharist less as a celebration and thanksgiving of the community and more as a ritual mediating the risen presence of the Christ seems to have developed more slowly. Ambrose of Milan became perhaps the major exponent, or at least the most influential mediator of this Eastern tradition for later Western theology. In his *De sacramentis*, a collection of addresses given to catechumens, Ambrose argued that the creative Word of God caused the living and vivifying body and blood of the Lord to become present in the ritual elements of bread and wine:

In order to answer you, therefore, there was no body of Christ before the consecration, but after the consecration I say to you that there is now the body of Christ. He Himself said it, and it has been done. He Himself ordered it, and it has been created. You yourself were, but you were an old creature; after you have been consecrated, you had begun to be a new creature.[7]

For Ambrose, just as the newly baptized catechumens had been re-created in Christ, so too the bread and wine were given a new and salvific identity by their consecration.

Hilary of Poitiers stressed the presence of the risen Lord in the Eucharist in his argument against the Arians in his *De trinitate*. Hilary argued that if the union of the Son with the Father was a union of will alone, then our sacramental union with the Son, our joining of his flesh with ours, would be to no salvific purpose. In fact, however, the Eucharist creates a perfect unity of believer, Father, and Son. 'Accordingly, this is the cause of our life, that we, who are carnal, have Christ dwelling in us through His flesh, and through Him we shall live in that state in which He lives in the Father.'[8] This work, too, was to have a profound influence on later writers.

The earlier emphasis on community celebration retained its force in the West through the influence of the great Bishop of Hippo. Augustine, while not denying the reality of the presence of the Lord in the ritual, preferred to stress the community itself as the true body of Christ, present to the world through its acts of faith and charity. Augustine described this approach in his commentary on John's Gospel:

The Lord, about to send the Holy Spirit, called Himself the bread of heaven exorting us that we might believe in Him. To believe in Him; this is to eat living bread. Whoever believes, eats; invisibly he is nourished, because invisibly he is reborn.[9]

We have said, brothers, that the Lord had commended to us the eating of His body and the drinking of His blood in order that we might remain in Him and He in us. We remain in Him when we are His members; He remains in us, when we are His temples. In order that we might be His members, unity bonds us together. In order that unity might bond us, what is there except charity?[10]

For Augustine, to share in the ritual of Eucharist entailed and symbolized the community's life of faith and charity.

Whatever incompatibilities may have existed in these different emphases by the Fathers in their discussions of the Eucharist seem to have gone unnoticed during their lifetimes. The theological efforts of the era were directed, for the most part, toward the great Christological and soteriological controversies. Questions concerning the celebration and explanation of the Lord's Supper were discussed in catechetical settings or as they contributed to the larger controversies. In general, the ritual of the Lord's Supper would not have been considered as an action separated from the larger life of the community, and similarly discussions of the Eucharist would not have been separated from larger theological issues.

The First Treatises on the Eucharist

The first theological treatise devoted specifically to a doctrinal rather than a ritualist treatment of the Eucharist was the *De corpore et sanguine domini* written *c.*831-833 by Paschasius Radbertus, a monk of Corbie, for the education of the Saxon monks. The work appeared to have little circulation until the author, now the Abbot of Corbie, presented a revised version to the newly crowned Emperor Charles the Bald in 844.[11] The outstanding characteristic of Paschasius's work was his strong identification of the presence of the Lord in the sacrament with the terrestrial, risen, and now glorified body of Christ.

About the same time (843/4), the Emperor Charles wrote to another monk of Corbie, the scholar Ratramnus, asking him to consider certain doctrinal questions concerning the Eucharist.[12] Ratramnus responded in a work also entitled *De corpore et sanguine domini*, expounding an understanding of the sacrament very different from that of his abbot, Paschasius. Ratramnus emphasized the Eucharist as an effective sign of the presence of the Lord, without identifying the elements of the ritual, the bread and wine, with the risen body of the Lord.[13]

The juxtaposition of the two works, both in time and space, has led most later commentators to speak of these authors as the principal protagonists in a ninth-century 'controversy' over the understanding of the Eucharist. Heriger, Abbot of Lobbes from 990 to 1007, would be the first scholar to recognize the potential disagreement between the two scholars of Corbie. In the eleventh century, and again in the sixteenth, and so on into the twentieth century, the appearance of these two works, the first to appear specifically on the doctrine of the Eucharist, has been described in terms of controversy.

Jean-Paul Bouhot, in his recent study of the scholarly career of Ratramnus has suggested that the juxtaposition of these works does not necessarily indicate that the two scholars were the centre of any controversy.[14] Certainly, there are indications that there was not a doctrinal conflict here of any major pro-

portion. Paschasius's work existed, apparently available to
Ratramnus, for some fourteen years before Ratramnus responded with his own work, and then Ratramnus's work does
not seem to be a response to his abbot, but to certain quite
specific questions addressed to him by the Emperor. Further,
no councils were held or called for, and no condemnations
appeared. The theology of Paschasius and Ratramnus seemed
to have existed in relative harmony at the monastery of Corbie.

If neither of the two treatises produced at Corbie resulted in
ecclesiastical action, action was taken during the ninth century
on the matter of the proper teaching on the Eucharist. At the
Council of Quierzy in 838, some of the teachings found in the
De officiis of the liturgical commentator, Amalarius of Metz,
were found to be heretical. Among the condemned propositions
was the explication of the threefold fraction of the bread as
signifying a threefold existence of the body of Christ. The
opposition to Amalarius's teaching, led by Florus, a deacon of
Lyon, argued that Amalarius's distinction between the presence of Christ in the sacrament, the presence of Christ in the
Church, and the presence of Christ on earth and in heaven
constituted a separation of the one person of the Lord.[15] Bouhot
suggests that the questions asked by Charles the Bald of Ratramnus arose not from Charles's reading of Paschasius's gift,
but from the Emperor's concern to settle the political and
theological issues raised by the condemnation of Quierzy.[16]
Whether or not Bouhot is correct in his interpretation of these
events, or indeed in his larger claim that the treatise of Ratramnus was not intended to refute his abbot's earlier work, the different explanations of the presence of the Lord in the sacrament
as well as the condemnation of Amalarius demonstrate that the
diversity of the patristic period had developed into a more conscious sense of incompatibility.

The major theological issue concerning the Eucharist in the
ninth century centred on the mode of presence assumed in the
sacrament. Several works attest to a concern for a more uniform understanding of this presence among Carolingian theologians. Rabanus Maurus, Abbot of Fulda and Archbishop of
Mainz, wrote a warning to Heribald of Auxerre around 855
concerning those: 'who, incorrectly judging, recently have said
that the sacrament of the body and blood of the Lord is the

same body and blood of the Lord which was born of the virgin Mary, and which suffered on the cross, and which is risen from the grave'.[17] John Scotus Erigena, head of the palace school at Laon, similarly cautioned his readers 'about those who wish to assert the visible Eucharist to signify nothing else but itself'.[18] Rabanus and Erigena might well have been directing their remarks to the teaching of Paschasius, but such brief references make any identification tenuous. No doubt exists, however, in identifying the object of the attack launched by Gottschalk, a wandering monk eventually exiled to the monastery of Haut-villers for his teaching on predestination. In his work, *De corpore et sanguine domini*, Gottschalk accused Paschasius of advocating a realism which bordered on cannibalism in which Christ underwent suffering at the hands of the faithful.[19]

If some theologians feared a too close identification of the presence of the Lord in the Eucharist with his earthly existence, others feared that any disassociation would be a denial of true eucharistic presence. Paschasius's work contained two references to a person or persons with whom he disagreed (in one reference labelled *haeretici*) who denied that the risen and enthroned Christ could now be received by the faithful, and who argued that the reception of the Lord was efficacious for the soul but not for the body.[20] Hincmar, Archbishop of Reims from 845 to 882, listed certain teachings against the truth of catholic faith that he seems to have attributed to Erigena. Among them is the opinion 'that the sacraments of the altar might not be the true body and true blood of the Lord, but only a remembrance of the true body and His blood'.[21] Adrevald, a monk of Fleury, went further than Hincmar, and entitled his florilegia of patristic texts on the Eucharist, *De corpore et sanguine christi contra ineptias ioannis scoti.*[22] Paschasius again defended his position in relation both to the treatise of Ratramnus and to the attack of Gottschalk in a letter to a former student of his, Fredugard, who having read the work of the two scholars of his original monastery, was understandably quite confused.[23]

The references in these works are for the most part too inexact to be easily classified into pro-Paschasian and pro-Ratramnian camps. Indeed, at least the references of Paschasius to *haeretici* suggest that a group or groups of opinions then existed concerning the Eucharist which have not as yet been identified by historians of the period. What the references do suggest is that a diversity of opinions did exist during this period and that this diversity was beginning to be felt as a matter for theological concern.

Joseph Rupert Geiselmann traces the origins of this conflict to the different emphases in the approaches to the Eucharist found in the works of Ambrose of Milan and Augustine of Hippo. Both approaches to the sacrament coexisted in the West and were carried by different liturgical traditions. According to Geiselmann, the Gallic liturgies used an 'Ambrosian' language emphasizing a change in the species of bread and wine into the salvific presence of the Lord. The Roman liturgy, on the other hand, taking an 'Augustinian' approach, spoke of the bread and wine as symbols through which the salvific presence of the Lord was made available to the believers. These two approaches to the Eucharist came into conflict with the introduction of the Roman liturgy into the Gallic churches by Pippin and Charlemagne. The differences in liturgical language became more apparent as a uniformity of liturgical practices was attempted. When the question arose of how the Lord was then to be understood as present in the Eucharist, different answers were forthcoming depending on whether theologians relied on the 'Ambrosian' or 'Augustinian' tradition.[24]

Rosamond McKitterick, in her study of the Carolingian reforms, lends some weight to Geiselmann's theory at least in so far as she demonstrates the importance which the reformers saw in the liturgy as a source of education and unity:

The motives for the remarkable liturgical activity in the ninth century are quite clear, and they are those of the Carolingian reform programme generally; the extirpation of paganism, promotion of unity, the proclamation of Christianity, and above all, the instruction of the people. The liturgy was one of the most crucial elements in the shaping of the Frankish society.[25]

Once the liturgy had been pressed into the service of the Emperor to provide education and unity, the diversity of the patristic period would not only be noticed, but would also be called into question. As Gottschalk remarked in his criticism of Paschasius: 'Thus the blessed Augustine disputes what the holy Ambrose has said, as if this would not have pleased him.'[26]

Another factor which may have contributed to the concern of the Carolingian theologians to explain the presence of the Lord in the Eucharist would be the shift noticed by some modern scholars of the liturgy in the focus of the celebration itself. These scholars point to a tendency beginning in the Carolingian Church and continuing throughout the Middle Ages to separate the action of the priest during the ritual from that of the people. Raphael Schulte in his *Die Messe als Opfer der Kirche*, points out that it is the commentaries on the liturgy written during the ninth century which first stressed the liturgical action as belonging properly to the priest, rather than to the people of God as a whole acting as the 'Body of Christ'.[27] The popularity of these *expositiones missae* in the ninth century, and indeed throughout the Middle Ages, would itself then be seen as an indication of the necessity to explain a ritual which had become, in the words of Joseph Jungmann, a new *disciplina arcani*.[28] The growth of private Masses, and the unintelligibility of the language of the liturgy, formed the laity into a passive audience whose only function would be that of adoring the Christ made present on the altar through the power of the priest. This sort of emphasis would in turn lead to a growing interest in how this miracle could take place, and in how exactly Christ could be present in what still looked, felt, and tasted like bread and wine.[29]

Some delicacy needs to be exercised, however, in accepting this explanation for the ninth-century interest in the Eucharist. Although participation in the sacrament might be quite different from the solemn pageantry of late patristic times, the laity adopted a new and in some ways more lively role in the liturgy. As O. B. Hardison demonstrates in *Christian Rite and Christian Drama in the Middle Ages*, the empathetic 'living out' of the liturgy urged by ninth-century ecclesiastics and their many medieval successors formed the origins for modern European drama.[30] To refer again to Dr McKitterick:

The drama of liturgical rites, architectural and pictorial innovation, the demand for material offerings from the people, and the evidence we have for the encouragement of popular piety, singing and veneration of relics, all suggest that the Frankish clergy did believe they should make the effort to ensure that the laity were comprehending and even delighted participants in the offices of the Church.[31]

Secondly, a shift in the form of the participation of the laity in the liturgy alone says little about how the laity or clergy perceived their roles. If the community maintained a strong corporate identity, and there is some reason to think that it did,[32] then to speak of the priest as the focal point of the ceremonial drama might bespeak more iconographical than juridical language. The priest might have offered the gifts of the people and received God's grace in their name as symbol himself of the community. To have understood this focusing as a separation of clergy and laity might well have required a juridical precision and an understanding of individual worth the rise of which might be more easily attributable to the twelfth rather than the ninth century.[33] In any case, much more information about the self-understanding of laity and clergy in the ninth century would be necessary to assess properly the liturgical changes then taking place.

Again, there is no necessary connection between the gradual change in the role and understanding of clergy and laity and a devotion to a 'realistic' mode of presence of the Lord in the Eucharist. Indeed, the very different understandings of that presence evinced by two members of the same monastery, presumably attending the same liturgy, would indicate that the change in liturgical roles which took place in the ninth century could and did support quite different theologies.

A growing awareness of the diversity present in the writings of the Fathers, the attempt to enforce a more uniform and political conception of the Church and a change in the function of the liturgy itself all seem to have contributed, to some degree, to the interest in the Eucharist shown by Paschasius, Ratramnus, and their contemporaries. Other factors might be, and have been, mentioned, such as the influx of scarcely Christianized pagans into the Church and the influence of monastic devotion on the understanding of the liturgy.[34] Whatever factors or complex of factors contributed to the ninth century in the Eucharist, it must be remembered that this 'concern' was, to ninth-century theologians at least, minor in comparison to the much larger issues of the instruction of the people, the need for unity, Western debates over predestination and reordination, and the controversy with the East over the *Filioque* clause.[35] Only one of the works on the doctrine of the Eucharist, that of Paschasius, rose above the level of an occasional treatise. Yet, because of the later importance of both this work and the shorter reply of Ratramnus to Charles the Bald, a brief mention should be made of the theologies which they contain.

The Theology of Paschasius and Ratramnus

Paschasius's understanding of the Eucharist was in many ways innovative. He was the first theologian to present a comprehensive theology of the sacrament, and despite his heavy reliance on Hilary and Ambrose, his approach goes far beyond any previous explanation of the role of the sacrament in Christian life.[36] Paschasius insisted that the body of Christ present in the Eucharist was the same as that born of Mary.[37] Indeed, this claim was essential for his theology. According to Paschasius, the divine-human existence of Christ received by the faithful in the Eucharist becomes united 'naturally' with the body and soul of the believer thus making possible the believer's participation in Christ's divinity, and hence ensuring his or her salvation. This salvific function of the sacrament formed, in an important sense, the soteriological and Christological framework and rationale for Paschasius's insistence that the God-Man in his essential nature was received in the Eucharist. The warrant for this approach came from Hilary, which Paschasius acknowledged in his letter to Fredugard,[38] but the conclusions drawn from Hilary's work were Paschasius's own. The following paraphrase of chapter eight of the *De trinitate* demonstrates how Paschasius would make use of Hilary's thought:

And in fact Christ is rightly said to remain in us daily not solely through agreement of wills, but also to remain through His nature in us as we also in Him. If the Word had become flesh, and we truly consume the Word as flesh in the Lord's food, how can it not be justly judged that He dwells in us by His nature, who being God born man, has assumed the inseparable nature of our flesh, and has mingled the nature of His flesh to His eternal nature in the sacrament (*sub sacramento*) of the flesh that was to be communicated to us? And therefore in this way, we all are one in God the Father and the Son and the Holy Spirit, because it has been shown that the Father is in Christ and Christ is in us. On this account, it is that we are made one body naturally with Christ.[39]

Paschasius repeated this claim often. It appeared perhaps in its crudest form in the letter to Fredugard: '(Christ) however lives on account of the Father, because He was born the only-begotten one of the Father, and we live on account of Him, because we eat Him.'[40] Paschasius denied that this eating could in any sense be understood as impugning the dignity of the risen Lord, and indeed insisted that this reception was a spiritual matter.[41] Paschasius resolved any difficulties attendant on this mode of presence of the glorified body in the Eucharist through reference to divine omnipotence. The divine was the author of, and not subject to, the laws of nature.[42] Paschasius assumed that the salvific contact achieved in the Eucharist could only be accomplished by those who were already united to Christ in faith and love; those who received unworthily did so unto their damnation.[43]

In short, Paschasius wished to assert the presence of Christ, as God and as man, in the Eucharist, for it was only through our contact with the nature of the God-man that our own nature could be redeemed. Paschasius's theology was a simple and unified attempt to explain the role of the Eucharist in the salvation of the Christian. Its simplicity which might in itself be seen as a virtue, may also well be its major vice, for although it could be understood as implying a spiritual contact of our natures with that of the true God-man, (as Paschasius seems to have intended), it could also be understood as the crassest kind of capharnaism (as Gottschalk seems to have understood it). For better and for worse, it would have a long and influential history.

Ratramnus, unlike Paschasius, was not concerned to give a complete theology of the Eucharist. His treatise was intended to answer two questions asked him by Charles the Bald. First, did the faithful receive the body and blood of Christ in mystery or in truth (*in mysterio fiat, an in veritate*); and secondly, was this the same body and blood as that born of Mary?[44] Ratramnus began the answer to the first question by distinguishing reality *in figura*, a form of reality which betokens another hidden reality, from reality *in veritate*, a form of reality in which the nature of that reality is clearly apparent.[45] The body and blood of Christ present in the Eucharist would be a reality of the first type, for the bread and wine that are sensed betoken the spiritual body and blood of Christ.[46] In a reality present *in figura*, there are actually two realities. The sensed reality points to the more important and, what appears to have been for Ratramnus, 'more real' reality.[47] This second mode of existence could be discerned, not by the senses, but by the mind, or in faith.[48] Ratramnus was quite concerned that the two realms of body and spirit should not be confused, although the exact relationship between the two was not clarified. In the specific instance of the Eucharist, the exterior objects discerned by the senses are the bread and wine, the interior reality understood by faith is the living Christ. Thus it is in mystery, i.e. through the use of bread and wine, that we apprehend the life-giving Saviour.[50] Even before his incarnation, death, and resurrection, Christ was able to mediate, through exterior signs such as manna, spiritual and salvific food and drink to the Hebrews in the desert.[51] The spiritual working of the Word was salvific here, rather than any corporeal sensed reality. This distinction appears to be at the centre of Ratramnus's understanding of the Eucharist:

This is confessed most plainly by saying that in the sacrament of the body and blood of the Lord, whatever external thing is consumed is adopted to refection by the body. The mind, however, invisibly feeds on the Word of God, Who is the invisible bread invisibly existing in that sacrament, by the vivifying participation of faith.[52]

In answer, then to Charles's first question, the faithful received Christ in the Eucharist 'in mystery', that is under the tokens, the signs of bread and wine; not 'in reality', that is, by consuming the external, sensible body and blood of Christ. Following the same mode of thought, Ratramnus denied that the body of Christ born of the Virgin was that present in the Eucharist. The differences between the presences ought to be obvious. The body born of Mary was made up of bones, nerves, flesh; the spiritual flesh received in the Eucharist was invisible, impassible, and appeared under the physical reality of bread and wine. The first was truly a body; the second an interior spiritual reality betokened by an exterior physical sign.[53]

Ratramnus's short treatise did not provide the completeness and unity of Paschasius's presentation, nor indeed was this its intent. Nor did Ratramnus's work receive the attention that

Paschasius's work received. Apart from Fredugard, Paschasius, and, presumably, Charles the Bald, no other contemporary readers are known. Indeed, the known medieval readers of this work are few and even they gave it little acceptance.[54] The importance of Ratramnus's work lies not so much in its influence on later thought as in its witness to the diversity of thought on the Eucharist current in the ninth century. Only two works on the Eucharist of any completeness exist from this, the period in which such works first appear, and it is significant that they espouse quite different approaches. That they do so appears to reflect the diversity already noted in the works of Amalarius, Erigena, Rabanus Maurus, Hincmar, Gottschalk, and Adrevald.

The major difference between the works of Paschasius and Ratramnus can be demonstrated by comparing their different understandings of the salvific function of the Eucharist. For Ratramnus, the salvific union achieved, or rather symbolized, by the Eucharist, was a spiritual union between the divine Christ with the soul of the believer achieved by faith. Certainly there was no need here for the God-Man in his divine and human natures to be present in the sacrament. Nor indeed would this be consistent with Ratramnus's understanding of *natura*. Sensible objects remained what they appeared to be, even if they could point beyond themselves to more important spiritual realities.[55] In some ways, Ratramnus played the role of the conservative in this regard, invoking, if not explicating, a theology similar to that of Augustine, upon whom he relied heavily.[56]

For Paschasius, on the other hand, the salvific union was achieved by means of the eucharistic reception itself. The nature of the God-Man, incarnate and now risen, was joined with the nature of the believer. This too had been described as a spiritual union, but here nature was completely subject to, and enveloped in the spiritual realm. Not only was it necessary in Paschasius's thought for the God-Man to be naturally present in the Eucharist; this was consistent with an understanding of nature under the sentence of the divine. The nature of the bread and wine could be replaced by divine power with the nature of the God-Man, in itself impassible and unrestricted by particular location. How this occurred was hidden from humans living in a divine world.

The diversity of the patristic period was not lost in the ninth-century discussions of the Eucharist, but it was noted, and noted with some concern. The coexistence, even if in disagreement, of Paschasius and Ratramnus at Corbie demonstrated that this concern had not yet reached a state where plurality would become intolerable. During the next two centuries, however, this plurality would slowly be lost, to be replaced by a dominant and Paschasian understanding of the Eucharist.

The Tenth Century

If the ninth century has received a great deal of attention from scholars of eucharistic theology, the tenth century has been practically ignored. The little research dedicated to this period, however, indicates that the theological questions raised by the Carolingian scholars continued to be discussed.[57] Heriger of Lobbes, writing at the end of the century, would remark concerning the Eucharist that there were still contemporaries willing to continue the dissension of the earlier century.[58] Most mentions of the Eucharist continued to appear, as in the ninth century, in the context of larger theological treatments or in occasional works. Atto II, Bishop of Vercelli from 924 to 961, in his commentary on I Corinthians, and Aelfric, teaching at Cerne Abbas from 987 to 1005, in his Easter sermon, both spoke of the Eucharist in terms reminiscent of Ratramnus.[59] Ratherius, Bishop of Verona intermittently from 932 to 968 in his *Dialogus confessionum* and Remigius, master at the cathedral school at Auxerre from 876/77 to *c*.908 in his *De celebratione missae* both preferred a theology of the Eucharist similar to that of Paschasius.[60]

Three more important works were written during the course of the century which dwelt specifically and exclusively with the Eucharist. The shortest work was the anonymous *Responsio cuiusdam de corpore et sanguine domini*, written some time before it was used by Heriger of Lobbes at the end of the century.[61] The author wrote in response to the question 'when we receive in the breaking of the bread and the drinking of the chalice, in what fashion is (the body and blood of the Lord) preserved in us having passed through the natural and bodily condition?'[62]

The question of how digestion might affect the body and blood of the Lord received in sacrament raised here had occasioned some slight notice by earlier writers. Paschasius, having read a passage in the Pseudo-Clementine letters suggesting that the sacred body would be subject to digestion, dismissed the idea as 'frivolous'.[63] Amalarius mentioned in a letter to a young priest scandalized by Amalarius's habit of spitting after communion, that whatever happened to the body and blood after communion was not nearly so important as our interior respect for the sacrament.[64] Around 855, Rabanus Maurus responded to Heribald of Auxerre's question of whether the body and blood were digested like other food. Rabanus warned Heribald against those who took too literal an understanding of the Lord's presence and assured him that digestion affected only the exterior form of the sacrament, not the interior spiritual reality.[65]

Apart from these brief dismissals, no mention occurred of the question as a serious theological problem. Indeed, perhaps, as in Amalarius's letter, this short tract might represent only a studied response to a scrupulous soul. Charles Shrader, in his study of tenth-century eucharistic tracts, has suggested another source, however, for this question. He argues that the question arose among certain 'neo-manichean' groups whom he identifies as stercoranists, who wished to discredit any notion that the Eucharist could be of material rather than spiritual value.[66] Certainly the *Responsio* was used by Heriger of Lobbes to refute the argument that the body and blood were subject to ordinary digestion.[67] Shrader attempts to identify at least one such group of dissidents at the monastery of Göttweig. The identification is tenuous, however, and little information was provided by the *Responsio* as to the source of this question.[68] Heriger, on the other hand, seemed to be addressing his remarks to the letter of Rabanus Maurus, which Heriger read as suggesting that the Lord's body and blood underwent digestion.[69] Certainly by the twelfth century, what would be then known as the stercoranist argument would be commonly used by the Cathars to attack the Eucharist, and as early as 1015 in Orleans and 1025 in Liège, dissident groups would be tried for denying the value of the Eucharist. Yet neither the *Responsio* nor Heriger's response to Rabanus's letter provide adequate

information to assert the existence of a tenth-century stercoranist heresy, and modern scholars find no real evidence for
the existence of neo-manichean groups in the West in the tenth
century.[70]

The answer the anonymous author of the *Responsio* provided
to the problem was simple and straightforward. We should
never say that the body of Christ suffers any kind of decom-
position in the sacrament, for the presence here is a spiritual
presence.[71] Several times the author repeated that both the
effect of the sacrament and the presence of the Lord in the
Eucharist concern only the spiritual and not the material
realm.[72] Although the treatise hardly provided a complete
understanding of the sacrament, it does demonstrate that
interest in the Eucharist had not disappeared in the tenth
century.

Gezo, Abbot of the monastery of SS. Peter and Martian at
Tortona from the mid-tenth century, produced a lengthy
treatise on the Eucharist for the edification of his monks.[73] If
the author of the *Responsio* left few clues to his over-all view of
the sacrament, Gezo left no doubt. Twenty-three of the seventy
chapters of the book were taken directly from the *De corpore et
sanguine domini* of Paschasius.[74] Gezo set Paschasius's work
into a specifically Christological setting. In the first seven chapters, he established that Christ was the incarnate Deity, partaking fully in the divine and human natures. From here, Gezo
could easily espouse the same theology of natural union as
Paschasius:

As (Christ) is in the Father through the nature of divinity, we, on the
other hand, are in (Christ) through His bodily nativity, and He again
is believed to be present in us through the mystery of the sacraments,
and thus a perfect unity through a mediator has been taught, with us
remaining in Him, He might remain in the Father, and remaining in
the Father, He might remain in us.[75]

Gezo, again relying heavily on Hilary, took up Paschasius's
theology and set it into a more explicit trinitarian setting.

Borrowing both from Gezo and the *Responsio*, Heriger, the
Abbot of Lobbes, would provide the first explicit attempt at
a reconciliation of the theologies of Paschasius and Ratramnus.
Familiar with both of these authors as well as Rabanus Maurus,

Heriger wished to attempt to provide a theology which could provide some unity to what he perceived as divisions in contemporary understandings of the sacrament.[76] As already mentioned, he also wished to respond to those, and he referred specifically to Rabanus here, who believed the body and blood of the Lord received in the sacrament was subject to digestion.[77]

Heriger distinguished between 'natural' references to the Lord's body and 'special' references to the Lord's body. Those who refer to the Lord's body 'naturally' simply refer to the one body of the Lord without specifying the mode of its existence. Those who distinguish between the Lord's body as it was on earth, as it is in the Eucharist, and as it is in the Church, are referring 'specially' to the mode of existence of the body of the Lord.[78] Since the body of the Lord remains one despite these two ways of speaking of the Lord, they are not in opposition. To distinguish, then, between the Lord's body born of Mary and the Lord's body present in the Eucharist, as Augustine did, is only to distinguish modes of presence of the one body of the Lord, and not to deny that the body present on the altar is the same as that born of Mary.[79]

Like Gezo, Heriger adopted Paschasius's general approach to the salvific function of the sacrament:

Wherefore it is thus to be understood: No one ascends to heaven with flesh unless he descends with divinity. To this end, (Christ) has been made a participant of our humanity, having assumed our flesh from the Virgin, in order that we, that is the Church, having been made participants of His divinity, might be united to His body assumed from the Virgin by means of the mediating and confirming Eucharist which is consumed at the altar.[80]

Heriger understood Paschasius's theology in a slightly more physical way than his predecessors. The question of digestion for Heriger was a serious theological issue, as he believed that the Lord's body was absorbed into the body of the faithful thus ensuring its immortality. What Heriger wished to deny, and what he believed Rabanus to have affirmed, was that the Lord's body and blood might somehow not be completely absorbed by the body and thus be subject to excretion.[81]

The work of Heriger, Gezo, and the anonymous writer of the *Responsio* provide witness to a continued discussion of the

Eucharist in the tenth century. Although a plurality of approaches continued to exist, it is worth noting that the only two works which provided a more or less complete theology of the sacrament relied heavily on the work of Paschasius. The theology of Paschasius appears as at least the dominant approach to the Eucharist by the end of the tenth century.[82] It was in the eleventh century that the theology of Paschasius, for a number of related political and theological reasons, received its strongest advocacy and official ecclesiastical sanction.

The Berengarian Controversy

It was perhaps inevitable that a crisis should eventually be reached in the teaching on the Eucharist in the Western Church. The plurality which existed from the time of the Fathers was used to support different theories of the Eucharist in the ninth century. Different explanations of the function of the Eucharist in salvation underlie different understandings of mode of presence of the Lord in the sacrament. These different approaches continued to exist, albeit uneasily, throughout the ninth, tenth, and into the eleventh centuries.[83]

In the mid-eleventh century, however, the unresolved tensions found a focal point when Berengar, the *scholasticus* of the church of St. Martin in Tours *c*.1040-1080, raised serious objections to the now dominant theology of Paschasius. Basing his teaching on the *De corpore et sanguine domini* of Ratramnus, which he wrongly attributed to Erigena, Berengar was held to maintain that the body and blood of the Lord were not present in the Eucharist. The controversy between Berengar and his opponents was long and bitter, and as that story has been told better elsewhere, only the outline of its history will be given here.[84]

By 1049, Berengar's flamboyant manner and popularity as well as his teaching on the Eucharist caused much opposition from his fellow theologians. Heading the opposition during this early phase of the controversy were the scholars of the Norman monastery of Fécamp, led by the abbot, John, and his cross-bearer, Durand. Word of Berengar's teaching reached Pope Leo IX, who condemned Berengar's teachings at the Council of Rome in 1050, destroying Ratramnus's book (under the

name of Erigena). Leo then summoned Berengar to defend his
teaching at the Council of Vercelli that same year, but Berengar was prevented from attending by Henry I of France, who
incarcerated him for political reasons. Once again, Berengar
was condemned unheard at Vercelli. He continued to expound
his teaching, however, and received support especially from
his bishop, Eusebius Bruno of Angers. Meanwhile, discussion
of Berengar's theology took place at councils in Brionne,
Chartres, and Paris. At the Council of Tours in 1054, Berengar
signed a compromise creed, proposed by himself and accepted
by the papal legate, Hildebrand, who hoped thus to settle the
matter until it could once again be referred to Rome.

For five years, the theological controversy continued without
judicial intervention, but in 1059, Berengar was again called to
appear before the Roman Synod. Berengar came, but instead
of defending his theology, he was presented with an oath drawn
up by Humbert, Cardinal-bishop of Silva Candida. The confession of 1059, which Berengar very reluctantly read, contained the strongest statement of physical presence yet put
forward by any author:

. . . the bread and wine which are laid on the altar are after consecration not only a sacrament but also the true body and blood of our lord
Jesus Christ, and they are physically taken up and broken in the
hands of the priest and crushed by the teeth of the faithful, not only
sacramentally but in truth.[85]

This statement settled the judicial question of the first phase
of the controversy, but its effect went far beyond an attempted
resolution of the Berengarian affair. The confession passed into
canon law collections, and so received wide distribution as an
orthodox statement on the Lord's presence in the sacrament.[86]
The confession, crude as it was, could not easily be ignored by
medieval theologians. This blunt statement of the reality of the
Lord's presence in the sacrament represented the furthest extreme to which the identification, first made by Paschasius, of
the eucharistic and historical presence of the Lord would be
taken in credal statements. Yet even at the time of its promul-
gation, it was an embarrassment in more learned circles, and
with very few exceptions, it would be the subject of reinterpre-
tation and rationalization by later theologians.[87]

After the Council, Berengar returned to Tours, and soon repudiated his oath as taken under duress. He circulated a pamphlet attacking the oath of Humbert, and again defended his earlier views. Around 1063, Lanfranc of Bec, one of Berengar's old opponents, took up the leadership of the opposition to Berengar by publishing a rebuttal to Berengar's pamphlet. Berengar responded with a long and rambling reply, and the theological controversy was once again rekindled. Judicial intervention, this time, was slow in coming. Finally, Gregory VII, who as Hildebrand had once reached a reconciliation with Berengar, now once more called the controversial teacher to Rome. The outcome was an oath accepted by Berengar at the Synod of Rome in 1079. The oath moderated considerably that of 1059:

> . . . the bread and wine which are placed on the altar . . . are changed substantially into the true and proper vivifying body and blood of Jesus Christ our Lord and after the consecration there are the true body of Christ which was born of the virgin . . . and the true blood of Christ which flowed from his side, not however through sign and in the power of the sacrament, but in their real nature and true substance.[88]

The oath demonstrated the technical expertise which had developed throughout the controversy. Here the technical terms of Aristotelian philosophy were introduced to describe the mode of presence which the Lord undertook in the sacrament. The sophistication which later theologians would develop as they rediscovered the use of Aristotelian concepts such as *substantia*, would continue to evolve new and more nuanced understandings of a sacramental terminology which would remain remarkably unchanged. Hans Jorissen, in his excellent study of the use of the term *transsubstantiatio* in eucharistic theology, has shown how this same word might mean very different things, say, for Innocent III and William of Auxerre.[89] The Berengarian controversy had established a terminology for further discussions of the Eucharist, but this terminology itself would be open to new developments.

The Berengarian affair was the first true controversy in the Western Church over the proper understanding of the Eucharist. The theological exchange which it entailed provided not

only the framework for most medieval discussions of the sacrament and began a period of lively interest in that topic, but also
provided an impetus and an outlet for the more general rise in
learning which marked the eleventh century.[90]

One cause of this controversy was the growing interest in
and mastery of the disciplines of logic, grammar, and dialectic.
These would provide the weapons by which Berengar attacked
and Lanfranc defended the theology of Paschasius. The debate
was also formed by less intellectual factors however. In the
early stages of the controversy, much judicial action taken
against Berengar appeared to be equally directed at Berengar's
protectors, Eusebius Bruno, Bishop of Angers, and Geoffrey
Martel, Count of Anjou, as a form of political chastisement.[91]

J. R. Geiselmann has further argued that Humbert's harsh
treatment of Berengar sprang from Humbert's involvement in
the azymite controversy.[92] In 1059, Humbert was deeply involved in the controversy with the East over the use of leavened
or unleavened bread in the Eucharist. Indeed, only five years
earlier Humbert had dramatically placed a writ of excommunication on the altar of Hagia Sophia, thus ending his disastrous mission to avoid schism. The Greeks defended their use
of unleavened bread by claiming that it symbolized the Trinity,
the Spirit represented by the leaven, while the unleavened
bread of the West would be a *corpus imperfectum et inanimatum.*[93]
In reply, Humbert and others insisted that only the salvific
body and blood of Christ were present here; to suggest the presence of the Trinity would be tantamount to Monophysitism.
Further, to speak of the bread *symbolizing* anything would be a
deep error. Firstly, because after the consecration, there would
be no true bread present and, secondly, somehow to think that
there would be a presence of the Lord in the bread different
from that of the incarnate, risen Lord, would split the unity of
Christ. Given this background, Humbert may well have intended the oath of 1059, with its extreme insistence on the
presence of Christ, as a rebuke not only to Berengar, but also
to the Greeks. As Geiselmann points out, the controversy with
the East may have lent an added edge to the opposition to
Berengar, and not all the arguments in the polemical works
may have had the teacher of Tours as their only target.[94]

The oath of 1079 also seemed to have a political motivation

behind it. Gregory VII who had so long taken a more moderate position in the Berengarian affair, may well have acted to demonstrate his own orthodoxy. The German bishops who supported Henry IV were looking for grounds for Gregory's deposition, and one such ground mentioned by them in 1080 was that Gregory espoused the heresy of Berengar. [95]

Granting the political nature of the dispute and its overlap with the Eastern problems, the central issue of the controversy remained theological and Western. The teaching of Berengar has been preserved in the responses of his critics, in his letters, and most especially in his refutation of Lanfranc, the *De sacra coena adversus Lanfrancum*. [96]

Berengar's theology appears to have been, as was Ratramnus's, based on a separation of the earthly and the divine. For Berengar, as for Ratramnus, the reception of the Lord's body and blood in the Eucharist was a spiritual matter. As humans are made up of an inferior body and superior soul, so in the Eucharist their souls receive spiritual bread in the Lord's body, and their bodies receive common bread. [97] Berengar insisted that the presence of the Lord was a spiritual presence, perceived in faith, and constituted by a faithful recollection of the mystery of the Lord's life, passion, and resurrection. [98]

In Berengar's understanding the bread and wine remained present in the Eucharist as visible signs (*sacramenta*) of the spiritual reality of the Lord (*rei sacramenta*). 'Eternal salvation is produced in us if we accept with a pure heart the body of Christ, i.e., the reality of the sign (*rem sacramenti*) while we accept the body of Christ in sign (*in sacramento*), i.e., in the holy bread of the altar, which has a temporal function.' [100]

Given this understanding of the function of the sacrament, Berengar would have seen no need for an insistence on the presence of the body and blood of the incarnate, risen Lord in the sacrament. Indeed, for Berengar, to assert this presence would not only be nonsense but blasphemy. It was on these two grounds that Berengar based his strongest attacks on what he understood as his opponent's theology. To say that the body and blood of Christ were physically present after the consecration was nonsense, because it was apparent to the senses that no such change in the bread and wine had taken place. [101] Further, it was a basic principle of Berengar's understanding of change, that if a subject changed, the qualities or accidents (*qualitates, accidentia*) of the subject also must change. To say, as Lanfranc had, that the qualities of colour and taste of the bread and wine remained after the consecration, but that now the body and blood were present, was sheer philosophical incompetence.[102]

More than just inane, however, such claims would be blasphemous. To believe in such a presence, would mean that 'little bits' (*portiuncula*) of Christ's flesh would then be placed on the altar and be daily subject to the indignity of being, in Humbert's phrase, 'broken in the hands of the priest, and crushed by the teeth of the faithful.'[103] This would be also mean that a new body of Christ came to be each day, and there would actually accumulate more and more 'body of Christ' as thousands of Masses were said.[104] Would not such a presence of the body of Christ on earth entail the faithful in a kind of cannibalism, to say nothing of the indignity of digestion, or desecration by rot, fire, or animals?[105] Surely, Christ was now incorruptible and seated at the right hand of the Father?[106] To assert a presence on earth as a sign of the presence in heaven, as Lanfranc wished, would be to split the body of Christ and to assert the existence of two Christs.[107]

Berengar spared no venom in his attacks on what he felt to be the stupidity of Paschasius, Humbert, and Lanfranc. In fact, his theology appears, in the bits of it which survive, to have been directed more towards destruction of his opponents' position than towards the construction of a positive theology of his own. This should hardly be surprising as the major work of Berengar to survive was meant as a rebuttal to an attack by Lanfranc. Yet, despite its ultimate defeat in 1079, Berengar's theology had an important impact on later discussions of the Eucharist. His description of a sacrament as the visible form of an invisible grace (*inuisibilis gratiae uisibilis forma*) would become accepted in medieval theology as the standard definition. Berengar's use of Aristotelian categories of subject and accidents, as well as his insistence on the distinction between *sacramentum* and *rei sacramentum* helped these terms become the standard terminology of a later age.[108] Exercising influence in another fashion, the arguments of Berengar used to demonstrate the blasphemy involved in asserting the body of Christ to be sensually present on the altar would be picked up and used by the Cathars in their attacks on the sacrament.[109]

Indeed, it may well be this connection that occasioned references to the 'heresy of Berengar' in the twelfth-century writings. On the whole it seems that the general approach to the sacrament taken by Berengar never exerted a wide influence in the twelfth century. As a general rule, the 'heresy of Berengar' refers to any teaching that denies the real presence, and not to any direct link with Berengar. Just as the term 'Arian' or 'Manichean' was applied to medieval heretics without suggesting a continuous connection with those ancient heresies, so, too, these 'Berengarians' were seen as new exponents of an old evil. As early as 1054, Berengar's name was being linked with heretics in Liège who denied the real presence.[110] Peter the Venerable, in his tract against the Petrobrusians accused these heretics in such terms,[111] and almost certainly when Gregory of Bergamo speaks of a new uprising of the Berengarian heresy, he is directing his remarks against one of the heretical sects which were beginning to infiltrate Northern Italy.[112] Even the orthodox teachings of Peter Lombard and of Alger of Liège were accused of being a revival of this heresy.[113] The constant reference to Berengar throughout the theological literature of the twelfth century has led some scholars to argue that the devotional practices, especially the elevation of the Host, were introduced to wean the people away from a lingering belief in the teachings of Berengar.[114] As suggested in Chapter 4, these devotions might better be explained as an outgrowth of that new devotion to the human Jesus prevalent in the twelfth century. If both the practices and the teaching of the Church with respect to the real presence took on a particular urgency, it came not from any aftermath of the Berengarian controversy, but from the very real conflict with the Waldenses and Cathars.

It was the teaching of Berengar's opponents that prevailed in the late eleventh and early twelfth centuries. Despite Berengar's fame as a teacher and apparent popularity, very few of his students seem to have continued to expound his teachings on the Eucharist. Certainly references to followers of Berengar abound in the twelfth century, but when these attributions are pressed, one soon finds that they could cover any eucharistic teaching of which an author did not approve. Even the reports

concerning students of Berengar during his own lifetime should
be received with caution. Guitmund of Aversa, for instance,
described the followers of Berengar as stercoranists in terms
which are strongly reminiscent of the tenth-century tract of
Heriger of Lobbes on the same subject.[115] It is difficult to know
if students of Berengar actually believed this teaching, or if
Guitmund attributed either contemporary or historical accounts
of this heresy to his enemy. Only one reference to an actual
twelfth-century master who is credited with teachings on the
Eucharist similar to those of Berengar has come to my attention.
Master Gerland, *scholasticus* and Canon of St. Paul's in
Besançon, *c*.1131-1148, is accused in a letter addressed to him
by Hugh Metel of teaching that Christ is present in the Eucharist in figure only.[116] Hugh does not describe Gerland as a student or follower of Berengar, however, and the records that do
exist concerning Gerland speak of him as a well-respected
master of liberal arts.[117] If the views of Berengar continued to
be propounded, it was not in the schools, but among the growing number of heretical groups formed during the eleventh,
twelfth, and thirteenth centuries.[118] From the evidence that
remains, it appears that the teaching of Berengar was not a
respectable theological option by the beginning of the twelfth
century.

To say that the theology of Berengar died with him, is not to
say that his teachings existed in some sort of historical vacuum,
out of touch with either past or future. Certainly many of his
major themes had been present in Ratramnus's thought, and
Ratramnus's theology in turn had been based on the Fathers.
The insistence that the eucharistic meal was an exclusively
spiritual affair had continued to find advocates during the tenth
and early eleventh century. Nor was this general approach to
the sacrament to die with Berengar. If during the twelfth and
thirteenth centuries no orthodox theologian would deny, as
Berengar had, that Christ was substantially present in the
Eucharist, several theologians would understand that substantial presence to have spiritual form and function quite similar
to that of Berengar.[119] His emphasis on the incorruptibility and
impassibility of the body of Christ would not be lost, and when
Berengar argued that 'in sign the body of Christ is broken, in
sign the body of Christ is accepted; nothing here is asserted

against the incorruptibility and impassibility of the body of Christ', he anticipated what would become the standard explanation of the theologically embarrassing oath of 1059.[120]

Berengar's major difficulty appeared to have been an inability to conceive of the presence of the body and blood of Christ in any but physical terms, and this sort of presence he simply could not accept in the Eucharist. Here at least he was at one with his contemporaries. They, too, while wishing to assert an 'essential' or 'natural' presence (and one must remember that an exact terminology has not been worked out here), were hard pressed to answer Berengar's objections because of their own physical understandings of presence. Only with a greater sophistication in metaphysics would a more adequate expression for a 'real' but yet not sensed presence be reached, and certainly to speak of 'a more adequate expression' is not to suggest that modern discussions of the sacrament are any less problematic than those of their medieval forebears.

The immediate future, however, lay with Berengar's opponents and it would be their refined articulation of Paschasius's theo-logy that would form the earliest model in scholastic theology for understanding the role of the Eucharist in the life of the Christian.

II

THE PASCHASIAN APPROACH TO
THE EUCHARIST

THE theology of the Eucharist developed by Paschasius and handed on by the theologians of the tenth and eleventh centuries found its fullest development among the writers of the late eleventh and early twelfth centuries. The writers who espoused this theology were not a completely heterogeneous group by any means. Rupert of Deutz, for instance, accused Alger of Liège of adopting Berengar's teaching despite both authors' insistence on the Paschasian approach. Yet these writers' similarity in their use of that approach would set their theology off from the theologies of the Eucharist taught during the later twelfth and early thirteenth centuries. To a large extent, the proponents of a Paschasian theology developed their theology in opposition to Berengar's heirs. Therefore, it is with the opponents of Berengar that a study of this theology ought rightly to begin.

Tracts Directed Against Berengar or 'Berengarians'

The leaders of the opposition to Berengar in the earlier stages of the debate, culminating in the oath of 1059, were the abbot of the monastery of Fécamp, John, and his cross-bearer, Durand, later Abbot of Troarn.[1] In his *Confessio fidei*, John attacked those who attempt reasonably to explain the mystery and miracle of the Eucharist.[2] Stating that the form of reception of the Lord's body is a spiritual reception,[3] John nevertheless insisted that the body and blood of the Lord were truly present, truly eaten, and truly drunk.[4] He explained that the same body which could pass through the Virgin's womb and walk upon the water, could certainly become present in the food broken by the teeth of the recipients.[5] Yet the salvific power of Christ's presence affects only the just; sinners receive unto damnation.[6] John described this salvific power in Paschasian terms. Christ has given us his flesh to eat, so that 'we might be made participants of the divine unity, because God remains in us and we in God.'[7]

One of the strongest theological reasons for the opposition to Berengar's teaching lay in this fundamental precept of Paschasian theology. Christ's 'natural' presence in the Eucharist unites us to Christ in his very nature, and hence salvifically to God. To deny this form of presence would be to deny us salvation itself. Hugh of Langres, writing about the same time as John of Fécamp, accurately described the problem: 'Nevertheless, then, if from their essences and natures, they (the bread and wine) do not have the power of salvation, they have the contrary of it, and thus, as long as they remain in their nature, it (the Eucharist) will be an impotent sign' (*impotens sacramentum*).[8]

Durand of Fécamp followed the tenth-century theologians by setting this objection into the framework of a theology of the Incarnation.[9] The Word became flesh in order that we might receive that flesh in the Eucharist and thus be joined naturally (*naturaliter*) to Christ. It is through this union that we become partakers in Christ's divinity.[10] The movement of the redemptive act becomes closely tied to the natural presence. Christ specifically took on flesh in order that we might be joined to his Godhead through consuming that flesh.[11] To deny the natural presence of Christ in the Eucharist undermines the highest salvation of mankind, and the whole of Christian religion.[12] Like his abbot, Durand insisted that the natural presence must not be understood crudely; this presence is a divine and spiritual reality.[13] It was Berengar who misunderstood this when he believed the sacred elements to undergo digestion, and Durand thus accused Berengar of stercoranism.[14] For Durand, the visible species were mere appearances (*similitudines*) given to the substance of the body and blood in order to make them more palatable for squeamish humans.[15] Again following his abbot, Durand insisted that this presence is both natural and spiritual in a way that transcends all human efforts to comprehend.[16] Durand's theology is thoroughly dependent on that of Paschasius, whom he calls, 'the most diligent Catholic investigator and expounder of the divine sacraments.'[17] Yet, under pressure from Berengar, Durand was forced to address a problem which seems not to have arisen for Paschasius. How could one claim that the presence of Christ in the Eucharist was a natural presence, and then describe that same presence as not subject to the ordinary laws of nature? Berengar had posed the question in a most pointed way, and the problem would remain a major obstacle to Paschasian theology.

Lanfranc, then Abbot of St. Stephen at Caen and later Archbishop of Canterbury, led the opposition to Berengar from the 1060s on.[18] Lanfranc began his rebuttal of Berengar's teaching, *De corpore et sanguine Domini*, written *c.*1163, by contending that Berengar stood condemned because of his flaunting of the received tradition of the entire Church, especially as propounded by the Council of Rome in 1059.[19] He then proceeded to attack a now lost tract of Berengar on a somewhat piecemeal basis. Lanfranc's approach, effective as it may have been in countering Berengar, does not easily lend itself to systematic analysis. Lanfranc made, for instance, no general statements on the purpose of the Eucharist such as one finds in Durand of Fécamp or Alger of Liège.

Yet Lanfranc's theology remains important for the distinctions which he used in attempting to clarify the relationship between the body of Christ in heaven, the body and blood present on the altar, and the sensed reality of bread and wine. It was, of course, in determining these relationships that Berengar made one of his most telling arguments. If the body of Christ is naturally present, why is it not sensed? How can the Fathers speak of a presence in sign (*in sacramento*) if the reality itself is present? Lanfranc took up the terms *sacramentum* and *rei sacramentum* introduced by Berengar from Augustine, but preferred to use them in a less specific way than Berengar.

Although Lanfranc listed several meanings for the word *sacramentum*,[20] he spoke in general terms of the entire ritual of the Mass as the *sacramentum* or *mysterium* of the Passion of Christ.[21] More specifically, he designated the visible species as the *sacramentum* of the flesh and blood of Christ present on the altar.[22] He also spoke of the flesh and blood of Christ present on the altar as the *sacramentum* both of the complete body and blood of Christ present in heaven, and of the body and blood crucified for us.[23] In this sense, he referred to Christ as a *sacramentum* of himself.[24] Both the flesh and blood on the altar and the body and blood of Christ in heaven are essentially the same, but have different *qualitates*.[25] In communion, the good receive both these bodies, while the evil receive only the flesh and blood.[26] Lanfranc's usage remains difficult and unclear, and the problem compounded itself for later writers when Alger of Liège copied passages of Lanfranc's treatment of this matter from Ivo of Chartres' *Decretum* believing them to have come from Augustine.[27] Despite his lack of clarity, Lanfranc offered a terminology which answered Berengar's use of the Fathers while yet protecting the Paschasian insistence on a natural presence.

Lanfranc also attempted to clarify and reconcile the insistence of most commentators on the Eucharist that this was a spiritual reception and the Paschasian insistence that a natural union was formed by reception. According to Lanfranc, there are two kinds of reception of the Lord's body and blood. The first, purely corporeal (*corporaliter*), involves only the sacramental reception, i.e. reception of the true flesh and blood of Christ. The second, a spiritual reception (*spiritualiter*), entails a faithful recollection of the deeds of salvation and is required for the salvific effect of the Eucharist.[28] In his references to the spiritual reception of the Eucharist, however, Lanfranc spoke both of the results of the sacrament, and the necessary disposition for proper reception without distinguishing the two.[29] Both a corporeal and spiritual reception are necessary to receive worthily,[30] and therefore only those who recall and imitate the Passion of Christ in purity and love receive unto salvation.[31]

Without specifically alluding to Paschasian theology, Lanfranc did include contact with the humanity of Jesus as one of the principal results of the reception of the Eucharist[32] In the Eucharist, we receive the *essentiam* and *virtutem* of Christ.[33] The reception of the body of Christ in the sacrament of the Eucharist is necessary for salvation. Spiritual union with Christ is not enough; all Christians of the age of reason must receive the true body and blood to be saved.[34]

Lanfranc's own use of dialectic allowed him to meet Berengar's arguments by introducing distinctions which integrated the patristic terminology offered by Berengar into the current Paschasian understanding of the Eucharist. Lanfranc did not, however, offer as an argument the necessity of a 'natural union' in the sacrament. Important as his contribution will be to later theology of the Eucharist, Lanfranc alone it would seem among the opponents of Berengar, does not explicitly advert to the role of the Eucharist in salvation as that role is delineated in Paschasian theology.[35]

If Lanfranc made no reference to the Paschasian approach to the Eucharist in his rebuttal of Berengar, his student and fellow monk Guitmund certainly did. Guitmund, later Bishop of Aversa from 1088 until his death *c*.1090-1095, wrote a tract directed against Berengar and his 'followers' while a monk at Bec, *c*.1073-1075.[36] Guitmund argued that if man fell by the eating of real fruit, then it is fitting that man be saved by the eating of the real fruit of the cross, Christ's body.[37] What would be the purpose of the Eucharist, if Christ himself were not received? It is the true body of Christ which carries the richness of salvation, and in which we hope.[38] How could man be substantially one with Christ, as St. Hilary said, if we receive only the shadow of Christ? An effect does not flow from the shadow of a thing, but from the substance of it. To remain substantially one with Christ, we must receive the substance of Christ.[39] Christ gives us the same substance of his body which he took from the flesh of Mary, and in which he walked on earth, in order that we might be saved.[40]

Guitmund placed himself firmly within the Paschasian tradition in adopting these views. Just as Durand of Fècamp or Hugh of Langres, Guitmund argued that the major objection to Berengar's position must be that it robs us of our salvation. If Christ's substantial body is not present in the Eucharist, the necessary salvific union of that body with our own cannot take place.

Guitmund used many of the same distinctions as his master in replying to the arguments of Berengar. In a long passage directed against Berengar's use of *signum-res*, he responded that the Mass is a *signum* of the Passion of Christ.[41] The Eucharist is always a sign of our Redemption, and even Christ is a sign of his own role as Redeemer.[42] Similarly in discussing effective reception of the sacrament, Guitmund argued that although all receive corporeally, only those who also receive spiritually, i.e. worthily, receive unto salvation.[43]

It is in his discussion of the implications of a substantial presence of Christ in the Eucharist that Guitmund went far beyond any of his predecessors. The earliest of the anti-Berengarian tracts merely asserted the incorruptibility of the risen Christ, thus denying that any change could affect his body. Responding to Berengar's argument that a substantial presence would involve sacrilege, Guitmund insisted that the true body and blood remain even when the bread and wine appear to rot or putrefy. Just as our Lord took on the form of a gardener to teach Mary Magdalene, and that of a pilgrim to teach the disciples at Emmaus, so he takes on the form of putrefied bread and wine to admonish us for improper care of the reserved species.[44] If an animal is seen to eat the species, this too is for our edification, nor should we be shocked to think of Christ as descending into the bowels of an animal, as he himself once descended into a tomb of stone.[45] It is difficult to tell if Guitmund ascribed any self-subsistent reality to these 'appearances'. When he discussed what happens to the Host if it is burned, Guitmund allowed that the 'sensible qualities' remain behind, while the true body ascends to heaven.[46] He denied, however, that any part of the species can be digested, and that if certain of the Fathers lived on communion alone for many years, this was only by means of a miracle.[47]

In his insistence on a substantial presence of Christ in the Eucharist, Guitmund denied any true reality to what might be sensed in the sacrament. Any external appearances are merely taken up by Christ to cloak what would ordinarily appear as his substantial body. Further, Guitmund understood that 'natural' or, in his terminology, substantial, presence in what seems to be far more corporeal terms than Paschasius or even his predecessors in the Berengarian dispute. Rather than deny the substantial presence of Christ in the Eucharist, Guitmund was prepared to accept the logical consequences of his highly corporeal understanding of such a presence, even if that meant that a mouse really did eat the body of Christ when he poached from the tabernacle.

Alger, Canon of St. Lambert's in Liège, wrote his *De sacramentis corporis et sanguinis Domini c.*1110-1115 in order to combat *varii errores, variaeque haereses.*[48] Among these teachings he included not only Berengar's teaching, but also impanation; the teaching that the bread and wine are changed not into Christ,

but into a certain holy 'son of man'; the teaching that immoral
priests cannot worthily consecrate; the teaching that those who
receive unworthily receive only bread and wine, and finally,
stercoranism.[49] Not all these teachings can be laid at the door
of Berengar, and some attempt will be made later in this work
to place the writings of Guitmund, Alger, and others into a
context which might better explain who their adversaries might
be. Alger's work would be highly regarded by later authors.
Peter the Venerable would account Lanfranc, Guitmund, and
Alger as the most learned of writers on the Eucharist, and
Alger the most learned of the three.[50]

Even more than Lanfranc or Guitmund, Alger made the
Incarnation the mainstay of his eucharistic theology. He began
his treatise with a description of the Incarnation as God's
greatest work; that is the unification of man to God and the
exaltation of Christ.[51] As sharers in the same human nature as
the God-man, we can also hope to become Sons of God.[52]
The Eucharist unites the Church 'not in name only, but in
His true body' to Christ, thus allowing us to share the same
dignity granted to Christ through the Incarnation.[53] The logic
is simple: Christ as man is joined to the Father through his
divinity. In the sacrament of the Eucharist, we are joined to the
body of Christ. We then become sharers in the union of the
Father and the Son through our own union with the Son.[54]

Alger, more than Lanfranc or Guitmund, set out to address
himself systematically to the problem of the relationship of sign
to reality in the Eucharist. He set out as a general rule that
the species of bread and wine are the *sacramentum* of the body
and blood present on the altar, and this body and blood are
the true *res sacramenti* of the Eucharist.[55] The body of Christ,
however, can be spoken of in three ways, as the historical body
of Christ which suffered; as the invisible, spiritual body of the
risen Christ, and as Christ whose body is the Church.[56] A *sacramentum* can signify a *res* either through similitude, or through
some external action performed in respect to the *res*.[57] The
bread and wine are *sacramentum* of both the risen body and of
the Church through similitude.[58] Because the actions of the
Mass represent the Passion of Christ, the invisible risen body
present on the altar can be called the *sacramentum* either of the
historical body of Christ, or of the Church according to the

second use of this term.[59] According to this usage, the body
of Christ can be referred to as a *sacramentum significans et significatum* (a signifying and signified sign).[60]

Alger added some precision to the usage of Lanfranc, but his
terminology remains unwieldly. His basic principle stresses the
central importance of the real presence as the *res* of the Eucharist, in line with the oath of Berengar: the body and blood are
not *solummodo sacramenta* (only signs). Yet he did not abandon
traditional language which spoke of the Mass as a commemoration of the Passion, or of the Eucharist as the sign of unity
in the Church. His solution is not a happy one, but it is the
best which the anti-'Berengarian' tracts will produce.

Alger followed Lanfranc in his understanding of worthy and
unworthy reception. The good and evil alike receive the body
of Christ, but only the good receive unto salvation.[61] Alger
also described spiritual reception as the commemoration of
the Passion of Christ, and the imitation of his Passion in our
lives.[62] Although Alger argued that spiritual communion is
more worthy than sacramental communion, he insisted, as
Lanfranc had, that both forms of reception are necessary for
salvation. Where Lanfranc had stated that simple sacramental
reception was inadequate, Alger insisted that spiritual reception could not alone suffice for salvation.[63] Alger may have
been directing his remarks against the teaching coming from
the school at Laon, which admitted the possibility of a salvific
union of God and believed in spiritual reception alone.[64] If
Alger copied Lanfranc's teaching on spiritual reception, he
followed Guitmund more closely in denying any reality to the
appearances of bread and wine. He underlined this teaching by
arguing that digestion and putrefaction cannot take place
naturally in the species because there is no substance left in the
species to undergo such a change.[65] Alger, unlike Guitmund,
left no doubt that for him, these changes in the appearances of
bread and wine are only an illusion.[66]

The latest work written specifically against 'Berengarians'
was that of Gregory, Bishop of Bergamo, writing in 1146.[67]
Gregory's work was not only the latest, but in many ways, the
least impressive of these occasional treatises. Rather than
follow the lead of Alger in attempting to simplify the terminology involved in describing the sacrament, Gregory offered his

own elaborate and somewhat difficult terminology. He specified three elements in each of the sacraments of the Church:
(1) *res quae sacramentum est* (the thing which is a sign), (2) *res
cuius sacramentum est* (the thing of which there is a sign), and
(3) *res quae virtus sacramenti est* (the thing which is the power of
the sign).[68] In the Eucharist, the *res quae sacramentum est* is the
true body and blood of Christ.[69] The *res quarum sacramentum est*
are the Passion and death of the Lord, true peace, the unity of
concord, and the Church which is the Body of Christ.[70] The *res
quae virtus sacramenti* is the remission of sin, and the natural
union of the faithful with Christ.[71] Gregory's analysis is not a
little confusing, as he himself realized.[72] In the constant repetition of the words *res* and *sacramentum*, one can quickly forget
which *res* is which. Gregory's terminology died with him, and
Christianity certainly need not bemoan the loss. It is interesting to note, however, that unlike Lanfranc, Guitmund, or
Alger, Gregory did not use *sacramentum* for the visible species,
possibly because he accorded them no real existence.[73]

In the other facets of his eucharistic theology, Gregory
offered little new. He copied Alger when he treated of the
effects of the sacrament. When we are incorporated into the
humanity of Christ in communion, we are joined through his
divinity to the Father.[74] Gregory also included the distinction
of Lanfranc between spiritual and corporeal reception, and in
his confession of faith emphasized that both forms of reception
are necessary for salvation.[75] Like Guitmund and Alger before
him, Gregory too spoke of the species of bread and wine as
mere external features adopted by Christ for use in the Eucharist.[76]

The tracts arising from the Berengarian conflict, as well as
those arising from opposition to what were felt to be extensions
or revivals of Berengar's teaching, did much to clarify and
categorize the Paschasian theology of the ninth and tenth
centuries. The natural union so essential to Paschasian theology acquired the more technical description of a 'substantial'
union, and hence it was a 'substantial' change that was said to
occur in the ritual. This particular description of the change
would become the standard terminology for the eucharistic
change, even though more sophisticated understandings of
'substance' might modify considerably the understanding of

such a change.[77] Further, the work of Lanfranc and Alger would go far to clarify the patristic terminology of *sacramentum/ res* introduced by Berengar. It was their work that would form a basis for the distinction among *sacramentum, res et sacramentum*, and *sacramentum* used by Peter Lombard and thus standardized for later centuries.[78] Guitmund, despite his strongly corporeal approach, at least attempted to deal with the questions raised by Berengar concerning natural processes affecting the bread and wine. These tracts did much to establish the terminology and the questions which would occupy theologians for at least the coming century. Yet the terminology, and more particularly the questions introduced by the Berengarian controversy remained current, not through mere theological conservatism, but because theologians continued to be challenged by other movements, certainly more numerous and probably more dangerous to Christianity than Berengar and his supporters could ever have been seen to be.

The Continuing Challenge

The tracts on the Eucharist discussed above, spanning a period of nearly a century, were clearly occasional works defending the Paschasian theology against what their authors saw as mistaken approaches to the sacrament. In each of the works, references to the 'heresy of Berengar' appear. Yet only the works of John, Durand, and Lanfranc were written specifically against the known teachings of Berengar. Indeed, Alger and Gregory wrote long after Berengar's death. If not against Berengar himself, then against whom were these tracts directed? One possibility would be students of Berengar who perhaps spread or even popularized his teaching. If this was indeed the case, however, few records of any such students remain. As discussed above, there appear to be no records of masters who actually espoused Berengar's teaching, apart from the rather doubtful example of Gerland of Besançon.[79]

A more likely background for these occasional works, and for the numerous references to the 'heresy of Berengar' throughout the twelfth century, are the appearance of popular religious movements which sprang up in the late eleventh, twelfth, and into the thirteenth centuries. As Herbert Grundmann and others have shown, these movements were often inspired by a longing for a purer Christian life. Some found acceptance, albeit reluctantly, by ecclesiastical officials. Other movements found themselves clearly in opposition to the official Church, and perhaps more often than not, genuine confusion prevailed.[80] Writers directing themselves against popular preachers, or even masters in the schools, could, and did, brand any teaching about the Eucharist with which they disagreed as a revival of Berengar's old errors. Such unlikely bedfellows as Peter of Bruys, Peter Lombard, and Alger of Liège, were accused of 'Berengarianism'.[81]

For this reason it would be difficult to explain the views on the Eucharist held by the various popular preachers of this time. Yet both the teaching and practices of the Church took on a particular urgency, not perhaps because of any aftermath of the Berengarian controversy, but because of the very real conflict with the Waldensians and Cathars. Moreover, controversy with the East continued throughout the twelfth and into the thirteenth century. Tracts against the Greeks continued to appear, and although the heat of the eleventh-century controversy cooled as time past, authors as late as Innocent III would take up the old arguments of the azymite controversy.[82] Cardinal Humbert of Silva Candida, author of the 1059 oath of Berengar, seems to have been the first to coin the phrase *stercorista* to describe those who dared to argue that the Lord's body might undergo the normal digestive processes, and, interestingly enough, he used the term to condemn both the teaching of Berengar and that of the Eastern Church.[83] Guitmund relied upon the arguments of Heriger of Lobbes to condemn the 'stercoranists' of his day, although he gave no hint as to who these 'Berengarians' might have been.[84] Alger of Liège was more specific, identifying the Greek 'heretics' as those who are rightly called *Stercoranistae*.[85] Although the identification of the Greek Church as stercoranist heretics will not appear as clearly in later works as in Humbert and Alger, the charge had been made, and therefore, the possibility always existed that the authors who spoke against this heresy were responding to the (in their minds) always recalcitrant Church in the East.

The wandering heretical preachers of the late eleventh and early twelfth centuries were frequently charged with a denial of the validity of the sacrament. In Ivois, near Trier, *c.*1122[86] and in Soissons, *c.*1114,[87] small bands of heretics are reported as having rejected the Eucharist. The same accusation is made of the preacher Ramihrdrus killed in Cambrai in 1074[88] and of the much-discussed preacher Tanchelm, who taught in Utrecht and Antwerp, *c.*1100-1115.[89] A problem arises, however, as to what exactly these men did preach. More likely in the cases of Ramihrdrus and Tanchelm, they rejected the validity of the sacrament when confected by unworthy priests.[90] The reform papacy of the late eleventh and early twelfth centuries urged the faithful to refrain from receiving the body and blood of Christ from unworthy ministers,[91] and it was a thin line, not too clearly distinguished by the theologians of the time, between invoking this injunction and preaching a form of Donatism which denied any validity to the sacraments performed by unworthy ministers. The situation presented grave problems in the twelfth century, and in order to demonstrate the fine distinction here between orthodoxy and heterodoxy, two examples will be given: the less well-known case of Albero of Merke and the more important phenomenon of Waldes of Lyon and his followers.

The only witness to the heretical teaching of Albero of Merke (near Cologne) comes from an anonymous tract directed against him, and dated *c.*1154-1177.[92] Albero is accused of precisely the teaching in question; that of denying the validity of the sacrament when confected by unworthy priests.[93] Albero referred specifically to the injunctions of Nicholas II, Alexander II, and Gregory VII in defending his case.[94] If, in fact, Albero was directing his attack against schismatics, he stood in good company. Gerhoh of Reichersberg, writing about the same time, from the same country, and same political situation, denied repeatedly the validity of the sacraments confected by simoniacs, schismatics, and even priests living in concubinage.[95] The author of the tract did explain that Albero has confused here the validity of sacraments performed by heretics, schismatics, and excommunicates, and the validity of sacraments offered by unworthy priests within the Church.[96] Since we do not know to whom Albero's attack was directed, the case of his orthodoxy on this point remains a delicate one. Albero also taught that if the believers accepted the Eucharist from a priest they knew to be in sin, they did not receive worthily. If, however, they received in ignorance, the sacrament had a salvific effect.[97] Again, Albero here stands in good company. Honorius Augustodunensis, a student of St. Anselm, writing earlier in the century,[98] denied that the Eucharist offered by an unworthy priest can have any good effect for the participants, even if they remain ignorant of their crimes.[99] Gerhoh's teaching on the subject was closer to that of Albero. If the faithful receive worthily, ignorant of the state of the minister, they receive the effect of the sacrament, even from schismatics.[100] Another of the condemned teachings of Albero denied that a Mass offered by an unworthy priest can be of any help to the dead.[101] The teaching once more parallels a similar teaching of Honorius.[102] Finally, Albero is accused of teaching that not angels, but demons accompany the sacrifices of unworthy priests.[103] This strong language is not unlike that of Honorius, who may actually be the source of Albero's teaching on this point.[104]

Albero may have indeed taught, as his accuser insisted, a kind of Donatism, holding that the state of the minister of the Eucharist determines the validity of the sacrament. He may also have been a defender of papal reform, directing his teaching against lax and perhaps schismatic clergy. In either case, he seems to have been a man familiar with the teaching of the Church, but perhaps too zealous in his interpretation of that teaching. The differences between the teachings of Albero, Honorius, and Gerhoh are slight, and yet, Albero was condemned as a heretic, while Honorius and Gerhoh were accepted as orthodox teachers.

One of the most numerous and influential heretical sects in the late twelfth and early thirteenth centuries was that founded by Waldes, a wealthy merchant from Lyon. Some time between 1173 and 1176, Waldes, having provided for his family, gave up his possessions and began to preach a form of *vita apostolica*, urging poverty and clerical reform. Waldes himself remained orthodox at least until 1180-1181, but in 1182/3 he and his followers were excommunicated and driven from Lyon. The Poor of Lyon, or Waldensians, moved south, and by the 1220s were firmly established, in different forms, in Languedoc and Northern Italy.[105] Basically, the Waldensians' errors concerning the Eucharist stem from the desire for a reformed clergy. They denied the validity of the sacrifice offered by unworthy ministers,[106] but accepted the sacraments from those orthodox priests who met their standards of morality.[107] At first, at least some of the Waldensians required the minister of the Eucharist to be a validly ordained priest,[108] but gradually their teaching expanded to admit the validity of a Mass offered by any worthy layman or laywoman.[109] Even in this extreme position they may have been following a twelfth-century teaching which attributed power to the words of consecration irrespective of the grade or intention of the minister.[110]

The Waldensians eventually adopted their own ritual for the Mass, which, like their teaching on the validity of the sacraments, appears to have evolved from an over-emphasis on certain traditions which remained orthodox.[111] At the centre of the ritual was a sevenfold repetition of the Lord's Prayer.[112] Quite probably, the Waldensians were here following the medieval tradition that the Mass first consisted of only this prayer used as the prayer of consecration.[113] They consecrated the elements by means of a sign of the cross.[114] Again, theologians earlier in the century accepted the benediction as one of the elements effecting the consecration, and then current theological opinion accepted the theory that Christ himself may have consecrated the elements in this way.[115] Both of these elements in the ritual seem to have been a deliberate attempt to recover the earliest form of Christian worship as this was presented in medieval tradition. In terms of how at least some scholars of the Middle Ages understood the Last Supper and early Christian worship, the Waldensian liturgy could be seen as a kind of 'liturgical renewal'; an attempt to recover the original form of the Eucharist.

One of the major heretical attacks on the sacrament of the Eucharist in this period came then not from a rejection of the sacrament itself, but from an over-zealousness for its value and purity; in short, from the explosive new devotion to the Eucharist, a force which carried some people into a head-on collision with the established Church.

A much more serious attack, not only on the Eucharist, but on the whole sacramental system of the Church, came from the various dualist sects which arose in the twelfth and thirteenth centuries. Appearing sporadically early in the twelfth century, they came to control much of Southern France and Northern Italy by the end of the century. Scholars debate the origins of these groups here referred to under the general name of Cathars, but most agree that by the 1160s at least some groups of Cathars were influenced by kinds of mitigated and unmitigated dualism coming from Eastern Europe and Constantinople. By the early decades of the thirteenth century, two general kinds of dualism existed; an unmitigated dualism which condemned all matter as evil, and a mitigated dualism which saw matter as created by God (that is, not evil *per se*) but as fallen, and ineffectual towards salvation.[116] As a basic principle, however, the Cathars of both groups completely rejected the real presence and the efficacy of the Eucharist for salvation.[117]

By their absolute rejection of the sacrament, the Cathars forced the orthodox theologians to rethink their arguments for the real presence, and not surprisingly, the objections advanced by the heretics are found as questions in the theological tracts. Even a brief review of the arguments put forward by the Cathars makes this clear. One of the most consistent criticisms by the heretics insisted that the amount of matter necessary to feed all the faithful far exceeds that of the body of Christ.[118] Another common group of arguments used by the Cathars held that the pronoun *Hoc* in the words of institution referred not to the consecrated bread but either to Christ himself or to the Church.[119] Arguments often occurred that involved the problem of desecration of the body of Christ by its digestion or consumption by an animal.[120] Again, the Cathars argued that scriptural references to the reception of the body and blood of Christ were to be taken figuratively.[121] All these arguments were discussed and re-discussed in the theological tracts of the early scholastic period, from the time of Berengar onwards.[122] The similarity between the objections raised by the Cathars to dispute the orthodox teaching on the Eucharist, and the questions discussed by the early scholastic theologians on the same subject show, even in this brief summary, that the early scholastic theologians were not merely undertaking a painstaking process of the gradual precision of doctrine, but attacking and re-attacking what was then felt to be a real threat to the sacramental life of the Church.[123]

Nor would this threat have been seen as discontinuous with the Berengarian controversy by contemporary theologians. Each of the arguments described above as belonging to the Cathars can be found either in Berengar's own teaching, or in teachings ascribed to him by Lanfranc, Guitmund, or Alger. Berengar certainly did question how it would be possible to feed all the faithful with the one body of Christ, and also raised the problem of desecration by animals or digestion.[124] His adversaries at least accused him of versions of the other teachings ascribed to the Cathars.[125] It should be no wonder that Gregory of Bergamo, writing in Northern Italy in 1146, at a time and in a place where the Cathars were first beginning to appear, should have spoken of 'the new Berengarians of this time.'[126]

The Cathars, the Waldensians, Albero of Merke, and the other heretics discussed here only serve as representatives of a large band of dissidents who rejected one or the other teaching on the Eucharist during this period. Peter of Bruys, teaching *c*.1112-1131, was said to assert that the body and blood were confected only once at the Last Supper and never again.[127] Henry of Le Mans, a wandering monk active *c*.1119-1145, was accused of teaching that unworthy priests could not confect the Eucharist.[128] Hugh Speroni and his small group of followers in Piacenza *c*.1177-1185 were held to deny that either the Last Supper or the Mass contained the body and blood of Christ, but held that to 'eat' Christ meant to imitate him in love.[129] Finally, mention should be made of the followers of Amalric of Bène condemned in Paris in 1210 for believing the Eucharist to be no longer necessary to those endowed by the Spirit.[130]

Since some of the heresies were stimulated by a too zealous manifestation of the growing piety towards the sacrament, and by a corresponding increase in readiness to criticize unworthy priests or to reflect on the possible meanings of the Eucharist, they in turn demanded a closer theological explanation of the issues raised. The heresies of this period, by challenging the orthodox approaches to the Eucharist, kept the questions surrounding the sacrament alive and urgent. Their denials and

the criticisms they received in turn provide a useful indication of
the attitudes to the sacrament current in the twelfth century.
They supply the context without which some of the theological
tracts and devotional practices of this period may appear as so
much shadow play.

The Commentaries on Scripture

Not only in the tracts directed specifically against 'Berengarianism' was the Paschasian approach to the Eucharist
espoused. In several mostly anonymous commentaries on Scripture from the late eleventh or early twelfth centuries, a similar
theology appeared. A series of four commentaries on Psalm 21,
all stemming from the same source, make up one group of these
glosses. The patristic source upon which these works depend is
the commentary of the so-called 'Ambrosiaster' on 1 Cor.
11:26.[131] The Ambrosiaster gloss was adopted by a commentary
on Psalm 21 attributed to Remigius of Auxerre, and now contained in Admont, Stiftsbibliothek Cod. 99, fols. 19v-20r.[132]
Three other glosses on this psalm depend on the Admont commentary. The first is a commentary, again attributed to Remigius, and now printed in Migne, *Patrologia Latina*, vol. 131.[133]
A second gloss, attributed to St. Bruno, founder of the Car-
thusians, also copied the Admont commentary.[134] The third,
attributed to Gilbert the Universal, exists in Loan MS 117.[135]
    The dating of these commentaries varies greatly. Rupert
Geiselmann, the first to discuss the matter, would date the
Admont gloss before 1076,[136] while Damien Van Eynde has
suggested the mid-twelfth century for the same gloss.[137] No
certain attribution exists for any of these glosses. Without
deciding the particular question of either dating or authorship,
the commentaries can be said to belong to the group of writings
which carried the Paschasian theology of the Eucharist into the
twelfth century. As in the tracts discussed above, all the commentaries contain some reference to eucharistic heretics against
whom they are directing their remarks.[138]
    The teaching on the Eucharist contained in all four commen-
taries is similar. Through the consumption of the Lord's body,
we become sharers in his immortality. The blood of Christ
represents his Soul, and therefore, it is through the reception

of Christ's Blood that our soul are redeemed.[139] In their commentary on Psalm 77:25, both the Bruno and the Pseudo-Remigius glosses placed this reception of the sacrament into a theology of the incarnation. The Word became Flesh in order that we might be saved through the consumption of the body of the God-Man.[140] We accept both the body and blood as sustenance for our present life and as a pledge of future glory.[141] A great emphasis was placed by these glosses on the inviolability of the body and blood as they exist under the sensual appearances of bread and wine. Christ exists undivided and entire in each part of the species.[142] All the glosses mentioned that the water mixed with the wine is a symbol of our sharing in the Passion of Christ.[143] They made some distinction between reception by the faithful and unfaithful,[144] and linked the salvific reception by the faithful to their life of faith and love.[145] Finally, all the glosses elaborated on the symbolism of bread and wine as a sign of the union of Christ and his Church.[146]

The same theological teachings are contained in a commentary on the Song of Songs by John, *grammaticus* of Mantua writing *c*.1081-1083.[147] John included a short treatment of the Eucharist in his commentary on Chapter 1, verse 13 in order to warn his patron, Matilda, Countess of Tuscany, against the heresy of Berengar.[148] As in the commentaries on Ps. 21, John saw the salvation of our bodies linked to reception of Christ's body and the salvation of our souls to the reception of Christ's blood.[149] The bread and wine cease to exist in all but external features so that we might be joined to Christ by reception of his sacramental presence.[150] Like the commentators on Ps. 21, John placed great emphasis on the indivisibility and inviolability of the body of Christ present under the appearance of bread and wine.[151] He also appears to be the first advocate of the concomitance of Christ under each species.[152] Although John did not cover all the points treated by the commentaries on Psalms mentioned above, those teachings which he does have in common suggest that a late eleventh-century dating of the gloss contained in Admont MS 99 is certainly possible.[153]

If these commentaries on Psalms present problems of dating and attribution, a set of commentaries on 1 Cor. 10:16 from roughly the same period present even greater problems. Again based on the commentary of Ambrosiaster on 1 Cor. 11:26, similar passages exist in two commentaries. One of these, extant in several manuscripts, has been edited under the name of St. Bruno the Carthusian.[154] A second and closely related commentary is that attributed to a certain *Gratiadei*.[155] So far no certain dating or authorship for either commentary has been determined, although one exemplar of the *Gratiadei* gloss appears to have been written *c*.1102.[156] Coterminous with these glosses are a number of *sententie* which contain the same passage found in the commentaries. The *sententie* exist in the work known both as the *Sententie magistri A.* and the *Compilationes Ailmeri*,[157] in the commentary on 1 Corinthians by Robert of Bridlington,[158] and in several manuscripts which also contain *sententie* associated with the school at Laon under the famous master, Anselm.[159] In one instance, a version of the *sententie* is attributed to a certain 'Manegold'.[160] The following versions of this passage have been used in this study: (1) that found in the *Compilationes Ailmeri* and *Sententie magistri A.* (version A), (2) that edited from several occurrences of the *sententie* by Heinrich Weisweiler (version B), (3) that attributed to 'Manegold' and edited by Odo Lottin (version C), (4) that copied by Robert of Bridlington (version D), and (5) that attributed to Anselm of Laon and also edited by Odo Lottin (version E).[161] A sixth version of the passage, found in Paris, Bibliothèque nationale, lat. MS 564 and edited by Philippe Delhaye will be discussed below.[162]

The work done on the relationship between these different works has been extensive, and is as yet far from complete.[163] According to the most recent research, the text attributed to Anselm of Laon (version E) is considered to be the oldest of the *sententie* versions of this passage.[164] Serious objections raised by Anselme Stoelen concerning this attribution still exist, however, and it would be perhaps rash at this stage too quickly to attribute the teaching contained here to Anselm or his students.[165] That this teaching would appear in collections of *sententie* also containing Anselm's teaching would not be unusual since the school at Laon did use the *Sententie magistri A.* as a source-book.[166] In the commentary on the Letters of Paul known to be written by Anselm, that contained in the *Glossa ordinaria*, no reference to this *sententie* occurs. In fact, the same passage from Ambrosiaster upon which the teaching is based, does appear in the *Glossa*, in a much different form; not in commenting on 1 Cor. 10:16, but in its proper place as a gloss on 1 Cor. 11:29[167]

The commentary of Robert of Bridlington used both the *Glossa ordinaria*, attributing it to Anselm, and the *Gratiadei* gloss without providing an attribution. His gloss on 1 Cor. 11:26 provides an example of how Robert used both glosses. Robert first quoted the entire gloss from the *Glossa* beginning with the *sigillum* 'An'.[168] Robert then inserted a passage from Paschasius: 'But because the whole man, who consists of body and soul was redeemed, therefore by the Body of Christ as well as the Blood, it is nourished. The soul, however, is not alone refreshed by this mystery, as some wish, but the body also is restored to immortality and incorruptibility.'[169] A passage from the *Gratiadei* gloss on 1 Cor. 10:16 then follows which corresponds to that copied by the different *sententie*.[170] This is not the only place where Robert quoted the *Gratiadei* gloss, but it is one place where he perhaps provided his motive for doing so.[171] The students of Anselm, if not Anselm himself, adopted a particular approach to the Eucharist which accepted that a man could be saved and united to Christ through a good life alone, apart from sacramental reception of the Eucharist; that is to say, through 'spiritual reception'.[172] Robert may have been objecting to this teaching, as does the *Gratiadei* gloss.[173] Man as a bodily creature would require a bodily union with Christ to ensure his immortality.

This passage provides only one indication that the gloss of Anselm and that of *Gratiadei* are at least two very different commentaries. In order to determine more closely the problems of dependence involved here, a study is necessary not only of the relationship of the Bruno and *Gratiadei* glosses on Paul, but also that of the *Glossa ordinaria* and the commentary of Robert of Bridlington. These works ought then be set into the larger context of the similar passages found in the commentaries on Psalms and of John of Mantua as well as the tracts of Lanfranc, Guitmund, and Alger. The object here, as with the commentaries on Psalms, will not be to untangle this complicated web of textual interrelationships, but to present the eucharistic theology present in all these instances as another set of witnesses to that particular approach to the sacrament which stresses the necessity of a bodily union between Christ and the believer.

As in the glosses discussed earlier, all of these witnesses spoke of the reception of the body of Christ as salvific for our bodies and the reception of his blood as salvific for our souls.[174] Again, the commentaries all stress the inviolability and indivisibility of Christ as he existed completely in each of the species.[175] Any harm which might seem to befall the body of Christ under the appearances of bread and wine is an illusion, affecting only our senses.[176] The *Gratiadei* gloss and all the different *sententie* spoke of the water added to the wine as a symbol of the people joined to Christ.[177] The *Gratiadei* gloss and all but version D of the *sententie* discussed the difference between worthy and unworthy reception.[178] The Bruno gloss, the *Gratiadei* gloss, Robert of Bridlington, and version B of the *sententie* linked worthy reception with a life of faith, hope, and love.[179] The *Gratiadei* gloss and versions A and B of the *sententie* described the results of reception as an aid for our present life and as a guarantee of our share in Christ's immortality.[180] Both glosses and version B of the *sententie* strongly insisted on the necessity of sacramental reception.[181] Finally, these same three sources spoke of the necessary salvific union achieved in sacramental reception between our bodies and that of the Word made flesh.[182]

None of these commentaries, whether on Psalms, the Song of Songs, or on the Letters of Paul, present as complete a theological treatment of the Eucharist as one finds in Lanfranc, Guitmund, or Alger. The treatment which they do provide, however, indicates that the approach they assumed in regard to the sacrament was quite similar to that adopted by these three authors. The substantial presence and reception of Christ was of central importance for salvation. The species of bread and wine were mere appearances; illusions to allow us to consume Christ's flesh and blood without repulsion. The reality of Christ present under the species persisted unscathed through any mishap, even reception by an unworthy individual. From the dates attached to these glosses, meagre though they be, this corporeal approach appears to have survived as a respectable approach to the Eucharist at least until the mid-twelfth century. Apart from John of Mantua in the late eleventh century and Robert of Bridlington in the mid-twelfth century, however, the authors of these glosses remain at best shadowy figures. Fortunately, not all the exponents of this stance maintained such anonymity.

Honorius Augustodunensis, Rupert of Deutz, and Hervaeus of Bourg-Dieu

One of the advocates of the corporeal understanding of the Eucharist of whom some record exists was the elusive figure, Honorius 'Augustodunensis'. Probably not connected with Autun (as his name might suggest), Honorius appears to have spent the early part of his career in England, (*c*.1098-1102/3) where he came under the influence of St. Anselm.[183] Scholars usually connect his later life (*c*.1102/3-1130/1133) with southern Germany or Austria, particularly Regensburg.[184] Three works of Honorius treat of the Eucharist. Of these, the *Elucidarium*, a dialogue between pupil and master, definitely belongs to Honorius's stay in England. The other works, the liturgical commentary, the *Gemma animae*, and the *Eucharisticon* probably belong to Honorius's later work in Germany, but have some English affiliations.[185]

Honorius adopted the Paschasian explanation of the value of the sacrament in all three of his treatments of the sacrament. Christ took on human nature, so that through the reception of his flesh in the Eucharist, we might be naturally joined to him, and through this union joined to the Godhead itself.[186] In the *Elucidarium*, Honorius so valued the power of this union that he did not admit that the wicked receive the body and blood at all, but only ashes.[187] In the *Eucharisticon*, Honorius changed this teaching, admitting that the unworthy do receive the 'essence' of Christ, but not his true living body.[188] Honorius upheld the indivisibility and incorruptibility of Christ in the sacrament,[189] and associated salvation of the body with reception of Christ's body and redemption of the soul with reception of his blood.[190]

Another theologian who would spend much of his life in Germany, Rupert, Abbot of the Benedictine monastery at

Deutz, *c*.1120-1132, developed his own particular version of
the corporeal approach to the Eucharist. A fiery and controversial figure, he wrote three works which dealt with the
Eucharist while a monk at the monastery of St. Laurent in
Liège.[191] The first of these works, the *Liber de divinis officiis*,
completed *c*.1111, earned him a mild rebuke from William,
later Abbot of St. Thierry, a student of Anselm of Laon.[192]
Rupert would clash with Anselm himself over questions concerning both predestination and the Eucharist some five or six
years later.[193] Rupert wrote at length about the sacrament for
a second time in his commentary on the Gospel of John which
appeared *c*.1115.[194] In this work, he attacked several teachings
on the Eucharist with which he disagreed. Guntram Bischoff
has argued that at least one of Rupert's targets was his fellow
townsman, Alger of Liège. He appears to have had more than
one adversary in mind, however, and there is some evidence
that he here renewed his attack on Anselm and his students.[195]
In 1117, Rupert completed the last work of his which would
treat of the Eucharist, the massive analysis of scripture, *De
santa Trinitate et operibus eius*.[196] In later life he wrote to Cuno,
Abbot of Siegburg, his friend and patron, re-dedicating his
commentary on John and still voicing his discontent with Alger
and Anselm.[197]

Along with his fellow townsman, Alger, Rupert is one of the
strongest advocates of the Paschasian understanding of the
Eucharist. In all three of his treatments of the sacrament, he
describes the salvific union of our body to that of Christ as
accomplished by sacramental reception. The Word became
flesh in order that through reception of that flesh in the Eucharist, we would be joined both to Christ's humanity and his
divinity.[198] This reception and the resulting unity is essential
for salvation.[199] Rupert strenuously attacked those who denied
the necessity of sacramental reception, and it is quite likely
that he was here addressing his adversaries at Laon.[200] Rupert
was so insistent on this point, that he argued that the souls of
the just received Christ's body when he descended into hell
in order that they could share in salvation.[201] As in the writings
of Lanfranc, Guitmund, and Alger, Rupert distinguished between the reception of the just and the unjust. The unjust
receive the true Body and Blood, but only a life of faith and

love allows us to share in the effects of the sacrament.[202]

In Rupert's explanation of the relationship of the species of bread and wine to the body and blood of Christ, he offered a unique and confusing terminology. In the *Liber de officiis,* he distinguished between the animal life 'of the sacrifice of the altar', dead and ineffective, and the 'spiritual life' of the Risen Christ, living and efficacious.[203] William of St. Thierry questioned this terminology. Did Rupert mean to suggest that Christ was not fully present on the altar, or that the bread and wine somehow still existed after the consecration?[204] Rupert clarified his terminology somewhat in his commentary on Exodus 3:11. The inanimate body of which he spoke referred to that which the senses revealed; the living body of Christ referred to the reality present on the altar.[205] Taking the several passages in which Rupert treated of this matter together, it appears that he adopted much the same position as Guitmund. The externally sensed species of the bread and wine are merely a covering, a veil, taken up by Christ because of our natural repugnance to eating flesh and drinking blood.[206] Despite this individual terminology, several other teachings characteristic of the Paschasian approach to sacrament appear in Rupert's works. He too stressed the indivisibility and incorruptibility of Christ present on the altar.[207] He spoke of the body of Christ as efficacious for the salvation of the body; his blood as salvific for the soul.[208] The effect of reception would ensure the life of the soul in the present life, and the future resurrection of the body.[209]

The Paschasian understanding of the Eucharist found its finest exponents in Alger at St. Lambert, and Rupert, at St. Laurent; both in Liège and both writing in the second decade of the twelfth century. Rupert certainly would not have understood Alger's theology as similar to his own. On the contrary, in his dedicatory letter to Abbot Cuno, he accused Alger of defending Berengar.[210] Yet both authors offered a Paschasian understanding of the sacrament. Christ's body must be joined naturally to our own in order to be saved. Although this particular approach would begin to appear less and less frequently from this time onwards, it continued to find adherents into the second quarter of the twelfth century. Gregory of Bergamo and Robert of Bridlington, both writing *c.*1150, are two such witnesses. Another espouser of this theory was the Benedictine monk, Hervaeus of Bourg-Dieu, who died *c*.1150.[211] In his commentary on 1 Corinthians, most of the major themes of the Paschasian theology of the Eucharist emerge. The substance of the body of Christ received in the sacrament passes into our bodies effecting a salvific union.[212] The body of Christ provides the salvific link necessary for the salvation of our bodies; the blood provides that which is necessary for the salvation of our souls.[213] Although all receive the true body and blood of Christ, only those who imitate the life of Christ receive unto salvation. Like Alger and Rupert, Hervaeus insisted that both sacramental reception and a good life were necessary to establish the salvific link to Christ.[214] Hervaeus's commentary on 1 Corinthians does not provide a complete theology of the Eucharist, but the few references which it does offer, place it among those works which espoused a Paschasian understanding of the role of the Eucharist in the salvation of humankind.

The Continuing Influence

By the mid-twelfth century, the Paschasian understanding of the salvific function of the Eucharist had already ceased to play a major role in sacramental theology. The discussions of the sacrament provoked by the Berengarian controversy and continued by the rise of the Cathars were taken up by the influential centres of learning at Laon and Paris. The different approaches to the Eucharist proposed by the masters at these schools would come to dominate thought on the sacrament by the end of the century.

Long after the general approach of Lanfranc, Alger, and Rupert had been abandoned, however, their theology continued to influence thought on the sacrament. By far the most important and enduring contribution of this theology was its repeated insistence on the identification of the body of Christ born of Mary and present in heaven, and the bodily presence of Christ on the Altar. The victory of the theology of Lanfranc and Guitmund over that of Berengar was complete by the early decades of the twelfth century, and despite the many differing interpretations given to it, no orthodox theologian of the Middle Ages would seriously challenge the 'real' presence which this identification implied. The theological importance of the salvific function of that presence would fade, but insistence on the presence itself would continue as an abiding and unquestioned feature of sacramental theology.

Certain themes characteristic of the Paschasian approach to the Eucharist also continued to appear in theological treatises throughout the twelfth and into the thirteenth century. One of these was the teaching that the body of Christ effected the salvation of the body, while the blood of Christ effected the salvation of the soul. In phrases similar to those used by these earlier writers, the teaching occurs in the *Glossa ordinaria* on John 6:56,[215] in the commentaries on 1 Corinthians by Peter Lombard and by the Pseudo-Hugh of St. Victor,[216] and in the *Sententie divinitatis*.[217] Mention of this symbolism appears in several other treatises, but at least by the early thirteenth century, the way in which the authors approach the subject indicates that they no longer subscribed to the Paschasian theology that once lay behind the symbol.[218]

The emphasis on the real presence of the body and blood of Christ continued to cause problems for the theologians when they attempted to explain the fraction of the Host, and corruption of the reserved species. As the oath required by Berengar by the Synod of Rome in 1059 shows, the earliest opponents of Berengar believed the Body of Christ to be actually broken and torn during the celebration of Mass. This theory was not without its adherents in the twelfth century. Walter of St. Victor, writing *c*.1178, decried later interpretations of what might happen to the Body, and demanded a return to the literal meaning of the oath.[219] A tract on the Eucharist by an unknown abbot Abbaudus emphatically argued the same point,[220] and at least one passage in the writing of Robert of Melun would appear to uphold a similar teaching.[221] Guitmund of Aversa had taught the somewhat less literal interpretation that all changes in the species are mere illusion, and this is the more common teaching of those who adopted the Paschasian approach to the sacrament. This stance found advocates throughout the twelfth century, most notably in the School of Gilbert of La Porrée.[222] Two interesting variations of this teaching appear in *sententie* from the mid-twelfth century. A certain unidentified *Magister Walterius* argued that the accidents of bread and wine actually adhere in the substance of the body and blood of Christ.[223] The fraction must be illusory, therefore, because otherwise Christ would suffer and this would be impossible.[224] Among the *sententie* included in Hague, Museum Meer-manno-westereenianum MS 10.B.33, fols. 197[v]-199[v], a sentence dealing with the Eucharist occurs based on the text of 1 Cor. 11:20.[225] The author argued that not only is Christ present in substance, but also in accident.[226] Although the accidents of bread seem to be present, this is an illusion, just as a stick placed in water appears to be bent, to the senses, even though the mind knows it to be straight.[227]

The Paschasian explanation of the role of the Eucharist in salvation history found its finest expression in the aftermath of the Berengarian controversy and continued to exercise influence on sacramental theology for several centuries afterwards. The essential feature of this theology, the importance of the 'natural' union of the body of Christ and the body of a worthy recipient effected by sacramental reception, however, slowly faded from the theology of the Eucharist. Not far from Liège, and during the lifetimes of Alger and Rupert, another way of understanding the sacrament was already being discussed at Laon, and it is from here that another approach to the Eucharist developed.

The Theology of the Paschasian Model

The essential function of the Eucharist in a Paschasian understanding is to mediate the presence of the risen Lord to the believer so that the believer might be united to the Lord and hence saved. The image used here is biological. Just as the food we eat becomes part of ourselves, so we, in a sort of divine reversal, become part of Christ when we receive the Eucharist.[228] Paschasius made this perfectly clear, 'we become part of Christ because we eat him.[229]

This model for explaining the function of the sacrament in salvation demands that Christ be 'really', 'naturally', 'substantially', present. To suggest that Christ is not so present, as Berengar was understood to do, would undermine our very salvation, and Berengar was charged on just such grounds.[230]

Because of this insistence on the presence of the risen Lord in the sacrament which this model entails, and because of their own strong focus on theories of the change that takes place in the sacrament, Geiselmann and, following him, many others, have described the theologians who adopted this model as 'metabolists' in opposition to theologians such as Ratramnus or Berengar who would be deemed 'Augustinian spiritualists'.[231] This nomenclature can be misleading for at least two reasons. First of all, to insist that the risen Christ be present, even present 'really', 'naturally', or 'substantially', need not necessarily entail a highly corporeal understanding of that presence. The meaning of 'substantial presence' will differ depending upon an individual theologian's understanding of substance, and as Jorisson has shown there were quite divergent understandings of substance in the twelfth century.[232]

Secondly, it would seem possible that a theologian might insist on the 'real', 'natural', or 'substantial' presence of the risen Christ in the Eucharist, and yet not understand that presence as directly causing our salvation. In other words, one might insist that Christ is present in the Eucharist, but not that a salvific union is formed between that presence and the believer. As subsequent chapters hope to show, many theologians did in fact adopt such a position.

If subsequent theologies differed from the Paschasian model for explaining the sacrament, they did so not because they rejected the Paschasian insistence on a 'real' presence, but because they offered a different understanding of the role which the Eucharist played in the salvation of the believer.

It is not surprising that different theologies should so appear. First of all, the Middle Ages inherited a diversity of teachings on the Eucharist from the Fathers, and as the Fathers came to be rediscovered and re-appropriated in the burgeoning academic settings of the twelfth century, this diversity was likely to be rediscovered as well. Secondly, the Paschasian theology did present some severe problems, especially when pressed to its limits under the dialectical scrutiny of Berengar. Since the Paschasian theology depends on a biological metaphor, the temptation exists to think of the presence of the risen Christ in extremely corporeal terms. A host of problems follow from this. Does Christ then suffer at the hands (and teeth) of the

III

THE MYSTICAL APPROACH
TO THE EUCHARIST

Anselm of Laon, William of Champeaux, and the 'School of Laon'

THE Paschasian understanding of the Eucharist received its clearest enunciation in the early decades of the twelfth century, but even by this date the fundamental assumptions of this approach were being challenged. Another, more mystical understanding of the sacrament began to appear during the same period. The origins of this theology, based more on Augustine than Hilary, are not completely clear, but almost without exception, its earliest advocates are associated in some fashion with the cathedral school at Laon.

The circle of scholars grouped around Anselm, the Chancellor, Deacon (*c.*1109—1114), and later Archdeacon (1115-1117) of Laon, include some of the most illustrious teachers of early scholasticism. Abelard, William of Champeaux, William of St. Thierry, and Gilbert of La Porrée are only the most famous students of the master of Laon.[1] The teaching of Anselm himself, however, survives only in fragments. Most important for his teaching on the Eucharist are his commentaries on 1 Corinthians and on the Gospel of John which were to become part of the *Glossa ordinaria.*[2] Apart from these commentaries, there are series of *sententie* which can be attributed with more or less certainty to Anselm.[3] Together they give at best only an indication of what Anselm's teaching may have been. These indications are important, however, for understanding the teaching of Anselm's students. In the commentary of John 6:29, one of the central points of Anselm's theology is explained. The true work of God, the beginning and end of all good, is faith working through love. Even when the facility for good works fails, the desire to do them suffices.[4] Applied to the Eucharist, this means that true reception consists in receiving with faith working through love.[5] The essential unity achieved in the sacrament is the unity of charity, of the spirit, and thus to be united is truly to be a member of Christ.[6] Some indications also appear that Anselm offered a connection between this kind of reception and the larger plan of salvation history. For Anselm, the body of Christ received in the Eucharist was the same as that upon which the angels feed in heaven through contemplation.[7] Since we are incapable of this kind of spiritual reception, the Word became Flesh to provide us with more palatable food until we too reach heaven.[8]

These few passages provide the bulk of what has remained as identifiably the teaching of Anselm on the Eucharist. Among the *sententie* attributed to him, a few other teachings occur. It appears that Anselm considered sacramental reception extremely important,[9] that he taught the concomitance of Christ in both species,[10] and that he believed the body of Christ received by the apostles at the Last Supper to be immortal and impassible.[11] In the one passage in these *sententie* where the subject is treated, proper reception of the sacrament is described as the union of wills between Christ and the faithful.[12]

From the material which can be more or less identified with Anselm, no clear eucharistic theology emerges. A strong emphasis, though, on the sacrament as a sign of spiritual unity, of a union effected by faith working through love does stand out, and this will be one of the central teachings of Anselm's students.

The first of the members of the school of Laon to add to the teachings of Anselm on the efficacy of the sacrament of the Eucharist was William of Champeaux. The two names of Anselm of Laon and William, Bishop of Champeaux from 1113 to 1121, have been closely linked as the two leading teachers of the school at Laon. William, a student of Anselm, taught in the cathedral school of Paris, and founded both the priory and the school of St. Victor.[13]

Like his teacher, his works exist only as sentences, collected and included in florilegia. O. Lottin has collected and published the sentences attributed to William along with those of Anselm.[14] Like Anselm, William insisted that the body which Christ gave to his disciples at the Last Supper was immortal and impassible by nature, having been conceived without sin.[15] The real body and blood of Christ are substantially present on the altar, but it is the *species et qualitates* which remain after the change that undergo the fraction and other changes.[16]

In two areas, William went beyond the teaching of Anselm. He insisted much more strongly on the presence of the entire Christ, body, soul, and divinity, in each of the species, and argued that to insist that reception of both species is necessary for a proper reception of the sacrament is heretical.[17] The most important of William's teachings treats of the salvific effects of Christ's Passion in relation to the Eucharist. Christ died once to save all the just; past, present, and future. Therefore, those just persons born before the time of Christ were saved by faith, and by the sacraments which prefigured the sacraments of the Church. Those born after Christ share in his passion through its re-enactment in the Eucharist.[18] The teaching of William contradicts that of Rupert of Deutz on this subject, emphasizing the faith of the believer, not the sacramental action, as the essential requisite for salvation. This *sententia* may well record one of the issues at stake in Rupert's dispute with the masters at Laon.[19] While the known teaching of Anselm and William on the Eucharist is scanty and unclear, that of the anonymous material surrounding the two masters is large and quite distinctive.

Although large collections of *sententie* have been associated with Anselm's school at Laon,[20] a serious question remains as to the existence of a 'School of Laon' as represented by anonymous sentence collections. Dr V. I. J. Flint has suggested that these books of sentences may in fact have been compiled to meet the pastoral needs raised by the reform movements of the late eleventh and early twelfth centuries, rather than to preserve the teaching of Anselm, William, and the other masters and students at Laon.[21] The fact that a certain *sententia* recorded in a particular book of *sententie* can be associated with the teaching of Anselm or William would not then necessarily establish that book as a product of Anselm's school at Laon, nor demonstrate that all the other *sententie* contained in that book come from Anselm and his colleagues. Miss Flint's caveat seems well taken, and in order to establish as clearly as possible which of the teachings contained in the books of *sententie* associated with the 'School of Laon' might actually correspond to the teaching of Anselm, William, and the other scholars at Laon, the *sententie* described here will be compared with the more or less certain work of Anselm and William, and with the teaching of the known students of the cathedral school at Laon. It is remarkable, in fact, how similar most of the teachings found in these different works are, and yet, complete agreement does not exist. The so-called 'letter of Anselm on the Eucharist' for instance, which is found in several sentence-collections attributed to the 'School of Laon' put forth a Paschasian theology much more in agreement with certain Scripture commentaries of the late eleventh and early twelfth centuries than with the theology known to be taught by Anselm, William, and the identifiable students of Laon. [22]

Several different *sententie* and sentence-collections have been used in this study, but the most important of these are (1) *sententie* 375 and 193 of the *sententie* edited by Lottin, (2) a *sententie* attributed to Anselm and edited by Philippe Delhaye, [23] (3) the sentence-collection *Dubitatur a quibusdam*, [24] (4) the *Sententie Atrebatenses*, [25] and (5) the *Sententie Anselmi*. [26]

The most important subject dealt with by these authors in their treatment of the Eucharist concerns the terminology used to describe the relationship of the different realities signified by the Eucharist. In the two collections, *Dubitatur a quibusdam* and the *Sententie Anselmi*, the *res* of the Eucharist was described as both the true body and blood of Christ, and as the *panis celestis*, the heavenly bread on which the angels feed. The first *res*, the true body and blood, is a sign of the second *res*, the *Panis celestis*. [27] Although all who receive the sacrament receive the true body and blood, only the good receive the *panis celestis*, by which one is joined to Christ in faith and love. [28] In a similar fashion, the *Sententie Atrebatenses* described the *res sacramenti* as both the body and blood of Christ, and the union in faith and love symbolized by them. [29] As in the commentaries by Anselm, the anonymous *sententie* stressed the union in faith and love achieved by reception of the *panis celestis*, the spiritual body of Christ symbolized by his physical presence in the sacrament.

Corresponding to these two *res* found in the sacrament, the *sententie* spoke of two forms of reception. In the *Dubitatur* and the *sententia* edited by Delhaye, they were described as sacramental reception, and 'real' reception. [30] Sacramental reception is accomplished by all, good or evil, who receive the true body and blood in the sacrament. Real reception takes place when the just receive in faith and love.[31] This same distinction occurred in *sententia* 193 edited by Lottin, only instead of sacramental and real reception, the older differentiation between sacramental and spiritual reception was used.[32] The emphasis of these *sententie* was clearly on the spiritual union in faith and love. The term *res*, reserved by the theologians advocating a Paschasian understanding of the sacrament for the true body and blood has been extended to include the *panis celestis*, the union in faith and love; the 'real' reception of the Eucharist.

The *Sententie Anselmi* went further than the other *sententie* by describing three kinds of reception in the Eucharist: sacramental reception alone, sacramental and real reception, and real reception alone.[33] Sacramental reception alone referred to reception by the wicked who receive the true body and blood, but unto damnation, for they do not receive in faith and love.[34] Sacramental and real reception described the good who receive both the true body and blood and the *panis celestis*, the union in faith and love, and the wicked who receive the body and blood unto damnation.[35] Real reception alone referred to those just who receive the *panis celestis* and are joined to Christ in faith and love, even if they do not receive the true body and blood in the sacrament.[36] Here a mystical interpretation of the Eucharist takes over completely. The union in faith and love effects the salvific function of the sacrament. This teaching explicitly contradicts the central efficacy of the natural union stressed in Paschasian theology. The true *res* of the Eucharist is the spiritual union of God and believer, accomplished by faith and love, and this union need not necessarily involve sacramental reception. In fact, in a way very different from that described by the advocates of the Paschian approach, sacramental reception alone is imperfect.[37] The structure of the Eucharist as described by the *Sententie Anselmi* in effect transfers the 'reality' of the Eucharist from the physical presence of Christ to the spiritual union of God and the Christian.

None of the other *sententie* was as explicit on this point as the *Sententie Anselmi*, but other indications of the importance of a spiritual union are apparent in them. *Sententia* 375 edited by

Lottin also spoke of a salvific reception of the *rem sacramenti* apart from sacramental reception.[38] *Sententia* 198 edited by Lottin copied the teaching of Fulgentius of Ruspe that children who die without receiving the Eucharist are still saved,[39] and *sententia* 222 held that those who unknowingly receive unconsecrated species at the hands of an unordained priest, are saved through faith alone.[40] Finally, in the sentence-collection *Sententie Anselmi* as well as *sententia* 381 edited by Lottin, a description of the practice of spiritual communion appeared, probably the first such description in the history of Western spirituality.[41]

The *sententie* treated also of other matters, such as concomitance,[42] the immortality of the body of Christ received at the Last Supper,[43] and the continued existence of the accidents of the bread and wine after the consecration,[44] but their major contribution remains their clear explanation of the Eucharist as salvific, not because of the union formed by sacramental reception, but because of that formed by spiritual reception. These works are anonymous, however, difficult to date, and therefore not completely reliable witnesses to the teaching of the masters at Laon. Fortunately, the works of several of Anselm's identifiable students have survived, and they contain a remarkably similar approach to the sacrament.

Students of the School at Laon

The school at Laon continued to exert an influence in the early decades of the twelfth century not only through the sentences and sentence-collections attached to Anselm, William, and their school, but also through the teaching and writing of the pupils who studied at Laon. Leaving aside for the moment the students of Anselm and William who were later to form their own 'schools', a number of the less famous students of Laon came to discuss the Eucharist in the course of their careers.

Hugh Metel, a student of Anselm at Laon, and later a canon of St. Leo's in Toul, has remained one of the least well-known of the students of Anselm, despite his correspondence with most of the leading figures of his day.[45] Hugh wrote two short letters discussing the Eucharist. The first letter, addressed to a certain *Gerardo probati spiritus Monacho*,[46] answers two questions directed to Hugh. First, should the body of Christ be received daily? Secondly, is the body present on the altar the *figura* of the body present in heaven?[47] Hugh answered both questions as a true student of the masters at Laon. Discussing the many meanings of the phrase 'daily bread,' he answered that we receive the 'daily bread' of Christ's body and are daily incorporated into that body if we have faith working through love, even if we do not daily receive the sacrament.[48] Hugh answered the second question by distinguishing between the outward action of the Mass, and the spiritual union of the faithful. Only the faithful joined to Christ in faith and love receive the *rem sacramenti*, not only the *sacramentum* of the Eucharist.[49] Hugh in effect distinguished here between *comestio sacramentalis* and *comestio spiritualis*.[50]

Hugh's second letter was addressed to a certain Gerland who has been identified with *Magister Gerlandus* canon and *scholasticus* of Besançon.[51] Here Hugh dealt with a much more serious problem. *Magister Gerlandus* seems to have been teaching certain positions similar to Berengar's.[52] Gerland asserted that the words of Christ speaking of his body and blood are only figurative, and that Augustine supports this interpretation.[53] That which is performed on the altar is a sign, not the object of a sign.[54] Hugh answered that one must distinguish here between the sacramental body of Christ and incorporation into Christ which is signified by the body.[55] When Augustine spoke of a sign or figure, he was referring to *comestio spiritualis*, not to *comestio sacramentalis*.[56] Hugh offered several passages from Augustine which support his interpretation.[57]

Hugh stood firmly within the tradition of the school at Laon. He answered the questions directed to him by referring to the school's teaching on *comestio sacramentalis* as a sign of *comestio spiritualis*. The presence of the body and blood is the *sacramentum* of the true *res* of the Eucharist, the incorporation of the worthy into Christ through faith and love.

Unlike his fellow student, the canon of Toul, Hugh of Amiens led an active public life. After studying in Laon, Hugh held several important posts. He was appointed Prior to Saint-Martial in Limoges *c.*1115, the Prior of St. Pancras in Lewes. In 1123, he became Abbot of Reading, and in 1130 Archbishop of Rouen, a position which he held until his death in 1164. As archbishop he participated in several councils and synods.[58]

Hugh's main theological work, *Dialogorum seu questionum theologicarum libri septem*, written c.1125-1133,[59] depends heavily on the teachings associated with Laon.[60] Hugh's theology of the Eucharist as found in Book 5 of his *Dialogi* also follows this teaching. Like William of Champeaux, Hugh argued that although God allowed different *sacramenta* at different times, it is always faith working through love that saves.[61] Even those who did not formally receive these *sacramenta* could be saved if they offered their lives for their faith.[62] Only those who are members of Christ in faith receive worthily, and whoever perseveres in faith will be saved.[63] Hugh offered the teaching of Anselm on the impassible body of Christ received at the Last Supper,[64] asserting both the concomitance of the body and blood under the species of bread and wine,[65] and the substantial change.[66] Hugh of Amiens, like Hugh Metel, offers a clear witness to teaching of the school at Laon.

Guibert, Abbot of Nogent-sous-Coucy, near Laon, from 1104 to 1124, offers one of the most interesting approaches to the Eucharist among that group of writers who may be included loosely within the influence of Anselm's teaching. Guibert, born at Clermont in 1053, entered the monastery of Saint-Germer de Flay in 1064, where he studied under the then Prior of Bec, Anselm, the great teacher and future Archbishop of Canterbury.[67] It was probably not from this Anselm, but from the Archdeacon of Laon of the same name that Guibert learned his eucharistic theology.[68] Guibert certainly knew both Anselm and his brother Ralph, and spoke of their teaching ability in glowing terms.[69]

Guibert has two treatments of the Eucharist, both written before 1119-1120.[70] The shorter treatment is contained in a letter to Siegfried, Prior of Saint Nicolas near Laon, *Epistola de buccella Judae data et de veritate dominici corporis*. The major part of this treatise is concerned with the question whether Judas received the true body and blood at the Last Supper, a question which Guibert answered in the affirmative. It is interesting to note that this is one of the teachings attacked by Rupert of Deutz in his commentary on John.[71] He then went on to answer certain *objectiunculas* ('little objections') which the sender has concerning the real presence.[72] Guibert offered several arguments in favour of the real presence, and affirmed the substantial change of the bread and wine,[73] the concomitance of the body and blood under the species,[74] and the efficacy of spiritual reception.[75]

It is in Guibert's attack on the worship of spurious relics, *De pignoribus sanctorum*, that he offered a complete treatment of the sacrament of the Eucharist. Guibert was basically concerned in this tract in disproving the claims of the abbey of St. Médard in Soissons to relics of the body of Christ.[76] According to Guibert, if any part of the true body still existed on earth, the Eucharist would be unnecessary.[77] He dedicated the second book of the tract to a complete treatment of the sacrament which replaces all need for relics of Christ.

Guibert argued that there are three bodies of Christ, that which died and suffered on earth, that which is present on the altar, and that which sits on the right hand of the Father.[78] The body on the altar is 'derived' from the body that suffered and died,[79] having a 'vicarious identity' with the former,[80] and a 'conformity' with the body in heaven.[81] Although the true body and blood are present on the altar, the purpose of the sacrament is to lead us from a terrestial understanding to a divine understanding of Christ; thus from his terrestial presence (on the altar) to his mystical presence (in heaven and in our hearts).[82] To receive worthily, one must conform one's life to that of Christ, receiving the inner inspiration of Christ.[83]

Guibert, however, added a distinctive touch to the teaching that true reception is reception in faith and love. Christ determines the grace given in the sacrament,[84] and it is only the elect, the predestined, who receive this grace.[85] Even if one of the elect receives in sin, the grace is stored up for him until such time as the sin is removed.[86] Like many of the students at Laon, Guibert admitted that it is possible to receive the effects of the Eucharist without receiving sacramentally.[87] Also in line with the teaching of Laon, he accepted the concomitance of the species,[88] and gave a long defence of the impassible and immortal body which Christ received at birth.[89] Guibert also held that animals or corruption damaging the Host affect neither the *sacramentum* nor the *res sacramenti* since this sacrament is operative only through faith.[90] Relying on the inverse of this principle Guibert argued that the sinners who received unconsecrated bread still sin mortally if they believe themselves to be receiving the body and blood of Christ.[91] This question will become important for later theologians.[92]

Guibert's approach to the Eucharist stands within the influence of the masters and students at Laon.[93] His basic structure of the sacrament is the same. The *sacramentum*, that is the true body and blood, are only a sign of the mystical union of Christ and the believer through faith and love. The purpose of the sacrament is to lead us to this union, which can be effected outside the sacramental reception. On the other hand, Guibert added some ideas to this general overview that are distinctly his own. The explanation of the relationship between the three bodies of Christ and his teaching that only the predestined receive the grace of the sacrament are, it seems, unique contributions to the theology of the Eucharist in the twelfth century.

Hugh Metel, Hugh of Amiens, and Guibert of Nogent all present teachings on the Eucharist that correspond in a greater or lesser degree to the teaching on the same subject found in the sentences and sentence-collections associated with the 'School of Laon', but their membership in this 'School' should not be overstressed. In each case, these men wrote their treatments of the sacrament after they had left the master at Laon. They do not mechanically reproduce the teaching of Anselm, William, or one of the anonymous sentence-collections. Especially in the case of Guibert, the over-all approach of the 'School' of Laon is set in an individual framework, and the work of these men should be seen not only as witnesses to the influence of the teaching of the masters of Laon, but also as the individual reflections of educated clergymen on the role of the Eucharist.

Hugh of St. Victor and his School

Of all the masters of the twelfth-century schools, none produced a theology of the Eucharist as rich and consistent as that of Hugh, master of the school of the Augustinian canons of St. Victor at Paris. Of Hugh's fame and excellence as a teacher, theologion, and philosopher, volumes have been written; of his origins and public life, very little is known.[94] The first reference to Hugh shows him already a canon of St. Victor in 1127, where he may have learned the teachings of the founder of the

abbey, the famous William of Champeaux. Hugh appears to
have spent the rest of his life at the abbey, teaching up until his
death in 1142.[95] His two main treatments of the Eucharist
appear in his commentary on the *Celestial Hierarchy* of Pseudo-
Dionysius, and in his famous theological compendium, the *De
sacramentis christianae fidei*. Both works come from the later years
of his career, the central passage on the Eucharist from the
commentary having been copied into the somewhat later work,
the *De sacramentis*.[96]

For Hugh, the central salvific act of Christ's death and
resurrection supplies to humankind the graces of faith and love
through the working of the Holy Spirit.[97] Faith and love, in
turn, lead us toward our final spiritual union with the Father.[98]
The sacraments of the New Testament, especially baptism and
the Eucharist, are signs and carriers of the graces bestowed by
the Spirit.[99] The power of the Redemptive act also empowers
the sacraments of the Old Law, making them salvific in retro-
spect for those who had faith.[100] The sacrament of the Eucharist is the greatest of all the sacraments because it is itself an
efficacious sign of the central act of our salvation, the death
and resurrection of Christ.[101] The sensible species and the
presence of the body and blood of Christ are signs of the power
and purpose of the Eucharist which is the internal spiritual
union with Christ, perfected by faith and love.[102] The outward
physical presence of the Eucharist, like the presence of Jesus on
earth leads us by his physical appearance to his spiritual existence and hence to a mystical union in faith and love.[103] This
spiritual union in faith and love, toward which all salvation history tends, is by far the most important aspect of the Eucharist
for Hugh. To receive the sacrament worthily one must receive
in faith and love.[104] Further, if one cannot receive the outward
sign of the Eucharist, faith and love alone are sufficient to gain
the spiritual union with Christ.[105]

The influence of the school at Laon on Hugh's theology is
immediately apparent in his emphasis on the Eucharist as pri-
marily a sign of the salvific spiritual union with Christ achieved
through faith and love. In a much more systematic way than
the other inheritors of this tradition, Hugh provided a consistent framework for this approach. The whole of salvation
history moves toward the spiritual union with Christ made

possible by the graces won through the redemptive act. The Eucharist in particular signifies this act in order to lead us from the sensual to the spiritual realm, and to provide us with the grace necessary to do so. The emphasis of the movement is on faith and love and the union which they achieve. This union is far more important than, and can indeed exist apart from, either the outward ritual or the real presence. As one might expect, the questions concerning the maltreatment of the species are of little interest to Hugh, who was much more interested in directing his readers away from this sensual reality toward the spiritual reality which it signified.[106] In Hugh of St. Victor, the mystical approach to the sacrament found its greatest exponent, and his theology would continue to reverberate in the work of his followers well into the second half of the twelfth century.

One of the works which most closely follows the teaching of Hugh on the Eucharist is the *Summa 'Inter cetera alicuius scientie'* contained in Vatican City, Biblioteca Vaticana, Vat. lat. MS 1345, fols. 4r-211v.[107] Following Hugh, this anonymous author distinguished between the *sacramentum* and the *res* and the *virtus sacramenti*.[108] The *virtus sacramenti* is received only by the good, who imitate the life of Christ.[109] Although the tract spoke of the effect of the Eucharist for both soul and body, it insisted that it is basically food for the soul received in faith and love.[110] The *Summa* contains two sections treating of the difference between sacramental and spiritual reception. In one the phrase *perceptio sacramentalis et realis* from the teaching of Laon is used, and in the other more common distinction between reception *corporaliter* and *spiritualiter*.[111] In both sections, the author emphasized that spiritual reception is undertaken only by the just who imitate Christ in faith and love.[112]

Included among the most important and influential of those works associated with the School of Hugh of St. Victor appears a well-ordered, compact sentence-collection entitled the *Summa sententiarum*. The work has survived in several different manuscript versions, and probably more than one recension of the collection existed. Several of the manuscripts attribute the work to a *Magister Otho*, some manuscripts adding that he gathered his material from the works of Anselm of Laon and Hugh of St. Victor. However, the authorship and history of the work remain unclear. The dating of the *Summa* is uncertain, but roughly ascribed to the second quarter of the twelfth century.[113]

The most important contribution of the *Summa* is its use of the terms *sacramentum tantum, res et sacramentum,* and *res tantum* for distinguishing the appearances of bread and wine, the body and blood of Christ, and the spiritual union of God and man effected by worthy reception.[114] This usage, similar to that used by the different works associated with Laon, would become the standard terminology for discussing the structure of the Eucharist.[115] The *Summa* described two forms of reception, sacramental and spiritual.[116] The anonymous author stressed the importance of spiritual reception without sacramental reception.[117]

Another work attached to the School of St. Victor, the anonymous commentary on the Mass, the *Speculum de mysteriis ecclesiae*, depended on both the *De sacramentis* of Hugh and the *Summa sententiarum* for its discussion of the Eucharist. The *Speculum*, written *c*.1160-1175, appears to have been a popular book in the twelfth century, and formed one of the sources for Simon of Tournai's theological *summa*.[118] The *Speculum* copies the *Summa sententiarum* both on the structure of the sacrament and on spiritual and sacramental reception.[119] The tract also included Hugh's discussion of the physical presence of Christ in the species after reception, and his description of the movement from the terrestrial to the spiritual presence of Christ.[120] The *Speculum* insisted even more strongly than either of its sources on the possibility of spiritual union outside sacramental reception, and accepted as salvific the practice of spiritual communion when sacramental reception was unavailable.[121]

An unidentified commentary on the Gospel of John, published in Migne, *PL* 175 after the second book of the *Liber exceptionum* of Richard of St. Victor contains a eucharistic theology similar to that of Hugh and his students.[122] Like Hugh, this author spoke of our reception of the Spirit through the body of Christ. The participation in the Spirit through faith is the cause of our salvation, without which we would be able to do nothing.[123] Like the students of Hugh, he spoke of spiritual reception as a life of faith and love which unites us to Christ even apart from sacramental reception.[124]

The teaching of Hugh of St. Victor and that of those works

closely associated with him continued the particular approach to the Eucharist found among the works associated with Anselm's school at Laon. The Eucharist here contributes to the salvation of humankind by providing a ritual representation of the saving union with Christ in faith and love. Going beyond this teaching, Hugh set this emphasis on spiritual union into a framework of salvation history, in which Christ draws us to his own spiritual reality of faith and love through the use of sensually perceived images of that reality. This interpretation of the sacrament would find no more eloquent advocate but would survive among many lesser masters to influence writers well into the thirteenth century.

Devotion to the Eucharist

It has already been suggested that the Paschasian theology of the Eucharist was likely to be joined by other theologies of the Eucharist as theologians both rediscovered the diversity of patristic teaching and realized the limits of Paschasian theology.[125] But just as the challenge of different heterodox approaches to the Eucharist form a background to the continued insistence of medieval theologians on the substantial presence of Christ in the sacrament, so too it is a popular movement outside the realm of academic theology that forms a context for the insistence of certain theologians on a salvific mystical union of faith and love formed between the believer and Christ. Beginning in the early twelfth century, a new phenomenon in the history of the Western Church began to appear, a devotion to Christ present in the sacrament. This form of devotion, which by the thirteenth century was to become commonplace throughout Europe, appears to have few antecedents in previous centuries. At least according to Peter Browe and Édouard Dumoutet, the two scholars who have done the most research in this area,[126] the devotion to Christ present in the Eucharist, a devotion often seen as typically medieval, arose suddenly and dramatically between the death of Berengar and the opening of the Fourth Lateran Council.

The most obvious manifestation of this devotion consisted in the tremendous proliferation of miracles, visions, and miracle-stories surrounding the sacrament. Stories of this kind were not unknown before the twelfth century, but now the accounts became more and more frequent, and were stories not of ancient times, but of present events.[127] The change in attitude is quite striking. Guitmund of Aversa, in his *De corporis et sanguinis Christi veritate*, recounted such a miraculous change of appearance of bread and wine into those of the flesh and blood witnessed by his master, Lanfranc. When the bishop was consulted as to what should be done with the miraculous objects, he ordered that they be perpetually reserved in the middle of the altar as great relics.[128] A hundred years later, in 1171, the community of Fécamp removed just such a relic of miraculous blood, placed in the altar in the preceding century, in order to display it to the faithful.[129] What had been reverently concealed in the eleventh century, would be equally reverently revealed in the later twelfth century.

The question of the rise of miracle-stories in the twelfth century has been admirably treated by Peter Browe in his book, *Die eucharistichen Wunder des Mittelalters* where he discusses over one hundred references to visions, miracles, and wondrous occurrences attributed to the Eucharist by twelfth- and early thirteenth-century writers. The overwhelming impression given by these stories is of a great desire to see, to communicate somehow with the Lord present in the sacrament.

It would be impossible to discuss all of the many miracles recounted by Browe, and one representative case will have to suffice. The miracle Host of Arras must be one of the best-attested instances of miraculous change in the species in the twelfth century. Gerald of Wales described the story behind the miracle Host, which he himself saw, having passed through Arras only eight days after the event.[130] On Easter Day, 1176, a woman removed the Host from the church, and wrapped it in a cloth, hiding it in a well. The Host revealed itself by shining through the cloth, and when the cloth was unwrapped, the Host was seen to have partly changed into bloody flesh.[131] The story does not stop there, but the realm of the miraculous then entered into the all too harsh reality of canon law. It seems that the Bishop of Arras realized the value of the Host as an object of pilgrimage, and ordered it to be brought to the cathedral church. The local priest protested. The case was settled by Alexander III himself, and the decision recorded in at least one of the ancient collections of decretals.[132] A miracle Host was no longer a relic to be piously removed from sight; it was an object to be seen and revered, worthy to be the object of a pilgrimage. Sometime between the end of the eleventh century, when Guitmund wrote, and the 1170s a complex and important change in the attitude toward the Eucharist had taken place. People wanted to see Christ as he existed in the sacrament. This was the greatest of all relics on earth, and by 1176, like most relics in the Middle Ages, it had become big business.

The devotion to the Eucharist manifested itself not only in the growing occurence of and reverence for miracles surrounding the sacrament, but also in a number of new liturgical practices which demonstrated the change in attitude toward the sacrament. This subject has been treated at length by Browe and Dumoutet, and our objective here will be to present and update their findings.[133] Already in the eleventh century sanctuary lamps had been introduced into some churches, but it is in the twelfth century that the first references have been found to the practice of burning a perpetual light before the reserved species.[134] To the twelfth century also belong the first witnesses to prayer before the reserved species, a custom which would become more common in the beginning of the thirteenth century.[135] Both Gerhoh of Reichersberg and Peter the Venerable defended the adoration of Christ present in the Eucharist.[136] By far the most important liturgical change came with the introduction of the elevation of the Host in the twelfth century.[137] A custom had already developed earlier in the twelfth century of raising the Host during the words of consecration,[138] but the earliest clear witness to a major elevation after the consecration comes from a synodal statute attributed to Odo of Sully, Bishop of Paris from 1196 to 1208. The statute refers to the practice as already in existence.[139] The custom quickly spread, and had become a common practice by the middle of the thirteenth century.[140] At about the same time, churches began to signal the consecration and elevation of the species by ringing of the church bells.[141] These two customs are the clearest witnesses to the desire of the people to see the miraculous presence of Christ on earth, or if that were not possible, at least to know of and acknowledge that presence. At the moment of elevation, the people came as close to seeing Christ as possible in this life, and here they brought their petitions to place before him. William of Auxerre, in his *Summa de officiis*, described the ritual in precisely these terms: '. . .the priest elevates the Body of Christ in order that all the faithful might both see it and seek what is necessary for salvation.'[142]

Of all the exponents of this new devotion to the sacrament, the most fervent devotees were a group of Flemish women who lived in the late twelfth and thirteenth centuries. The central figure in the movement was a laywoman, Marie of Oignies. Married at the age of fourteen, she pursuaded her husband to join her in a chaste life dedicated to the care of lepers. When her fame spread, she gained the consent of her husband to retire to the Augustinian house at Oignies, where the later cardinal Jacques de Vitry was appointed her spiritual adviser.[143] He greatly admired Marie, and wrote her *Vita* shortly after her death in 1213.[144] The group of holy women who came under the influence of Marie demonstrated an extraordinary devotion to the Eucharist, as did she herself. Miracles, visions, and a sometimes excessive desire to be joined to Christ in the sacrament characterized their spiritual lives.[145] St. Juliana of Liège, who came under the influence of Marie's circle, received a vision *c*.1209 urging the Church to adopt a special feast in honour of Christ present in the Eucharist. Jacques Pantaleon, then Archdeacon of Liège, supported Juliana's request and secured the new feast for the diocese of Liège in 1246. Later as Pope Urban IV, he extended the feast of Corpus Christi to the entire Church in 1264.[146]

This extensive devotion to the sacrament represented a completely new attitude toward the Eucharist. Before the twelfth century no similar devotion to the real presence appears in the history of Western Christianity. Yet by the middle of the thirteenth century, most of the liturgical, devotional, and even superstitious forms which this attitude would take had been established.[147]

One form which this devotion did not take, however, was that of more frequent reception. In fact, the opposite occurred. The sacrament was so revered that frequent reception was discouraged. One first finds evidence in the twelfth century for an insistence on a proper devotional disposition for reception. Confessors expected not just a formal cleansing from mortal sin, but a true longing for union with Christ demonstrated by acts of penance and charity.[148] Some theologians actively discouraged frequent reception on the grounds that this kind of familiarity with the sacrament would breed indifference.[149] At least in the thirteenth century, special permission from one's confessor was required to receive the Eucharist outside the required days.[150] The exception to this reluctance, almost fear, to approach the sacrament, proves the general rule. The exception, not surprisingly, came from the circles of holy women of Brabant and Flanders, who practically waged war against their confessors and superiors to attain permission to receive the sacrament daily or even weekly.[151] In some instances, Christ himself was reported to have miraculously appeared to distribute the Eucharist when more earthly permission to receive had been refused.[152] Apart from the exceptional devotion of these women from the Low Countries, the general attitude toward reception of communion during this period was determined by two opposing forces: a strong social pressure to receive on the required feasts, and an equally strong fear of approaching unworthily Christ present on earth.[153]

That this personalized devotion to Christ present in the Eucharist appeared for the first time in the twelfth century cannot be denied, but why such a devotion should spring up at such a time, and with such fervour, presents a difficult historical question. Three theories have been presented to account for this phenomenon. The oldest of these theories, dating back at least to the eighteenth century, described the appearance of eucharistic devotional practices, especially the elevation, as deliberate introductions on the part of the Church to counter the teachings of Berengar.[154] Several circumstances argue against this theory. First, Berengar died some hundred years before the first known witness to the elevation occurred, and there is no evidence that he ever had a large academic or popular following.[155] Secondly, the first mention of the elevation does prescribe the ritual, but gives instructions to ensure the proper usage of a practice already in use.[156] Finally, it seems unlikely that the Church would be able to foment the great number of miracles, visions, stories, and liturgical practices which grew up around the Eucharist without an audience already strongly disposed toward this form of devotion. There is an element of truth, however, in this particular approach. Since the time of the Berengarian heresy, theologians had insisted on the real presence of Christ in the Eucharist, and this insistence, once it reached the popular level, could certainly have stimulated a reverence for Christ in his sacramental presence. Again, many of the miracle stories were told to combat heresy; not however the heresy of Berengar, but rather the heresy of the Waldensians and Cathars.[157] An explanation of this rise in devotion must include as one of its elements the insistence on the real presence, asserted from the time of the Berengarian heresy, and reasserted again and again in opposition expecially to the Cathars.[158]

The teaching that Christ exists somehow just behind the veil of the species, an understanding supported by the more corporeal examples of Paschasian theology, may well have interacted with popular devotion. In order to have a strong devotion to Christ present in the Eucharist, one must first have a strong belief that in some very real way Christ *is* present. The particular approach to theology advocated by Lanfranc, Guitmund, Alger, and the *Gratiadei* gloss firmly insisted on a nearly tangible presence, and this insistence ought to be considered as one important factor underlying the rise in popular devotion to the sacrament.

A second explanation for the rise of eucharistic devotion in the second half of the twelfth century has been put forward by Albert Mirgeler. He suggests that the reverence for the Eucharist was an offshoot and refinement of the earlier practice of relic worship which was popularized during this period by the new Cistercian order.[159] Certainly, the connection between reverence for relics and reverence for the Eucharist existed. Miracle Hosts were treated precisely as relics.[160] The problem is that Hosts, miraculous and otherwise, had been treated as relics before the twelfth century.[161] The importance of Mirgeler's insight lies in his description of this devotion as a refinement of the practice. A reverence that had been limited to relics (and to the Eucharist as a relic) shifted now to focus on the central sacrament of the Church. The miracle Hosts were not just stowed away with the other church treasures, but exhibited in clear glass reliquaries,[162] while the consecrated Host was held aloft for the people to see. The importance lay in the actual 'seeing' of Christ, alive and present, rather than, as was the case with relics, in mere possession of the dead remains of sanctity. But if Mirgeler is correct in showing that the Eucharist had somehow taken over and changed the role traditionally played by relics in the earlier Middle Ages, this leaves unanswered the question of why such a change took place at that time, and in that particular way.

A third and more adequate theory accounting for the sudden rise in devotion to the Eucharist has been advanced by Édouard Dumoutet. According to Dumoutet, the same interest that underlay the devotion to the human Christ, and to his Passion and death focused on the Eucharist as the one point of contact with Christ physically present on earth.[163] He sees in the theology of this time, in the devotional literature, and even in the Grail Legends, a growing desire to see Christ as he exists in the Eucharist;[164] a desire which Dumoutet interprets as consistent and synonymous with the appearance of a personal devotion to the Blessed Virgin, and especially to the Passion.[165]

The theory has much to recommend it. In speaking of the characteristics of the rise in learning and literature which took place during the twelfth century, scholars have noted the new and intense interest of twelfth-century authors in psychology, friendship, and contact with the Beloved. So, too, the devotion to the Eucharist is a devotion to the Human Christ, here present on earth out of love for his faithful. The thought behind this form of devotion has been beautifully expressed by Peter the Venerable:

[The human soul] is moved more by presence than by absence, is moved more by having seen Christ than by having heard Him; is moved to admiration, is moved to love, ... The sacrament of the Body and Blood of Christ ... is not superfluous, because not only through that which is God, but even through that which is human, He is with us until the consummation of the world. (The sacrament) is not superfluous, because He Who redeemed us through His Body, renews us through that same Body, in order that redeemed through His Body and renewed by His Body, we are nourished and fed by His humanity until that time when we will be filled with His deity and glory.[166]

Just as in other areas of twelfth-century life, so, too, in the devotional practices surrounding the Eucharist, the soul was moved to love and admiration by the presence and commemoration of Christ the Beloved. And just as in other areas, so, too, the devotion to the Eucharist can only be adequately explained as part of that whole move toward a new understanding of humanity that is generally held to characterize the twelfth century.[167]

Substitutes for the Reception of the Eucharist

A strong devotion to the Eucharist increased the desire for some form of contact with the Human Christ present in the sacrament, but at the same time for reasons which will be discussed in chapter four, actual reception of the sacrament became a difficult and infrequent practice. Not surprisingly, a series of practices grew up in the twelfth century which served as substitutes for eucharistic reception. The theologians disputed the value of these forms of spiritual communion, but in the popular mind at least, they were seen as a kind of participation in the benefits of the sacrament.

John Beleth in his *Summa de ecclesiasticis officiis*, described three substitutes for the reception of communion: the kiss of peace, the blessed bread (*eulogia*) distributed after Sunday Mass, and the *Oratio super populum*.[168] The first of these, the kiss of peace, had been closely connected with reception of the Eucharist from the earliest times, and remained tied to the reception of the sacrament throughout the period in question.[169] In some cases, the connection between the two practices was so close that the sign of peace was seen as necessary for reception.[170] It is very likely that because of the union of this act of reconciliation and the reception of the sacrament, some sharing in the benefits was ascribed to the kiss of peace, but very few writers actually describe this ritual as bestowing the graces belonging to proper reception.[171] The prayer over the people was given on fast days when it was impossible to distribute blessed bread, and so really represents a substitute ritual for a substitute reception. Apart from a few commentators on the Mass, little reference to this practice as a substitute for communion occurs.[172]

By far the most important physical substitute for communion

in the twelfth century was blessed bread, whether received after Mass in the traditional practice of distributing the *eulogia*, or outside Mass. Several writers speak of the reception of blessed bread as a substitute for communion.[173] Blessed bread seems to have been given for communion in cases where the consecrated species were not available or there was danger of irreverence,[174] and, according to Browe, came to be seen as a substitute for viaticum in the popular mind.[175] The theological dispute over this practice and over the results of such a reception will be discussed below. But if the theologians were divided over the question of what graces were received in the reception of blessed bread, the popular belief held that such a reception was somehow a share in the merits of sacramental communion.

With the introduction of the elevation, another replacement for communion entered the realm of popular devotion. Later in the Middle Ages, people would believe that the sight of the Host alone carried extraordinary graces.[176] The way for this belief had been prepared in the twelfth and early thirteenth centuries. William of Auxerre appears to have been the first of many thirteenth century theologians to ask whether a person in mortal sin could, without further sin, view the Host at the elevation.[177] The underlying assumption of this question would be a regard for the elevation equal, or nearly equal, to that for reception of the Eucharist itself. Even before William, however, Peter the Chanter had asked the related question of whether a priest in mortal sin could concelebrate and receive the Eucharist spiritually without committing further sin.[178]

At the heart both of the devotional substitutes for reception of the Eucharist and the discussions of the efficacy and reverence due to these rituals, lies a belief that somehow one could receive the graces resulting from the Eucharist without actually receiving the sacrament itself. All these practices were ritual forms of spiritual reception of the Eucharist, but even the ritual itself was not essential for spiritual communion. The necessity for such reception was a longing for union with Christ demonstrated by a life of faith and love.[179] William of Auxerre, for instance, recommended this form of spiritual communion to those too ill to receive the sacrament.[180] The connection here between these practices and the mystical approach to the Eucharist characteristic of the 'School of Laon' and the Victorine School seems clear. The authors associated with the cathedral school at Laon, the first to accept the possibility of a regular reception of the *res sacramenti* without the *sacramentum* were also the first witnesses to the actual practice of spiritual communion.[181] It would be too facile to say that the ritual forms of spiritual communion were merely the putting into practice of the Laon-Victorine theology, but certainly this theology justified such practices. It would be perhaps more precise to say that just as the devotion to the Eucharist in the twelfth and thirteenth centuries was one expression of a whole movement toward a more personal love for the Human Christ, so too the Laon-Victorine theology of the Eucharist was one complementary theological expression of the same desire.

The devotion to the Eucharist needed both a strong belief in the actual presence of Christ in the sacrament and a belief that somehow one could communicate with Christ thus present. The Paschasian approach to the sacrament expressed and encouraged the first belief, and the mystical approach to the sacrament expressed and encouraged the second.

The short treatment of eucharistic devotion and practice presented here hardly does justice to the diversity and range of the actual practice. The reality was both more colourful, and less ordered than such a systematic discussion could lead one to believe. The amorous priest who tried to use the consecrated Host as a love potion certainly believed Christ to be present in the sacrament, but by no stretch of the imagination could he be said to have been seeking a mystical union with the Human Christ.[182] On the other hand, the spiritual communion attributed to Hugh of St. Victor on his deathbed specifically concentrated on the union with Christ possible without his presence in the sacrament.[183] Despite the manifold forms that the devotion to the Eucharist manifested in the early scholastic period, however, the two consistent features of that devotion appear to be a strong belief in a real, nearly sensual, presence of Christ in the sacrament, and a growing interest in the Human Christ so present.

William of St. Thierry, Peter the Venerable
and Baldwin of Canterbury

Although the most important and influential centres for the
dissemination of the mystical approach to the Eucharist would
be Laon and St. Victor, other writers took up this kind of
theology during the twelfth century, each giving it their own
variations.

The earliest and most ambitious of these writers was William,
Abbot of St. Thierry from 1119 to 1135, and later a monk at
the Cistercian abbey of Signy (1135-1148). William, a native of
Liège, studied in this city during the time when Alger was
master there. Leaving Liège, William later studied under
Anselm of Laon, *c.*1105-1113. An imporant theological figure
in his own right, he was one of the moving forces in the condemnation of Abelard, and himself taught a form of mystical
theology based on the love of God.[184]

William's long work on the Eucharist, *De corpore et sanguine
domini* is difficult to date with accuracy. It was certainly written
after William's letter to Rupert of Deutz, correcting the eucharistic theology of Rupert's *De divinis officiis*, written *c.*1111.[185]
The *De corpore et sanguine domini* is dedicated to Bernard of
Clairvaux whom William first met in 1118,[186] and since
William probably wrote his tract soon after his letter to Rupert,
the work quite likely dates from the early years of his abbacy.[187]

William skilfully drew together strands of thought from the
different approaches of Alger and Anselm into a synthesis
which is entirely his own. Following the line of thought connected with the anti-Berengarian tracts, William asserted that
the presence of the body of the glorified Christ in the sacrament
is necessary to our salvation.[388] Sacramental reception of the
sacrament should not be neglected, for our bodies are prepared
for future immortality and resurrection through contact with
the body of Christ.[189]

Like the 'School of Laon', however, he placed his greatest
emphasis on spiritual reception.[190] He reviewed the history of
salvation as the history of God's love for man.[191] In the Eucharist, man truly receives the body of Christ when he recalls
God's love for man in Christ's Passion and death.[192] It is the
faithful, through their faith and love, who are joined to Christ.[193]

Quoting Fulgentius of Ruspe, William accepted salvation without sacramental reception, but only in cases of necessity.[194] William managed to reconcile the two opposing interpretations of Liège and Laon on the efficacy of spiritual and sacramental reception by relegating the efficacy of the corporeal reception to the future salvation of the body, while spiritual reception is necessary for the more important salvation of the soul.

But this is not William's only contribution to the eucharistic theology of his time. Equally important is his full explanation of the existence of the accidents of the bread apart from any substance. Since the substance of the bread and wine are gone after the consecration, and the accidents of the bread cannot inhere in Christ's substance, William posited that they exist without a substance by an act of God.[195]

William explained the structure of the Eucharist in terms of the three 'bodies' of Christ. The body of Christ *secundum essentiam* is the material body of Christ born of the Virgin, which is received by the worthy and unworthy alike.[196] This body is the *sacramentum* of the divine body of Christ present *secundum unitatem*.[197] Only the worthy, vivified by the Spirit, receive the divine body in faith and love.[198] The third body of Christ is the Church present *secundum effectum* and is the result of worthy reception.[199]

William's theology of the Eucharist is important for many reasons. Although he emphasized the importance of spiritual reception, he managed to reconcile this with an understanding of the importance of sacramental reception for the salvation of the body. In this, he offered a unique and imaginative approach to the Eucharist; one which recognized the discrepancy, even opposition, between the eucharistic theologies of Liège and Laon. William's teaching that the accidents have an independent existence apart from either the body of Christ or the bread and wine would be adopted by Peter Lombard, and hence gradually be accepted as the most popular approach to the question of the accidents in the later thirteenth century. With the introduction of William's position on the accidents an alternative was presented to the teaching of Guitmund and Alger who afforded no real existence to the sensed existence of bread and wine. The question continued to be discussed

throughout the century, and most theological tracts were con-
tent to cite the different options available without themselves
taking a stand. 200

Peter 'the Venerable', Abbot of Cluny from 1122 to 1156
remained, like his fellow abbot, William, in close touch with
the intellectual ferment of the mid-twelfth century. Although
a friend of Bernard of Clairvaux, he sheltered Bernard's foe,
Abelard, in Cluny after the latter's condemnation at Sens. 201
A scholar in his own right, one of Peter's most famous works is
his tract against the heretic, Peter of Bruys, written *c*.1139-
1140. 202 Here Peter defended the Eucharist against the charges
of the heretic, who claimed that Christ gave His Body as a sacrament only once at the Last Supper. 203 In a manner reminiscent of Hugh of St. Victor, Peter explained that the Eucharist
is necessary in order to lead our minds to the love of God
through the outward sign of the sacrament. 204 The Passion and
death of Christ ought to lead us to love him more and more,
but men need visual signs to recall these events, and so Christ
instituted the Eucharist not only to commemorate, but to represent his great offering. 205 Through this commemoration
and representation the necessary virtues of faith, hope, and
charity are strengthened. 206 True reception of the Eucharist,
according to Peter, consisted not in any sacramental reception,
but in the reception of the bread of angels, the Word on which
we will feed in heaven. 207 This is the same heavenly food upon
which all the faithful from the beginning of time have fed
spiritually. 208

Peter's theology, in its whole mystical movement from the
sensed to the spiritual recalls that of Hugh of St. Victor, as his
references to the *panis angelorum* reminds one of the teaching
of Anselm of Laon. Peter's theology remains unique, however,
in its strong emphasis on re-commemoration as the purpose of
the sacrament of the Eucharist and even, in some sense, the
cause of its effect. 209

A third one-time abbot, Baldwin, who headed the Cistercian
abbey of Ford from 1175 to 1180, and later became Archbishop
of Canterbury (1184-1190) also adopted the Laon-Victorine
approach to the Eucharist. Writing a good deal later than
William or Peter, (*c*.1160-1180), Baldwin composed a long
commentary on those passages in Scripture which were tra-

ditionally associated with the sacrament.[210] For Baldwin, the highest good and perfection to which the just are led by the Spirit is the faith that works in love.[211] The consummation of this faith is the knowledge and love of Christ, which finds its most perfect expression in the consumption of the *panis angelorum*, the word himself in his spiritual presence.[212] Again and again, Baldwin insisted that this spiritual reception of the Eucharist consists in living a life of faith and love and in imitating the sufferings of Christ.[213] Through such a reception, we will receive all that is necessary for salvation,[214] and through such a reception have all the just been saved.[215] Baldwin also asserted that this spiritual reception could, and did, take place apart from sacramental reception.[216]

Like William and Peter before him, Baldwin accepted the general approach of Anselm of Laon and Hugh of St. Victor, holding the salvific function of the Eucharist to exist in the spiritual union with Christ which the sacrament symbolized. Like his predecessors, Baldwin added his own nuance to this interpretation, particularly stressing the moral requirements demanded by such a union in faith and love. For Baldwin, to receive the Eucharist without living a good life would be to cut oneself off from the society of the just, the Body of Christ.[217]

William of St. Thierry, Peter the Venerable, and Baldwin of Canterbury are three witnesses not only to the survival and spread of the mystical approach to the theology of the Eucharist, but are also witnesses to the individual differences which that interpretation embraced. All three of these men spent as great a part of their lives as administrators as they did as scholars, yet each remained in touch with one of the major currents in sacramental theology and exhibited a knowledge of the subject profound enough to be individual. The theology of the Eucharist had not yet become the private reserve of the professional theologians. In the latter half of the twelfth century, especially at Paris, such a professional corps and corporation were slowly evolving. Although it would be some years before another champion of the Laon-Victorine theology of the Eucharist would emerge from the schools, its influence was continuous throughout the twelfth and into the thirteenth century.

The Continuing Influence

Although the Laon-Victorine approach to the Eucharist would find fewer and fewer advocates after the middle of the century, especially among the theological masters, a few authors still adopted, or copied the theology of the 'School of Laon' or of Hugh of St. Victor. Zachary, *scholasticus* of Besançon, copied the *Sententie Anselmi* on the structure of the Eucharist and spiritual reception into his synoptical commentary on the Gospels, written before 1161.[218] Adam, Premonstratensian canon of Dryburgh Abbey in Scotland, similarly copied Hugh of St. Victor when he spoke of the Eucharist in his *De tripartito tabernaculo* written *c*.1179-1180.[219]

Other authors, although not directly copying either Hugh or the 'School of Laon', emphasized spiritual reception as a life of faith and love and saw this form of reception as the salvific element in the Eucharist. William de Montibus, who taught in Paris, *c*.1170-1186, and then in Lincoln until his death in 1213 described spiritual reception as the imitation of Christ in good works.[220] Peter the Chanter, the famous Parisian master, whose academic career covered the years *c*.1170-1197, spoke of the Eucharist in many of his works.[221] For the most part, Peter confined his teaching on the sacrament to dialectical and canonical problems, and rarely treated the structure of the Eucharist or different forms of reception.[222] In the few references which do exist, he distinguished between reception of the true living Christ and mere reception of his flesh.[223] Reception of the living Christ is the purpose of the Eucharist, the Flesh being merely the instrument of that reception.[224] Peter insisted on the necessity of charity for a salvific reception of the sacrament,[225] and accepted the possibility of spiritual apart from sacramental reception.[226]

As far as can be determined from the few references available, it appears that the Chanter understood the salvific value of the Eucharist to reside in the spiritual reception of the living Christ rather than the sacramental reception of his body and blood.

The practice of spiritual communion as it developed in the twelfth and into the thirteenth century provided the theologians with an opportunity to discuss the efficacy of the Eucharist. Some, following the Laon-Victorine line of thought, accepted this form of reception as salvific. This position was taken by several theologians associated with the School of Abelard,[227] by Peter Comestor,[228] Peter of Poitiers,[229] and Raoul Ardens.[230]

As described above, spiritual reception often took the form of a kind of 'substitute' reception of the sacrament. In a *sententia* attributed to the School of Gilbert of La Porrée, the reception of blessed bread or even of grass is discussed as a spiritual alternative for viaticum.[231] The author argued that although such substitutes themselves are of no salvific value, they may signify a salvific spiritual reception on the part of the recipient.[232] Robert Pullen, an English theologian writing in Paris *c.* 1142-1144, discussed precisely the same question, and energetically denied the value of such a reception.[233] The whole question of spiritual reception and its value remained an open one among the twelfth-century theologians.

Peter of Poitiers was one of the theologians in the later twelfth century who defended the Laon-Victorine approach to spiritual reception. A master at Paris from at least 1168, he took Peter Comestor's chair of theology in 1169, a post which he held until he became Chancellor of Notre Dame in 1193. As chancellor from 1193 to 1205, he witnessed the first stirrings of a formal university at Paris.[234] His major theological work, the *Sententiarum libri quinque* dated from his early years at Paris, *c.*1170-1175.[235]

As has been mentioned, Peter accepted the possibility of spiritual reception as valid apart from sacramental reception.[236] Like Guibert of Nogent before him, Peter also discussed whether a priest ought to give simple bread to those whom he knew to be in mortal sin, and if sinners sin mortally by receiving such bread thinking it to be the Eucharist.[237] Peter answered, as had Guibert, that the person who received sins just as if he had received the true body of Christ.[238] Peter's answer not only dealt with what must have been a sticky pastoral problem, but clearly demonstrates the emphasis which Peter placed on the relationship between the spiritual state of the recipient and the efficacy of the sacrament. Just as one can receive worthily without sharing in the physical sacrament, so one can receive unworthily without actually partaking of the body and blood.

Stephen Langton, later the famous Archbishop of Canterbury, recorded some of the opinions of Peter of Poitiers in his *Questiones* written during his teaching career at Paris, *c.*1195-1210.[239] He discussed in two separate places in his *Questiones* (possibly two different recensions), problems concerning to whom the Eucharist ought to be given.[240] Both sections include the question asked by Peter of Poitiers concerning the sinner who unknowingly receives plain bread. Stephen recorded two answers. First, he gave the opinion of Peter of Poitiers without naming his source.[241] Secondly, he reported the opposite opinion attributing it to Paganus of Corbeil, a contemporary of Peter Lombard. Here Stephen did not decide between the two opinions.[242]

In a related question asking whether blessed bread may be given to the sick instead of the Eucharist, Stephen did offer his own opinion, or rather opinions, for the two versions differ slightly but significantly. In the first recension of the question, Stephen answered that blessed bread ought not be given instead of the Eucharist, nor could blessed bread supply the same grace as the Eucharist to the unknowing believer.[243] In the second recension, he gave a shorter version of the same answer adding, however, 'but nevertheless, it (this spiritual reception) would be valid for eternal life.'[224] In other words, the added graces and remission of sin which accompany sacramental reception are not bestowed by such a spiritual communion, but such a reception is valid for salvation. One is reminded strikingly of the words of the Porretan *sententia* on the same question.[245]

The examples of Peter of Poitiers and Stephen Langton demonstrate that although the dominant theological approach of the late twelfth century stressed the corporate salvation of the Church as a function of the Eucharist, the understanding of a personal relationship between the believer and Christ continued as a force in theology throughout that period.

The approach to the Eucharist emphasizing the spiritual union between the individual believer and God continued to influence theologians into the early years of the thirteenth century. William of Auxerre, one of the most famous of the early thirteenth-century masters, would recover and revive this approach, passing it on into the high scholastic period.[246] Before William was to write, however, yet a third approach to the Eucharist would appear to dominate the theological scene, advocated by no less than the important Schools of Abelard and Gilbert of La Porrée.

The Theology of the Mystical Model

Before introducing the third of the approaches to the Eucharist current in the twelfth century, again it might be well to draw out the theology behind the mystical approach. The model used by the theologians discussed above to describe the role the Eucharist plays in salvation might well be described as 'platonic', using that much-used term in this case to mean an approach to reality which understands the phenomena of this world to be imperfect and transitory reflections of an eternal and spiritual reality. One moves through sense data, is led by sense data, to higher divine realities. In the case of the Eucharist, this would mean that the sensed bread and wine, and even the substantial presence of the risen Christ, are but *sacramentum* of the divine reality (*res*) which the Eucharist signifies, the salvific union between the individual believer and Christ formed by faith and love.[247] This is clearly the meaning of the terminology introduced by the theologians of the Laon-Victorine milieu. *Sacramentum, res et sacramentum, res* indicate respectively, the sensed bread and wine, the substantial body of the risen Lord, and the union of faith and love. Only the last is *res et non sacramentum*, reality and not sign. This particular theological approach, at least in its general outlines was certainly not new. It relied heavily on Augustine and the Pseudo-Dionysius, recalled the theology of Ratramnus, and even revived the concerns, if not the theology, of Berengar.[248]

This more mystical approach to the Eucharist insisted that salvation came through a spiritual, mystical union with Christ rather than through a natural or substantial union, as the advocates of a Paschasian theology held. That the theologies of these different authors differed significantly on this point did not then result in any major dispute. On the whole, the basic dichotomy between the two theologies went unnoticed by the twelfth-century theologians themselves. Yet tensions existed and they expressed themselves in the differing opinions held on certain key issues. Most of the authors who adopted a mystical approach to the Eucharist attributed some salvific value to the practice of spiritual communion. Alger of Liège, Robert Pullen, and, most ardently, Rupert of Deutz, denied any such validity outside sacramental reception. Rupert also denied that the sacraments of the Old Testament could in themselves be salvific and he argued against those who believed the Hebrew sacraments to be so. William of Champeaux and Hugh of St. Victor, among others, held the Old Testament signs to be salvific in so far as they signified a life of faith and love. By the mid-twelfth century, advocates of a Paschasian theology were few and the tensions in eucharistic theology would take a new direction.

Just as in the Paschasian theology, the limits of this approach were to cause theological and pastoral problems for its advocates. The most obvious problem was that which accompanies many mystical approaches in religion. If the desired religious object is a mystical union with God which can be achieved outside any ritual function or ecclesiastical organization, why bother with such functions or organizations? While such eloquent theologians as Hugh of St. Victor or Peter the Venerable could explain the necessity of the senses, and of history (and hence of ritual and structure) to direct our human nature to the divine, other less well-versed theologians might miss this connection. The Waldensians were willing to dismiss those elements of the ecclesial structure which did not meet their spiritual expectations. Hugh Speroni denied the validity of all rituals since true union with Christ was achieved by imitating him in love. Amalric of Bène found signs such as the Eucharist unnecessary to those endowed directly by the Spirit.

On a pastoral level, what ought to be said about knights who administered themselves viaticum in battle by plucking and eating three blades of grass? If one substituted some form of spiritual communion for participation in the Eucharist, of precisely what value was this? Could one even be said to sin if one unworthily approached these substitutes for the Eucharist? All these questions, which appear to make little sense outside a mystical approach to the Eucharist, received consideration by twelfth-and thirteenth-century theologians.

This particular approach to the Eucharist stressed the individual relationship of each believer to the risen Christ present in and through the sacrament. It said little about the larger ecclesial and communitarian setting of what was meant to be, after all, a banquet celebrating and forming Christian unity. In an age when just such communitarian aspects of the Church were beginning to be forged into new and influential forms by the lawyers of Bologna and the Popes of Rome, it would be surprising indeed if these concerns were not expressed in the theology of the sacrament of Christian unity. In fact, it would be in conjunction with the formal institutional role which the Eucharist played in medieval society that yet another approach to the Eucharist would find advocates in the twelfth century.

IV

THE ECCLESIASTICAL APPROACH
TO THE EUCHARIST

By the mid-twelfth century, two distinct interpretations of the salvific function of the Eucharist existed. One, based on the theology of Paschasius Radbertus, and worked out by the tenth-century theologians, viewed the natural contact between the recipient and Christ as the cause of grace. This was the position taken up by the opponents of Berengar, Lanfranc, Guitmund of Aversa, and Alger of Liège. A second approach, expounded particularly by the schools at Laon and at St. Victor, determined the purpose of the Eucharist to be symbolic. The Eucharist symbolizes the salvific, spiritual union of God and the Christian effected by faith and love. The positions differ greatly on several important points. For the first group, the real presence of Christ is of supreme importance, and so questions concerning the mode of that existence are also important. Sacramental reception here is a necessity for salvation. For the second group, the presence of Christ on the altar, while never denied, symbolizes rather than directly causes salvation. Questions concerning the mode of that presence are less pressing, and most characteristically sacramental reception is seen as a sign of, rather than a necessity for, salvific union with God. These two approaches, different as they are, still do not exhaust the range of early scholastic thought on the Eucharist. A third interpretation of the sacrament would appear to dominate much of the theology of the sacrament in the second half of the twelfth century.

Gilbert of La Porrée and His School

Of the students of Anselm of Laon who went on themselves to establish academic careers, one of the most famous was Gilbert, later Bishop of Poitiers, c.1141-1154. Although Gilbert is best remembered for his philosophical works and his controversial views on the Trinity, he also dealt with questions concerning the Eucharist. Gilbert made mention of the sacrament in his commentaries on Psalms written while at Laon, and his commentary on the epistles of Paul, written *c*.1130.[1] Both works were based on commentaries of Anselm, and together with the later gloss of Peter Lombard, became famous as one of the most commonly used sets of commentaries on Paul and the Psalms.[2] Gilbert's teaching on the Eucharist exists in a more complete form in a set of *sentenie*, edited by Nicolaus Häring, which Professor Häring believes to be a record of Gilbert's teaching shortly before he was elected bishop.[3] These two sources give a fairly clear picture of Gilbert's rather distinctive teaching on the Eucharist.

Similarities certainly exist between Gilbert's theology of the Eucharist and that of Anselm. Gilbert spoke of the Eucharist as the *panis celestis* upon which the angels feed, now become flesh that we might partake of it.[4] The Old Testament faithful received the same spiritual food as we do, even though the species under which they received differed.[5] Gilbert also included in his commentary on 1 Corinthians 10: 16-17 the teaching of Fulgentius of Ruspe that baptized children who die without the Eucharist will still be saved.[6]

Gilbert understood the *res sacramenti*, the reality symbolized by the Eucharist somewhat differently from Anselm. Basing his teaching on that of Augustine, *In Iohannis evangelium*, tract. 26, Gilbert described the *res* not as a personal bond of faith and love with Christ, but as a bond of all the saved which is the Church.[7] The teaching formed an important part of Gilbert's teaching on the sacrament, and affected his other views on the Eucharist. In describing the different forms of reception possible, Gilbert's commentary on 1 Corinthians 11: 29 delineated two forms of reception, sacramental and spiritual.[8] His teaching as recorded in the *sentenie* spoke of four forms of reception: sacramental, spiritual, sacramental and spiritual, and neither sacramental nor spiritual.[9] The force of the teaching remains the same, however. To receive spiritually is to remain in the unity of the Church,[10] and this form of reception alone is salvific if one is prevented from receiving sacramentally.[11] One approaches the sacrament worthily only if one rightly believes, is free from sin, and remains within the bonds of the Church.[12] Gilbert's tendency here was to describe worthy reception more as good juridical standing in the Church, rather than the individual life of faith and devotion so stressed by the Laon-Victorine approach. Following this tendency, Gilbert argued that a person ought not be denied the Eucharist, even if the priest knew the person to be in sin, as long as the recipient was not a public sinner.[13]

Gilbert followed Guitmund of Aversa and Alger of Liège in describing the mode of presence of the risen Christ in the sacrament. The appearances of bread and wine are merely that, and if the bread appears to be broken on the altar, that is mere illusion, as a stick appears to bend when placed in water.[14] As long as the appearances and taste of bread and wine last, Christ remains with us corporeally. Once these appearances fade, the Lord remains only spiritually. To argue that the Eucharist follows the natural digestive process is heretical.[15]

The emphasis which Gilbert placed on the ecclesiastical dimension of the sacrament, on the reality of the sacrament as the union of Christ and his Church, will appear as well in a group of mostly anonymous works associated with the teaching of Gilbert. One of the most interesting witnesses to this teaching is an anonymous commentary on 1 Corinthians edited by Arthur Landgraf, who dates this work *c.*1150.[16] The commentary contains a lengthy discussion of the Eucharist. The author combined, in a way somewhat similar to William of St. Thierry, both the spiritual and corporeal approaches to the Eucharist.[17] According to the glossator, there are two results of proper reception of the sacrament: (1) a union in *spiritualis gratia* (spiritual grace) which is the corporeal union of Christ and the faithful,[18] and (2) a union in *spiritualis vivificatio* (spiritual animation), which is the spiritual union of the faithful who live in the spirit of Christ.[19] The second form of union (*spiritualis vivificatio*) effects the salvific union of the faithful with Christ, and without this union, reception is of no value.[20] The author made clear, however, that the result of both unions was obedient membership in the Body of Christ, which is the Church.[21] The commentator insisted on the necessity of sacramental reception,[22] but accepted the teaching that baptized children who die without the Eucharist will be saved.[23] The commentary goes on to discuss other problems concerning the Eucharist.[24] Despite the unwieldy terminology, the major contribution which it makes towards understanding the efficacy of the Eucharist is the merging of all three early scholastic approaches to the sacrament. Both the corporeal and the spiritual union of the faithful to Christ comprise that union of the saved which is the Church. No other twelfth-century author will come as close to reconciling these different approaches as the author of this commentary.

A second work connected with Gilbert's school, the so-called *Zwettl summa* appears to be the work of Peter of Vienna, a student of Gilbert's who lived in Vienna from *c.*1161 to his death in 1183. The work was written in France, before the author moved to Vienna.[25] Like the commentary on Corinthians, the *Zwettl summa* presents a combination of theologies, but in a perhaps more eclectic form.

Peter of Vienna was particularly concerned to explain that true and 'real' reception of the Lord's body and blood consisted in spiritual communion.[26] Although it is true that the Lord is present in the sacrament, present even in his 'proper human form',[27] it is not the reception of this bodily presence that is salvific.[28] If it were so, then even heretics and schismatics would be saved, for they too receive sacramentally.[29] Salvation, for Peter, consisted in the spiritual union of faith and love. His terminology often strongly suggests that of the Laon-Victorine writers.[30] Yet in several passages, he made it clear that the union of faith and love to which he referred was the community of the Church.[31] For Peter, the unity of the Church, the reality signified by the Eucharist, would be salvific even if one refrained from sacramental reception, for instance out of reverence for the sacrament.[32] Sacramental reception was important, nevertheless, as a visible sign of the unity of the Church.[33]

Peter was quite clear on the relation of the sensed species to the Lord's body and blood present on the altar. The species are images, like prophetic visions, of no reality in themselves.[34] They exist merely to lead us through faith to the true reality, Christ, 'whole and undivided who is seen and touched and as present is adored'.[35] Peter also argued that this sacramental presence is unaffected by any change in the species. Even sacramental reception would not affect Christ's proper body, as this reception ought to be understood as spiritual.[36]

Peter's teaching does not appear to have been completely consistent. He seems to have held both that Christ is received sacramentally by good and evil alike, and that sacramental reception is not of the body and blood of Christ. His insistence on the spiritual nature of reception appears incompatible with his strong insistence on a substantial presence. His understanding of spiritual communion (and hence of the *res sacramenti*) closely parallels both that of Gilbert and that of the Laon-Victorine writers. It is the teaching of Gilbert that dominates, however, for the life of faith and love of which Peter spoke was defined as membership in the Church. He also seems to have followed the Porretanian teaching that the appearances of bread and wine on the altar after the consecration are mere illusion. Unlike either Gilbert or the anonymous commentary on Corinthians, Peter's theology explicitly rejected the central Pachasian tenet that a natural union is formed between Christ and the believer in the Eucharist. Indeed, Peter's theology seems to have left little functional value to the real presence apart from adoration. Christ is truly present, but that presence has no salvific value, and it is not even clear in Peter's theology how such a presence affects or is affected by reception.

Two further books of *sententie*, both linked to the School of Gilbert, adopted this more ecclesiological approach to the Eucharist The *Sententie divinitatis* and the earlier *Summa 'Nostre iustitie et salutis'*, both dating from around the mid-twelfth century,[37] stressed the ecclesiastical union of Christ and the faithful as the *res* of the Eucharist and true reception.[38] The *Summa 'Nostre iustitie'* particularly described this union as bound together by faith and love.[39] Both collections of *sententie* accepted the possibility of spiritual reception apart from sacramental reception under certain conditions.[40] Like Gilbert, these theologians have much in common with the Laon-Victorine School. The difference between these theologians and those of the Laon-Victorine approach remained mainly one of emphasis. Both saw true reception as a spiritual and salvific union, but while Hugh of St. Victor and the other theologians of a more mystical approach saw this union as a personal, mystical union effected by both faith and love, the students of Gilbert's school saw the union basically as the Church itself, the society of the saved.

The distinction can be exemplified by the canonical approach of the *Sententie divinitatis* to the different kinds of reception. The author described three kinds of reception. Those innocent of any sin receive worthily; those who receive conscious of their sins, receive unworthily.[41] A third group, those who have confessed their sins, but not yet made restitution, receive neither worthily nor unworthily, for if they accept the sacrament in hope of God's mercy they will be saved.[42] The division here between worthy and unworthy reception of the Eucharist depends not so much on the spiritual disposition of the recipient, but rather on his canonical standing in the Church.

Of the later theologians traditionally recognized as connected with the School of Gilbert, several authors spoke, although briefly, of the Eucharist as essentially a sign of salvific membership in the Church.[43] The Parisian master, Simon of Tournai, in his *Disputationes*, written *c.*1170-1175,[44] described the *collegium ecclesiasticum* as the second and salvific body of Christ.[45] Alan of Lille, in his *Liber distinctionum theologicarum*, written during his stay in the Midi, *c.*1171-1185,[46] was more specific in his identification of worthy reception with membership in the Church. In his definition of the verb *bibere*, Alan asserted that this means to be united to the Church, apart from which there is no salvation.[47] Commenting on the partner verb *manducare*, Alan reasserted the basic meaning of this verb as union with the Church, and added that one does not receive spiritually unless he is joined to the Church.[48] A work attributed to Alan by some scholars, the *Summa de sacramentis 'Totus homo'* carries much the same theology as the works of Alan and Simon.[49] The *res* of the sacrament is the unity of Christ and the faithful. This union is the spiritual Body of Christ, membership in which is necessary for salvation.[50] Only the faithful who are in unity with Christ and the Church truly and salvifically receive the Eucharist.[51] Another master influenced by the teachings of Gilbert was Raoul Ardens who wrote his theological masterpiece, the *Speculum ecclesie*, near the end of his life, *c.*1191/1192-1215.[52] Again Raoul described the *res* of the Eucharist as the unity between Christ and the Church.[53] As in the *Sententie divinitatis*, Raoul spoke of the members of this union as those free from sin.[54] Both the author of *Summa 'Totus homo'* and

Raoul accepted the possibility of spiritual apart from sacramental reception.[55]

With the teaching of Gilbert of La Porrée and his students another and different approach to the Eucharist began to appear. Here the salvific effect of the sacrament lies not in the corporeal union of the body of Christ and the body of the believer, nor specifically in the spiritual union of Christ and the believer in faith and love, but in continuing membership in good standing in the Body of Christ which is the Church. Gilbert and those who later followed his teaching were not the only theologians to adopt this approach. Even before the middle of the century, this emphasis on the Eucharist as a sign of an ecclesiastical union would find one of its most outspoken exponents in the German theologian, Gerhoh of Reichersberg.

Gerhoh of Reichersberg

Gerhoh, Provost of the Augustinian House at Reichersberg in the diocese of Passau, from 1132 to his death in 1169, had spent a turbulent youth as a staunch supporter of the 'Gregorian' reform movement.[56] Gerhoh's first thoughts on the Eucharist, in fact, arose in connection with his opposition to the anti-pope Anacletus II (1130-1138). Gerhoh insisted, against the opinion of Bernard of Clairvaux, that the schismatics could not worthily confect the sacrament.[57] In 1135, he wrote a tract against the anti-pope, *Libellus de eo quod princeps huius mundi iam indicatus sit*, dedicated to Bernard and containing his first lengthy treatment of the Eucharist.[59]

Gerhoh's theology of the Eucharist stems from his general theology of the sacraments.[59] He made a basic distinction between two forms of effect found in the sacraments: *effectus passivus*, that by which the sacrament is effected, and *effectus activus*, that which the sacrament effects.[60] The first form of effect takes place whenever the proper rite is observed, the second takes place only within the Church.[61]

Speaking of the Eucharist in particular, Gerhoh first defined *sacramenta* as *rerum sacrarum signa*, and then carefully distinguished between the *signa* and the *res sacra*. The *signa* of the Eucharist are the bread and wine. The *res sacra*, which the sacrament effects, is the unity of the Church.[62] The *res* of the sacrament is not the true body of Christ, but the Body of Christ which is the Church, not 'the redeeming Body of the Lord' but the 're-deemed Body of the Lord'.[63] The *signa* or *sacramenta* can exist outside the Church, but not the *res*.[64] That is to say, the *effectus passivus* is possible outside the Church, but never the *effectus activus*.[65] The sacrament of unity cannot be efficacious outside the unity it represents,[66] and thus the Eucharist outside the Church is likened to a dead body without a soul. Salvation consists in the 'faithful participating worthily in the rituals (*sacramentis*) and persevering in unity through them'.[67]

In 1147, Gerhoh, involved in a Christological dispute with Eberhard II, Bishop of Bamberg, produced a work entitled *Liber contra duas haereses*.[68] In Chapter 3, Gerhoh quoted from a letter of Hugh of Amiens on the Eucharist which he discovered in Rome.[69] The work inspired Gerhoh to refine his earlier description of the Eucharist. He first noted the different mean-ings given to the *res sacramenti* of the Eucharist by various authors.[70] Gerhoh himself then made a fourfold distinction: (1) *species*, the species of bread and wine; (2) *essentia*, the true body of Christ; (3) *res* or *virtus*, the imitation of Christ's Passion by the believer; and (4) *effectus*, the salvific remission of sin.[71] The faithful who worthily participate in the Eucharist receive all four parts of the sacrament. The unworthy within the Church receive only the *species* and the *essentia* of the sacrament,[73] while those outside the Church receive the bare *species*.[74] Gerhoh mentioned several times that the *res*, not the *essentia*, constitutes the most important element in the Eucharist.[75] According to Gerhoh, whoever receives remission of sins in the Eucharist, acquires the salvific effect of this reception precisely when he passes into the Body of Christ, the Church.[76]

A third lengthy discussion of the Eucharist appears in Gerhoh's commentary on Psalms, especially Ps. 22.[77] Many of the elements from Gerhoh's other works reappear here although Gerhoh used both the work of Rupert of Deutz and Hugh of St. Victor in his commentary.[78] Gerhoh accepted that worthy reception of the Eucharist forms a corporeal union between the believer and Christ,[79] but this union was effected by the union of wills acting out of love which is the Church.[80] For Gerhoh, the true *res* and *virtus* of the Eucharist is the union of Head and members in the Body of Christ which is the Church.[81]

Gerhoh's writings on the Eucharist offer one of the first, and

most complete presentations of the ecclesiological approach to
the Eucharist which would characterize the second half of the
twelfth century. The *res* of the sacrament will come to be described as the unity, and the worthy participation, of the believer in the Church. Gerhoh did not identify the Church
automatically with salvation as there are many unworthy
recipients of the sacraments within the Church, but his entire
career witnessed his firm insistence that there can be no salvific participation in the sacrament outside the Church. This
same close association of the salvific participation in the sacrament and membership in the Church will appear more and
more frequently in the theologians of the mid-twelfth century.

The School of Peter Abelard

Of all the students who studied under Anselm and William,
probably none was more outspokenly critical of the teaching of
their masters than Peter Abelard. Already a brilliant dialec-
tician and a famous master in his own right, Abelard studied
theology under Anselm in 1113, when he openly criticized his
master. He came into conflict with William of Champeaux in
Paris both before and after his stay in Laon. Despite his con-
tentiousness, Abelard gathered students wherever he taught, at
Paris, Melun, Corbeil, St. Denis, and at his own monastery of
the Paraclete near Troyes.[82] But if Abelard attracted a great
following, he also attracted great opposition. Twice his theological teaching was condemned. Attacked by Alberic of
Rheims and Lotulph of Novara, both students of Anselm,
Abelard was forced to burn his *Theologia 'Summi boni'* by a
council at Soissons in 1121. Under more serious opposition by
William of St. Thierry and Bernard of Clairvaux, a series of
propositions attributed to Abelard were condemned by the
Council of Sens in 1140, and the condemnation was ratified by
Pope Innocent II. Abelard died shortly after this final attack
(*c.*1142) at the Cluniac priory of St.-Marcel near Châlon-sur-
Saône.[83]

Abelard himself has left no systematic treatment of the
Eucharist. The few references to his teaching on the sacrament
hint that he probably did treat of it during his teaching career.[84]
William of St. Thierry included among the doctrines which he

found objectionable in the works of Abelard, the teaching that the accidents of the bread and wine subsist in the substance of the air after the subtantial change has taken place in the Eucharist.[85] The teaching does not appear in any of the known works of Abelard. Bernard of Clairvaux did mention that Abelard's teaching on the sacrament of the altar appears in his 'sentences',[86] and it may well be that this teaching was contained in the lost work *Liber sententiarum*, posited by Dr Ostlender.[87]

If no treatment of the Eucharist has survived which can be attributed to Abelard himself, a number of works closely connected with him and his students discuss the sacrament at length. They are unanimous in adopting the same ecclesiastical approach to the Eucharist which was being expounded by the students of Gilbert of La Porrée and by Gerhoh of Reichersberg. Following Professor Luscombe in his book on the School of Abelard, these works can be divided into two groups: those students who wrote up his teaching while still studying under the master himself, and those writers who later drew on Abelard's teaching in their own works.[88] Three sentence-collections connected with this first group of students contain discussions of the Eucharist. The earliest of these collections, called the *Sententie Florianenses* witnesses to the teaching of Abelard in the mid-thirties of the twelfth century, before his condemnation at Sens.[89] The remaining two collections the *Sententie Parisienses I* and the *Sententie Hermanni* both appear to contain reactions to the criticisms levelled at Abelard, and can probably be dated after 1139.[90] Nothing is known about the authors of these works, except that the author of the third collection was a certain Hermann.[91]

The works are important because they supply the closest contact with the actual theological teaching of Abelard on the Eucharist. Yet caution must be taken here, for H. Ostlender has suggested that two of the works, the *Sententie Parisienses I* and *Sententie Hermanni*, were influenced by the lost *Liber sententiarum*, and the theology reflected in these books may come from Abelard at best second-hand.[92]

All three collections give a similar treatment of the Eucharist. The *sacramentum* of the Eucharist is the true body and blood; the *res sacramenti* the union of head and members in the Church.[93] Proper reception consists in this union,[94] and those

who belong to the Church can be saved even without sacramental reception.

These writings show a unique approach to the problem of the
species. True substantial change takes place,[96] but the form of
the species cannot reside in Christ. The form exists, then, in
the air,[97] and the breaking of the Host on the altar is an illusion
for the good of our faith.[98] This is the teaching which William
of St. Thierry attributed to Abelard.

The collections admit the concomitance of the bread and
wine,[99] but take no stand on the question of the body received
by the apostles at the Last Supper.[100] All three collections
adopt the teaching of Guitmund of Aversa on the corruption
and mistreatment of the species.[101]

Another work, written some time after 1153 by a student
who studied under Abelard and who recorded his teaching, is
the commentary on the letters of Paul known as the *Commentarius Cantabrigiensis*.[102] The commentator considered the
Eucharist in his gloss on 1 Cor. 10-11, using much the same
language as the three books of *sententie*. The *res* of the sacrament
is the union of the faithful which is the Church.[103] Truly to
partake of the sacrament is to belong to this union, whether one
receives the outward sign of the Eucharist or not.[104]

The teaching of these four works on the salvific function of
the Eucharist is straightforward. The end result of the sacrament is the union of Christ and the Church and it is this
union that effects salvation, even apart from sacramental
reception. The teaching, much more simply ecclesiastical in its
approach than that of either Gilbert or Gerhoh, would find
a warm reception among many theologians in the second half
of the twelfth century. The School of Abelard's teaching on the
accidents also achieved a wide recognition in the twelfth
century, and was still being discussed at the end of the thirteenth century.[105]

Apart from those works which contain material from students studying directly under Abelard, there are a number
of theologians whose work reflects the influence of Abelard and
of his School. Two such works are the *Sententie* of the two
Bolognese masters, Roland and Omnebene, both writing in the
mid-twelfth century.[106]

Magister Rolandus, formerly identified with Rolandus Bandinelli, the later Pope Alexander III, completed his *Sententie* before 1150.[107] In Rolandus's discussion of the *sacramentum* and *res sacramenti* of the Eucharist, he gave two different interpretations of the relationship of the Church to the sacrament. If the definition 'sign of a sacred thing' is used for *sacramentum*, then the bread and wine are the signs both of the true body and of the Church. If the definition 'visible sign of invisible grace' is used, then the body assumed by Christ is a sign of the unity of the Church.[108] Speaking of the twofold reception of the sacrament, corporeal and spiritual, Roland defines spiritual reception as union with the body of Christ.[109] Interpreted in light of his definition of *res sacramenti*, the reference here is to the Body of Christ which is the Church. Like the other works of the School of Abelard, he accepts the possibility of spiritual reception apart from corporeal reception.[110] The *Sententie* of Magister Omnebene record the same approach to the Eucharist. He, too, spoke of the *res* of the sacrament as the Church made up of the faithful.[111] Spiritual reception of the Eucharist consists in union with the Body of Christ which is the Church.[112]

Robert of Melun, a master at both Melun and Paris, is another theologian whose works show the influence of Abelardian teachings.[113] His works, as they now exist, offer little information on his teaching concerning the Eucharist.[114] Although, in his *Questiones de epistolis Pauli*, he did describe the *res tantum* of the sacrament as the body of the Church.[115] In his *Questiones de divina pagina*, Robert explained that the sacramental reception of the Eucharist was a sign of the ultimate heavenly union of the Church with God.[116]

Drawing on both the teachings of Abelard and Robert of Melun is an anonymous commentary on the letters of Paul written before 1180.[117] Here the Eucharist is treated at length. According to the commentator, the *res tantum* of the Eucharist consists of both the Church and the vivifying spirit of the Church which is charity.[118] In order worthily to receive a person cannot be in discord with Christ.[119] Faith is essential for effective reception,[120] and the author specified as worthy recipients those who are not in mortal sin.[121] Considering the subject of spiritual communion, the author accepted spiritual reception apart from sacramental reception as a possibility, but limited this form of reception to those near death who are deprived of the sacrament.[122]

The teaching of the School of Abelard on the salvific function of the Eucharist clearly emphasizes the sacrament as a sign of ecclesiastical union. Even apart from reception of the sacrament itself, it is membership in the Church which saves. Although this teaching on spiritual communion is similar to that of the Laon and Victorine Schools, the whole approach to the sacrament is quite different. In the Laon-Victorine estimation of the Eucharist, Christ is joined to each individual in a mystical union formed by faith and love. In the Abelardian explanation of the sacrament, the salvation signified by the Eucharist is corporate rather than individual. Worthy reception is a sign of membership in good standing in the body of the saved, the Church.

The Social Function of the Eucharist

The ecclesiastical emphasis found in the eucharistic theology of Gilbert of La Porrée, Gerhoh of Reichersberg, and the students of Abelard drew upon one of the oldest traditions of the Church in speaking of the sacrament. Paul, in his Letter to the Corinthians, and the great Western Father, Augustine, both stressed the role the Eucharist played in symbolizing and in forming the unity of all Christians. The ritual of the Eucharist itself had been from earliest times the symbol *par excellence* of the unity of the Christian community. To be excommunicate litterally meant that one was forbidden to attend and participate in the sign of Christian unity which is the Eucharist. But just as excommunication would come to entail ostracism from Western society, so too reception of the Eucharist came to play an important social function in Western society during the Middle Ages.[123] It is this social role which underlies and helps explain the importance and popularity of those theologies which emphasized the ecclesiastical dimension of the Eucharist.

The reception of the Eucharist for an ordinary layman or woman in the twelfth or early thirteenth century was an extraordinary event. Only on the great feasts of the liturgical year, and on the great days in one's public life did any lay person expect to receive the sacrament. The most common practice in the twelfth century required the faithful to receive the body and blood of Christ on the feasts of Christmas, Easter, and Pentecost.[124] Later in the twelfth century, a custom grew up in France of receiving only once a year at Easter.[125] In 1215, the Fourth Lateran Council regulated the local practices by ruling that Easter communion would be the minimum requirement for all adult Christians.[126] Apart from this required participation, people approached the sacrament only as a mark of the highest solemnity: upon coronation, or reception into knighthood, or the taking of religious vows.[127] Even among the religious orders, more frequent reception was unusual. The ordinary practice of both the Benedictines and Cistercians, for instance, seems to have been monthly communion.[128] Very seldom indeed does one hear of weekly or daily reception. Never in the history of the Church has the sacrament been received as infrequently as in the twelfth to the fourteenth centuries.[129]

The reasons for this reluctance to receive the sacrament cannot be ascribed merely to indifference. On the contrary, as has been shown, the whole period under discussion witnessed a remarkable devotion to the Eucharist. In fact, the reasons why people received only infrequently seemed to have stemmed more from reverence than from indifference. First and foremost, however, the reception of the Eucharist (or indeed of any sacrament) was a formal social occasion in the Middle Ages. Reception on the high feasts proved one's allegiance to the Church, especially to one's local church. Then it was that people paid their tithes and made offerings to the church.[130] These fees were very important to the parish churches, and were considered a requirement for reception of the sacrament. If the Fourth Lateran Council forbade payment of a fee before receiving a sacrament as simony,[131] later councils made it clear that payment could be legally exacted after reception.[132] In the long struggle between the secular clergy and the mendicant orders, one of the rights most zealously guarded by the parish priests was that of distributing the Easter communion, and the reason, unfortunately, was mainly financial.[133] The act of reception could almost be compared to a renewal of the bonds of fealty to the Church. It was a solemn and public declaration of faith in good standing, and like most public acts, required the payment of a fee.

Like other social acts, the Eucharist also required proper preparation. In the twelfth and early thirteenth centuries, the sacrament was approached with a growing awe and reverence. A recipient was expected to fast, sometimes for days in advance before approaching the altar.[134] Conjugal relations were forbidden for the days preceding reception.[135] Confession was (at least in theory) essential for worthy reception,[136] and in some parishes, priests were required to keep a list of parishioners who had confessed during Lent, so that they would know who was eligible to receive at Easter.[137] Parish priests were forbidden to give communion to strangers, partly so as not to infringe on another priest's right to tithes, but also lest he give communion to one not properly prepared. Robert of Melun sternly warned priests that to allow unworthy reception of the Eucharist, 'either out of favour or money', would be tantamount to killing Christ himself.[139]

Despite the expense and the difficulty involved in preparation, great social pressure was brought to bear on the individual to receive on the high feast days. Not to receive was a public admission of serious sin and public refusal of communion could easily arouse suspicion, even of heresy.[140] Odo of Ourscamp argued that a priest ought not publicly to deny the sacrament except to those who were declared excommunicate, because he might thereby cause false accusations.[141] Stephen Langton similarly stated that a priest should not publicly refuse anyone the sacrament, even if he knew him privately to be in serious sin: 'not only because of scandal, but especially that his crime not be made public'.[142] Several authors recorded the related practice of sinners or unbelievers receiving communion on the high feast days in order to avoid detection.[143] Churches empty on ordinary days, literally overflowed on these days.[144] The cup, which was first denied to the faithful during the twelfth century, was probably withdrawn because of the danger involved in distributing the wine to the large crowds.[145] In some cases, the species were distributed on side altars, or even after Mass, in order to maintain some semblance of order.[146]

The parish priest shouldered a great responsibility in distributing communion to his parishioners. Should he refuse the sacrament publicly to those he knew privately to be in sin, and thus perhaps cause them unjust social ostracism? In general, the theologians agreed with Odo of Ourscamp and Stephen Langton in urging the priest to admonish the secret sinner, but not to refuse him the sacrament.[147] In this case, though, would not the priest be contributing to the damnation of the sinner by allowing him to receive unworthily?[148] The problem was a grave one, and not surprisingly, a practice arose which avoided both difficulties. The priest would give the secret sinner an unconsecrated Host, thus deceiving both the congregation and the sinner.[149] Paganus of Corbeil, Peter of Poitiers, Stephen Langton, and William of Auxerre all discuss the morality of this practice. Does the priest sin by this act? Does the sinner still receive unworthily by intent? The opinions of these theologians, discussed above,[150] offer an excellent example of a theological issue which, at first glance, seems to be mere logic-chopping, but in fact deals with an important pastoral problem.

It takes little imagination to see this social aspect of the sacrament as intimately bound up with what has been described as an ecclesiastical approach to the Eucharist. The reception of the sacrament at Christmas, Pentecost, and especially Easter was a dramatic, and physically obvious witness to the unity of the Church. All members in good standing appeared in their parish churches, hopefully cleansed from sin, ready to partake of the effective sign of the unity of the community of the saved, and to pay the dues which that membership required. Many influences moulded that particular form of theology, but certainly one of the greatest must have been this actual living practice.

The teaching of the Schools of Gilbert of La Porrée and of Abelard, and that of Gerhoh of Reichersberg demonstrate the popularity of the ecclesiastical approach to the Eucharist even before the mid-twelfth century. In the second half of the century, this approach will become even more popular, not the least because of its adoption by the much-copied Parisian master, Peter Lombard.

Peter Lombard and his School

Peter, master of the cathedral school in Paris from before 1144 until his election as Bishop of Paris in 1159, was one of the most famous Parisian masters in the mid-twelfth century. Born in Lombardy, and educated at Reims and at St. Victor's in Paris, he is best known for his *Sententie* (written *c*.1155-1158) which became the standard theological text of the thirteenth and fourteenth centuries. The theology of the Eucharist contained in the *Sententie* comes for the most part from Peter's commentary on the Letters of Paul (written after 1148), and it is here that Peter's most complete discussion of the Eucharist occurs.[151]

Like that of Gerhoh of Reichersberg and the School of Abelard, the Lombard's theology focused on the union of the faithful, the Church, as the ultimate salvific union symbolized by the Eucharist. The *res* of the sacrament is the unity of the Church composed of all the predestined.[152] Thus, the Fathers of the Old Testament received the same spiritual food as do we because they too believed in Christ.[153] The Church is the union of the faithful with Christ bound together in faith, hope, and love.[154] Whoever remains outside that union of peace, bears witness against himself.[155] Whoever belongs to the union will be saved, even if he dies before receiving the sacrament of the Eucharist.[156] Anyone who remains in the unity of Christ and the Church spiritually eats Christ.[157]

Salvation, for the Lombard, consisted of membership in the Church as the body of the faithful from both Testaments. The Eucharist, including the real presence of Christ on the altar, signified this union, but was not necessary to effect it. The Lombard's theology in a sense adapts the Laon-Victorine framework to a more ecclesiological interpretation of the sacrament. Whereas, especially for Hugh of St. Victor, the Eucharist symbolized an individual, mystical union between the believer and God, in the Lombard's theology, the same sacrament signified the corporate and ecclesiological union between the Church and God. Both approaches, however, emphasized the *res sacramenti*, the union which the Eucharist symbolized and in part effected. The real presence of Christ on the altar, so important to the salvific union envisaged by Alger of Liège and

Rupert of Deutz, lacks this central role both in the theologies of Hugh of St. Victor and Peter Lombard.

In the second half of the twelfth century, the ecclesiological approach to the Eucharist espoused by the Lombard, Gerhoh of Reichersberg, and the School of Abelard would become the most common interpretation of the sacrament, making the identification of any one particular source for any particular work more difficult. Three works, at least, can be identified as closely following the Lombard's theology of the Eucharist. A certain Magister Bandinus made an abbreviation of Peter's *Sententie* some time in the second half of the twelfth century, in which he copied the master's eucharistic theology.[158] A more independent but equally unknown master, Udo, wrote a *Summa* (*c.*1165) following the *Sententie* of the Lombard which influenced such theologians as Peter of Poitiers and Magister Martinus.[159] Udo followed Peter Lombard in describing the *res* of the Eucharist as the unity of the Church.[160] True reception consists in receiving the true spiritual body of Christ, which is the unity of the Church.[161] Membership in this community constitutes salvific reception even for those faithful unable to receive sacramentally.[162] Like the *Sententie divinitatis* and the *Speculum ecclesie* of Raoul Ardens, Udo specified mortal sin as the impediment for proper reception.[163]

Magister Gandulphus, writing in Bologna, *c.*1160-1170, produced a book of *Sententie*, which like Udo's work, depended heavily on the *Sententie* of Peter Lombard.[164] Gandulphus copied the Lombard's definition of *res* as the unity of the Church, and condensed Peter's teaching on spiritual communion.[165] Going even further in associating worthy reception with membership in the Church than Udo, Gandulphus described the impediment to worthy reception as 'acts worthy of excommunication'.[166] Gandulphus held that sacramental reception is necessary because of the requirement of the Church that the Eucharist be received thrice yearly.[167]

By the middle of the twelfth century, the ecclesiological approach to the Eucharist had been adopted by a large and respectable group of scholars, challenging for popularity both the now declining approach of Alger and Rupert and the mystical interpretation of the sacrament of Hugh of St. Victor. One theologian after the other in the second half of the century would come to follow Gerhoh, the School of Abelard, and the Lombard. To discuss the teaching of all of these theologians would be needless repetition, and in any case, much too large a task for a study such as this. To give an idea of the forms which this particular approach to the Eucharist could take, the teaching of three of these theologians will be examined in more detail.

Arnold of Bonneval, Magister Simon, and Peter Comestor

Arnold, Abbot of Bonneval in the diocese of Chartres, was a contemporary and biographer of Bernard of Clairvaux.[168] He is the author of several spiritual works and in one of them, the *Liber de cardinalibus operibus Christi*, he discusses the Eucharist at length.[169] Since the work is dedicated to Pope Adrian IV, it can be dated within the years of his pontificate, 1154-1159.[170]

Arnold's theology offers an interesting variation on the basic theme of the ecclesiological union formed by the Eucharist. Describing how one can eat and drink the body and blood of Christ, Arnold explained that the bread, wine, body and blood are all different ways of describing Christ and the union of the Church with him in the Eucharist.[171] Arnold wished that there be no misunderstanding about how this union is achieved. The sacrament contains the humanity and divinity of Christ in order that proper devotion will be shown,[172] but recipients of the sacrament are in no way thus substantially united with Christ.[173] Only the Father is consubstantial with the Son.[174] Our union is one of wills, the union of the most pure society of the Church.[175]

Arnold's insistence that no kind of physical union between Christ and the believer occurs in the Eucharist demonstrates the difference between this approach and that of the anti-Berengarian tracts. The substantial union of God and man, essential to the Paschasian approach, is definitely rejected here. Arnold's theology adheres no more closely to that of the Schools of Laon and St. Victor. The union achieved in the Eucharist consists in the identity of Christ and the Church, not that of Christ and the individual believer.[176] Salvation takes place when Christ unites us to the society of eternal life, the Church.[177]

Arnold's work is important not only as an example of one form of the ecclesiological approach to the Eucharist. Although basically a devotional tract, Arnold's work contains certain elements which reappear in the early thirteenth-century theological treatments of the Eucharist. He spoke with emotion of the sweetness of the banquet of the altar, the delights of the spiritual palate on perceiving and receiving the Lord with desire and love.[178] Those who unworthily receive, although they partake of the gifts, are denied the sweetness of charity and of the Spirit.[179] The longing of the worthy soul for Christ and the description of the savours of worthy reception depicted by Arnold serve as an eloquent witness to the growing eucharistic devotion of the twelfth century. By the beginning of the thirteenth century, this devotion will have penetrated into the properly theological treatments of the sacrament in much the same form as it appeared in Arnold's work.[180]

While Arnold witnessed to the use of the ecclesiological approach to the Eucharist outside the proper theological schools, Magister Simon offers an excellent witness to this approach within the schools. Little is known about this master apart from his name, Simon. Some time between 1145 to 1160, he produced a work on the sacraments which presents a typical example of the ecclesiological approach to the Eucharist.[181]

In his introduction to the Eucharist, Simon described the purpose of the Eucharist as the union of the worthy recipients to Christ.[182] We receive under the species of bread as a sign of the second body of Christ present in the sacrament, the *corpus mysticum, quod est Ecclesia.*[183] In a long discussion of the two forms of reception, *sacramentalis* and *realis*, Simon described the union which he believed to take place in the Eucharist. The evil receive only the *sacramentum* of the Eucharist, which for Simon was both the species and the true body. The good, however, also receive the *rem, id est unionem corporis sui, hoc est Ecclesie.*[184] The evil do not receive worthily because they are not united to the Church.[185] The good receive worthily precisely because of the work they do within the Church.[186] In speaking of spiritual communion outside the sacrament, Simon allowed that in cases of necessity a person who is a worthy member of the Church receives the *rem* of the sacrament simply because he remains within the union of the Church.[187] For Simon, true reception of the Eucharist consisted in the salvific union of faith and will which is the Church.[188]

Simon, like Arnold, understood the Eucharist as the sign and seal of worthy membership in the Church. He identified more closely than most of his contemporaries the worthy reception of the Eucharist with active participation in the Church.[189] Those who are members of the Church receive the sign of that membership efficaciously in the sacrament and gain salvation from their membership even outside the sacrament.

Another more famous master, Peter Comestor, Chancellor of Paris from 1164 to 1178, also put forward a theology of the Eucharist which closely linked that sacrament to membership in the Church. Peter treated of the Eucharist at length not only in his work, *De sacramentis*, written *c*.1165-1170, but also in his commentary on the Gospels, written *c*.1152-1178.[190]

In both the *De sacramentis* and in his commentary on John's Gospel, Peter followed the Lombard in describing the *res sacramenti* of the Eucharist as the union of the predestined.[191] He particularly emphasized that this union included only those who would make up the glorified Church in heaven.[192] The Comestor also urged the necessity of faith for a worthy reception, and in one passage in his commentary on John, he spoke of a worthy reception in faith in much the same way as Hugh of St. Victor or the School of Laon.[193] For the Comestor, however, salvation came not from faith alone, but through membership in the Church. Through the Eucharist received in faith, one is incorporated into the salvific union of the Church and through this union is filled with the spirit of Christ.[194]

The Comestor, like Arnold of Bonneval, offered his own version of the ecclesiastical approach to the Eucharist, particularly stressing the role of the Eucharist as a symbol of the union in faith of the future glorified Church. Despite his individuality, however, the general approach to the sacrament remains the same as that of Simon and the Lombard. The Eucharist symbolized, for all these men, the one union in faith which is the Church, through which one alone could be saved.

The Continuing Influence

The ecclesiastical interpretation continued to influence, and even dominate theological discussions of the Eucharist during the second half of the twelfth and the beginning of the thirteenth century. The list of theologians who in one form or another, accepted the eucharistic thought of the Lombard, or the Schools of Gilbert of La Porrée or Abelard, reads like a compendium of later twelfth-century theologians.

In the mid-twelfth century, Robert Pullen, the Parisian master, discussed the Eucharist in a book of sentences.[195] He described worthy reception of the Eucharist as the union with Christ which makes up the Church.[196] The reception of the sacrament is death to all except true members of the Church.[197] Pullen attacked the opinion of the School of Gilbert of La Porrée which accepted as salvific the spiritual reception of blessed bread or of three blades of grass.[198] He insisted on sacramental reception of the Eucharist because of the statute of the Church requiring reception three times a year.[199] Pullen was perhaps the first of several theologians who in adopting the ecclesiological approach to the Eucharist valued sacramental reception not so much for its intrinsic value, but because such reception was demanded by the precepts of the Church. This teaching would best give formal theological expression to the social pressures brought to bear on required reception of the Eucharist.

Odo of Ourscamp, writing slightly later than Pullen (*c*.1145-1166/7) also identified the *res sacramenti* of the Eucharist with the unity of the Church.[200] The Church is the body of the elect which Christ came to redeem, and which is united through reception of the Eucharist.[201] In a *questio* found in Chalons-sur-Marne MS 72, attributed by O. Lottin to Hugh of St. Victor, an approach to the Eucharist similar to that of Peter Lombard and Robert Pullen appears.[202] The *res sacramenti* consists in the spiritual union of the predestined, which is the Church.[203] The anonymous author discussed both spiritual and sacramental reception of the Eucharist, and insisted on the necessity of sacramental reception.[204] His reasons for this insistence were clearly ecclesiological: 'Sacramental reception, however, is necessary at least once a year because it unites the church, remits sin, and defends against sin.'[205]

Peter of Poitiers, although retaining some aspects of the Laon-Victorine approach to the Eucharist, described the *res sacramenti* as ecclesiastical unity.[206] Stephen Langton, whose theology again includes some elements of the more mystical understanding of the sacrament, defined the *res tantum* as the unity of the Church, and urged sacramental reception for all Catholics.[207] The *Notule super IIII sententiarum* followed Langton in this teaching, as the *Summa* of John of Noyon would follow Peter of Poitiers in his teaching.[208]

Praepositinus, fellow master at Paris with Peter the Chanter and Alan of Lille and Chancellor of Paris from 1206 to 1210,[209] described the *res* of the Eucharist as the Body of Christ which is the Church.[210] In commenting on the words of the canon of the Mass, *Jube hoc proferri*, he explained that in this prayer, we pray that the Body of Christ which is the Church might be joined in heaven to the true body of Christ, the head of the Church.[211]

Writing shortly after Praepositinus, the Parisian master known as Magister Martinus discussed the Eucharist in two of his works.[212] In a manuscript of St. John's College, Cambridge, a series of questions precedes the *Summa* of Martinus entitled: *Summa magistri martini et questiones theologice a cantuar. disputatae.*[213] In one of the questions, Martinus insisted on the necessity of the Eucharist for salvation.[214] In his *Summa* written *c.*1190-1200, he discussed the necessity of sacramental reception at greater length. If faith suffices for salvation, why does a person need to receive the sacrament?[215] Martinus took the position of Robert Pullen on the question, arguing that reception is necessary because Church law demands it.[216] Referring to the teaching of some theologians that sacramental communion may be unnecessary, Martinus explained that spiritual communion suffices only in times of urgent necessity.[217] This discussion is important, for it demonstrates the awareness among at least some early scholastic theologians of the danger that too strong an emphasis on spiritual communion might obviate the need for sacramental reception. Like so many other theologians of his day, Martinus referred to the *res* as union, indicating the ecclesiastical union.[218]

The ecclesiological approach to the Eucharist continued to be propounded in the early years of the thirteenth century. Master Guy of Orchelles, writing at Paris, *c.*1215-1217, identified the *res* of the Eucharist with the unity of the Church.[219] Guy described spiritual communion as incorporation in the Body of Christ which is the Church.[220] He defined this incorporation quite closely. To remain in Christ does not demand divine charity, but sorrow for past sins and a desire to sin no more.[221] In short, as in the teaching of Gandulphus, to receive worthily is to receive conscious of no mortal sin, that is to say, to be a member of the Church in good standing.[222] Guy did not accept the teaching that a person legitimately hampered from sacramental reception can receive the grace of the sacrament through faith alone.[223]

Wolbero, Abbot of St. Pantaleon in Cologne *c.* 1147-1165,[224] Peter of Capua, the Parisian master, writing *c.* 1201-1202,[225] Gerard, later Bishop of Novara, writing *c.*1200-1209,[226] and Jacque de Vitry, writing *c.*1219-1225[227] should also be included among the scholars who accepted the ecclesiastical approach to the Eucharist.

The Theology of the Ecclesiastical Model

The basic metaphor upon which the ecclesiological approach to the Eucharist rests is formed from the traditional Judaeo-Christian notion of the community as the chosen people of God.[228] The community as such is saved; the individual appropriates salvation through membership in the community as saved. In the twelfth and early thirteenth centuries, membership in the community of the saved tended to be defined in increasingly juridical fashion as canon law procedures and statutes were codified and enforced. Not surprisingly, theologies of the Eucharist were affected by this move towards institutionalization. Those writers who described the Eucharist as a sign of corporate salvation would slowly come to see the community of faith and love more broadly defined as those free from mortal sin, or even those not publicly excommunicate.

The question of worthy reception tended to become a question of juridical standing rather than a question of spiritual intent.

Not all authors were equally influenced in this regard. Indeed, as among the exponents of other models, a great deal of diversity existed. For some writers, the Church was the community of faith and love, and the difference between these writers and those of the more mystical approach would be mainly one of emphasis. One group would stress the individual as saved through a life of faith and love, while the other group would understand the communal life of faith and love to constitute the community which Christ had saved. When writers began to apply juridical rather than moral and spiritual criteria for worthy reception of the sacrament, the differences between the two approaches would become more apparent, and this emphasis on juridical standards became more marked as the twelfth century waned.

The interpretation of the Eucharist which described the sacrament as a sign of the salvific union of the faithful in the Church dominated theological discussions of the sacrament in the second half of the twelfth century. The theology of Alger of Liège and Rupert of Deutz had all but disappeared from the scene, and the Laon-Victorine theology, while still finding adherents, appeared less and less frequently in the discussions of the masters as the twelfth century wore on.

Despite their loss of theological prominence, both of these earlier interpretations continued to exercise an important influence on the theology of the Eucharist. The insistence on the real presence of Christ in the Eucharist so strongly advocated by Alger and Rupert continued to be asserted and defended by later theologians. The practice of spiritual communion, a practice justified and advocated by theologians adopting the spiritual approach to the Eucharist, continued to grow in popularity throughout the twelfth century, despite the opposition of theologians like Robert Pullen, Magister Martinus, and Guy of Orchelles.

The coexistence of these three differing approaches made for an unresolved tension in the early scholastic theology of the Eucharist not always unnoticed by the contemporary theologians. The most apparent problem, at least to some contemporary observers, lay in the practice of spiritual communion. If a salvific bond of faith and love can be created apart from the sacramental reception of the Eucharist, why risk damnation through possibly unworthy reception of the sacrament? The point could be pushed to a logical and anti-sacramental extreme, and apparently was by men like Hugh Speroni and the Amalricians.[229] Even more important to theologians like the anonymous author of *questio* 39 attributed to Hugh of St. Victor was the anti-ecclesial nature of a too fervent advocacy of spiritual communion. If the Eucharist was a sign of the Church, then one ought not to exempt oneself from the Church's command to participate in this sign.

The difference here extends deeper than a disagreement over practice. Basically, the Laon-Victorine approach to the Eucharist envisages salvation as individual; the union symbolized by the sacrament is that of the good person and God. The ecclesiastical approach to the Eucharist sees salvation as basically corporate; the union symbolized is that of the Church and God. Membership in the Church saves rather than direct union with God. Too great an emphasis on individual salvation could contribute to a strong anti-clerical stand, and this emphasis appears to have at least partly influenced the teaching of the Waldensians.[230]

Another problem, perhaps less obvious to contemporaries, involved the real presence itself. Once the basic premiss of the corporeal approach to the sacrament disappeared, the almost sensual presence of Christ in the Eucharist lost much of its theological value. Why is Christ present, if this presence is not necessary for our salvation? A mystical approach to the sacrament such as that adopted by Hugh of St. Victor could and did handle this question gracefully by fitting it into the whole salvific movement from the sensed to the spiritual. Not all theologians were so skilled, however, and men like Arnold of Bonneval could only explain this presence as an aid to devotion. As the rapid rise in devotions to the real presence demonstrates, more and more people began to think like Arnold, and the real presence became more and more a metaphysical wonder and an object of veneration.

Thought on the Eucharist was far from unanimous in the early scholastic period. Very different interpretations of the purpose and necessity of the sacrament underlie a deceptively similar terminology. Between the different approaches to the Eucharist loomed important differences in the role of the Church, and of salvation itself. The situation made for an uneasy tension in the writing of theologians, and in the religious practices of the time.

The teaching of the early scholastic theologians formed the basis for the achievements of the great scholastic theologians, and it would be surprising indeed if the underlying problems and tension present in the earlier theology did not carry over into the latter. The eucharistic theology of one of the men often considered the first of the great scholastics, William of Auxerre, echoes the whole earlier scholastic treatment of the sacrament, and so in many ways provides a proper conclusion to a discussion of that treatment.

V

THE LEGACY OF DIVERSITY

WILLIAM of Auxerre, a Parisian master of the early thirteenth
century, holds a central position in the study of early scholastic
theology because of the influence of his *Summa aurea*, written
between 1215 and 1225.[1] Dom Odon Lottin has listed some
twenty-six theologians who are known to have used the *Summa
aurea*,[2] and one estimation of a recent study of William's work
has noted: 'It is becoming clear that William occupies a key,
pivotal position between the earlier scholastic theology of the
12th century and the full flowering of the scholastic genius in
the 13th.'[3] Certainly, this seems to be the situation in regard to
William's theology of the Eucharist. Not only did he preserve
the theologies of the twelfth century, with their inherent tension, for the later scholastic theologians, but he also introduced
into his works a more systematic discussion of the growing devotion to the Eucharist, and in so doing revived some of the teachings of the Laon-Victorine approach to the sacrament.

At first glance, William's theology seems to contain little
new. Like his predecessors, he described the *res* of the sacrament as the unity of the Church.[4] Both the bread and wine,
and the body and blood are symbols of the mystical Body of
Christ, which is the Church.[5] In William's discussion of the
different modes of receiving Christ, the originality of his position first appears. He discussed two kinds of reception, sacramental and spiritual.[6] To receive sacramentally is to receive
the body and blood of Christ under the species of bread and
wine.[7] William's description of spiritual reception came
straight from the Laon-Victorine tradition: '(the Body of
Christ) is spiritually received when through faith we are incorporated into Christ. Of this form (of reception) Augustine says:
Believe and you have eaten.'[8] William followed this definition
with a description of the proper stages of spiritual reception:
discernment, love, imitation, incorporation.[9] The discussion,
set in the form of a *questio*, offered a treatise on the spiritual
ascent to final incorporation with God.[10] Continuing in this

devotional vein, William next discussed the spiritual sweetness of worthy reception. The language he used is similar to that of Arnold of Bonneval, although again the format is that of the theological *questio*.[11] This section of William's treatment is very important, for here appeared what is perhaps the first introduction of this form of devotional language into a formal theological treatise on the Eucharist.

William may have realized that his treatment of spiritual reception differed from that of his immediate predecessors, for he offered what appears to be a deliberate attempt to amalgamate two approaches to this question, that of Laon and St. Victor, and that of the School of Abelard and the Lombard. In a further discussion of spiritual reception, he spoke of two kinds of spiritual reception. The first kind is simple incorporation into the mystical Body, the Church. This would be, of course, the usual explanation of the ecclesiastical approach. A second form of this reception includes a closer and closer incorporation into the Body of Christ. Both of these forms of spiritual reception are different modes of incorporation into the mystical Body of Christ, the Church.[12] William contrasted this means of spiritual reception with another kind, based on the Laon-Victorine teaching and again embodying the devotional attitude of the thirteenth century: 'To eat the Body of Christ according to this second mode is both to be united to and assimilated into Him through faith in His Incarnation, and to delight in this, that He became human for us.'[13]

William of Auxerre's discussion of sacramental reception preserved all three of the early scholastic approaches to the Eucharist. His teaching on sacramental reception upheld the basic insistence of the Paschasian analysis of the sacrament on the real presence of Christ in the Eucharist. His teaching on the two forms of spiritual reception as incorporation into the Church, the mystical Body of Christ, bore the mainstream teaching of the theologians of the late twelfth and early thirteenth centuries. His teaching on a form of spiritual reception in faith and love revived the teaching of Laon and St. Victor and gave expression to the growing devotion to the Eucharist during this period. William's discussion of spiritual communion presented a conglomeration, rather than a synthesis of earlier positions, preserving intact all the problems and tensions discussed earlier. The importance of his discussion lies in his juxtaposing the different explanations of the role of the sacrament, and thus transmitting them, with all their ambiguities, to the later scholastic theologians.

On other points concerning the Eucharist, William did present a particular stand, siding with the more spiritual and devotional apprehension of the sacrament. First, in his discussion whether simple bread ought to be given to those in mortal sin, William followed the teaching of Peter of Poitiers. A man who receives simple bread thinking it to be the true body of Christ sins as if it were the true body. Unlike Stephen Langton, however, he offered only Peter's opinion (as his own) and does not give the opposing view of Paganus of Corbeil.[14] On the question of the value of blessed bread as a substitute for viaticum, William accepted the teaching found in the second of Langton's discussions on this point. The blessed bread suffices for salvation because of the charity of the person receiving, but does not carry the same graces and remission of venial sin as combined sacramental and spiritual reception.[15] William admonished priests not to substitute blessed bread for viaticum, but to urge those in need to make a spiritual communion.[16] Finally, William presented the first formal theological discussion of the benefits derived from viewing the Host.[17] Since William was also the first of the commentators on the Mass to comment on the elevation, it is quite likely that this is the practice he had in mind during this discussion.[18] William affirmed that a person in mortal sin could view the body of Christ without further sin, and that this 'vision of the Body of Christ' both excites a person to greater devotion and provides the occasion for the granting of petitions.[19] Even more than Arnold of Bonneval's teaching, these comments by William show how far the real presence of Christ in the Eucharist had become of devotional rather than salvific importance. To receive the body of Christ unworthily was of no benefit, and even worthy reception was the sign of one or other higher union; to see the body of Christ in itself granted benefits to worthy and unworthy alike.

The teaching of William of Auxerre on the Eucharist provided in many respects a summary of the diverse discussions of the sacrament started by the Berengarian controversy and pursued continuously throughout the twelfth and into the

thirteenth century. If nothing else, the sheer volume of theologi-
.cal literature on the Eucharist from this period would provide
convincing witness to the strong contemporary concern with
the role of the Eucharist. But the discussions were not only vol-
uminous, they were divergent. The early scholastic theologians
were not in agreement on fundamental questions regarding the
Eucharist. From this point of view, William's work was not
only a finale, but a prelude to a continued discussion of the
Eucharist, a discussion which, like the teaching in the *Summa
aurea*, inherited the conflicts of earlier treatments of the sacrament.

William of Auvergne, for instance, in his *Magisterium divinale*,
written *c*.1223-1240,[20] included a discussion of the spiritual
delights of worthy reception,[21] and insisted on the union in
charity between God and man as esential for salvation.[22] He
even provided instructions in his treatment of the Eucharist for
profitable meditation on the sacrament.[23] Yet despite his emphasis on devotion, he set the union achieved and symbolized
in the Eucharist within the framework of the community of the
saved, the mystical Body of Christ, the Church.[24] William of
Middleton, in his *Questiones de sacramentis,* written *c*.1245-
1249,[25] followed much more closely the teaching of Laon and
St. Victor re-introduced by William of Auxerre. True reception exists only when faith is present working through love.[26]
William taught that this spiritual reception can take place outside the sacrament.[27] Albert the Great, on the other hand, in
his work, *De sacramentis*, written *c*.1240-1243,[28] denied that
spiritual reception can take place outside sacramental reception.[29] Thomas Aquinas, Albert's great pupil, followed his
master in this teaching. In his *Summa Theologiae, pars. 3*, written
1272-1273,[30] he admitted that spiritual communion by desire is
possible outside sacramental reception, but only in cases where
one is prevented from sacramental reception.[31] A man is clearly bound to receive sacramentally not only by the law of man,
but by the mandate of God.[32] The questions raised by early
scholastic discussions of the Eucharist continued to address
theologians long after the time of William of Auxerre, and it
would be both naïve and historically inaccurate to suggest a
kind of break or discontinuity between the work of the early
and later scholastic writers. But in the work of William the dif-

fering theologies of the Eucharist forged during the twelfth and early thirteenth centuries appeared juxtaposed, their contradiction intact, in a work which would become an important source for later thirteenth-century writers. The old discussions could be renewed by new antagonists.

Conclusion

The discussion of the theology of the Eucharist during the early scholastic period does not represent a continuous and harmonious development toward one or the other 'classic' teaching on the Eucharist, whether one sees that teaching embodied (or attacked) in Aquinas, Trent, Luther, Zwingli, Calvin, or the Thirty-nine Articles. When the question is asked what role the early scholastic theologians thought the Eucharist played in salvation, at least three general answers to that question appear. Lanfranc, Guitmund of Aversa, Alger of Liège, and Rupert of Deutz were the most important of a group of theologians who saw the natural contact between the receiver and Christ achieved in the Eucharist as essential for salvation. Based on the theology of Paschasius Radbertus, this formulation insisted on the real presence of Christ in the Eucharist, and on the necessity of sacramental reception for salvation. Although this form of eucharistic theology ceased to be popular by the mid-twelfth century, insistence on the real presence of Christ in the Eucharist continued to be stressed owing both to attacks on the validity of the Eucharist, especially by the Cathars, and to a growing devotion to Christ present on the altar.

Before the middle of the twelfth century, two other interpretations of the salvific role of the Eucharist appeared. One, espoused especially by works connected with the Schools at Laon and St. Victor, saw the Eucharist as a sign of the mystical union in faith and love between a worthy believer and God. For many members of this group, such a union could be achieved apart from the actual participation in the sacrament. Salvation was achieved individually, in a mystical ascent to God of which the Eucharist was a sign, but not a necessity. In the writings of these theologians first appear references to the practice of spiritual communion; reception of the salvific graces of the Eucharist by actions, prayers or meditation which are substitutes for reception of the sacrament. This approach to the Eucharist, although suffering a decline in popularity in the second half of the twelfth century, was revived in the teaching of William of Auxerre, and so continued to influence theologians in the thirteenth century.

A third group of theologians, including Gerhoh of Reichersberg, Peter Lombard, and members of the Schools of Peter Abelard and Gilbert of La Porrée spoke of the Eucharist as a sign of the unity of Christ and the Church. Salvation, according to this interpretation, consisted in membership in the union of the elect, the mystical Body of Christ. Some members of this group accepted the practice of spiritual communion as a sign of membership in the Church; others argued for the necessity of sacramental reception on the grounds that such reception was commanded by the Church. This ecclesiastical approach to the Eucharist expressed in theological terms the social importance of required participation in the Eucharist as a sign of membership in good standing within the Christian community. The ecclesiastical interpretation of the sacrament came into ascendancy in the late twelfth and early thirteenth centuries, and continued to be expounded well into the thirteenth century.

These different approaches to the Eucharist encompass numerous individual variations, and some theologians incorporated two or even all three general analyses in a single work. Despite these variations, and the theological eclecticism of some of the early scholastic theologians, there was some contemporary awareness that on basic issues, disagreement existed. Rupert of Deutz, Robert Pullen, and Guy of Orchelles, for instance, spoke out against the teaching and practice of spiritual communion as advocated by the Laon-Victorine approach to the sacrament. Hugh of St. Victor eloquently drew his students away from a useless concern with the physical presence of Christ on the altar. Arnold of Bonneval raised the question of the necessity for that presence at all, and Magister Martinus questioned the purpose of sacramental reception if spiritual reception sufficed. The different approaches to the sacrament assume attitudes toward salvation and towards the role of the Church and sacraments in salvation that are not easily reconcilable, and each of the teachings mentioned here demonstrates that at least some contemporary theologians sensed the problem.

On the whole, most twelfth-century theologians were more aware of their agreement about eucharistic theology than their disagreements. Their clearer disagreements were with the Greeks, the Waldensians, and above all the Cathars. But twelfth-century Latin theologians used different, even divergent models of the Eucharist. To identify and highlight each of these different models is to stress the diversity of the period: not to suggest dissension, but to point out tensions within a diversity of emphasis and approach. For these three models hardly existed in the neat isolation which separate chapter-headings unavoidably suggest. The authors discussed in these chapters were for the most part contemporaries. Few, if any, completely 'fit' one model. All were equally faced with the new trends in devotion, with the new forms of ecclesiastical structures, and all were at least aware of heterodox forces at work. The linear presentation offered here of the theologies of the period sacrifices the rich and even flamboyant liveliness of the period in the task of arguing that the diversities of the theologies of the period reflected this richness.

To be in Angers, as was Gerald of Wales, in the week following the miraculous change of the Host to flesh, would be to see theology and devotion in interaction; to view different models for understanding the Eucharist in living counterpoint. Pilgrims, like Gerald, flocked to see the miraculous revelation of the naturally present Lord of the sacrament. Here they would know the Lord to be near them, proving his presence, as Gerald explained, to silence the heretics. Yet this very devotion to the living Lord present to his people set in motion the ecclesial machinery necessary to determine which church would house the relic, for the Lord's presence was a presence for his people and his people were the juridically governed Church. All the forces and all the theologies described above existed in vibrant intermixture. To suggest that the early scholastic theology used different models for understanding the Eucharist is not to suggest isolated divisions within that theology, but rather a simultaneity of diverse approaches, a form of not altogether conscious pluralism.

Again, to suggest this diversity in early scholastic theology is not to argue that such diversity was witness to a lack of clarity, an immaturity, on the part of the early scholastic theologians. Certainly inaccuracies, incompleteness, and hesitation appear in the work of these writers, but perhaps no more or no less than might appear in the theological writers of any historical period. Writers of the insight and eloquence of Hugh of St. Victor are rare, the Gregorys of Bergamo are ubiquitous in the history of theology. The root of the diversity apparent in this period may in fact be clarity, not confusion. To represent patristic thought on the Eucharist clearly is to represent a diversity of approaches. Even more importantly, to begin to describe the mystery of the active and salvific love of the risen Lord present in the community's celebration of that love is to open oneself to a mystery of myriad dimensions. A clearer insight into the mystery may be gained by allowing the simultaneity of divergent approaches, each of which may fall short of the whole. Together they may indeed create a balance in tension closer to the whole of the mystery than any one approach could be. It is perhaps the theological presupposition that such mysteries ought to receive a definitive expression that results in the early scholastic period being seen as either confused or preparatory to the theology of the high scholastic period.

In this regard, a word ought to be said about the use of the word *transsubstantiatio* in the creed promulgated by the Fourth Latern Council in 1215.[33] The creed has often been referred to as 'defining' transubstantion.[34] As Darwell Stone, Hans Jorisson, and more recently and explicity, James McCue, have pointed out, the creed offered no definition of the term, and merely included what was common terminology to assert the real presence against the claims of the Cathars.[35] Duns Scotus was the first theologian to interpret this confession of faith as a dogmatic affirmation of transubstantiation. It was certainly not so understood by contemporaries of the council.[36] The creed of Lateran IV was neither the culmination of twelfth-century eucharistic theology nor a prohibition against further speculation about the mode of Christ's presence in the sacrament. To read the creed in either of these two manners, would be to impose sixteenth-century concerns on to this early thirteenth-century council. It was not the mode of presence which Innocent III wished to affirm here, but the presence itself; it was not theological discussion which he wished to curtail, but the spread of the heresy of the Cathars.

The purpose of this book has been to argue that the early scholastic period, the first period in Christian history to discuss the Eucharist at length, was witness to a diversity of approaches to the sacrament. Further, this diversity, with its tensions intact, continued into the high scholastic period. The myth that the early scholastic period presented a unified theology of the sacrament, despite its polemical importance in the past, ought now be laid to rest. For only when this lingering spectre of the Reformation polemics has at last been exorcized, will historians and theologians from the many Western Christian sacramental traditions begin to discern their own roots, and, more importantly, the roots of their diversity, embedded in the rich soil of medieval religion and theology.

NOTES

INTRODUCTION

1. Joseph de Ghellinck, 'Eucharistie au XIIe siècle en occident', *DTC* 5 (1924), 1233-1302.
2. See, for instance, ibid., 1234.
3. 'Dans l'histoire de la théologie de l'eucharistie, le XIIe siècle constitue une période de transition durant laquelle la valeur intrinsèque des ouvrages ne peut se mesurer à l'intérêt qu'ils suscitent de nos jours. Mais écrits et discussions ne s'élèvant guère au-dessus de travaux d'essais ou de tentatives d'approche: imprécisions de language, inexactitudes dans l'expression, tâtonnements dans les recherches, fléchissements dans la pensée, tout cela place ces productions fort en deçà de la perfection du siècle suivant.' *DTC* 5, 1233-4.
4. Ibid., 1301-2. Cf. ibid., 1234 and 1285.
5. A. J. MacDonald, *Berengar and the Reform of Sacramental Doctrine*, p. 364.
6. See ibid., Ch. 22, esp. p. 404.
7. Jean de Montclos, *Lanfranc et Bérengar*, p. 470.
8. Burkhard Neunheuser, *L'Eucharistie. II. Au moyen âge et à l'époque moderne*, pp. 57-93, esp. p. 67.
9. See, e.g., Joseph Powers, *Eucharistic Theology*, pp. 29-31. W. Dugmore and E. L. Mascall, while adopting this general approach, appear open to the possibility of a more diverse interpretation of this period. See Dugmore, *The Mass and the English Reformers*, pp. 39-42, 59; Mascall, *Corpus Christi*, pp. 185-8; and esp., Dugmore, 'The Eucharist in the Reformation Era', *Eucharistic Theology Then and Now*, pp. 71-3. See also Tad Guzie, *Jesus and the Eucharist*, pp. 64-8.
10. *A History of the Doctrine of the Holy Eucharist*, vol. i, p. 1.
11. *The Growth of Medieval Theology*, pp. 184-204.
12. Hans Jorisson, *Die Entfaltung der Transsubstantiationslehre bis zum der Hochscholastik*. See, e.g., pp. 155-6.
13. Ibid., Ch. 2. See also p. 155.
14. *Das Sakrament der Liebe im Mittelalter*, p. 5.
15. Ibid., p. 119.
16. The major works by Geiselmann on the Eucharist include *Die Eucharistielehre der Vorscholastik* and *Die Abendmahleslehre an der Wende der christlichen Spätantike zum Frühmittelalter*.
17. *Die Eucharistielehre der Vorscholastik*, pp. 290-406.
18. Ibid., pp. 431-41. See also p. 448: 'So war um 1100 inhaltliche wie formell im einzelnen so Reiches erarbeitet, daß, es zur Synthese drängte. Sie war das Werk der Schule Anselms von Laon, die damit den Auftrakt für die frühscholastichen Eucharistietraktate gab.'
19. 'Zur Eucharistielehre der Frühscholastik', *Theologische Revue* 29 (1930), 1-12. Geiselmann reviews here *Das Sakrament der Liebe im Mittelalter*, of which he gives an extremely unfavourable estimation.

20. *Corpus mysticum*, pp. 184-8.
21. Ibid., p. 288.
22. Ibid., pp. 117-18.
23. Ibid., pp. 252-67, pp. 274-77. See, for instance, pp. 256-7: 'Les belles considerations du passé, les symboles ruisselant de richesses doctrinales sont à leur tour relégués au second plan, quoique sans mépris formel. De la dialectique insidieusement négatrice, à laquelle on ne peut se contenter toujours d'opposer un recours à la Toute-Puissance, seule pourra triompher une autre dialectique. Après une séries de tâtonnements, celle-ci, deux siècles apres Bérengar, sera prête.'
24. This relationship is also treated in a quite abbreviated form by George Tavard, 'The Church as Eucharistic Communion in Medieval Theology', *Continuity and Discontinuity in Church History* (ed. F. Forrestor Church and Timothy George (Leiden, 1979)), pp. 92-103. Tavard seems unaware of de Lubac's work.
25. *Der Eucharistie und der mystische Leib Christi*, pp. 190-1.
26. Ibid., p. 239.
27. Ibid., p. 12.
28. Ibid., pp. 63-4, pp. 102-22. See, e.g., Holböck's discussion of the *Summa 'Inter cetera alicuius scientie'*, pp. 121-2: 'Hier ist also bei der Beschreibung der Wirkung der Eucharistie von keiner Incorporatio durch sie die Rede, sondern nur einer ethischen Angleichnung an Christus durch Glaube, Hoffnung und Liebe.' On this *summa* see Ch. 3, pp. 84, 184-5.
29. Ibid., pp. 126-40. See, e.g. p. 127: 'Der Eingliederung in der mystischen Leib wird nicht durch die Eucharistie oder durch die Taufe in Verbindung mit der Eucharistie bewirkt, sondern nur durch die Taufe allein. Die Eucharistie ist bloss Symbol des durch die Taufe auferbauten mystichen Leibes. Diese Betonung der Unwirksamkeit der Eucharistie fur die Einverleibung in der mystichen Leib ist der Schule abalards eigen.' On the School of Abelard see Ch. 4, pp. 114-18, 203-6.
30. For references to discussions of this question see Ch. 3, n. 167.
31. *Berengar and the Reform of Sacramental Doctrine*, pp. 406-14.
32. The premiss is taken from Bernard Lonergan, *Method in Theology* (New York, 1972), p. xi.
33. 'Church History as a Branch of Theology', *Church History in Future Perspective,* ed. Roger Aubert (Concilium, 57 (New York, 1970)), p. 87.
34. *Doing Theology on Dover Beach: An Inaugural Address* (Cambridge, 1978), p. 28.
35. *Method in Theology*, pp. 235-66.
36. 'Is Exegesis Without Presuppositions Possible?', *Existence and Faith. Shorter Writings of Rudolf Bultmann* (Cleveland, Ohio; 1960), pp. 289-96.
37. It might be well to recall the description of models given by Bernard Lonergan: 'By a model is not meant something to be copied or imitated. By a model is not meant a description of reality or a hypothesis about reality. It is simply an intelligible, interlocking set of terms and relations that is may be well to have about when it comes to describing reality or to forming hypotheses. As the proverb, so the model is

something worth keeping in mind when one confronts a situation or tackles a job.' (*Method in Theology*, p. xii.)

38. Shortly before the submission of this text for publication, Professor Walter Principe kindly reviewed an earlier version of the work. Among many excellent suggestions, he remarked that the book makes no mention of the Eucharist as a re-enactment of the sacrifice of Calvary. Again, lack of space makes a study of this important area difficult here. I have treated this matter in an unpublished paper given at the annual convention of the College Theology Society, 'Morality and the Eucharist in the Middle Ages', and hope to offer a more detailed study in the near future.

CHAPTER I

1. 1 Cor. 11: 23-6.
2. See, for instance, Hans Conzelmann, *1 Corinthians. A Commentary on the First Epistle to the Corinthians*, trans. James W. Leitch (Philadephia, 1975), p. 194.
3. On the problem of the authenticity and meaning of the passage in John see *The Gospel According to John* (i-xii), introduction, translation, and notes by Raymond E. Brown (The Anchor Bible (Garden City, N.Y., 1966)), pp. 268-92. Cf. Raymond E. Brown, *The Community of the Beloved Disciple* (New York, 1979), pp. 78-80.
4. Of the scholars who treat of this period, cf. Louis Bouyer, *Eucharist. Theology and Spirituality of the Eucharistic Prayer*, trans. Charles Underhill Quinn (Notre Dame, Indiana, 1968), pp. 103-19; Yngve Brilioth, *Eucharistic Faith and Practice Evangelical and Catholic*, trans. A. G. Herbert (London, 1961), pp. 18-34; and J. N. D. Kelly, *Early Christian Doctrines*, pp. 196-8; 212-16.
5. The importance of the understanding of the Eucharist for the Nestorian controversy has been pointed out by Henry Chadwick, 'Eucharist and the Christology in the Nestorian Controversy', *Journal of Theological Studies* N.S. 2 (1951), 145-64.
6. Cf. Henry Chadwick, *The Early Church* (The Pelican History of the Church, 1 (New York, 1967)), pp. 266-8; and J. N. D. Kelly, *Early Christian Doctrines*, pp. 440-55.
7. 'Ergo, tibi ut respondeam, non erat corpus Christi ante consecrationem, sed post consecrationem dico tibi quia iam corpus est Christi. Ipse dixit et factum est, ipse mandauit et creatum est. Tu ipse eras, sed eras uetus creatura; postquam consecratus es, noua creatura esse coepisti. Vis scire quam noua creatura? Omina inquit, in Christo noua creatura.' *De sacramentis*, 1.4, c. 16 (ed. Henry Chadwick, *Saint Ambrose On the Sacraments*, Studies in Eucharistic Faith and Practice (London, 1966), p. 33).)
8. *De trinitate*, l. 8, cc. 13-17 (*PL* 10, 245-249B).
9. 'Daturus ergo Dominus Spiritum sanctum, dixit se panem qui de caelo descendit, exhortans ut credamus in eum. Credere enim in eum, hoc est manducare panem uiuum. Qui credit, manducat; inuisibiliter

saginatur, quia inuisibiliter renascitus.' (*In Iohannis evangelium tractatus CXXIV,* tract. 26, c. 1 (edited by the monks of St. Peter's, Steenbrugge, Corpus christianorum, series latina, 36 (Turnhout, 1954), p. 260.)

10. 'Diximus enim, fratres, hoc Dominum commendasse in manducatione carnis suae et potatione sanguinis sui, ut in illo maneamus, et ipse in nobis. Manemus autem in illo, cum sumus membra eius; manet autem ipse in nobis cum sumus templum eius. Vt autem simus membra eius, unitas nos compaginat. Vt compaginet unitas, quae facit nisi caritas.' (Ibid., tract 27, c. 6 (ibid., p. 272).)

11. On the dating of Paschasius's work see the introduction to the edition of his *De corpore et sanguine domini* by Bede Paulus (Corpus Christianorum, continuatio medievalis, 16 (Turnhout, 1969)), pp. vii-x.

12. On the dating of this work, cf. Jean-Paul Bouhot, *Ratramne de Corbie. Histoire littéraire et controverses doctrinales* (Études augustiniennes, Paris, 1976), pp. 77-85.

13. The history of Ratramnus's text is discussed by Bouhot, *Ratramne de Corbie,* pp. 89-138; H. Peltier, s.v. 'Ratramne', *DTC* 13, 1783-4; and J. N. Bakhuizen van den Brink, 'Ratramn's Eucharistic Doctrine and its Influence in Sixteenth-Century England', *Studies in Church History,* 2 (1965), 54-77. For a discussion of modern estimations of Ratramanus's eucharistic theology see the conclusion to J. N. Bakhuizen van den Brink's edition of the *De corpore et sanguine domini* (Amsterdam, 1974), pp. 140-5.

14. Bouhot, *Ratramne de Corbie,* esp. pp. 77-99, 117-38.

15. For a discussion of the condemnation at Quierzy see Rosamond McKitterick, *The Frankish Church and the Carolingian Reforms 789-895* (London, 1977), pp. 151-3.

16. *Ratramne de Corbie,* pp. 85-8.

17. Epistola 56 (*MGH, Epistolae,* 5, 513).

18. 'Quid ergo ad hanc magni theologi Dionysii preclarissimam tubam respondent, qui uisibilem eucharistiam nil aliud significare preter seipsam uolunt asserere, . . .' (*Expositiones in ierarchiam coelestem,* cap. 1 (ed. J. Barbet, Corpus christianorum, continuatio medievalis, 31 (Turnhout, 1975), p. 17).

19. *De corpore et sanguine domini* (ed. C. Lambot, *Œuvres théologique et grammaticales de Godescalc d'Orbais* Spicilegium sacrum lovaniense, 20 (Louvain, 1945), pp. 324-6.

20. 'Ad uero quod ultimum est, si post resurrectionem hoc dedisset, dicturi essent heretici, quod incorruptibilis iam Christus et in caelo positus non posset in terris eius caro a fidelibus uorari.' *De corpore et sanguine domini,* c. 18 (Paulus, p. 100) and 'Denique non, sicut quidam uolunt, anima sola hoc mysterio pascitur, . . .' (Ibid., c. 19 (Paulus, p. 101)).

21. 'Sunt et alia quae vocum novitatibus delectantes, unde sibi inanes comparent rumusculos, contra fidei catholicae veritatem dicunt. Videlicet quod trina sit Deitas, quod Sacramenta altaris non verum corpus et verus sanguis sit Domini, sed tantum memoria veri corporis et sanguini ejus, . . .' (*De praedestinatione,* c. 31 (*PL* 125, 296D)).

22. Adrevald lived at Fleury until his death in 878; see St. Hilpisch, *LexThK* 1, 158. His work on the Eucharist is printed in *PL* 124, 947-954.

23. The letter has been edited by Bede Paulus in his edition of Paschasius's *De corpore et sanguine domini*, pp. 145-73.

24. *Die Eucharistielehre der Vorscholastik* (Paderborn, 1926), esp. pp. 3-55.

25. *The Frankish Church*, p. 154.

26. '. . . ita disputat beatus Augustinus, quasi non ei placuerit illud quod sanctus dixit Ambrosius.' (*De corpore et sanguine domini* (Lambot, p. 326).)

27. Schulte, *Die Messe* (Münster, 1958), esp. pp. 121-38. According to Marta Cristiani, 'La controversia nella cultura del secolo IX', *Studi medievali*, 3rd series, 9 (1968), 221-33, this separation of clergy and laity was accompanied by a corresponding understanding of the Church in which the Church would become more closely associated with the clergy alone.

28. *Missarum Sollemnia* i, 114, 143-50.

29. For a recent summary of the scholarship in this area, cf. *The Frankish Church*, pp. 138-47. Of the more important scholars who to a greater or lesser extent adopt this general approach, cf. Adolf Franz, *Die Messe im deutschen Mittelalter*, pp. 333-98; Joseph Jungmann, *Missarum Sollemnia* i, 112-16; Gregory Dix, *The Shape of the Liturgy*, pp. 589-98; and Joseph Powers, *Eucharistic Theology*, pp. 22-7.

30. O. B. Hardison, Jr., *Christian Rite and Christian Drama in the Middle Ages: Essays in the Origin and Early History of Modern Drama* (Baltimore, Md., 1969), esp. pp. 35-79.

31. *The Frankish Church*, p. 146.

32. On the strong sense of community in the early Middle Ages see, for instance, Colin Morris, *The Discovery of the Individual*, pp. 20-36.

33. See Ch. 3, pp. 92-3 and n. 167.

34. On the effect of pagan conversions see Dix, *The Shape of the Liturgy*, pp. 594-8 and Brilioth, *Eucharistic Faith*, pp. 84-7. On both these themes see Cristiani, 'La controversia', pp. 213-33.

35. See, for instance, *The Frankish Church*, p. 125, n. 25 above, and David Knowles and Dmitri Obolensky, *The Middle Ages* (The Christian Centuries, 2 (London and New York, 1969)), pp. 132-7.

36. For a discussion of Paschasius's originality, as well as his patristic sources, see Cristiani, 'La controversia', pp. 167-91.

37. *De corpore*, c. 1 (Paulus, p. 15) and c. 7 (pp. 38-9), *Epistola ad Fredugardum* (Paulus, pp. 145, 149, 159-60).

38. Paulus, p. 169.

39. *De corpore*, c. 9 (Paulus, p. 56).

40. Paulus, p. 173. Cf. *De corpore*, c. 1 (Paulus, p. 19), c. 4 (pp. 29-30), c. 9 (pp. 55-6), c. 16 (p. 96), c. 17 (p. 98), c. 18 (pp. 100-1), c. 19 (pp. 101-2); *Epistola* (Paulus, pp. 148, 160).

41. *De corpore*, c. 2 (Paulus, p. 23), c. 17 (pp. 97-8), c. 20 (pp. 106-7); *Epistola* (Paulus, pp. 146-7; 153).

42. *De corpore*, c. 1 (Paulus, pp. 13, 16-17); *Epistola* (Paulus, p. 156).

43. *De corpore*, c. 17 (Paulus, p. 98); c. 21 (p. 112, pp. 117-23).

44. 'Quod in ecclesia ore fidelium sumitur corpus et sanguis christi, quaerit vestrae magnitudinis excellentia in misterio fiat, an in veritate. . . . Et utrum ipsum corpus sit quod de maria natum est, et passum, mortuum et sepultum, quodque resurgens et caelos ascendens ad dexteram patris consideat.' (*De corpore et sanguine domini*, c. 5 (ed. J. N. Bakhuizen van den Brink, p. 44).)

45. *De corpore*, cc. 7-8 (van den Brink, p. 44).

46. *De corpore*, c. 9 (van den Brink, pp. 44-5), c. 16 (p. 47), and c. 49 (p. 55).

47. 'Exterius igitur quod apparet, non est ipsa res, sed imago rei, mente vero quod sentitur, et intellegitur veritas rei.' (*De corpore*, c. 77 (van den Brink, p. 62).) Cf. *De corpore*, c. 9 (p. 45), cc. 30-1 (pp. 50-1), cc. 48-9 (p. 55), and c. 66 (p. 59).

48. 'Non ergo sunt idem quod cernuntur et quod creduntur. Secundum enim quod cernuntur corpus pascunt corruptible, ipsa corruptibilia. Secundum vero quod creduntur, animas pascunt in aeternum victuras, ipsa immortalia.' (*De corpore*, c. 19 (van den Brink, p. 48). Cf. c. 49 (p. 55), c. 54 (p. 56), c. 58 (p. 57), cc. 65-6 (p. 59).)

49. 'Quantum differunt spiritalia, et corporalia, visibilia, et invisibilia, divina, atque humana.' (*De corpore*, c. 71 (van den Brink, p. 60).)

50. *De corpore*, c. 16 (van den Brink, p. 47).

51. See *De corpore*, cc. 21-8 (van den Brink, pp. 48-50).

52. 'Ista dicendo planissime confitetur, quod in sacramento corporis et sanguinis domini quicquid exterius sumitur ad corporis refectionem aptatur. Verbum autem dei qui est panis invisibilis invisibiliter in illo existens sacramento, invisibiliter participatione sui fidelium mentes vivificando pascit.' (*De corpore*, c. 44 (p. 54).)

53. *De corpore*, c. 72 (pp. 60-1).

54. Bouhot, *Ratramne*, p. 115-38.

55. Cf. *De corpore*, c. 14 (van den Brink, p. 46), c. 8 (p. 44), c. 54 (p. 56), c. 77 (p. 62).

56. For a discussion of the sources of Ratramnus's theology see Cristiani, pp. 192-207.

57. Geiselmann, pp. 258-81; MacDonald, pp. 244-9; Shrader, 'The False Attribution'.

58. 'Verum cum ad eos venerimus qui moderno tempore his contentionibus non timuerunt inservire, . . .' (*De corpore et sanguine domini*, c. 1 (*PL* 139, 180A)).

59. Cf. Geiselmann, pp. 218-19, 266-7; MacDonald, pp. 245, 247-9.

60. Geiselmann, pp. 259-63; MacDonald, p. 245; Shrader, pp. 184-5.

61. On the dating of this work see Geiselmann, pp. 263; Shrader, pp. 183-4.

62. '. . . fidei integritate manente provocamur respondere, . . . quod cum in panis fractione & calicis haustu accipimus, quo ordine, trajectum in nobis naturali & corporeâ conditione servetur.' (Luc d'Archery, *Spicilegium*, i, 149.)

63. *De corpore et sanguine*, c. 20 (Paulus, p. 107).

64. *Epistola ad Guntradum* (*PL* 105, 1338C-D).
65. *MGH* Epistolae i, 513-14.
66. Shrader, pp. 181, 200-3.
67. G. Morin, 'Les *Dicta* d'Heriger sur l'Eucharistie', *Revue bénédictine*, 24 (1908), 1-18; Geiselmann, p. 274.
68. Shrader, pp. 201-2, bases this identification solely on the reference to the unworthy canons of Göttweig in 1094 as 'filth' (foectorem stercoris) in the *Vita Altmanni.*
69. 'Et his quidem, qui dixerunt, secessui obnoxium . . . id est, Heribaldo Antisidorensi episcopo, qui turpiter proposuit, et Rabano Mogontino, qui turpius assumpsit, . . .' (*PL* 139, 179B).
70. On the incidents at Orleans and Liège see Jeffrey Barton Russell, *Dissent and Reform in the Early Middle Ages* (Berkeley and Los Angeles, 1965), pp. 21-53. On the subject of neo-manichean heresy in the West see R. I. Moore, *The Origins of European Dissent*, esp. pp. 23-45.
71. d'Archery, pp. 149-50. e.g. 'Absit tamen ut tantum mysterium secessui fiat obnoxium, in quo si fortè ordo naturae servatur, mysterium quod solâ fide conspicitur, humilietur.' (d'Archery, p. 149.)
72. d'Archery, pp. 149-50.
73. Shrader, p. 185.
74. *Capitula* 14-35. See Shrader, p. 185, Geiselmann, 'Der Einfluss', pp. 242-4.
75. 'Nisi ut cum ille in Patre per naturam divinitatis esset, nos contra in eo per corporalem ejus nativitatem, et ille rursum in nobis per sacramentorum inesse mysterium crederetur, ac sic perfecta per mediatorem unitas doceretur, cum nobis in se manentibus ipse maneret in Patre, et in Patre manens maneret in nobis. Et ita ad unitatem Patris proficeremus, cum qui in eo secnndum (*recte:* secundum) nativitatem inest, nos quoque in eo naturaliter inessemus, ipso in nobis naturaliter permanente.' (*PL* 139, 383C.)
76. '. . . pateat et tantos viros non dissentire, et in catholica Ecclesia unum et idem debere omnes sapere, et schisma non esse.' (*PL* 139, 180A.)
77. See n. 69 above.
78. *PL* 139, 183B-D, 185C-186B. Heriger may well have borrowed this distinction from Gottschalk, whose work he attributed to Rabanus. On this mistaken identification see Bouhot, pp. 132-3. Cf. Gottschalk, *De corpore* (Lambot, pp. 327, 333-5).
79. 'Et idcirco, sive secundum Hieronymum dupliciter, sive secundum Augustinum dicatur corpus Christi tripliciter, *specialiter* debeat dici, cum sit *naturaliter* unum.' (Emphases by editor, *PL* 139, 183C.)
80. *PL* 139, 186B-C.
81. *PL* 139, 187C-188D e.g. 'Quapropter cujus potenti virtute panis iste communis quem quotidie sumimus, cum sit candidus, . . . debeat reservari conformata.' (Ibid., 188B.)
82. Cf. Shrader, 'The False Attribution', p. 204, MacDonald, *Berengar*, p. 246.
83. On the early 11th-century teaching of Fulbert of Chartres and Gerard of Cambrai see Geiselmann, *Vorscholastik*, pp. 284-9, MacDonald, pp. 245-6.

84. The Berengarian controversy has been the subject of much recent scholarship. An excellent account of the affair is given in Margaret Gibson, *Lanfranc of Bec* (Oxford, 1978), pp. 63-97. Important also are Jean de Montclos, *Lanfranc et Bérengar*, Richard Southern, 'Lanfranc of Bec and Berengar of Tours', *Studies in Medieval History Presented to Fredrick Maurice Powicke*, pp. 27-48. See also Josef R. Geiselmann, *Die Eucharistielehre der Vorscholastik*, pp. 290-406 and Margaret Gibson, 'The Case of Berengar of Tours', *Councils and Assemblies*, G. J. Cuming and Derek Baker (eds.), pp. 61-8; André Cantin, '*Ratio* et *auctoritas* dans le première phase de la controverse eucharistique entre Bérengar et Lanfranc', *Revue des études augustiniennes* 20 (1974), 155-86; ibid., 'La «raison» dans le *De sacra coena* de Bérengar de Tours (av. 1070)', *Recherches augustiniennes* 12 (1977), 174-211, and Ovidio Capitani, 'L''affaire berengarienne' ovvero dell'utilità delle monografie', *Studi medievali*, 3rd series, 16, fasc. 1 (1975), 353-78.

85. Lanfranc, *Liber de corpore et sanguine Domini*, c. 2 (*PL* 150, 410D). I have used the translation given by Gibson, *Lanfranc*, p. 81.

86. The passage was copied into Ivo of Chartres, *Decretum*, and hence into Gratian, *Decretum III, De cons.* d. II, c. 42 (A. Friedberg, *Corpus Iuris Canonici* (Leipzig, 1879), vol. i, pp. 1328-9.

87. For references see Ch. 2, pp. 69-70, 173-4 and n. 120 below.

88. Gregory VII, *Registrum* (ed. Caspar, 2 vols. (Berlin, 1920-3)), 6, 17a (Caspar, 2, 426-7).

89. *Die Entfaltung der Transsubstantiationslehre bis zum Beginn der Hochscholastik* (Münster, 1965).

90. On the contribution of the Berengarian controversy to the development of theology in the early scholastic period see Joseph de Ghellinck, *Le Mouvement théologique du XIIe siècle*, pp. 72-8.

91. Gibson, *Lanfranc*, pp. 63-70, MacDonald, pp. 44-132.

92. *Die Abendmahlslehre an Wende der christlichen Spätantike zum Frühmittelalter*, pp. 73-85, 248-52. On the azymite controversy see Steven Runciman, *The Eastern Schism* (Oxford, 1955), pp. 40-54, and Mahlon H. Smith III, *And Taking Bread . . . Cerularius and the Azyme Controversy of 1054* (Théologie historique, 47 (Paris, 1978)).

93. See Geiselmann, *Abendsmahlslehre*, p. 77.

94. Ibid., pp. 75-9. See also Ch. 2, pp. 54, 157.

95. See Gibson, *Lanfranc*, pp. 94-5.

96. The brief analysis of Berengar's theology presented here will be based on the *De sacra coena*, which probably dates from the last years of Berengar's life. On the dating and identification of this work see R. B. C. Huygens, 'A propos de Bérengar et son traité de l'Euchar- istie', *Révue bénédictine* 66 (1966), pp. 133-9.

97. *De sacra coena*, c. 27 (ed. W. H. Beekenkamp (The Hague, 1941), p. 59). On the problems with this edition see Huygens, ibid.

98. Ibid., c. 31 (p. 77), c. 32 (p. 83), c. 39 (pp. 123, 124), c. 41 (pp. 132-3), and c. 42 (p. 141).

99. Ibid., c. 26 (p. 55), and c. 36 (p. 105).

100. 'Salus enim aeterna prouenit nobis si corpus Christi, i.e. rem sacra- menti, puro corde accipimus, dum corpus Christi in sacramento,

i.e. in pane sancto altaris, quod est munus temporale, accipimus.'
(Ibid., c. 45 (p. 158).)

101. Ibid., c. 32 (pp. 83-4).
102. Ibid., c. 20 (p. 35, 42), c. 21 (p. 43), c. 34 (pp. 91-2), c. 35 (p. 98), c. 36 (p. 103), c. 37 (p. 106), and c. 38 (pp. 117-18).
103. Ibid., c. 9 (pp. 13-14), c. 30 (p. 66), and c. 35 (p. 94).
104. Ibid., c. 20 (p. 41), c. 21 (pp. 44-5), c. 30 (pp. 67-8), and c. 37 (p. 109).
105. Ibid., c. 39 (p. 123), c. 42 (p. 141), c. 46 (pp. 159-60).
106. Ibid., c. 6 (p. 7), c. 37 (p. 58), and c. 30 (p. 67).
107. Ibid., c. 29 (p. 65), c. 38 (p. 110), and c. 41 (p. 137).
108. On Berengar's introduction of these terms see Nicolaus Häring, 'Berengar's Definitions of *Sacramentum* and Their Influence on Medieval Theology', *Mediaeval Studies*, 10 (1948), 109-11; Geiselmann, *Vorscholastik*, pp. 293 ff., and Montclos, pp. 144-6, *et passim*. On Berengar's use of Augustine for formulating these terms see Geiselmann, ibid., and Montclos, pp. 137-41; 172 n. 3, *et passim*. The entire question of the introduction of the Augustinian notion of *sacramentum* is discussed by Damien Van den Eynde, *Les Définitions des sacrements pendant la première période de la théologie scolastique* (*1050-1240*), pp. 3-16 and Ludwig Hödl, 'Sacramentum et res—Zeichen und Bezeichnetes. Eine begriffsgeschichtliche Arbeit zum frühscholastischen Eucharistietraktat', *Scholastik* 38 (1963), 161-82.
109. See Ch. 2, pp. 58-9, 161-2.
110. '. . . Bruno Andegavensis episcopus, item Berengarius Turonensis, antiquas haeresis modernis temporibus introducendo, astruant corpus Domini non tam corpus esse quam umbram et figuram corporis Domini, legitima conjungia destruant, et quantum in ipsis est, baptismum parvulorum evertant.' Letter from Theoduin, Bishop of Liège, 1048-75, to Henry I, king of France (*PL* 146, 1439B). Cf. Russell, *Dissent*, p. 41, and Ilarino da Milano, 'Le eresie popolari del secolo XI nell'Europa occidentale', *Studi gregoriani*, 2 (1947), 78-9.
111. 'Si heresis hec uestra Berengarianis limitibus contenta esset, que veritatem quidem corporis Christi sed non sacramentum uel speciem aut figuram negabat, facile me huius capituli labore expedirem . . .' (*Contra petrobrusianos* (Fearns, pp. 87-8)).
112. 'Loquor autem de novis hujus temporis berengarianis, . . .' (Gregory of Bergamo, *Tractatus de ueritate corporis Christi* (H. Hurter (ed.), p. 2)).
113. Peter Lombard is so accused by Walter of St. Victor in his *Contra quatuor labyrinthos Franciae*, l. 3, c. 11: 'Ecce dum catholicam fidem nulla prorsus distinctione indigentem solitis sibi argumentationibus distinguit, alterum se probat Berengarium' (P. Glorieux (ed.), p. 261). Rupert of Deutz applied the same name to Alger of Liège in a letter to Cuno, Abbot of Siegburg, written in 1115: 'Hinc approbare conati sunt beato me derogare Augustino contra illum sentiendo, quem in sui erroris patrocinium Berengarius citare consueuerat dicat eius malo sensu diripiendo' (R. Haacke (ed.), *Commentaria in evangelium sancti Iohannis*, p. 2).
114. See Ch. 3, pp. 90-1, 189.

115. Cf. Guitmund, *De corpore et sanguine Christi veritate in eucharistia*, l. 2 (*PL* 149, 1450D-1453C) and Heriger of Lobbes, *Libellus de corpore et sanguine Domini*, c. 9 (*PL* 139, 187C-188D). On the authorship and dating of Heriger's work see Shrader, pp. 178-204.

116. 'Quod si panis sanctificatus non corpus Christi, sed figura corporis Christi est, ut asseris, ut fert tecum multorum opinio, imo errantium multus error: . . .' (Charles Louis Hugo (ed.), *Sacrae antiquitatis monumenta historica*, . . . vol. ii, p. 373 = *PL* 188, 1274C). Siegfried, Prior of St. Nicholas near Laon, appears to have heard a similar teaching concerning which he consulted Guibert, Abbot of Nogent. Guibert recorded the question in his reply, c. 119: 'Sed quoniam de Domini corpore objectiunculas fieri epistolae auctor dicit, quod signum, et non veritas exstet, pauca etsi exilia, super eo contemplemur' (*PL* 156, 530C-D).

117. See the article on Gerland in the *Histoire littéraire de la France*, vol. xii, fols. 275-9.

118. See Ch. 2, pp. 53-60, 156-62, esp. pp. 59 and 162.

119. See Ch. 3.

120. *De sacra coena*, c. 45 (p. 156): 'Quod autem non simpliciter, sed cum additamento coniunctim dicitur, in sacramento frangitur, in sacramento accipitur Christi corpus, nichil contra incorruptibilitatem et inpassibilitatem corporis Christi intendit.' For a similar statement, cf. e.g., the text given in Ch. 2, n. 142. For the few theologians who would insist on a literal interpretation of the oath of 1059, see Ch. 2, pp. 69-70, 173-4.

   For a discussion of the treatment of the oath of 1059 by later theologians, see Gary Macy, 'The Theological Fate of Berengar's Oath of 1059: Interpreting a Blunder Become Tradition', *Interpreting the Tradition*, ed. Jane Kopas (The Annual Publication of the College Theology Society, 1983) (Scholars Press: Chico, California, 1984).

CHAPTER II

1. See J. Leclerq and J. P. Bonnes, *Un maître de la vie spirituelle au XIe siècle: Jean de Fécamp* (Paris, 1946), pp. 31-44, and Margaret Gibson, *Lanfranc of Bec*, pp. 67-8.

2. *Confessio fidei, Pars IV* (*PL* 101, 1087A-B).

3. Ibid. (ibid., 1088C-D, 1091D).

4. Ibid. (ibid., 1089A-B).

5. 'Iste est, qui non aperte utero virginis ingressus est mundum, qui cum vero corpore supra mare ambulavit, qui pauculas escas transitorias et visibiles sub dentibus edentium augeri fecit.' Ibid. (ibid., 1090C).

6. Ibid. (ibid., 1091C-D).

7. 'Ex his sane divinis mysteriis mundamur, et sanctificamur, et unius divinitatis participes efficimur, quia Deus in nobis, et nos in Deo manemus.' (Ibid. (ibid., 1089B).)

8. 'Porro autem, si ex sua essentia vel natura non habent salutis potentiam, habent ejus contrarium, sicque, dum in sua natura permanserit

(*recte*: permanserunt), erit impotens sacramentum' (*PL* 142, 1327). Two different claimants for the authorship of this tract exist: Hugh, the Bishop of Langres, who was deposed by the Synod of Reims in 1049, and died in 1050, and Hugh-Renard, Bishop of Langres, 1065-85. The problem is discussed by Montclos, p. 49 n. 2 and p. 50 n 2. Cf. MacDonald, pp. 273-9 for an evaluation of Hugh's theology on this point.

9. Durand wrote his treatise *De corpore et sanguine Domini c.*1053-4 while at the abbey of Fécamp. On his life and works see Raoul Heurtevent, *Durand de Troarn et les origines de l'hérésie bérengarienne*, and G. Poras, 'Durand de Troarn', *DHGE* 14 (1960), 1159-60. On his theology of the Eucharist see Heurtevent, pp. 217-51; Geiselmann, *Vorscholastik*, p. 320; MacDonald, pp. 280-1, and Ferdinand Holböck, *Der eucharistische und der mystische Leib Christi*, pp. 11-33.

10. *De corpore* (*PL* 149, 1382B).

11. *De corpore* (*PL* 149, 1383B-C). Durand's source for this linking of the Incarnation and the real presence in the Eucharist is Hilary of Poitiers, *De Trinitate*, l. 8, cc. 13-17 (*PL* 10, 245B-249B). Durand gave what is virtually a summary of Hilary's teaching in *pars tertia* of the *De corpore et sanguine Christi*, twice referring to the *De Trinitate* by name (*PL* 149, 1382B-C, 1383A = *De Trinitate*, l. 8, c. 13, *PL* 10, 246A).

12. 'Sicut enim in his solidus catholicae fidei vigor et salutis humanae summa consisti, ita his ademptis nihil sanctitatis, nihil meriti reliquum fuerit' (*PL* 149, 1377C-D).

13. Cf. *PL* 149, 1379A-B; 1380B; 1391A; and 1408C-1410C.

14. Ibid., 1377B; 1382A-B.

15. Ibid., 1388B-1389A; 1396A-D and 1410A-1411B.

16. Ibid., 1399A-1400C; 1417A-1418B. Durand's use of miracle stories also placed the Eucharist in the realm of the miraculous. See c. 8 (ibid., 1418B-1421B).

17. 'Quod Paschasius quoque, divini sacramenti scrutator diligentissimus discussorque catholicus, . . .' (ibid., 1389C-D).

18. On Lanfranc's career see Margaret Gibson, *Lanfranc of Bec*. On Lanfranc's role in the Berengarian controversy see Gibson, pp. 63-97 and Montclos, pp. 249-432, as well as Geiselmann, *Vorscholastik*, pp. 365-75; MacDonald, pp. 289-99, and Southern, 'Lanfranc and Berengar', pp. 28-31.

19. Lanfranc, *De corpore* (*PL* 150, 409C).

20. Lanfranc, *De corpore*, c. 13 (*PL* 150, 423A-B) and c. 20 (ibid., 437D-438A).

21. *De corpore*, c. 20 (ibid., 437C). Cf. *De corpore*, c. 5 (ibid., 415A) and c. 14 (ibid., 425A).

22. '. . . sacrificium scilicet Eccesiae duobus confici, duobus constare, visibili elementorum specie, et invisibili Domini Jesu Christi carne et sanguine, sacramento et re sacramenti; . . .' (*De corpore*, c. 10 (ibid., 421B-C)).

23. *De corpore*, c. 5 (ibid., 415A) and c. 14 (ibid., 424B).

24. *De corpore*, c. 14 (ibid., 424C) and 'Veritas et sacramentum quod hic habetur, id est, Christus, qui est veritas et sacramentum, manifeste

magnus est.' (Lanfranc, *In Pauli epistolas commentarii,* 1 Tim, 3:16 (*PL* 150, 353, No. 18).) On Lanfranc's commentary on Paul see Margaret Gibson, 'Lanfranc's "Commentary on the Pauline Epistles"', *The Journal of Theological Studies,* N.S. 22 (1971), 86-112.

25. *De corpore,* c. 14 (*PL* 150, 424B).

26. *De corpore,* c. 15 (ibid., 425B-426A).

27. See Nicolaus Häring, 'Berengar's Definition of *Sacramentum*', pp. 111-12, and idem, 'The Sacramentology of Alger of Liège', p. 73 who argues that Lanfranc used only a very general definition of the word *sacramentum,* and refused to accept the closer usage of Berengar. Montclos, pp. 392-403 disagrees with Häring, and holds that Lanfranc did accept a more precise definition of the word as used by Berengar, but applied this definition to several different *sacramenta* in the Eucharist. However Lanfranc's usage is interpreted, its lack of precision presented problems for the 12th-century theologians, especially since one of the key passages on this subject, *De corpore,* c. 14 (*PL* 150, 423D-424A) appeared in the *De sacramentis* of Alger of Liège under the heading 'Augustinus in libro sententiarum Prosperi' (*PL* 180, 792D). On the history of this text see Häring, 'Sacramentology', pp. 41-78.

28. '. . . ore corporis, et ore cordis, hoc est corporaliter ac spiritualiter manducari et bibi. Corporali siquidem ore corporaliter manducamus et bibimus, quoties de altari Dominico ipsum Dominicum corpus per manum sacerdotis accipimus; spirituali vero ore cordis spiritualiter comeditur et hauritur, quando suaviter et utiliter, sicut beatus Augustinus dicit, in memoria reconditur quod unigenitus Dei Filius pro salute mundi carnem accepit . . .' (*De corpore,* c. 17 (*PL* 150, 429B-C)). The main sources for Lanfranc's distinction here are Augustine, *Tractatus XXVI in evangelium Iohannis,* nn. 11-13 (Corpus christianorum. Series latina 36, pars 8, pp. 264-7) and Gregory the Great, *Homilia XXII in evangelium,* c. 7, (*PL* 76, 1178A-D).

29. Montclos, pp. 430-1, offers a very convincing argument for this interpretation. See esp. *De corpore,* c. 17 (*PL* 150, 429B-430C).

30. In a letter to Dunan, Bishop of Ireland, written *c.*1070-4, Lanfranc accepted the proposition that baptized children who die without receiving the Eucharist may be saved, but as a general rule, he asserted that all Christians of the age of reason must receive the sacrament for salvation (*PL* 150, 533B). The short work, *Sermo sive sententiae* attributed to Lanfranc, also asserts that baptized children may be saved without the Eucharist, quoting Fulgentius of Ruspe, *Epistola* 12 (J. Fraipont (ed.), Corpus christianorum. Series latina, 41 (Turnhout, 1968), pp. 380-1 = *PL* 150, 640B). See Montclos, pp. 326-7, 339-40, 424-6.

31. *Epistola* 33 (*PL* 150, 533B). Cf. n. 28 above.

32. '. . . Ecclesia congregata, quasi sponsae sponsus adhaesit, cum qua unigenitus (*recte:* unitus) est in carne una; quia carnem quam de Virgine sumpsit, in missa et celebritatibus, quotidie Ecclesia sumit.' (*In Pauli epistolas commentarii,* Ephesians 5: 22 (Montclos, p. 430 n. 5 = *PL* 150, 304, No. 22).) Montclos (p. 431) places great emphasis on this aspect of Lanfranc's thought.

33. *De corpore* (*PL* 150, 430C).
34. See n. 30 above.
35. On Lanfranc's style of argument see Gibson, pp. 81-91. On Lanfranc's contribution to the larger theological issues raised by Berengar see Gibson, p. 97: 'Lanfranc made one fundamental point at the right time: that without a sound patristic basis the theologian was lost. Beyond that he did little to clarify the technical problems of eucharistic definition.'
36. On Guitmund, cf. Réginald Grégoire, *NCE* 6, 858-9; Montclos, pp. 462-4: Geiselmann, *Vorscholastik*, pp. 375-96; MacDonald, pp. 341-56; Holböck, pp. 11-13, and Gibson, pp. 95-6.
37. *De veritate*, l. 1 (*PL* 149, 1432C-D).
38. Ibid., l. 3 (ibid., 1490A-B).
39. Ibid., l. 3 (ibid., 1478A-C) Guitmund quoted Hilary more extensively than Durand, and with greater respect. Cf. *PL* 149, 1474B-C, 1476A, 1478C-D).
40. Ibid., l. 2 (ibid., 1462B). Guitmund was here commenting on Augustine, *Enarratio in psalmum* 98: 9 (Corpus christianorum. Series latina 39, p. 1385). On Heriger of Lobbes's use of this same passage see Geiselmann, *Vorscholastik*, p. 269 and Shrader, p. 182.
41. Ibid., l. 2 (ibid., 1455B-1461B).
42. Ibid. (ibid., 1458A-B).
43. Ibid., l. 3 (ibid., 1492B).
44. Ibid., l. 2 (ibid., 1445C-1448C). He concluded: '. . . ita si quando putredo, vel aliud simile indecens quid in Ecclesiae sacramentis appareat, ad negligentiam ministrorum puniendam vel corrigendam, vel certe ad fidem dilectionemve probandam, ut diximus, valet: veritatem tamen essentiae Dominicae carnis et sanguinis evacuare non potest' (*PL* 149, 1448B). Guitmund borrowed the idea that Christ took on different forms in speaking to Mary and the disciples from Lanfranc, *De corpore* (*PL* 150, 424C), although Lanfranc did not use the example for this purpose. See Montclos, pp. 462-4, Geiselmann, *Vorscholastik*, pp. 387-8, and MacDonald, pp. 348-9.
45. *De veritate*, l. 2 (*PL* 149, 1448C-1449C), e.g.: 'Sed Christi corpus, sicut jam diximus, in lapide jacuit, et terram calcavit: non igitur propter aliquam vilitatem cujuscunque animalis corpus horrescit' (ibid., 1449C).
46. Ibid. (ibid., 1450A-B).
47. *De veritate*, l. 2 (ibid., 1451A-1453B).
48. *De sacramentis, prologus* (*PL* 180, 739D). On Alger's career see Louis Brigué, *Alger de Liège*, pp. 1-27 and Nicolaus Häring, 'Alger of Liège', *NCE* 1, 315-16. According to Guntram Bischoff, 'The Eucharistic Controversy Between Rupert of Deutz and His Anonymous Adversary' (Unpublished dissertation, Princeton Theological Seminary, 1965), the *terminus ad quem* for Alger's work would be 1115 when Rupert of Deutz replied to Alger's work in his commentary on the Gospel of John. On Alger's theology of the Eucharist see MacDonald, pp. 379-89; Brigué, pp. 59-110, Holböck, pp. 22-31; Montclos,

pp. 464-70, and Nicolaus Häring, 'A Study in the Sacramentology of Alger of Liège', *Mediaeval Studies* 20 (1958), 41-78.

49. *De sacramentis, prologus (PL* 180, 739D-740C). Brigué, pp. 54-8, suggests that Alger may have at least in part been addressing a heresy of which he had first-hand knowledge.

50. *Contra Petrobrusianos* (Fearns, p. 88).

51. *De sacramentis*, l. 1, c. 1 *(PL* 180, 743B-744D).

52. Ibid. (ibid., 745A).

53. '. . . non nomine tenus tantum, sed in veritate sui corporis, vere sibi concorporatum: . . .' (ibid., l. 1, c. 3 (ibid., 747C)).

54. Ibid. (ibid., 748A-B).

55. Ibid., l. 1., c. 5 (ibid., 752B-C).

56. Ibid., c. 17 (ibid., 790C-791D).

57. Ibid., c. 19 (ibid., 794A-B).

58. Ibid. (ibid., 794C).

59. Ibid. (ibid., 796B).

60. Ibid., c. 18 (ibid., 792C).

61. Ibid., c. 20 (ibid., 797B-798B).

62. Ibid., c. 20 (ibid., 797D).

63. 'Quamvis igitur spiritualis comestio corporis Christi prior et dignior sit quam corporalis, . . . cum utraque tamen sit ad salutem necessaria, . . .' (ibid., c. 21 (ibid., 798B)). 'Diximus superius non minus ore corporis quam ore cordis corpus Domini esse sumendum . . .' (ibid., l. 2, c. 1 (ibid., 807B)).

64. See Ch. 3, pp. 76-82, 178-82.

65. *De sacramentis*, l. 2, c. 1. *(PL* 180, 807B-814B). e.g. '. . . quia cum illae species sine panis et vini substantia sint, quomodo mucescere et putrescere magis quam digeri possint, non facilis patet causa' (ibid., 813C).

66. e.g.: 'Possunt tamen videri mucidae et putridae, quamvis ita non sint, sicut Christus hortulanus, peregrinus, prout erant intuentium mentes; . . .' (ibid. (ibid., 813D)).

67. Gregory was a Vallombrosan monk of the monastery of Astino near Bergamo. He was elected Bishop of Bergamo in 1133, a post which he held until his death in 1146. On his life see Mario Lupi, *Codex diplomaticus civitatis, et ecclesiae bergomatis*, vol. ii (Bergamo, 1799), cols. 977-1071, and Giuseppe Ronchetti, *Memorie istoriche della citta e chiesa di Bergamo* . . . , vol. iii (Bergamo, 1837), pp. 58-80. Two sources associate the *Tractatus de veritate corporis Christi* with Gregory. According to Joseph de Ghellinck, 'Eucharistie au XIIe siècle en occident', *DTC* 5, 1237-8, the work survives in a single copy of a now lost MS made by J. A. Casari, a Vallombrosan monk, for Jean Mabillon, now Paris, Bibliothèque nationale latin MS 17187. The MS gives Gregory, Bishop of Bergamo as the author. Bartholomeus de Peregrini, *Opus divinum de sacra ac fertili Bergomensi vinea* (Brescia, 1553), *pars* 1, c. 29, fol. 7^r-v mentions that Gregory had written a tract on the Eucharist dedicated to Humbert, Archbishop of Milan: 'Hic edidit volumen de veritate corporis Christi, quod dedicauit Humberto 83. Archiepiscopo mediolanensi.' The tract

as printed by H. Hurter, *Scriptorum veterum de eucharistia opuscula selecta*, carries the dedication: 'venerandi Christi presul Omberti', whom Hurter identifies as Humbert, Archbishop of Milan. Humbert was elected and consecrated archbishop in January of 1146 (*Storia di Milano*, Fondazione Trecani degli Alfieri per la storia de Milano (eds.), vol. iii (Milan, 1954), p. 383). Since Gregory died a violent death later in the same year, the tract must date from 1146.

68.   '. . . in unoquoque sacramento tria esse distincte servanda inveniemus: rem scilicet quae sacramentum est, rem cuius sacramentum est, et rem quae virtus sacramenti est.' (*Tractatus*, c. 14 (Hurter, p. 59).)

69.   'Re igitur vera pariter et mira verum corpus Christi per visibilem, quam gerit, speciem panis et vini, sacramentum profecto collgitur esse corporis Christi.' (*Tractatus*, c. 18 (Hurter, p. 74).)

70.   'Porro de re, sive potius de rebus, quarum hoc sacramentum est, in anterioribus schedulis prolocuti sumus, quas esse passionem mortemque dominicam, pacem non fictam, unitatem sive concordiam evidenter ostendimus.' (*Tractatus*, c. 18 (Hurter, pp. 73-4).)

71.   'Res igitur, cujus sacramenti virtus dicitur, eadem est, quia per hoc sacramentum si religiose sumamus, absolutionem peccatorum indubitanter consequimur, nec non ipsi Christi per esum suae carnis potumque sui sanguinis conjungimur.' (*Tractatus*, c. 20 (Hurter, pp. 82-3).)

72.   Gregory felt that the reader might need help with his categories: 'Sed meminerit diligens lector meus atque benevolus, quod supra monuimus, ut cum audit dici rem, quae sacramentum est, rem intelligat quae sacramentum aliquod significat; cum vero rem legit, cujus est sacramentum, sacramentum illud quod significatur noverit sentiendum.' (*Tractatus*, c. 15 (Hurter, p. 64).)

73.   *Tractatus*, cc. 8-10 (Hurter, pp. 34-43). e.g.: '. . . sed neque semper et ubique species (panis et vini) ad aliquid refertur, quoniam et nonumquam pro veritate ponitur, . . .' (Hurter, p. 40).

74.   '. . . dum per communionem corporis et sanguinis sui ejus humanitati concorporamur, divinae quoque ejus substantiae, quae ei est una cum Patre, non solum fide, sed naturaliter participamus.' (*Tractatus* (Hurter, p. 84).

75.   '. . . ipsumque verum corpus et sanguinem Christi non solum ore cordis sed etiam ore corporis de mensa dominica sumi a communicantibus, . . .' (*Tractatus*, c. 21 (Hurter, p. 85)). See also c. 31 (Hurter, pp. 116-18).

76.   *Tractatus*, cc. 8-10 (Hurter, pp. 34-43).

77.   On the different understandings of 'substance' current in the 12th century and their effect on theology of the Eucharist, see Jorissen, *Die Entfaltung der Transsubstantiationslehre*.

78.   On the theology of the Lombard, see Ch. 4, pp. 122-4, 209-11.

79.   See Ch. 1, pp. 42, 151.

80.   We cannot hope to present a complete picture of the heretical movements of the 12th and early 13th centuries, and we rely heavily on the work of others. The main sources for this study are: Herbert Grund-

mann, *Religiöse Bewegungen im Mittelalter*; Arno Borst, *Die Katharer*; Jeffrey Burton Russel, *Dissent and Reform in the Early Middle Ages*; Christine Thouzellier, *Hérésie et hérétiques. Vaudois, cathares, patarins, albigeois*; Walter Wakefield, *Heresy, Crusade and Inquisition in Southern France, 1100-1250*; Raoul Manselli, *Studi sulle eresie del secolo XII*, 2nd rev. edn., and R. I. Moore, *The Origins of European Dissent.*

81. See Ch. 1, nn. 111 and 113.

82. See Geiselmann, Vorscholastik, pp. 21-73, and de Ghellinck, 'Eucharistie au XIIe siècle', cols. 1283-4. Peter of Vienna could write *c.*1160: 'Latinus non est increpandus a Greco tanquam non sacrificans aut male sacrificans eo quod uel in albo uino uel in pane azimo sacrificat. Nec est a Latino contempnendum sacrificium Greci tanquam vacuum quoniam in uino rubeo et fermentato pane sacrificat.' (*Summa*, l. 4, c. 285 (N. Häring (ed.), *Die Zwettler Summe*, pp. 192-3).)

83. Shrader, 'The False Attribution', p. 202 n. 129.

84. *De corporis*, l. 2 (*PL* 149, 1450D-1453C).

85. 'Non sunt igitur observanda Graecorum haereticorum, qui merito Stercoranistae vocantur, . . .' (*De sacramentis*, l. 2, c. 1 (*PL* 180, 810B)).

86. '. . . fuerunt eo tempore haeretici, qui substantiam panis et vini, quae in altari per sacerdotes benedicitur, in corpus et sanguinem Christi transmutari negabant . . .' (*Gesta Trevirorum* printed by Paul Frédéricq, *Corpus documentorum Inquisitionis haereticae neerlandicae*, vol. i, p. 19). The incident is discussed in Borst, p. 85; Russell, *Dissent*, pp. 54-6; and Moore, *Origins*, pp. 66-7.

87. The information comes from the autobiography of Guibert of Nogent, l. 3, c. 17 (Georges Bourgin (ed.), p. 212). Cf. Borst, p. 84; Russell, *Dissent*, pp. 78-81; and Moore, *Origins*, pp. 67-9. See also Ch. 1, n. 70 for earlier witnesses to such heretical groups.

88. Ramihrdrus is discussed by Russell, *Dissent*, pp. 43-4; Illarino da Milano, 'Le eresie', pp. 80-2; Moore, *Origins*, pp. 62-3, and Norman Cohn, *The Pursuit of the Millennium*, pp. 46-50.

89. The references to Tanchelm have been collected by Frédéricq, *Corpus documentorum*, vol. i, pp. 15-18, 22-9. The incident is discussed by Borst, pp. 84-5; Russell, *Dissent*, pp. 56-68; and Moore, *Origins*, pp. 63-6.

90. For discussion of the intentions of these men see the references cited in nn. 88 and 89.

91. The earliest such injunction was that of the Synod of Rome in 1059, c. 3: 'Ut nullus missam audiat presbyteri, quem scit concubinam indubitanter habere, aut subintroductam mulierem' (Mansi 19, 897D). Cf. also the Council of Rome in 1079 (Mansi 20, 413C); the Council of Constance in 1094 (Mansi 20, 795A-B); the Council of London in 1103 (Mansi 20, 1230C); and the Council of Reims in 1119, c. 5 (Mansi 21, 236B). This teaching occurs in the following letters of Gregory VII; *epistolae* 2, 61 (Erich Caspar (ed.), *MGH, Epistolae selectae*, vol. ii, fasc. 1, p. 216); 2, 66 (Caspar, p. 222); 2, 67 (Caspar, pp. 224-5).)

92. The work is edited by E. Martène and U. Durand, *Veterum scriptorum et*

monumentorum. . . . Amplissima collectio, 9, 1251-70. Russell, *Dissent*, follows Albert Hauck, *Kirchengeschichte Deutschlands*, vol. iv (Leipzig, 1903), p. 860 n. 3 in dating this work *c*.1154-77. See also Moore, *Origins*, pp. 187-90.

93. '. . . a sacerdote criminoso corpus Domini non confici docere praesumsit' (*Amplissima collectio*, 9, 1253C).

94. Ibid., 1253D, 1259C, 1261A.

95. 'Ex his colligitur quod in Ecclesia sola corpus Christi praesentatur, ubi a sacerdotibus catholicis missa ritu ecclesiastico celebratur. In quorum consortio non reputantur Simoniaci, et sub excommunicatione interdicti; Nicolaitae videlicet sacerdotes et reliqui altaris ministri manifeste incestuosi.' (*Liber de gloria et honore filii hominis, c.* 14 (*PL* 194, 1123B).) Cf. also Gerhoh's *Liber de simoniacis* (Emil Sackur (ed.), *MGH*, Libelli de lite, 3, 243) and his *Liber contra duas haereses* (E. Sackur (ed.), pp. 284-5).

96. *Amplissima collectio* 9, 1262C-D, 1263B-D.

97. '. . . Sacramenta a criminoso sacerdote confecta, nec defunctis nec vivis crimina sacerdotis scientibus, sed ignorantibus dumtaxat prodesse.' (Ibid., 1260A.) Russell, *Dissent*, pp. 87-8 argues that Albero was inspired here by the distinction made by the Council of Piacenza in 1095 between priests knowingly and unknowingly consecrated by simoniacal bishops. Albero could just as easily have borrowed from his countryman and contemporary Gerhoh, or even from Honorius, who may have spent much of his career in Germany.

98. On Honorius's life and works see pp. 65, 169-70.

99. '. . . imo communicando eis comitantur, cum iisdem etiam poenis participantur. . . Et ideo qui eis, quamvis inscii, communicant, tamen ab eis contaminantur . . .' (*Elucidarium*, l. 1, cc. 188-9 (Yves Lefevre (ed.), p. 397)). Honorius assumes here that simoniacs and nicolaitans are automatically excommunicate. He modifies his statement later in the same work: 'Si quis vero eorum opera mala exsecrans et bonum Christi venerans simpliciter ab eis communicat, et hunc credo hac fide salvari, . . .' (c. 193 (ibid., p. 398)).

100. Gerhoh, unlike Albero, specifically made the connection with the teaching of the Council of Piacenza, although he referred rather to Nicolas II: 'Quae cum ita se habeant, liceat nobis dicere, quod, sicut Nicolao papa distinguente non omnes ordinati a symoniacis ordinantur symoniace, ita non omnia sacramenta, quae celebrant precisi, fiunt in precisione.' (*Epistola ad Innocentium papam* (E. Sackur (ed.), *MGH*, Libelli de lite 3, 223).) See also his *Liber de simoniacis* (Sackur, p. 264).

101. 'Deine quod defunctis criminosorum sacerdotum sacramenta non prodesse dicit, . . .' (*Amplissima collectio* 9, 1263D).

102. 'Oratio eorum non suscipitur, sed fiet in peccatum, quia non exaudiet eos Dominus. Benedictio eorum in maledictionem convertitur, ut dicitur: Conventam benedictionem vestram in maledictionem, ait Dominus (2 Esdras 13: 2).' (*Elucidarium*, l. 1, c. 194 (Lefèvre, pp. 398-9).)

103. 'Addit denique somniator noster, quod . . . inter hoc sacrum mys-

terium semper daemonum, raro sanctorum angelorum praesentiam haberi' (*Amplissima collectio* 9, 1264D-E).

104. 'Hos abhorret angelorum conventus, hos fugit ipse Dominus, . . .' (*Elucidarium*, l. 1, c. 194 (Lefèvre, p. 398)). The teaching that angels are not present at Masses celebrated by those outside the Church has been attributed by Raoul Ardent, *Speculum universale*, l. 1, c. 28 to Augustine: 'Super hoc ait augustinus . . . Omnipotens deus iube hec perferri per manus sancti angeli tui in sublime altare tuum. Idcirco nisi angelus uenerit missa nequaquam uocari potest. Nunquid enim si hoc ministerium hereticus fuerit ausus usurpare angelum de celis mittit deus oblationem eius consecrare?' (Vatican City, Biblioteca Vaticana, Ottoboniana MS 880, fols. 9ᵛ2-10ʳ1). I have been unable to locate this passage in Augustine. The same teaching is recorded in the *Summa de sacramentis* '*Totus homo*', *De Eucharistia*, c. 30 (Umberto Betti (ed.), pp. 67-8). Both works date from the late 12th century.

105. On the early history of the Waldensians see Borst, pp. 109-10; Christine Thouzellier, *Catharisme et valdéisme en Languedoc à la fin du XIIe et au début du XIIIe siècle*, pp. 16-44; Kurt-Victor Selge, *Die ersten Waldenser*, i, 228 ff.; and Moore, *Origins*, pp. 228-31.

106. Selge, i, 159-63, 174-5. One example of a source which attributes this teaching to the Waldenses is the *Contra haereticos libri quatuor* of Alan of Lille, l. 3, c. 8: 'Aiunt etiam praedicti haeretici quod magis operatur meritum ad consecrandum vel benedicendum, ligandum et solvendum, quam ordo vel officium' (*PL* 210, 385A).

107. Selge, i, 149-50, 175, 307. The *Summa contra hereticos* attributed to Peter Martyr of Verona, and written *c.*1235 contains this teaching: 'Quod quidam ipsorum videntes indignati dixerunt quod nullus poterat sacrificare corpus et sanguinem Christi nisi esset sacerdos ab ecclesia romana institutus, . . .' (edited in Thomas Kaeppeli, 'Une somme contre les hérétiques de s. Pierre Martyr (?)', *Archivum fratrum praedicatorum* 17 (1947), 334. Kaeppeli discusses in this article the authorship and dating of this *Summa*).

108. Selge, pp. 159-61; Wakefield, *Heresy*, pp. 46-7, and n. 107 above.

109. Selge, p. 160, and Thouzellier, *Catharisme*, pp. 177-8. e.g., Raynier Sacconi, *Summa de catharis et a pauperibus de Lugduno*: 'Item dicunt quod simplex laicus potest consecrare corpus domini. Credo etiam quod idem dicunt de mulieribus, quia haec non negaverunt michi.' (Ed. Antoine Dondaine, *Un traité néo-manichéen du XIIIe siècle*, p. 78. Dondaine dates this work *c.*1250.)

110. Peter Abelard mentions such a teaching in his *Theologia christiana*, l. 4, c. 80: 'Nouimus et duos fratres qui se inter summos connumerant magistros, quorum alter tantum uim diuinis uerbis in conficiendis sacramentis tribuit, ut a quibuscumque ipsa proferantur aeque suam habeant efficaciam, ut etiam mulier et quislibet cuiuscumque sit ordinis uel conditionis per uerba dominica sacramentum altaris conficere queat.' (*Petri Abaelardi opera theologica*, (E. Buytaert (ed.), p. 302).) The two brothers mentioned here have been identified as Bernard and Thierry of Chartres. On the whole question of this teaching as a form

of 'grammatical platonism' see M.-D. Chenu, 'Un cas de platonisme grammatical au XIIe siècle', *Revue des sciences philosophiques et théologiques* 51 (1967), 666-8.

111. The rite, which took place on Holy Thursday, has been described by Anselm of Alexandria, *Tractatus de hereticis* dated by the editor Fr. Dondaine *c.*1260-80, 'La hiérarchie cathare en Italie. II. Le Tractatus de hereticis d'Anselme d'Alexandrie, O.P.', *Archivum fratrum praedicatorum* 20 (1950), 257. This witness is late for our study, but Anselm specifically referred this rite to a period before the split between the French and Lombard factions, i.e. before 1218 (Dondaine, p. 321.) Cf. Thouzellier, *Catharisme*, pp. 175-6. The practice of receiving the sacrament on Holy Thursday was considered an ancient custom by the 12th-century Church. See Gratian, *Decretum*, De cons. 2, c. 17 (Friedberg, i, 1320).

112. Anselm of Alexandria, *Tractatus de hereticis* (Dondaine, p. 321).

113. The tradition stems from Gregory the Great, *Epistola* 11, c. 12: 'Orationem vero Dominicam idcirco mox post precem dicimus quia mos apostolorum fuit ut ad ipsam solummodo orationem oblationis hostiam consecrarent. Et valde mihi inconveniens visum est ut precem quam scholasticus composuerat super oblationem diceremus, et ipsam traditionem quam Redemptor noster composuit super eius corpus et sanguinem non diceremus' (*PL* 77, 956D-957A). This teaching is copied by Bernold of Constance, *Micrologus* (*c.*1085, *PL* 151, 984D-985A); Honorius Augustodunensis, *Gemma animae* (*PL* 172, 572B); Rupert of Deutz, *De divinis officiis*, l. 2, c. 18 (R. Haacke (ed.), p. 52); John Beleth, *Summa de ecclesiasticis officiis*, c. 98 (Douteil, p. 181); Robertus Paululus, *De officiis ecclesiasticis*, l. 2, c. 11 (*PL* 177, 418C), and Sicard of Cremona, *Mitrale*, l. 3, c. 1 (*PL* 213, 91C).

114. Anselm of Alexandria (Dondaine, p. 321).

115. Several commentaries on the Mass from this period speak of the sign of the cross made over the species as part of the effecting ritual. To name a few: Hildebert of Lavardin, *De mysterio missae*: (A. B. Scott (ed.), *A Critical Edition of the Poems of Hildebert of Le Mans* (Oxford, Bodleian Library, MS D. Phil. d. 2403, p. 393). Odo of Cambrai, *Expositio in canone missae* (*PL* 160, 1062B-C); *Speculum ecclesiae*, c. 7 (*PL* 177, 370C), and Richardus Premonstratensis, *Tractatus in canone misse*, c. 1: (*PL* 177, 459A). The question of how Christ consecrated the bread and wine at the Last Supper was much discussed by the early scholastic theologians. One of the theories proposed suggested that Jesus consecrated the bread in the blessing, and only gave the words of institution to the apostles to be used in later celebrations. Peter of Poitiers, *Sententiarum libri quinque*, gives one of the most complete presentations of the question, l. 5, c. 11 (*PL* 211, 1244C-1245B), e.g.: 'Sed istud ulterius dixit quod videtur ex serie verborum Evangelii, et antequam hoc diceret, facta erat transsubstantiatio, in benedictione scilicet quae jam erat praemissa' (ibid., 1244D). Cf. Jacques de Vitry, *Historia occidentalis*, c. 38 (Hinnebusch, p. 226), and *Notule* (Vat. Reg. lat. MS 411, fol. 68^r).

116. For a general history of the Cathars and their teachings see Borst, pp. 81-122, 240-53, Thouzellier, *Catharisme*, pp. 12-16, Wakefield, *Heresy*, pp. 14-43; and Moore, *Origins*, pp. 139-96. Moore's argument that heresy in the West can be seen as an indigenous development preceding the arrival of Bogomil missionaries (*c.*1140) seems, at least to this author, the most reasonable of those explanations put forward to describe the rise of heresy in the 11th and 12th centuries.

117. The basic objection of the Cathars rested in their belief that matter was evil. Cf. Borst, p. 217: 'Die Eucharistie wird den üblichen abend-ländischen Argumenten verworfen; aber vor allem deshalb, weil die Materie in den Augen der Bogomilen böse ist.' See also Moore, *Origins*, pp. 139-67.

118. Borst, p. 217 n. 4 gives several references to this teaching. To these we can add Alan of Lille, *Contra haereticos*, l. 1, c. 57 (*PL* 210, 359A) and Georgius, *Disputatio inter catholicum et paterinum haereticorum*, c. 8 (ed. Edmond Martène and Ursin Durand, *Thesaurus novus anecdotorum*, vol. v, p. 1729B). The work is by an unknown layman and· dates *c.*1240-50. Cf. Antoine Dondaine, 'Le Manuel de l'Inquisiteur (1230-1330)', *Archivum fratrum praedicatorum* 17 (1947), 174-80. This teaching is also mentioned by Durand of Huesca, *Liber anti-heresis*, l. 1 (ed. Selge, ii, 51). The work, by a Waldensian who was later converted, was written before 1207 (Thouzellier, *Hérésie*, p. 40).

119. Alan of Lille, *Contra Haereticos*, l. 1, c. 60 (*PL* 210, 364D-365A) mentions this teaching. Ermengaud of Béziers, *Contra haereticos*, c. 11 (*PL* 204, 1251D) also records this objection. Ermengaud wrote his work *c.*1200-20. For a recent study of Ermengaud's work see further Christine Thouzellier, 'Le "Liber antiheresis" de Durand de Huesca et le "Contra hereticos" d'Ermengaud de Béziers'. *Revue d'histoire ecclésiastique* 55 (1960), 130-41. The teaching is also mentioned by Ébrard of Béthune, *Liber antiheresis*, c. 8 (M. LaBigne, *Maxima biblio-theca veterum patrum* . . . , vol. xxiv, p. 1571). Ébrard wrote his book before 1212 (cf. Borst, p. 9). See also Georgius, *Disputatio*, c. 8 (Martene, *Thesaurus*, v, 1731); Moneta of Cremona, *Adversus catharos et valdenses*, l. 4, c. 3 (Thommaso Ricchini (ed.), p. 296). Moneta wrote *c.*1241-4 (see Borst, pp. 17-19).

120. Alan of Lille, *Contra hereticos*, l. 1, c. 57 (*PL* 210, 369D-360A): Durand of Huesca, *Liber antiheresis* (Selge, ii, 52) and Ébrard of Béthune, *Liber antiheresis*, c. 8 (LaBigne, *Maxima bibliotheca*, xxiv, 1548C-D).

121. Ermengaud of Bézier, *Contra hereticos*, c. 11 (*PL* 204, 1253B-C); Ébrard of Béthune, *Liber antiheresis*, c. 8 (*Maxima bibliotheca*, xxiv, 1547E-H); Georgius, *Disputatio*, c. 8 (*Thesaurus*, v, 1730D-E, 1731C), and Moneta of Cremona, *Adversus catharos et valdenses*, l. 4, c. 3 (Ricchini, pp. 301-2).

122. Joseph de Ghellinck, 'Eucharistie au XIIᵉ siècle en occident', *DTC* 8 (1924), 1242-3 lists several theologians from this period who discuss the problems raised by the heretics. An excellent discussion which specifically refers to the objections as coming from the heretics occurs in Jacques de Vitry, *Historia occidentalis*, c. 8 (Hinnebusch, pp. 224-7).

123. De Ghellinck, ibid., col. 1239, makes this same point. The early

scholastic theologians were aware of the dangers involved in purely speculative questioning of eucharistic teaching. Jacques de Vitry specifically condemned useless discussion of the sacrament, deigning to answer these questions only if raised by heretics: 'Hec et consimilia superuacuum et curiosum reputaremus discutere, nisi importunitati hereticorum oportet nos respondere.' (*Historia occidentalis*, c. 38 (Hinnebusch, p. 240).)

124. See Ch. 1, pp. 40-1, 150. Cf. Guitmund, *De corporis*, l. 1 and 2 (*PL* 149, 1450B-C, 1430B, 1448C, 1450D); Alger, *De sacramentis*, l. 2, c. 1 (*PL* 180, 811A-B).

125. Cf. Lanfranc, *De corpore*, c. 6 (*PL* 150, 415D), c. 20 (ibid., 436A ff.); Guitmund, *De corporis*, l. 2 (*PL* 149, 1461D ff., 1463B ff.).

126. 'Loquor autem de novis hujus temporis berengarianis, qui haeresim Berengarii ab Ecclesia catholica jamdudum convictam atque damnatum resuscitare conantes, . . .' (*Tractatus, prologus* (Hurter, p. 2)).

127. Peter the Venerable, *Contra petrobrusianos* (Fearns, p. 87). On Peter of Bruys, cf. Russell, *Dissent*, pp. 74-5, and Manselli, *Studi*, pp. 79-92.

128. '"Corpus Christi, ut asseris, per indignum ministerum non conficitur" . . .', Tract against the errors of Henry, *c.*1133-5, ed. R. Manselli, 'Il monacho Enrico e la sua eresia', *Bullettino dell' Instituto storico italiano per il medio evo e archive muratoriano*, 65 (1953), 53. On Henry's career, cf. Russell, *Dissent*, pp. 68-77; Manselli, *Studi*, pp. 93-109, and Moore, *Origins*, pp. 82-114.

129. The only record of Hugh's teaching is a tract written against him by his former schoolmate, Vacarius. The entire affair is discussed and Vacarius's tract edited by Ilarino da Milano, *L'eresia di Ugo Speroni nella confutazione del maestro Vacario*. On Hugh's teaching about the Eucharist see, e.g. 'Tu vero, econtra, quod nec caro Christi nec eius sanguis ore participetur vel communicetur, ex eo probare niteris quod sufficit sola dilectio Dei ut Verbum Dei manducetur, ita et in carne Christi' (da Milano, p. 530). See also Richard W. Southern, 'Master Vacarius and the Beginning of an English Academic Tradition', *Medieval Learning and Literature*, esp. pp. 264-6, and Peter Stein, 'Vacarius and the Civil Law', *Church and Government in the Middle Ages*, esp. pp. 131-3.

130. 'Vnde dicunt, quod, si aliquis esse spiritualis, et haberet illam ueritatis cognitionem, quam se habere dicunt: et cessarent omnia sacramenta, quia sacramenta ecclesie signa sunt, sicut cerimonialia in ueteri lege; et sicut adueniente christo cessauerunt, ita nunc per spiritum sanctum aduenientem in eis hec signa debent cessare.' (*Contra Amaurianos* (Clemens Baeumker (ed.), p. 48).) The authorship of this tract is disputed. It may be the work of Garnernius of Rochefort, or Rudolph of Namur. The whole question of the Amalricians and the sources for their heresy is discussed by G. C. Capelle, *Autour du décret de 1210: III. Amaury de Bène. Étude sur son panthéisme formel*. See also N. Cohn, *The Pursuit of the Millennium*, pp. 152-6.

131. 'In cuius typo (*recte*: typum) nos calicem mysticum ad tuitionem corporis et animae nostrae percipimus, quia sanguis domini sanguinem

nostrum redemit, id est totum hominem salvum fecit. Caro enim salvatoris pro salute corporis, sanguis vero pro anima nostra effusus est, sicut prius praefiguratum fuerat a Moyse. Sic enim ait: caro, inquit, pro corpore vestro offertur, sanguis vero pro anima, ideoque non manducandum sanguinem.' (Heinrich Vogels (ed.), *Ambrosiastri qui dicitur commentarius in epistulas Paulinas*, vol. ii, *In epistolas ad Corinthios*, Corpus scriptorum eccesiasticorum latinorum, vol. lxxxi, part 2 (Vienna, 1968), p. 128.) This passage was also copied and used to support the eucharistic theology of Gezo of Tortona in the 10th century; cf. his *Liber de corpore et sanguine Christi*, c. 36 (*PL* 137, 387D-389B).

132. On the Admont gloss see Josef Geiselmann, 'Zur frühmittelalterlichen Lehre vom Sakrament der Eucharistie', *Theologische Quartalschrift* 116 (1935), 373-94; and Damien Van den Eynde, 'Complementary Note on the Early Scholastic *Commentarii in Psalmos*', *Franciscan Studies* 17 (1957), 149-72. The Commentary on Psalm 21 is edited by Geiselmann, ibid., pp. 397-403.

133. This gloss has long been recognized as wrongly attributed to Remigius. For a short history of the scholarship on this work see Van den Eynde, 'Complementary Note', p. 166. On the dependence of the gloss on Admont 99 see Geiselmann, 'Zur frühmittelalterlichen Lehre', pp. 351-73; Van den Eynde, ibid., pp. 150-2.

134. The authenticity of this attribution is still undecided. For a recent evaluation see Anselm Stoelen, 'Les commentaires scripturaires attribués à Bruno le Chartreux', *RThAM* 25 (1958), 177-247. On the dependence of this gloss on the Admont commentary see Geiselmann, 'Zur frühmittelalterlichen Lehre', pp. 351-73, and Van den Eynde, 'Complementary Note', pp. 152-4.

135. On this commentary and its attribution to Gilbert see Beryl Smalley, 'Gilbertus Universalis, Bishop of London (1128-34), and the Problem of the "Glossa Ordinaria"', *RThAM* 8 (1936), 51-9, Damien Van den Eynde, 'Literary Note' on the Earliest Scholastic *Commentarii in psalmos*', *Franciscan Studies* 14 (1954), 124-8, has demonstrated the dependence of this gloss on those of Anselm of Laon, Gilbert of La Porrée, and Lietbert of Lille. Originally dating this work *c.* 1130-40, Van den Eynde revised this dating to a decade later in his discussion of this work in 'Complementary Note', pp. 171-2.

136. 'Zur frühmittelalterlichen Lehre', pp. 373-88.

137. 'Complementary Note', pp. 161-4. Van den Eynde's dating of the other three glosses depends heavily on this estimation of the date of the Admont gloss.

138. Admont 99 gloss on Ps. 21: 26 (Geiselmann, p. 401). Gilbert gloss on Ps. 21: 26 (Smalley, 'Gilbertus', p. 57). Cf. Ps-Remigius gloss on the same psalm and verse (*PL* 131, 259C). The Bruno gloss has a long discussion of eucharistic heretics, cf. Ps. 21: 26 (*PL* 152, 725A-C) and Ps. 77: 18-22 (ibid., 1038B-1039C).

139. 'Cum vero corpus a fidelibus accipitur, signum est corpora nostra adhuc mortalia per Christi passionem esse reparanda. Per sanguinis acceptionem animarum intelligimus reparationem. Circa sanguinem

namque potius anima commoratus.' (Admont 99 gloss on Ps. 21: 26 (Geiselmann, p. 402).) Gilbert gloss on Ps. 21: 26 (Smalley, p. 58). Cf. Ps.-Remigius gloss on Ps. 21: 26 (*PL* 131, 206A) and Bruno gloss on Ps. 21: 26 (*PL* 152, 725D-726A).

140. Ps.-Remigius gloss (*PL* 131, 553B) and Bruno gloss (*PL* 152, 1038B).

141. Ps. 21: 26 (Geiselmann, p. 402). Gilbert gloss on Ps. 21: 26 (Smalley, p. 58). Cf. Ps.-Remigius gloss on Ps. 21: 26 (*PL* 131, 260B) and Bruno gloss on Ps. 21: 26 (*PL* 152, 725D), Ps. 21: 31 (ibid., 726B-C) and Ps. 103: 15 (ibid., 1180D-1181A).

142. Admont 99 gloss on Ps. 21: 26 (Geiselmann, p. 402). This problem is discussed as a separate question in the Gilbert gloss (cf. Smalley, p. 58). The glossator concluded: 'Et sicut est ineffabile sacramentum, quod multi cum suscipiunt tamen perseverat unus et integer, ita est illud ineffabile, quod nullam corruptionem neque aliam divisionem suscipit cum sit immortale et impassibile, et tamen sacramentum in partibus dividitur, et dentium fidelium atteritur' (Smalley, p. 58). Cf. Ps.-Remigius gloss on Ps. 21: 26 (*PL* 131, 260A-B), and Bruno gloss on Ps. 21: 26 (*PL* 152, 726A) and Ps. 77: 18 (*PL* 152, 1038D).

143. Admont 99 gloss on Ps. 21: 26 (Geiselmann, p. 402). Cf. Gilbert gloss (Smalley, p. 58), Ps.-Remigius gloss (*PL* 131, 260A) and the Bruno gloss (*PL* 152, 725D) on the same verse.

144. 'Et pauperes Christi hoc modo intelligentes edent, sc. hoc sacrificium, et saturabuntur i. imitabuntur, si opportuerit, et hoc modo laudabunt dominum, . . . Edere commune est omnium, saturati fidelium.' (Admont 99 gloss on Ps. 21: 26 (Geiselmann, p. 402).) The Gilbert gloss copied Lanfranc on this point. Cf. Smalley, p. 58 and Lanfranc, *De corpore*, c. 15 (*PL* 150, 425B-C). Cf. also Ps.-Remigius gloss on Ps. 21: 27 (*PL* 131, 260C-D), and the Bruno gloss on Ps. 77: 25 (*PL* 152, 1043A-B).

145. Admont 99 gloss on Ps. 21: 26 (Geiselmann, p. 402). Gilbert gloss on Ps. 21: 26 (Smalley, pp. 57-8). Cf. Ps.-Remigius gloss on Ps. 21: 26 (*PL* 131, 260A), and Bruno gloss on Ps. 21: 27 (*PL* 152, 726B, 726D-727A). e.g.: 'Et quia non sufficit comedere, addit: *Et saturabuntur,* id est replebuntur, re, id est significatio sacramentorum scilicet unitate fidei, spei et dilectionis, . . .' (*PL* 152, 726B).

146. Cf. Admont 99 gloss on Ps. 21: 26 (Geiselmann, p. 402), Gilbert gloss on Ps. 21: 26 (Smalley, p. 57), Ps.-Remigius gloss on Ps. 21: 26 (*PL* 131, 259D-260A) and Bruno gloss on Ps. 21: 26 (*PL* 152, 725C-D).

147. The commentary exists in Berlin, theol. lat. oct. MS 167, and is partially edited by Bernard Bischoff, 'Der Canticumkommentar des Johannes von Mantua für die Markgräfen Mathilde', *Lebenskräfte in der abendländischen Geistesgeschichte*, pp. 37-48. On the dating and identification of this commentary see Bischoff, ibid., pp. 22-36 and Friedrich Ohly, *Hohelied-Studien*, pp. 106-8.

148. 'Apud te enim est, quem, quia mundi gloriam fugit, nominare timeo, qui Berengariam heresim his sententiis repugnantem cum aliis sanctis episcopis catholico destruxit presidio . . . Huic crede et in tanta re eum consule' (Bischoff, p. 40).

149. 'Sed ideo bis idest in duobus sacramentis totus sumitur diversitatem unius quodammodo designantibus, ut animadvertamus animam et corpus nostram eius perceptione liberari. In sacramento enim sanguinis anima nostra docetur liberari, que in sanguine dicitur versari. In sacramento carnis nostrum corpus docetur salvari, ita tamen, ut in utroque totus suscipiatur' (ibid.).

150. '. . . nichil remaneat nature panis et aque et vini. Nulla enim creatura unita est divine excepta humana, quia sola erat redimenda. . . . Ista ergo non existit botrum . . . ut satis sint Christo sociati' (ibid.).

151. The matter is treated at length, see Bischoff, pp. 39-40. e.g.: 'Neque orribile debet esse, si a quibusdam irrationabilibus creaturis tangatur, cum nihil coram deo sit inmundam excepto peccato, et multa etiam inanimata ut vestea et terra eum tetigerunt. Inmundior enim coram deo est peccator omni creatura. Inde etiam gaudet huius botri sponsa, quod uno et eodem tempore in diversis locis sumitur vivus et integer' (ibid.).

152. 'Sed neque caro videtur posse sumi sine sanguine neque sanguis sine corpore; sed cum in specie panis sumitur, totus accipitur, cum autem in specie vini participatur, de toto anima sponse saginatur' (Bischoff, p. 40). The text would antedate by several years those discussed as the earliest witnesses to the teaching on concomitance cited by James Megivern, *Concomitance and Communion*, p. 105.

153. Two more recent studies have disputed Van den Eynde's late dating of several other commentaries on Psalms similar to those discussed here by showing their dependency on and similarity to other late 11th- and early 12th-century works. On this subject see Wilfried Hartmann, 'Psalmenkommentare aus der Zeit der Reform und Frühscholastik', *Studi gregoriani* 7 (1972), 315-66 and V. I. J. Flint, 'Some Notes on the Early Twelfth Century Commentaries on the Psalms', *RThAM* 38 (1971), 80-8.

154. For an excellent summary of the scholarly research on this commentary, as well as an estimation of its alleged authorship, see Anselme Stoelen, 'Les commentaries scripturaires attribués à Bruno le Chartreux', *RThAM* 25 (1958), 177-247, and idem, 'Bruno le Chartreux, Jean Gratiadei et la "Lettre de S. Anselme" sur l'eucharistie', *RThAM* 34 (1967), 18-83.

155. The attribution occurs in Paris, Bibliothèque nationale, lat. MS 14442: 'Incipiuntur glos(u)le epistolarum pauli ab illo uidelicet cuius nomen gratia dei interpretatur in anno quo cons(u)l pictaviensis de iherusolima rediit.' Stoelen discusses the similarities between the two glosses at length in 'Bruno le Chartreux', where he edits the text of both glosses on 1 Cor. 10.

156. According to M. F. Vallaid, the Count of Poitiers to which the inscription refers is William the Young (1086-1126). He returned from the crusades in 1102. See Stoelen, 'Les commentaires', p. 186 n. 13.

157. On the identification of this sentence-collection see Heinrich J. F. Reinhardt, 'Literarkritische und theologiegeschichte Studie zu den Sententie magistri A. und deren Prolog (Ad iustitiam credere

debemus)', *Archives d'histoire doctrinale et littéraire du moyen âge* 36 (1969), 23-56; idem, 'Die Identität der Sententiae Magistri A. mit dem Compilationes Ailmeri und die Frage nach dem Auto dieser frühscholastischen Sentenzensammlung', *Theologie und Philosophie* 50 (1975), 381-403. Although Reinhardt remains cautious in drawing any final conclusions, he argues in favour of the attribution of the *Compilationes* to Elmer, Prior of Canterbury from 1128-37. Reinhardt, 'Die Identität', p. 398 would date this work *c.*1120 or earlier, if Elmer is the author. The *Sententie magistri A.*, as the same work is known in continental as opposed to English MS tradition, has long been recognized as an important source-book for the School of Laon. See Reinhardt, 'Literarkritische Studien', and Nicolaus Häring, 'The Sententiae Magistri A (Vat. MS lat. 4361) and the School of Laon', *Mediaeval Studies* 17 (1955), 1-45.

158. The passage occurs in the *Compilationes in epistolas pauli apostoli* of Robert, Prior of Bridlington in his commentary on 1 Cor. 11: 25. Robert's commentary, written probably 1150-60, is famous for its reference to earlier glossators by name. A longer discussion and description of this particular gloss occurs below. On Robert and the possible dating of his work see Beryl Smalley, 'Gilbertus Universalis', *RThAM* 7 (1935), 248-51; 8 (1936), 32-4, 159.

159. The research on this *sententia*, sometimes referred to as the 'Letter of St. Anselm on the Eucharist' due to its original mistaken attribution, is extensive. For a review of earlier materials and modern estimations of the problem see Odo Lottin, 'La soi-disant "Lettre de saint Anselme de Canterbury sur la Cène"', et sa source', *Psychologie et morale au XIIe siècles*, v, 143-6; Stoelen, 'Bruno le Chartreux', esp. pp. 77-83; and Ludwig Hödl, 'Die ontologische Frage im frühscholastischen Eurcharistietraktat Calix benedictionis', *Sola ratione. Anselm-Studien für Pater Dr. h.c. Franciscus Salesius Schmitt*, pp. 87-110.

160. The text contained in Oxford, Bodleian Library, Laud. Misc. MS 216, has been edited and discussed by Lottin, 'La soi-disant "Lettre"', pp. 146-53. See also Stoelen, 'Bruno le Chartreux', pp. 66-77.

161. The text used for version A will be that of Cambridge, University MS Ii. 4. 19, fol. 62^r (*Compilatio Ailmeri = C*) and that of Vatican City, Biblioteca Vaticana, Vaticana lat. MS 4361, fols. 112^r1-113^r1 (*Sententie magistri A. = A*). The text for version B will be that of Heinrich Weisweiler, *Das Schrifttum der Schule Anselms von Laon und Wilhelms von Champeaux in deutschen Bibliotheken*, pp. 192-8. Version C will be the text given by Lottin, 'La soi-disant "Lettre"', pp. 147-9, while version D will come from Cambridge, University Library MS Dd. 8. 14, fol. 120^r1-2 and version E from Lottin, *Psychologie et morale*, v, 147-9.

162. The *sententie* is edited in part in Delhaye's article, 'Un dossier eucharistique d'Anselme de Laon à l'abbaye de Fécamp au XIIe siècle', *L'Abbaye Bénédictine de Fécamp,* ii, 155-8.

163. Cf. Stoelen, 'Bruno le Chartreux', pp. 66-83; Hödl, 'Die ontologische Frage', pp. 90-5 and Reinhardt, 'Die Identität', for an estimation of recent work on this subject. For further discussion of these commen-

taries see G. Macy, 'Some examples of the Influence of Exegesis on the Theology of the Eucharist in the Eleventh and Twelfth Centuries', to appear in *RThAM* in 1985.

164. The research has been carried out by Frau Dr P. Maas in her unpublished thesis, 'Voorbereidende studies voor het uitgeven van het Liber Sententiarum Magistri A.' (Nijmegen, 1968), and the conclusions reported by Hödl, 'Die ontologische Frage', pp. 90-2 and Reinhardt, 'Die Identität', pp. 395-6. According to Hödl, p. 91, Maas rests her conclusions on the use by this *sententia* of the Bruno gloss which, in her judgement, preceded that of *Gratiadei*.

165. 'Bruno le Chartreux', pp. 77-83. Stoelen concludes: 'De cet examen des sentences recueilles pour prouver l'existence d'un commentaire paulinien d'Anselme de Laon, il faut retenir que les extraits 27 (the Valenciennes *sententia*) et 56 proviennent du commentaire de Gratiadei, tandis que les autres extraits lui sont étrangers. La conclusion s'impose: si tous ces textes, et notamment la "lettre", ont Anselme pour auteur, le maître de Laon doit avoir écrit non pas un, mais au moins deux commentaires de S. Paul, sans compter la glose *Pro altercatione*. On ne l'admettra pas facilement, d'autant moins que l'attribution de la "lettre" à Anselme de Laon se heurte encore à une autre difficulté.'

166. For a discussion of the whole question of the relationship of these *sententie* to Anselm's school at Laon see Ch. 3, pp. 75-6, 176.

167. The passage reads: '*Ego enim accepi.* Ostendit misterium eucharistie inter cenandum celebratum non cenam esse. Medicina enim spiritualis est et memoria redemptionis ut maiora consequamur, quia morte christi liberati sumus, huius in edendo et bibendo memores esse debemus. Nouum testamentum in hoc consecuti quia beneficii diuini, sanguis testis est. Unde ad tuitionem corporis et anime percipimus, quia caro christi pro salute corporis, sanguis pro anima nostra. Ideoque non manducandum esse sanguinem lex predixit' (Cambridge, Pembroke College MS 214, fol. 45^r).

168. Cambridge, University MS Dd. 8. 14, fol. 120^{r}1-2. Robert added the text of Leviticus 7: 26-7 referred to by the *Glossa.*

169. 'Nam quia totus homo qui ex corpore constat et anima redimitur; ideo carne Christi simul et sanguine saginatur. Non enim ut quidam uolunt anima sola hoc misterio pascitur; uerum etiam caro per hoc ad immortalitatem et incorruptionem reparatur' (Cambridge, U.L. Dd. 8. 14., fol. 120^{r}2). Cf. Paschasius, *De corpore*, c. 15 (Paulus, p. 101).

170. The passage begins: 'Item. Quia tota humana . . .' and ends '. . . qui per sanguinem christi a peccatis emundatur' (U.L. Dd. 8. 14, fol. 120^{r}2-120^{v}1) and corresponds to that section of the *Gratiadei* gloss edited by Stoelen, 'Bruno le Chartreux', pp. 44, line 494—p. 46, line 550.

171. For other instances of Robert's use of the *Gratiadei* gloss, cf. the commentaries on 1 Cor. 10: 16-17 (U.L. Dd. 8. 14, fol. 114^{v}2 = Stoelen, p. 49, line 622—p. 50, line 643; U.L. Dd. 8. 14, fol. 115^{r}1 = Stoelen, p. 50, line 644 p. 50, line 673).

172. See Ch. 3, pp. 76-82, 176-82.

173. Cf. the texts cited in n. 181.

174. For the text of both the Bruno gloss and the *Gratiadei* gloss on this topic see the edition by Stoelen of their commentaries on 1 Cor. 10: 16 ('Bruno le Chartreux', pp. 44-5). Cf.: 'Quia humana natura et in anima et in corpore erat corrupta, oportuit ut deus qui utrumque liberare uenerat utrique uniretur, et anima per animam, corpus uero per corpus competenter redimeretur. Ideo etiam in altari ad utrumque representandum panem et uinum ponimus, ut per panem corpus factum et a nobis digne sumptum, nostrum corpus corpori Christi inmortalitate et impassibilitate (*A* = inpassione) quandoque conformandum credamus et similiter per uinum sanguinem (*A* = in uerum sanguinem) conuersum, et similiter a nobis acceptum, animas nostras anime Christi credamus conformes fieri et in presenti quodammodo dum a peccatis prout possumus abstinemus, et maxime in dissolutione corporis, cum in beatitudine anime nostre cum anima christi constituentur. Anima autem christi per sanguinem qui anime sedes est conuenienter representatur.' (Version A (*C*, fol. 62^r; *A*, fol. 112^{r}1-2); version B (Weisweiler, pp. 192-3); version C (Lottin, pp. 147-8); version D (U.L. Dd. 8. 14, fol. 120^{r}2-^{v}1), and version E (Lottin, pp. 27-8).) Cf. also nn. 138 and 148 above.

175. For the texts of the Bruno and *Gratiadei* glosses see Stoelen, 'Bruno le Chartreux', p. 45. Cf.: 'Non tamen intelligendum quod in sanguine solam animam et non etiam corpus, uel in pane solum corpus et non animam accipiamus, sed in sanguine totum christum dominum (*A* = deum) et hominem et in pane totum (*A* = hominem) similiter accipimus. (A = Et.) Quamuis separatim sanguinem non tamen bis sed semel christum accipimus.' (Version A (*C*, fol. 62^r; *A*, fol. 112^{r}2); version B (Weisweiler, pp. 193-4); version C (Lottin, p. 148); version D (U.L. Dd. 8. 14, fol. 120^{v}1), and version E (Lottin p. 28).) Cf. also nn. 98 and 108 above.

176. For the text of the Bruno and *Gratiadei* glosses see Stoelen, 'Bruno le Chartreux', pp. 46-7 and the commentary of *Gratiadei* on 1 Cor. 11: 24: 'Accipite et comedite. Hoc quod uobis porrigo quod purum panem sensus exteriores uobis renuntiant sed fides uestra sciat esse corpus meum' (Oxford, Bodleian Library, MS lat. theo. c. 28, fol. 43^{v}2). Cf. 'Nec remanere substantiam panis et uini, speciem enim tamen uidemus remanere de hoc quod prius fuerat, scilicet formam, colorem et saporem. Et secundum speciem remanentem quedam ibi fiunt que nullomodo secundum hoc quod est possunt fieri (*A* = fieri possit), uidelicet quo conteritur, in uno loco concluditur, a mure roditur, in uentrem trahicitur. Ideo uero quod non est apparet, at quod est celatur, quia si quod est uideretur et saperetur (*A* = separetur), homines sumere uererentur.' (Version A (*C*, fol. 62^r; *A*, fol. 112^{v}1-2) version B (Weisweiler, pp. 194-5); version C (Lottin, p. 148) and version E (Lottin, p. 28).) Compare these texts to those given in nn. 142 and 150 above.

177. For the text of the *Gratiadei* gloss see Stoelen, 'Bruno le Chartreux', p. 46. Cf.: 'Aqua cum uino ideo in sacramento ponitur ut aqua que

cum sanguine de latere christi fluxit representetur. Que aqua populum significat uel baptismum in quo populis per effusionem sanguinis christi purgatur, mundatur (A - christi mundatur).' (Version A (*C*, fol. 62^r; *A*, fol. 112^{v}1); version B (Weisweiler, p. 194); version C (Lottin, p. 148); version D (U.L. Dd. 8. 14, fol. 120^{v}1), and version E (Lottin, p. 28).) Cf. also n. 143 above.

178. For the text of the *Gratiadei* gloss see Stoelen, 'Bruno le Chartreux', pp. 47-8. Cf.: 'Secundum (*A* - Sed) hoc uero quod in specie potest accipi, equaliter accipitur a fideli et infideli. Boni (*A* = Homines autem fideles) autem quodammodo singulari accipiunt, scilicet quod cum iam sint conformes christo per innocentiam . . . Quomodo accipiendi infideles omnino carent, nec tamen negandum quin et mali verum corpus accipiant, unde quidam dubitant propter eorum inmunditiam et sacramenti dignitatem. Sed sacramentum illud tam dignum (*A* = magnum) est ut nec propter mundum locum mundior (*A* - mundius) existat, nec ab inmundo uase (*A* - loco) aliquis (*A* = aliquid) inmunditie contrahat.' (Version A (*C*, fol. 62^r; *A*, fols. 112^{v}2-113^{r}1); version B (Weisweiler, pp. 195-6); version C (Lottin, pp. 148-9) and version E (Lottin, pp. 28-9).) Cf. also n. 143 above.

179. For the text of the Bruno and *Gratiadei* gloss see Stoelen, 'Bruno le Chartreux', pp. 50-1. Cf. version B (Weisweiler, pp. 197-8). Robert copied the *Gratiadei* gloss anonymously as part of his commentary on 1 Cor. 10: 17, e.g. 'Ita nos per corpus christi in fide, spe et caritate manentes unum facti sumus ex diversis personis. Sumus etiam unum corpus secundum executionem dilectionis et secundum sumministrationem mutue possibilitatis' (U.L. Dd. 8. 14, fol. 115^{r}1). Cf. n. 145 above.

180. See texts in n. 163 above.

181. For the text of the Bruno and *Gratiadei* glosses see Stoelen, 'Bruno le Chartreux', pp. 28-9, 51-2. Cf. also the commentary of the Bruno gloss on 1 Cor. 11: 34 (*PL* 153, 1860D); and that of the *Gratiadei* gloss on 1 Cor. 11: 24. '*Et dixit accipite* per conformitatem hunc anime cibum acceptabilem, et iocundum ac saluti uestre necessarium et postmodum etiam *comedite* ipsum sacramentum. Non enim sufficit accipere per conformationem nisi et comedamus, neque comedere nisi accipiamus' (Bodl. theo. lat. c. 28, fol. 43^{v}2). See also version B (Weisweiler, p. 198). Both the *Gratiadei* gloss (Stoelen, p. 52) and version B (Weisweiler, p. 198) quoted the passage of Fulgentius to the effect that baptized children who died without communicating would be saved. This was also the opinion of Lanfranc, cf. n. 30 above.

182. For the texts of the Bruno and *Gratiadei* glosses see Stoelen, 'Bruno le Chartreux', pp. 42-3, 49-50, 51, and 56. Cf. the Bruno gloss on 1 Cor. 5: 7: (*PL* 153, 148A), and version B (Weisweiler, p. 197).

183. This theory was first presented by Franz Bliemetzrieder, 'L'œuvre d'Anselme de Laon et la littérature théologique contemporaine. I. Honorius d'Autun', *RThAM* 5 (1933), 275-91. Cf. also Richard Southern, *St. Anselm and His Biographer*, pp. 209-17; O. Lottin, *Psychologie et morale*, v, 446 and Yves Lefèvre, *L'Elucidarium et les lucidaires*, pp. 214-30.

184. This theory was first put forward by Joseph Endres, *Honorius Augusto-dunensis.* See also V. I. J. Flint, 'The Career of Honorius Augusto-dunensis: Some Fresh Evidence', *Revue bénédictine* 82 (1972), 63-86, who suggests a connection between Honorius and Worcester in England and Lambach in Austria. See also idem, 'The Place and Purpose of the Works of Honorius Augustodunensis', *Revue bénédictine* 87 (1977), 97-127.

185. For a recent evaluation of the dating of these works see V. I. J. Flint, 'The Chronology of the Works of Honorius Augustodunensis', *Revue bénédictine* 82 (1972), 215-42; and Marie-Odile Garrigues, 'Quelques recherches sur l'œuvre d'Honorius Augustodunensis', *Revue d'histoire ecclésiastique* 70 (1975), 388-425.

186. *Elucidarium,* l. 1, c. 83 (Lefèvre, *L'Elucidarium,* p. 395); *Gemma animae,* l. 1, c. 36 (*PL* 172, 552B-C). See also *Eucharisticon,* c. 4 (*PL* 172, 1252B). The similarity between Honorius's theology of the Eucharist and that of the 'Letter of St. Anselm' has been pointed out by Endres, *Honorius,* pp. 41 f. See also Holböck, *Der mystische Leib,* pp. 53-62.

187. '. . . hi autem qui in Christo non manent, quamvis videantur ad os porrigere, corpus Christi non sumunt . . . Corpus autem Christi per manus angelorum in caelum defertur; carbo vero a daemone eis in os projicitur, . . .' l. 1, c. 195 (Lefèvre, p. 399).

188. In the *Eucharisticon,* Honorius taught that two unions were effected by worthy reception. The corporeal union between the body of the receiver and the Humanity of Christ, and a spiritual union in faith and love between the faithful and Divinity of Christ. The wicked received the true body and blood, but lacked this second and salvific union. See cc. 7-9 of the *Eucharisticon* (*PL* 172, 1254A-1255B). Honorius may have been influenced here by William of St. Thierry, see Ch. 3, pp. 96-7, 192-3.

189. *Eucharisticon,* c. 5, 10 (*PL* 172, 1253A; 1255B-D).

190. *Elucidarium,* l. 1, c. 180 (Lefèvre, pp. 394-5); *Gemma animae,* l. 1, c. 34 (*PL* 172, 555A); *Sacramentarium,* c. 88 (ibid., 795A-B), and *Eucharisticon,* c. 12 (ibid., 1256C-1258A).

191. Rupert involved himself in both theological and political disputes throughout his life. As a young man, he strongly supported the Gregorian reform movement, refusing ordination from his simoniac abbot. He would eventually cross swords with such important figures as William of St. Thierry, Anselm of Laon, and Norbert of Xanten. For a recent study of his life and works see Wolfgang Beinert, *Die Kirche-Gottes Heil in der Welt,* pp. 12-22.

192. On the date of this work see Beinert, p. 16 and Rhaban Haacke, *Ruperti Tuitiensis liber de diuinis officiis,* pp. ix, xliv. William of St. Thierry's letter to Rupert is printed in *PL* 180, 341-4.

193. Rupert disagreed with Anselm about God's predestination of evil, about whether Judas received the Eucharist, and about the use of the categories *res-sacramentum* introduced by Berengar. Cf. Rupert's *Epistola ad Cunonem* (Rhaban Haacke (ed.), *Commentaria in euangelium sancti Iohannis,* pp. 1-2), and *In regulam sancti Benedicti,* l. 1 (*PL* 170, 482 f.). On this dispute see Beinert, pp. 16-17, Herbert Silvestre, 'A propos de la lettre d'Anselme de Laon à Héribrand de Saint

Laurent', *RThAM* 28 (1961), 5-25, and idem, 'Notes sur la controverse de Rupert de Saint-Laurent avec Anselme de Laon et Guillaume de Champeux', *Saint-Laurent de Liège*, pp. 68-80.

194. On the dating of this work see Haacke, *Commentaria in euangelium sancti Iohannis*, p. vii.

195. Guntram Gerhard Bischoff, 'The Eucharistic Controversy Between Rupert of Deutz and His Anonymous Adversary' (unpublished dissertation, Princeton Theological Seminary, 1965). Rupert often used the plural in describing his adversaries, however, and in one case referred to 'nimium festini lectores et immaturati praeripuere doctores' (Haacke, *Commentaria in Iohannis*, p. 159).

196. On the dating of this work see Beinert, p. 16 and Haacke, *De sancta Trinitate et operibus eius*, p. vii.

197. See the reference to this letter, written *c*.1126, in n. 193 above.

198. *De officiis*, l. 2, c. 9 (Haacke, p. 41). Cf. *De sancta Trinitate*, l. 34, sect. 3, c. 20 and c. 24 (Haacke, pp. 1928, 1932) and *Commentaria in Iohannis* 6: 52 and 6: 57 (Haacke, pp. 325, 343).

199. *De sancta Trinitate*, l. 36, sect. 3, c. 26 (Haacke, p. 1934). Cf. *De sancta Trinitate*, l. 9, Ex. 2: 9 (Haacke, p. 645).

200. 'Hoc fundamento fidei non bene custodito illam praedicationem Domini dicentis: *Qui manducat carnem meam et bibit sanguinem meum in me manet et ego in eo*, quidam ita reciprocant. Qui manet in me et ego in illo, hic manducat carnem meam et bibit sanguinem meum, illo sensu praeoccupati, quod manere in unitate fidei hoc sit manducare carnem et bibere sanguinem Christi, et ideo non necessariam sibi arbitrantur esse ad salutem corporalem dominicae mensae communicationem . . . Pereat igitur a corde christiano hic sensus, quem importat haec inutilis reciprocatio . . . Manducare namque et bibere causa efficiens est, effectum autem, ut *in me manent et ego in eo*, . . .' (*In Iohannis* 6: 32 (Haacke, p. 342).) Rupert repeated his accusation *In Iohannis* 6: 53 (Haacke, pp. 359-60). On Anselm's teaching and that of his students see Ch. 3, pp. 73-82, 174-82.

201. *De sancta Trinitate*, l. 34, sect. 3, c. 20 (Haacke, pp. 1927-8). Rupert discussed the question at length in his commentary on John 6: 32 (Haacke, pp. 338-40).

202. *In Iohannis* 6: 32 (Haacke, p. 343). Cf. *De officiis*, l. 2, c. 9 (Haacke, pp. 41-2), and *In Iohannis* 6: 27 (Haacke, p. 325). Rupert specifically rejected the teaching that the evil do not receive the true body and blood; see *De sancta Trinitate*, l. 36, sect. 3, c. 22 (Haacke, pp. 1930-1).

203. e.g. 'Est enim uita animalis, est et uita spiritualis. Animalis uita quinque sensibus fungitur, uisu, auditu, gustu, odoratu et tactu . . . Solam ergo uitam spiritualem in sacrificio nobis administrare sapientiam eius decebat, et nostrae necessitati expediebat, quae est sanctificatio et benedictio, *misericordia et ueritas, iustitia et pax* (Ps. 84: 11)' (Haacke, pp. 43-4).

204. *Guillelmi epistola ad quemdam monachum* (*PL* 180, 341-4).

205. 'Colligat unusquisque quae sufficiunt, id est credat uerba Domini spiritum esse et uitam, et per ea panem et uinum exteriori specie non

mutata transferri in ueram uiuentis corporis et sanguinis Christi substantiam.' *De sancta Trinitate*, l. 12 (Haacke, p. 702).

206. Cf. *De sancta Trinitate*, l. 36, sect. 3, c. 21 (Haack, pp. 1929-30); idem, l. 11, *In Exodum* 2: 10 (Haacke, p. 647); *In Iohannis* 6: 63 and 6: 52 (Haacke, pp. 373, 357); and *Epistola ad Cunonem* (Haacke, *Commentaria in Iohannis*, pp. 3-4). For a recent discussion of Rupert's theology, esp. in regard to its use by the 16th-century reformers, see Haacke, 'Zur Eucharistielehre des Rupert von Deutz', *RThAM* 35 (1965), 20-42.

207. Cf. *De divinis officiis*, l. 2, c. 2 (Haacke, p.34); *De sancta Trinitate*, l. 11, *In Exodum* 12: 6 (Haacke, p. 637); idem, *In Exodum* 16: 17-18 (Haacke, pp. 707-8); *In Iohannis* 6: 32 (Haacke, p. 341) and esp. *In Iohannis* 6: 64 (Haacke, p. 375).

208. *In Iohannis* 6: 52 (Haacke, pp. 356-7).

209. Ibid., and *In Iohannis* 6: 63 (Haacke, p. 375).

210. See Ch. 1, n. 133.

211. For a recent estimation of Hervaeus's life and works see Guy Oury, 'Essai sur la spiritualité d'Hervé de Bourg-Dieu', *Revue d'ascétique et de mystique* 43 (1967), 369-80, and idem, 'Hervé de Bourg-Dieu', *DSAM* 7 (1969), 373-5. On Hervaeus's commentary on the letters of Paul see Artur Landgraf, 'Der Paulinenkommentar der Hervaeus von Bourg-Dieu', *Biblica* 21 (1940), 113-32.

212. 1 Cor. 10: 18 (*PL* 181, 918B). Cf. 1 Cor. 11: 27-9 (ibid., 936D-937A).

213. 1 Cor. 10: 15-17 (ibid., 917A). Cf. 1 Cor. 11: 23-4 (ibid., 934D).

214. 1 Cor. 11: 23-4 (ibid., 933C-D). Cf. 1 Cor. 10: 1-5 (ibid., 910B) and 1 Cor. 11: 27-9 (ibid., 936B-937A).

215. *Textus biblie*, 5: fol. 206^v.

216. Ps.-Hugh, *Questiones super epistolam primam ad Corinthios*, q. 89 (*PL* 175, 530D-531A); Peter Lombard, *Collectanea in Pauli epistolas*, 1 Cor. 11: 26 (*PL* 191, 1164D). The passage is repeated in his *Sententie*, l. 4, d. 11, c. 4 (Collegium s. Bonaventurae (eds.), pp. 805-6).

217. *Tractatus* 5 (Bernhard Geyer (ed.), p. 138).

218. Cf. Gerald of Wales, *Gemma animae*, c. 8 (J. S. Brewer (ed.), p. 26); Peter the Chanter, Commentary on Ps. 22: 5 (London, British Library, Royal MS 10, c. 5, fol. 32^{v}1); *Notule super IIII sententiarum* (Vatican City, Biblioteca Apostolica, Reginensis lat. MS 411, fol. 69^r-69^v); *Summa de sacramentis 'Cum multa sint sacramenta noue legis'* (ibid., Palatino MS 619, fol. 7^r); *Summa 'Inter cetera alicuius scientia'*, c. 13 (ibid., Vaticana lat. MS 1345, fol. 94^v), and *Ysagoge in theologiam*, l. 2 (Artur Landgraf (ed.), p. 206). For an example of how later commentaries treat this symbolism see e.g., the gloss on 1 Cor. 11: 23 now contained in Vatican, Biblioteca Apostolica, Ottobiana lat. MS 445, fol. 116^r: 'Notandum tamen primo et sane intelligendum quia in fine cuiusdam glosa super hunc locum habetur: quia caro christi pro salute corporis; sanguis pro anima nostra. Nonne utrumque hoc est caro christi et sanguis utrumque in nobis operatur, hoc est salutem anime et corporis? . . . Consimiliter dictum est quia caro christi salutem corporis et animae salutem operatur; sanguis licet utrumque utriusque salutem operetur in nobis.'

219. The teaching which Walter was attacking was that of Peter Lombard, *Sententie*, 1. 4, d. 12, cc. 2-4 (Collegium S. Bonaventura, p. 810). Walter concluded his argument against the Lombard: 'Catholica tamen indubitanter ei et in eum credit qui propriis manibus proprium et uerum corpus tenens et frangens nichilominus integer et uiuus manens dedit tunc illud ipsum hodieque dat in toto terrarum orbe, non tantum sacramento sed et in veritate, . . .' (*Contra quatuor labyrinthos Franciae*, 1. 3, c. 11 ed. P. Glorieux, 'Le Contra quatuor labyrinthos Franciae de Gauthier de Saint-Victor. Edition critique', *Archives d'histoire doctrinale et littéraire du moyen âge* 27 (1952), 261. Glorieux discusses the date of this work, pp. 194-5).

220. e.g. 'Itaque qui vere frangi corpus Christi non concedit, totam fidem tanti sacramenti, quantum in se est, fregit.' (*De fractione corporis Christi* (*PL* 166, 1344C-D).) The editor of this work, Jean Mabillon, *Vetera analecta* (2nd rev. edn., Paris, 1723), p. 52 dated it as contemporaneous with the works of Abelard against whom Mabillon thought this tract to be addressed. Most modern scholars follow Mabillon's dating. See, e.g., St. Hilpisch, 'Abbaudus', *LThK* 1, 8. There is no particular reason to single out Abelard here, as many scholars were teaching that the fraction occurred only in the species. See, e.g., the discussion of William of St. Thierry below. The date of this work can be assigned no more closely than to the 12th-century period generally.

221. 'Cum autem conteritur dentibus, quod in confessione Berengarii habetur, integer tamen manet modo mirabili; sed sic se res habet.' (*Questiones (theologice) de epistolis Pauli*, 1 Cor. 10: 16 (ed. R. M. Martin, p. 211).)

222. See Ch. 4, pp. 108, 109, 118, 200.

223. 'In quo ergo subiecto fundantur? . . . Michi tamen videtur quod in ipso corpore Christi sint.' (Ed. John R. Williams, 'The Twelfth Century "Questiones" of Carpentras MS 110', *Mediaeval Studies* 28 (1966), 318.) Williams discusses the dating (*c.*1160-80) and possible authorship of these questions, pp. 321-7.)

224. 'Videtur quidem fractio fieri in substantia corporis, nec tamen fit, nec ibi fractio est, set tantum videtur fieri. Si enim frangeretur corpus Christi, et pateretur. Christus autem semel mortuus est, iam non moritur' (Williams, p. 319).

225. The tract has been edited by P. C. Boeren, 'Un traité inédit du XIIᵉ siècle, *Convenientibus vobis in unum* (1 Cor. 11.20)', *Archives d'histoire doctrinale et littéraire du moyen âge* 45 (1978), 181-204.

226. '. . . quoniam ibi uere est Christus et in eadem sui corporis forma in qua resurrexit de sepulchro et est in celo. Est utique in altari et ibi corpus suum in proprio colore et propria quantitate et sanguis in proprio colore et sapore, sed hec non comparent sensibus' (Boeren, p. 199).

227. 'Sed in hoc sacramento quicquid appareat sensui, ratio tamen fideliter et ueraciter indicat de integritate rei, sicut *cum baculus ponitur in aqua* apparet quidem fractus oculis aut tortuosus, et tamen non est prestigium, quia quamvis sensus frustretur, ratio tamen non fallitur.'

(Boeren, p. 201.) This was the teaching of Gilbert of La Porrée, see Ch. 3, p. 108. On this teaching in the 12th century see Boeren, 'Un traité eucharistique', p. 191; p. 201, n. 1 and N. Häring, 'Die Sententie magistri gisleberti pictavensis episcopi', *Archives d'histoire doctrinale et littéraire du moyen âge* 45 (1978), 91.

228. See, for instance, the encyclical letter of Urban IV extending the feast of Corpus Christi to the entire Church: 'Hic panis sumitur, sed vere non consumitur; manducatur, sed non transmutatur, quia in edentem minime transformatur, sed, si digne recipitur, sibi recipiens conformatur.' (Clement V, *Const.* lb. 3, tit. 16, c. 1 'Si Dominum' (*Corpus juris canonici*, ed. E. Friedberg, ii, 1176).) The same idea was expressed by Augustine, *Confess.* I. viii, c. 10.

229. See Ch. 1, p. 28 and n. 40.

230. See p. 45 above.

231. *Metabolismus* or *Metaboliker* denotes according to Geiselmann those theologies of the Eucharist that insist upon a metaphysical change to make Christ present in the sacrament. It is used in counterdistinction to *Realismus* and *Augustinismus*. *Augustinismus* can further be understood as *realistische Augustinismus, dynamische Augustinismus* and *symbolisch-spiritualische Augustinismus*. See *Eucharistielehre*, esp. Ch. 2.

232. *Die Entfaltung.*

233. Historians who have dealt with the not uncommon medieval question of what happens when a mouse eats the consecrated Host have often described the medieval discussion as purely academic. Especially given a Paschasian understanding of the sacrament, the issue becomes an important pastoral concern as well. For a classic presentation of this issue see Artur Landgraf, 'Die in der Frühscholastik klassiche Frage *quid sumit mus*', *Dogmengeschichte der Frühscholastik*, vol. iii, pp. 207-22.

234. Among modern theologians, Gustave Martelet, *The Risen Christ and the Eucharistic World* (New York, 1976) seems to advocate a form of Paschasian theology based on just this difficult premiss.

CHAPTER III

1. For Anselm's life see A. Wilmart, 'Un commentaire des Psaumes restitué à Anselme de Laon', *RThAM* 8 (1936), 340-3. On the 'School of Laon' see Joseph de Ghellinck, *Le Mouvement théologique du XIIe siècle*, pp. 133-48, and Artur Landgraf, *Introduction à l'histoire théologique de la scolastique naissante*, pp. 67-78.

2. On Anselm's authorship of the commentaries on Psalms, the Gospel of John, and the letters of Paul, see Beryl Smalley, 'Gilbertus Universalis, Bishop of London (1128-34), and the Problem of the "Glossa Ordinaria"', *RThAM* 8 (1936), 24-49; idem, *The Study of the Bible in the Middle Ages*, pp. 56-66, and idem, 'Les commentaires bibliques de l'époque romane: glose ordinaire et glose perimées', *Cahiers de civilisation médiévale* 4 (1961), 16. See also Beryl Smalley, 'Some Gospel Commentaries of the Early Twelfth Century', *RThAM* 45 (1978), 147-80; idem, 'Peter Comestor on the Gospels and His Sources',

RThAM 46 (1979), 84-129, and Ermengildo Bertola, 'La Glossa ordinaria biblica ed i suoi problemi', *RThAM* 45 (1978), 34-78.

3. These have been printed by Odo Lottin, *Psychologie et morale aux XIIe et XIIIe siècles*, v, 9-121. I have used here only those sentences considered as authentic or plausibly authentic by Lottin. The sentences which he includes as possibly attributable to Anselm, I will deal with when I treat of the 'School of Laon'. I have already discussed the attribution of *sententia* 27 of the sentences printed by Lottin, see Ch. 2, pp. 62-4, 166-9.

4. '*Hoc est opus dei*. Fides per dilectionem operans est opus: quia si desit facultas non queritur nisi voluntas. Merito etiam fides que per dilectionem operatur opus dicitur: que est initium et finis totius boni' (*Textus biblie*, 5: 205^r).

5. '*Qui mandu. car. meum*. Exponunt quidam de commestione altaris et bene dicunt: sed querunt quomodo fiat in vitam eternam: cum quidam ad mortem ut dicit apostolus. Si quis comedit in altari cum hac comestione de qua agit hic. scilicet. cum fide operante et dilectione: hic comedit in vitam eternam.' (John 6: 55 (*Textus biblie* 5: 206^v).) Cf. the commentary on 1 Cor. 11: 24: '*Accipite*. id est gratum et acceptum intelligite et fide comedite' (Cambridge, University Library MS Ff. 4. 40, fol. 56^r).

6. '*Ver*. etc. Quibus dixi manducandum me esse: manere in me et me in ipso. Ut autem aliquis maneat in christo ut membrum et christus in ipso ut in templo: unitas facit. Unitas autem ex charitate est: charitas autem ex spiritu: ergo spiritus qui vivificat conpaginata membra separata.' (John 6: 64 (*Textus* 5: 207^r).) '*Quoniam unus panis*. Unus panis, unione fidei, spei et caritatis, corpus per subministrationem caritatis, quia unum sumus, unum sentire debemus ut fides una unum habeat sensum et opus.' (1 Cor. 10: 17 (U.L. MS Ff. 4. 40, fol. 53^v).) The source for this gloss appears to be Augustine, *In Iohannis evangelium, tract*. 26, n. 13 (edition by the monks of St. Peter's, Steenbrugge, Corpus christianorum. Series latina 36 (Turnhout, 1954), pp. 266-7).

7. '*Panes celi*. Cas. Non aliter quam christus de quo celestes .id est. angeli reficiuntur eius contemplatione: et hunc panem .id est. verbum quo grandi cibo pascuntur angeli per carnem factum: lac edit homo.' (PS. 77: 24-5 (*Textus* 3: 199^r).) Cf. also the gloss on Ps. 131: 15 (*Textus* 3: 285^r).

8. '*Panis enim versus*. Angeli purum verbum solidum cibum comedunt: Nos vero verbum: sed in lac versum: quia si non possumus comedere: possumus sugere: Nisi enim incarnaretur: a nobis non cognosceretur: a nobis non gustaretur.' (John 6: 33) (*Textus* 5: 205.) The source for this teaching, as for the gloss on Ps. 77, is Cassiodorus, *Expositio psalmi* 77: 25 (M. Adriaen (ed.), Corpus christianorum. Series latina 48 (Turnhout, 1958), p. 718), and Augustine, *Ennarratio ad psalmum 33, sermo* 1, c. 6 (edition by the monks of St. Peter's, Steenbrugge, Corpus christianorum. Series latina 38 (Turnhout, 1956), p. 277).

9. '. . . dominicum corpus necessario recipitur in uitam eternam. Unde ratio uidetur exigere ut pueris renatis ex aqua et Spiritu dominicum corpus detur.' (*Sententia* 61 (Lottin, p. 55).)

10. *Sententia* 62 (Lottin, p. 55).

11. *Sententia* 62 and 137 (Lottin, pp. 55-6, 105-6). *Sententia* 138 on the same subject is not from Anselm, but Ivo of Chartres, *Epistola* 287 (*PL* 162, 285C-286C).

12. '. . . id est unam uoluntatem cum proximis habentes, id est eis cupientes quod et nobis et in ipsa etiam perceptione cognoscentes hoc significari per illud quo debemus in ipso esse, ut ipse ait: *quia manducat carnem meam et bibit sanguinem meum in me manet et ego in eo* (John 6: 57).' (*Sententia* 139 (Lottin, p. 108).)

13. On William's life see Jean Châtillon, 'Chronique. De Guillaume de Champeaux à Thomas Gallus: chronique d'histoire littéraire et doctrinale de l'école de Saint-Victor', *Revue du moyen âge latin* 8 (1952), 141-6.

14. Lottin, *Psychologie*, v, 189-227.

15. This teaching appears in 3 of the sentences attributed to William published by Lottin, Nos. 271, 274, and 275 (*Psychologie*, v, 217-19).

16. This teaching appears in Nos. 272 and 273 of the sentences attributed to William published by Lottin, *Psychologie*, v, 218.

17. The teaching occurs in sentence No. 270 published by Lottin (*Psychologie*, v, 216-17) and attributed to William. William stated his teaching on concomitance twice, lines 9-13 and 34-42. It is the 2nd of these passages that is strongest in tone: 'Quod ergo dicitur utramque speciem oportere accipi heresis plane est. Quamuis enim sacramenta ibi sint secundum fractionem et odorem et colorem et saporem, tamen in utraque specie totus est Christus . . .'.

18. The teaching occurs in sentence No. 260 edited by Lottin, *Psychologie*, v, 211-13, and is attributed to William. Cf. esp. lines 70-6: 'Christus uero oblatus totius mundi pecatis, et preteritis, et presentibus, et futuris sufficiens, digna hostia factus, perfectam salutem fecit, et priores a tenebris eripiens posterioresque, si huic fidei perseueranter adhereant, omnino ab eiusdem penis immunes efficiens. Et ipse quidem semel occisus est, sed illius sue passionis recordatur Ecclesia participatione corporis et sanguinis eius.'

19. See Ch. 2, pp. 66, 170-1.

20. For a bibliography to date on the extensive research done on the 'School of Laon' and the sentence material connected with it, see H. J. F. Reinhardt, 'Literarkritische und theologiegeschichtliche Studien zu dem *Sententiae magistri A* und deren Prolog "Ad iustitiam credere debemus"', *Archives d'histoire doctrinale et littéraire du moyen âge* 36 (1969), 24-6.

21. 'The School of Laon: A reconsideration', *RThAM* 43 (1976), 89-110.

22. See Ch. 2, pp. 60-5, 162-9.

23. The *sententia* occurs in a collection of sentences headed by the title: *Optima sententia de corpore et sanguine Domini* now contained in Paris, Bibliothèque nationale, lat. MS 564, fols. 115ʳ-119. This *sententia* is a version of that group of sentences which closely follow the commentary on 1 Cor. 10: 16 by *Gratiadei*. The commentary appears to have been interpolated, the author adding material from one of the Anselmian sentence-collections. Philippe Delhaye has edited the interp-

olations, 'Un dossier eucharistique d'Anselme de Laon à l'abbaye de Fécamp au XIIe siècle', *L'Abbaye bénèdictine de Fécamp* ii, 155-8. Delhaye has argued that this *sententia* is the original version of Anselm's commentary on 1 Corinthians. The argument appears untenable in light of later research on the whole question of this commentary, see Ch. 2, pp. 60-5, 162-9.

24. Heinrich Weisweiler has described and edited this sentence-collection in his study on the 'School of Laon', *Das Schrifttum der Schule Anselms von Laon und Wilhelm von Champeaux in deutschen Bibliotheken*, pp. 269-81, 314-58.

25. The *Sententie Atrebatenses* has been edited by Lottin, *Psychologie*, v, 403-40. This sentence-collection is a later collection than the *Dubitatur a quibusdam* or the *Sententie Anselmi*, but depends on much older material for its treatment of the Eucharist. See H. Weisweiler, 'Die ältesten scholastischen Gesamtdarstellungen der Theologie. Ein Beitrag zur Chronologie der Sentenzenwerke der Schule Anselms von Laon und Wilhelm von Champeaux', *Scholastik* 16 (1941), 243-4, 247.

26. The *Sententie Anselmi*, although certainly not written by Anselm, is the most important work attributed to the 'School of Laon'. It has been edited by Franz Bliemetzrieder, *Anselms von Laon systematische Sentenzen*. For a recent evaluation of its importance see Heinrich Weisweiler, 'Die Arbeitsweise der sogenannten Sententiae Anselmi. Ein Beitrag zum Entstehen der systematischen Werke der Theologie', *Scholastik* 34 (1959), 190-232.

27. 'Utrumque enim sacre rei est signum: visibilis species ipsius corporis; corpus vero illius panis celestis et spiritualis, quo vivunt angeli, qui versus est in lac assumpta humanitate, ut inde possent et homines vivere.' (*Dubitatur a quibusdam* (Weisweiler, p. 350).) 'Corpus enim eius, quod diuersis respectibus uisibile et invisibile dicitur, res est uisibilis sacramenti; sacramentum panis celestis et inuisibilis, quo uiuunt angeli.' (*Sententie Anselmi* (Bliemetzrieder, pp. 116-17).) A similar teaching occurs in the *Sententie 'Augustinus. Semel immolatus est Christus'* (Weisweiler, *Schrifttum*, p. 282), and the *Sententie 'Tribus ex causis'* (Weisweiler, *Schrifttum*, p. 312) based on the *Sermo evangelii Johannis*, c. 1 attributed to Augustine (G. Morin, *Sancti Augustini sermones post Maurinos reperti* (Rome, 1930), pp. 375 ff.). The entire section on the structure of the Eucharist and the different forms of reception from *Dubitatur a quibusdam* was copied into the sentence-collection *Voluntas Dei relata ad ipsum Deum* (see Lottin, *Psychologie*, v, 350).

28. 'Hic vero panis celestis et spiritualis a solis bonis sumitur, qui in susceptione sui corporis per fidem et dilectionem ei couniuntur.' (*Dubitatur a quibusdam* (Weisweiler, p. 351).) 'Sola realis (comestio) bonorum est tantum quia, etsi sub uisibili sacramento carnem Christi non sumant, tamen fide dilectioneque panem celestem manducant et ei conueniunt.' 'Unde Augustinus: Quid paras dentem et uentrem? Crede et manducasti.' (*Sententie Anselmi* (Bliemetzrieder, p. 119).) The quotation from Augustine comes from *tractatus* 25, c. 12 of *In Iohannes*

evangelium (Corpus christianorum 36, p. 254) and recurs frequently among authors who adopt a more spiritual approach to the sacrament during the early scholastic period.

29. 'Res autem huius sacramenti Christus est, . . . Uel res sacramenti est unio et uinculum caritatis que confertur in hoc sacramento ad uitam (eorum qui) predestinati sunt; . . .' (Lottin, p. 434).

30. 'Cumque in eodem sacramento duo, scilicet sacramentum et res sacramenti, attendantur, duplex etiam comestio scilicet sacramentalis et realis ostenditur.' (*Dubitatur a quibusdam* (Weisweiler, p. 350).) 'Cumque dominici corporis comestio alia sit sacramentalis, alia realis, . . .' (Delhaye, p. 158).

31. 'Comestio sacramentalis et quantum ad visibilem speciem et quantum ad corporis Christi veritatem bonis et malis communiter convenit; sed bonis quidem in salutem vite eterne, qui per eius susceptionem in fide et in dilectione pani celesti et invisibili coniunguntur.' (*Dubitatur a quibusdam* (Weisweiler, p. 351).) '. . . sacramentalis (comestio) est aeque communis bonis et malis quia utrique verum corpus Christi suscipiunt, quod est sacramentum. Realis, vero, id est participem esse de membris Christi solis convenit justis.' (Delhaye, p. 158.)

32. 'Notandum quia due sunt manducationes: una sacramentalis, altera spiritualis. Sacramentalis illa est talis quam boni et mali accipiunt; . . . Spiritualis autem manducatio est illa qua, per fidem que ex dilectione operatur, credimus nos uniri Deo, . . .' (Lottin, p. 131). This *sententia* also appears as an addition to the *Sententie 'Deus de cuius principio et fine tacetur'* ed. Heinrich Weisweiler, 'Le recueil des sentences "Deus de cuius principio et fine tacetur"', *RThAM* 5 (1933), 269.

33. 'Modus etiam sumendi tripliciter diuiditur. Comestio enim alia sacramentalis tantum, alia tantum realis, alia sacramentalis et realis.' (Bliemetzrieder, p. 119.)

34. 'Sola sacramentalis malorum est tantum, qui, etsi in uisibili specie elementorum corpus Christi accipiant, tamen, quia nec uere credunt nec diligunt, pani celesti couniri non possunt.' (Ibid.)

35. 'Que uero utrumque est, bonis et malis conuenit, sed diuersis respectibus; realis enim malorum ad solam Christi susceptionem pertinet, realis uero bonorum etiam ad panis celestis communionem. Comestio igitur alia est ad mortem, que scilicet panem uite non potest contingere, alia ad uitam, que facit unum cum uerbo uite.' (Ibid.)

36. 'Sol realis bonorum est tantum, quia, etsi sub uisibili sacramento carnem Christi non sumant, tamen fide dilectioneque panem celestem manducant et ei conueniunt. Unde Augustinus: Quid paras dentem et uentrem? Crede et manducasti.' (Ibid.)

37. 'Illa (comestio) tantum dupliciter fit, quantum ad sacramentum uisibile, corpus Christi inuisibilis, et ideo imperfecta; . . .' (Ibid.)

38. 'Item alibi Augustinus: non manducans manducat et manducans non manducat; id est, non manducans sacramento manducate re, id est unione (ecclesie).' (Lottin, p. 278.) This phrase, often quoted by later theologians, does not appear to be from Augustine. The earliest datable (*c*.1135-43) use of this phrase which I have found is in

Lombard's commentary on 1 Cor. 11: 26 (*PL* 191, 1643D). The text of
Lombard's commentary closely resembles that of *sententia* 375 of the
sentences edited by Lottin (*Psychologia*, v, 278, lines 35-52 = *PL* 191,
1643D-1644A).

39. Lottin, pp. 133-4. For reference to this text see Ch. 2, n. 30.

40. 'Si autem aliquis ordinatum esse putans eius missam audierit, et
figuram, non dominicum corpus, de manu eius sumpserit, per solam
fidem saluabitur.' (Lottin, pp. 140-1.)

41. Bliemetzrieder, pp. 119-20; Lottin, p. 280. The passage compares the
process of spiritual eating with that of corporeal eating.

42. Cf. *sententia* 375 (Lottin, pp. 277-8); *Sententia Atrebatenses* (Lottin, p. 434)
and *Dubitatur a quibusdam* (Weisweiler, p. 350).

43. Cf. *sententie* 194, 271, 274, 275, and 526 (Lottin, pp. 132-3, 217-19,
364); *Sententie divine pagina* (Bliemetzrieder, p. 46); *Sententie Atrebatenses*
(Lottin, p. 434), and *Sententie 'Potest queri'* (Weisweiler, *Schrifttum*,
p. 268).

44. See, for instance, *sententie* 193 and 375 (Lottin, pp. 131-2, 278).

45. On Hugh's life and writings, cf. Jean Mabillon, *Vetera analecta*, p. 476
(repr. *PL* 188, 1269-1272); Charles Louis Hugo, *Sacrae antiquitatis
monumenta historica*, . . . , vol. ii, pp. 312-424; *Histoire littéraire de la
France*, vol. xii, pp. 493-511; Marquis de Fortia d'Urban, *Histoire et
ouvrages de Hugues Métel né à Toul en 1080*; H. Boehmer, *Hugonis Metelli
Opuscula*, *MGH*, Libelli de lite, vol. iii, pp. 711-12; and L. Ott,
Untersuchungen zur theologischen Briefliterature der Frühscholastik, pp. 47-8.
Hugh's correspondents include Bernard of Clairvaux, William of St.
Thierry, Pope Innocent II, Abelard, and even Héloise.

46. *Epistola* 26 (Charles Hugo (ed.), Monumenta historica, 2, 361-3).

47. Hugo, pp. 361-2.

48. 'Panis iste, panis dicitur quotidianus, quem etsi quotidie non
sumimus, quotidie tamen à Deo petere debemus, ut digni simus, quem
etiam quotidie nobis incorporamus, si fidem per dilectionem operantem habemus, per quam capiti nostro unimur' (ibid., 361-2).

49. 'Sed vir spiritu Dei plenus, ad intentionem Christi oculum convertit, &
sub appellatione Corporis & Sanguinis figuratâ locutione, fidem
Passionis suae incredulis obumbrari voluit, & amicis revelari, fidem
scilicet operantem per dilectionis societatem scilicet capitis &
membrorum, & unionem spiritualem scilicet comestionem non sacramentalem, rem Sacramenti non Sacramentum, virtutem Sacramenti &
efficaciam non Sacramentum, quod ipsa veritas . . .' (ibid., 362).

50. Hugh spoke of *comestio sacramentalis* to which he opposed *unionem
spiritualem scilicet comestionem non sacramentalem* (cf. n. 49), e.g. 'Quod
excludit aperte sacramentalem comestionem, quam quidam sumunt ad
sui confusionem' (ibid., 362).

51. *Epistola* 33, ed. Hugo (ii, 372-4); also ed. Mabillon, *Analecta*, p. 475,
and repr. *PL* 188, 1273B-1276B. Mabillon has argued that the *Gerardus*
of *epistola* 33 is actually an error in transcription of *Gerlandus*, and that
both letters are directed to the same person. Hugh did mention in
epistola 33 that he intended to write a second letter on the subject:

(*PL* 188, 1276B; Hugo, p. 374). Serious doubts, however, have been cast on this identification. For a discussion of the question cf. Ott, *Briefliteratur*, p. 53. On the identification of Gerlandus, cf. Ott, ibid.; D'Urban, pp. 182-7.

52. Hugh did not actually accuse Gerland of being a follower of Berengar, although he warned him that his teaching might be heretical: 'Verba quae seminas in populo de corpore et sanguine Domini, haeresim sapiunt, plurimosque, te duce, in abyssum erroris traxerunt' (*PL* 188, 1273C = Hugo, 372). See also Ch. 1, pp. 42, 151.

53. *PL* 188, 1273C = Hugo, 372.

54. *PL* 188, 1273D = Hugo, 372.

55. *PL* 188, 1273D-1274A = Hugo, 372.

56. *PL* 188, 1273C = Hugo, 372.

57. Cf. *PL* 188, 1274A-B = Hugo, 372-3 and *PL* 188, 1275B-1276A = Hugo, 373-4.

58. For a recent biography and bibliography of Hugh see Guy Oury, 'Hugues de Rouen', *DS* 7 (1969), 896-900 and Luchesius Spätling, 'Die Legation des Erzbischofs Hugo von Rouen (1134/35)', *Antonianum* 43 (1968), 195-216.

59. Hugh wrote 2 versions of this work, the 2nd containing an introductory letter to his cousin, Matthew, Cardinal and Bishop of Albano, and a 7th book added to the original six. Damien Van den Eynde, 'Nouvelles précisions chronologiques sur quelques œuvres théologiques du XIIe siècle', *Franciscan Studies* 13 (1953), 74-7 dates the 2 versions *c.*1125-33.

60. For the dependence of Hugh's theology on the 'School of Laon' see F. Bliemetzrieder, 'L'œuvre d'Anselme de Laon et la littérature théologique contemporaine. II. Hugues de Rouen', *RThAM* 6 (1934), 261-83; 7 (1935), 28-51; O. Lottin, 'Les théories du péché originel au XIIe siècle. III. Tradition Augustinienne', *RThAM* 12 (1940), 238-9, and idem, 'La doctrine d'Anselme de Laon sur les dons du Saint-Esprit et son influence', *RThAM* 24 (1957), 290.

61. *PL* 192, 1200A.

62. 'Ex hac fide salvi facti sunt qui, dum minime sacramenta perceperunt, praeventi tamen pro Christo passi sunt' (ibid., 1201C).

63. Ibid., 1212C, 1214C.

64. *PL* 188, 1201A.

65. Ibid., 1210B-C.

66. Ibid., 1209C.

67. For a recent biography of Guibert, cf. Klaus Guth, *Guibert von Nogent und die hochmittelalterliche Kritik an der Reliquienverehrung*, pp. 40-51, and Jacques Chaurand, 'Guibert de Nogent', *DS* 6 (1967), 1135-9. The standard study remains the introduction to Georges Bourgin's edition of Guibert's *De vita sua, Guibert de Nogent. Historie de sa vie (1053-1124)*. For a recent discussion of Guibert's theology see Jaroslav Pelikan, 'A First-Generation Anselmian, Guibert of Nogent', *Continuity and Discontinuity in Church History*, pp. 71-82.

68. Klaus Guth, *Guibert*, p. 94 n. 340 argues that Guibert's theology of the Eucharist may have been based on that of Anselm of Canterbury.

Although it would be difficult to deny this with certainty, since Anselm left little record of his thoughts on the Eucharist, the parallels between Guibert's work and that of the 'School of Laon' are evident. See, for instance, the discussion of this point by J. Geiselmann, 'Die Stellung des Guibert von Nogent in der Eucharistielehre der Frühscholastik', *Theologische Quartalschrift* 110 (1929), 66-84, 279-305, who presents an excellent analysis of Guibert's theology.

69. Cf. Bourgin, p. xiv, and the preface to Guibert's *Proemium ad commentarios in Genesim* (*PL* 156, 19C-20C).

70. Bourgin (pp. xiv-xx) dates the letter to Siegfried as before 1120 and the *De pignoribus sanctorum c.*1119.

71. The question was much debated in the early 12th century. It was, for example, one of the questions about which Rupert of Deutz disputed with Alger of Liège. See the references given in Ch. 2, n. 193. A discussion of this letter of Guibert is given by Ott, *Briefliteratur*, pp. 17-18.

72. As in the case of Hugh Metel's letter to Gerland, the author seems to be combating a form of teaching similar to Berengar's. See Ch. 1, pp. 42, 151.

73. *PL* 156, 534C-D.

74. Ibid., 534D, 529D.

75. Ibid., 535C.

76. See Guth, *Guibert*, pp. 73-5, and Guibert, *De pignoribus sanctorum, Epistola nuncupatoria* (*PL* 156, 607D-608D).

77. *PL* 156, 631B.

78. '. . . ergo tria corpora habet Deus. Erit itaque, primo, conceptum corpus ex Virgine; secundo, illud quod sub figura agitur in pane et calice; tertio, quod impassibile, imo glorificatum jam assidet paternae dexterae' (ibid., 650B).

79. '. . . primum (corpus) tamen principaliter verum est, quod causam subministrat illi, quod ab eo derivatum est' (ibid., 630B).

80. 'Alterum ergo sicut nascendo de Virgine, patiendo in cruce aliquantula temporum mora praecessit, dedit causas alteri, quod ad ejus, ut sic dicam, vicariam identitatem sub ejus exemplo successit' (ibid., 629D-630B).

81. 'At quoniam de conformitate hujus quod in sacra mensa conficitur corporis antelibavimus, hoc diffinire debemus, quod corpori illi omnino conveniat quod jam apud Patrem immortale incorruptibileque conregnat' (ibid., 643D).

82. 'Superius dictum est, quod ad exercitationem fidei nostrae, a principali corpore ad mysticum Dominus noster nos voluit traducere, et exinde quasi quibusdam gradibus ad divinae subtilitatis intelligentiam erudire' (ibid., 650A; cf. 609C).

83. 'Manducare mihi nihil aliud videtur, quam ad seipsum Jesu vitam exemplificare, et hoc est quod dicit "me", ac si diceret: "Me" non manducat, qui non se mihi uniendo concorporat. Mihi non credatur, nisi verba Dominica meis consonare probentur' (ibid., 639A, cf. ibid., 639B-C).

84. '. . . haec cui vult Deus infundit, cui vult obserat, pro intentione

videlicet ac merito accedentis, et cohibet et dat' (ibid., 637D). '. . . omnibus, juxta pietatis a Deo indultae mensuram, in nullo clauda est sufficientia tanti doni' (ibid., 632D).

85.   'Ergo panis iste qui et dicitur angelorum, quis audeat dicere quod alicui pertineat reproborum? Soli itaque sorti conceditur electorum.' (Ibid., 639B-C.) A similar teaching appears in a work entitled *Epistola de sacramentis haereticorum∫* (Ernest Sackur (ed.), p. 18). The work was written by a certain 'magister G.' around the first decade of the 12th century, and is usually associated with Gerhoh of Reichersberg. See Peter Classen, *Gerhoh von Reichersberg,* p. 443. Possibly the work belongs rather to Guibert, who would certainly have been active during this period.

86.   'Ex quo vigilanter et pulchre a Domino temperari dicuntur, quia multi sine re sacramenti haec suscipere aestimantur, qui, Deo eorum correctionem providente, vitae exinde aeternae nutriuntur, dum aliud longe in Dei sedet arbitrio quam hominum temeritas arbitratur, cum proba initia fine improbo demutantur, aut bona initia termino ignobili decoquuntur.' (*PL* 156, 642D-643A.)

87.   'In quibus tamen duobus id refert ut sine aqua aut sanguine Christianus esse non valeat, sine Eucharistia vero esse possit, si tamen in ejus constanter fide permaneat' (ibid., 613B).

88.   Ibid., 632C.

89.   See *PL* 156, 644A-646B.

90.   Ibid., 640D.

91.   'Ad quod ego inferam: Si panis ille nihil in se sacrum praeter quam panis communis haberet, ille tamen qui id sumit corpus esse Dominicum aestimaret, . . . non minori procul dubio judicio succumberet quam si Jesu verissimum corpus esset' (ibid., 636B-C), cf. ibid., 635C.

92.   See this chapter, pp. 101, 102, 195, 196.

93.   See Geiselmann, 'Die Stellung des Guibert von Nogent', pp. 299-305.

94.   For a complete bibliography on Hugh and his work see Roger Baron, *Science et Sagesse chez Hugues de Saint-Victor,* pp. 231-63, updated by the same author, 'Hugues de Saint-Victor', *DS* 7 (1969), 937-9. For more recent studies on Hugh's theology of the Eucharist see Erich Kleineidam, 'Literargeschichtliche Bemerkungen zur Eucharistielehre Hugos von St. Victor', *Scholastik* 24 (1949), 564-6; Heinrich Weisweiler, 'Sakrament als Symbol und Teilhabe. Der Einfluß des Ps.-Dionysius auf die allgemeine Sakramentenlehre Hugos von St. Victor', *Scholastik* 27 (1952), 321-43; idem, 'Hugos von St. Victor Dialogue de sacramentis legis naturalis et scriptae als frühscholastisches Quellenwerk', *Miscellanea Giovanni Mercati,* ii, 180-208, 211-19; Holböck, *Der mystische Leib,* pp. 114-18, and Heinz Robert Schlette, 'Die Eucharistielehre Hugos von St. Victor', *Zeitschrift für katholische Theologie* 81 (1959), 67-100, 163-210.

95.   On Hugh's life at St. Victor see Fourier Bonnard, *Histoire de l'abbaye royale et des chanoines reguliers de St.-Victor de Paris,* vol. i (Paris, 1908), p. 89 n. 1. R. Baron sees Hugh as intimately connected with the School

of Anselm of Laon and William of Champeaux. See esp. his 'Étude sur l'authenticité de l'œuvre de Hugues de Saint-Victor d'après les MSS Paris Maz. 717, BN 14506 et Douai 360-366', *Scriptorium* 10 (1956), 219-20.

96. On the dating of the *De sacramentis* see Roger Baron, 'Hugues de Saint-Victor', *DS* 7, 912; idem, 'L'œuvre de Hugues de Saint-Victor du point de vue chronologique', *Études sur Hugues de Saint-Victor*, p. 88, who dates this work *c*.1130-42. Damien Van den Eynde, *Essai sur la succession et la date des écrits de Hugues de Saint-Victor*, pp. 100-3, 214 dates the same work *c*.1130-7. Van den Eynde, *Essai*, pp. 58-65, 214 would date the *In hierarchiam caelestem* before 1125, but Baron, 'L'œuvre', pp. 78-80, argues against Van den Eynde's dating, offering what seems to be the more convincing dating of *c*.1130-42. For the section of the *In hierarchiam caelestem* copied into the *De sacramentis* compare *PL* 175, 951A-953D to *PL* 176, 465C-468A.

97. *De sacramentis*, l. 2, *pars* 2, c. 1 (*PL* 176, 415B-416B).

98. *De sacramentis,* l. 1, *pars* 10, c. 9 (*PL* 176, 342D). Cf. *De laude charitatis (PL* 176, 974A-C, 975C-D).

99. 'Qui enim non habet Spiritum Christi non est membrum Christi . . . Per fidem membra efficimur, per dilectionem vivificamur. Per fidem accipimus unionem; per charitatem accipimus vivificationem. In sacramento autem per baptismum unimur, per corpus Christi et sanguinem vivificamur.' (*De sacramentis*, l. 2, *pars* 2, c. 1 (*PL* 176, 416B).)

100. 'Passio namque Salvatoris quae primo loco sacramenta gratiae ad effectum salutis sanctificat, mediantibus istis etiam illa prioris temporis sacramenta sanctificabat, ut eadem salus esset, et his qui recta fide signa futurorum in illis venerati sunt, et his qui effectum salutis in istis percipiunt.' (Ibid., l. 1, *pars* 11, c. 2 (ibid., 343C-D).) Cf. *De sacramentis*, l. 1, *pars* 10, c. 6 (ibid., 335A-336C).

101. 'Sacramentum corporis et sanguinis Christi unum est ex his in quibus principaliter salus constat, et inter omnia singulare; quia ex ipso omnis sanctificatio est. Haec enim hostia semel pro mundi salute oblata, omnibus praecedentibus et subsequentibus sacramentis virtutem dedit, ut ex illa sanctificarent per illam liberandos omnes.' (Ibid., l. 2, *pars* 8, c. 1 (ibid., 461D).)

102. 'Ergo divinissima Eucharistia quae in altari et secundum panis et vini speciem et secundum corporis et sanguinis Christi veritatem visibiliter et corporaliter tractatur, sacramentum est et signum; et imago invisibilis et spiritualis participationis Jesu, quae intus in corde per fidem et dilectionem perficitur.' (Ibid., c. 7 (ibid., 476A-B).) Cf. *In hierarchiam caelestem*, l. 2 (*PL* 175, 951B).

103. *De sacramentis*, l. 2, *pars* 8, c. 13 (*PL* 176, 470C-471C), e.g.: 'Sic ergo in sacramento suo modo temporaliter (Christus) venit ad te, et est eo corporaliter tecum, ut tu per corporalem praesentiam ad spiritualem quaerendam exciteris, et inveniendam adjuveris' (ibid., 470D). On this role of the sacraments in general see *De sacramentis*, l. 1, *pars* 9, c. 3 (*PL* 176, 320A-322A).

104. 'Quae tamen corporis et sanguinis sumptio quia sola sine spirituali effectu salutem non conferat, . . .' (*De sacramentis*, l. 2, *pars* 8, c. 8 (ibid., 467C).) See also c. 5 (ibid., 465B).

105. 'Qui sumit sacramentum habet, qui credit et diligit, rem sacramenti habet. Melius ergo est illi qui credit et diligit, etiam si sumere et manducare non possit, quam illi qui sumit et manducat et non credit, nec diligit; vel si credit non diligit.' (Ibid., c. 5 (ibid., 465C).) On the sacraments in general see *De sacramentis*, l. 1, *pars* 9, c. 5 (ibid., 324C-D). Schlette, 'Die Eucharistielehre', p. 188 n. 57, and idem, *Die Lehre von der geistlichen Kommunion bei Bonaventura, Albert dem Grossen und Thomas von Aquin*, p. 16 denies that Hugh of St. Victor accepted the practice of spiritual communion. Holböck, *Der mystische Leib*, p. 116, argues that Hugh did accept such a practice. No specific reference to a practice of this kind appears in Hugh's work, although he certainly insisted on the premiss upon which such practices were based; that is that sacramental reception was not essential to effect the spiritual union symbolized by them.

106. 'Dicit ergo tibi cor tuum: Quid factum est de corpore Christi, postquam illud sumpsi et manducavi? Audi ergo. Corporalem praesentiam Christi queris? In coelo quaere.' (*De sacramentis*, l. 2, *pars* 8, c. 13 (*PL* 176, 470C).) See also cc. 11 and 12 (*PL* 176, 469B-470B).

107. The work borrowed from Ivo of Chartres, *Panormia*, and the *Summa sententiarum*. See A. Landgraf, 'Die Summa Sententiarum und die Summe des Cod. Vat. lat 1345'. *RThAM* 11 (1939), 260-70 and the later corrections to that article by Heinrich Weisweiler in his review of Landgraf's article, *Scholastik* 16 (1941), 123-5, and by Damien Van den Eynde, 'La "Summa Sententiarum" source des "Sententiae Sidonis" *Vat lat 1345*', *RThAM* 27 (1960), 136-41.

108. 'Inter sacramentum et rem sacramenti ac uirtutem sacramenti est notanda distinctio. . . . Est itaque sacramentum quod uidetur, res quod intelligitur, uirtus quod operatur.' (*Pars* 10, c. 11 (Vat. lat. 1345, fol. 94^r).)

109. 'Boni autem manducant christum, et in sacramento et in re. Hoc est enim re manducare, quod ei conformari. Manducant igitur christum in re quia uite innocentia et puritate pro modo humane fragilitatis ei conformantur.' (Ibid. (ibid.).)

110. 'Spiritualis dicitur eo quod spiritualiter tantum manducatur. Solius enim spiritus et anime est credere et amare. Quia ergo cibus iste sola fide et caritate ueraciter manducatur, nec corpus implet sed animam reficit, spiritualis dicitur.' (Ibid. (ibid.).)

111. 'Modus sumendi est duplex. Perceptio enim corporis et sanguinis domini alia sacramentalis et realis.' *Pars* 10, c. 12 (ibid., fol. 94^v). 'Corpus christi duobus modis manducatur, corporaliter scilicet et spiritualiter.' (*Pars* 10, c. 13 (ibid.).)

112. 'Sacramentalis et realis (perceptio) est bonorum qui non solum sacramentum suscipiunt, uerum etiam rem sacramenti qua uniuntur et conformantur christo quia percipiunt illud in triplici uirtutum susceptione, id est fidei, spei et caritatis in quibus uirtutibus unitas et conformitas

christi habetur quod non mali percipiunt.' (*Pars* 10, c. 12 (ibid.).)
'Spiritualiter autem christum manducare est ei unire et conformari.'
(Ibid. (ibid.).)

113. The best introduction to the state of scholarship on the *Summa senten-tiarum* is that of Roger Baron, 'Note sur l'enigmatique "Summa Sententiarum"', *RThAM* 25 (1958), 26-41, but see also R. Baron, *Science et sagesse*, pp. 249-50 for earlier studies, and Artur Landgraf *Introduction à l'histoire de la littérature théologique de la scolastique naissante*, pp. 98-100, for a more recent evaluation of scholarship. To the list of MSS of this work cited by Baron ('Note', pp. 37-8) should be added three Cambridge MSS: Trinity College MS 0.10.26, fols. 210^r-271^r (12th century): Gonville and Caius College MS 210 (225), fols. 33^r-58^r (12th/13th century), and Corpus Christi College, MS 209, fols. 180 ff. (13th century).

114. *Tractatus* 6, c. 3 (*PL* 176, 140A-B).

115. This terminology would be copied by Peter Lombard, *Sententie*, l. 4, dist. 8, Nos. 6-7 (PP. Collegium S. Bonaventurae (eds.), p. 790), and hence carried on into the high scholastic period. See Joseph de Ghel-linck, 'Eucharistie au XIIe siècle en occident', *DTC* 15, 1270.

116. *Tract.* 6, c. 8 (*PL* 176, 143D-144A).

117. 'Itaque virtutem sacramenti habent qui corde credunt sive sacra-mentum suscipiant, sive non.' (Ibid. (ibid., 143C). Cf. also reference given in n. 116 above.)

118. On the dating, sources, and influence of this work, see Barthélemy Hauréau, *Les Œuvres de Hugues de Saint-Victor*, pp. 199-203; Heinrich Weisweiler, 'Zur Einflusssphäre der "Vorlesungen" Hugos von St. Victor', *Mélanges Joseph de Ghellinck, S.J.*, pp. 534-70; Damien Van den Eynde, 'Deux sources de la Somme théologique de Simon de Tournai', *Antonianum* 24 (1949), 19-42, and idem, 'Le *Tractatus de sacramento altaris* faussement attribué à Étienne de Baugé', *RThAM* 19 (1952), 241. Haureau, *Les Œuvres*, pp. 201-2, lists 15 MSS of this work, to which the following Cambridge MSS can be added:
> Corpus Christi College MS 461, fols. 144^v ff. (13th c.)
> Magdalene College MS 15, fols. 95^r ff. (13th c.)
> Pembroke College MS 111, fols. 135^v-160^v (12th/13th c.)
> Trinity College MS 0.1.59, fols. 56 (62)^r ff. (12th/13th c.)
> Trinity College MS 0.1.30, fols. 30^r ff. (13th c.)
> Trinity College MS B.14.8, fols. 104^v ff. (12th c.)
> University Library MS Ff.1.11, fols. 137^r-154^v (13th c.)
> University Library MS Kk.2.22, fols. 216^v ff. (15th c.)
> University Library MS Kk.4.4, fols. 34^r ff. (15th c.)

119. *Speculum ecclesie*, c. 7 (*PL* 177, 365B-C) = *Summa sententiarum*, tract. 6, c. 3 (*PL* 176, 140A-D); *Speculum ecclesie*, c. 7 (*PL* 177, 365D-366B) = *Summa sententiarum*, ibid. (*PL* 176, 140C-D) and c. 7 (*PL* 176, 143D-144A).

120. *Speculum ecclesie*, c. 7 (*PL* 177, 364C-365B) = *De sacramentis*, l. 2, *pars* 8, c. 13 (*PL* 176, 470C-471C).

121. 'Qui credit et diligit, etsi manducare sub sacramento non possit, rem

tamen sacramenti habet, et spiritualiter manducat, et veraciter Christo incorporatur, . . . Quidam autem licet corporaliter sumere non possint tamen spiritualiter manducant spiritalem carnem Christi, hoc est efficientiam sacramenti, sine qua non est vita spiritualis' (*PL* 177, 366B-C).

122. The work as printed in *PL* 175 makes up Book 5 of the *Allegoriae super novum testamentum*. Books 1-4 are actually part of Richard of St. Victor's *Liber exceptionum*: while Books 6-8 make up a commentary on the letters of Paul by the same author who wrote the *Quaestiones in epistolas Pauli* (*PL* 175, 431-643) (see Ch. 4, n. 117 below). The commentary on Paul exists as a separate unit under the title *Notule in epistolas Pauli* in several MSS, and there appear to be no grounds for connecting this work with the commentary on John. See Glorieux, 'Essai sur les "Questiones in epistolas Pauli" du Ps-Hugues de St. Victor', *RThAM* 19 (1952), 48-59; J. Châtillon, 'Le contenu, l'authenticité et la date du *Liber exceptionum* et des *Sermones centum* de Richard de Saint-Victor', *Revue du moyen âge latin* 4 (1948), 43 n. 36; Philip S. Moore, 'The Authorship of the *Allegoriae super vetus et novum testamentum*', *New Scholasticism* 9 (1935), 213 n. 19, and A. Landgraf, 'Die Quaestiones super epistolas s. Pauli und die Allegoriae', *Collectanea franciscana* 16 (1946), 196-200.

123. *PL* 175, 851D.

124. 'Ex fide enim diligimus; ex dilectione Christo unimur, qui est vita nostra. Hic igitur panis spiritualis fide gustatus etiam sine perceptione sacramentali quotidie ad vitam proficit: . . .' (John 6: 13 (*PL* 175, 850C)). Cf. the commentary on John 6: 49 (ibid., 831D-832A).

125. See Ch. 2, pp. 71-2.

126. The major works of Peter Browe include *De frequenti communione in ecclesia occidentali usque circa 1000* (Rome, 1932), *Die Verehrung der Eucharistie im Mittelalter* (Munich, 1933), *Di eucharistischen Wunder des Mittelalters* (Breslau, 1938), *Die häufige Kommunion im Mittelalter* (Münster, 1938), and *Die Pflichtkommunion im Mittelalter* (Münster and Regensburg, 1940). Those of Édouard Dumoutet include *Le Désir de voir l'hostie et les origines de la dévotion au saint-sacrement* (Paris, 1926), *Le Christ selon la chair et la vie liturgique au moyen-âge* (Paris, 1932), and *Corpus Domini: Aux sources de la piété eucharistique médiévale* (Paris, 1942).

127. Peter Browe, *Die eucharistischen Wunder*, refers to many of the eucharistic miracles of the patristic era and early Middle Ages, but demonstrates that the real period of interest in such stories first occurs in the 12th century.

128. *PL* 149, 1449D-1450A.

129. The incident is discussed by Browe, *Wunder*, pp. 151-2.

130. Browe, *Wunder*, p. 19 gives the references to the many witnesses to the Arras miracle. Gerald of Wales recorded the story in his *Gemma ecclesiastica*, d. 1, c. 11, describing the miracle as a sign sent to disprove the teaching of the Cathars (J. S. Brewer (ed.), *Giraldi Cambrensis opera*, 2, 40-2).

131. Brewer, p. 40.

132. Gerald recorded the dispute: 'Accidit etiam ut crebrescentibus ibidem miraculis, et multiplicatis ex devotione fidelium oblationibus, episcopus urbis ejusdem hostiam illam ad cathedram ecclesiam deferri fecisset et honorifice reponi. Unde et epistolam Papae Alexandri III., cujus hoc tempore contigerat ad querimoniam canonici personae, scilicet ecclesiae praedictae, super restitutione facienda judicibus de legatis transmissam, legimus, et inter alias ejusdem papae decretales scriptam, satis et vidimus et habuimus' (Brewer, p. 41). The letter of Alexander III to the Bishop of Arras is included in the *Compilatio prima*, lib. 3, tit. 26, c. 30 of the *Quinque compilationes antique* (Emile Friedberg (ed.), p. 38).

133. Browe, 'Die Elevation in der Messe', *Jahrbuch für Liturgiewissenschaft* 9 (1929), 20-66; idem, *Die Verehrung der Eucharistie im Mittelalter*; Édouard Dumoutet, *Le Désir de voir l'hostie*; idem, *Corpus Domini*, pp. 8-111.

134. Browe, *Verehrung*, pp. 1-11; Dumoutet, *Corpus Domini*, pp. 88-9.

135. Browe, *Verehrung*, pp. 11-25; Dumoutet, *Corpus Domini*, pp. 92-9.

136. 'Sed ecce nostro in tempore rursum Photinus atque Nestorius emergit ab inferis in hominibus hominem Christum sua divinitate spoliantibus et carnem Christi latria indignam judicantibus eamque non adorandam sed Verbo coadorandam quasi alterum alteri blasphemantibus.' (Gerhoh of Reichersberg, *De investigatione Antichristi*, l. 2, c. 33 (Friedrich Scheibelberger (ed.), *Gerhohi Reichersbergensis opera hactenus inedita*, vol. i, p. 260).) 'Quod enim honorari, quod adorari debeat, fidelibus omnibus certum est, . . .' (Peter the Venerable, *Adversus petrobrusianos hereticos* (Fearns, p. 122)).

137. The research done on the history of this rite is extensive. For a summary of work up to 1940 see Gerard G. Grant, 'The Elevation of the Host: A Reaction to Twelfth Century Heresy', *Theological Studies* 1 (1940), 228-50. See also V. L. Kennedy, 'The Moment of Consecration and the Elevation of the Host', *Medieval Studies* 6 (1944), 121-50. A possible influence on the introduction of this practice might have been the use of low altar screens particularly during the 12th century. This suggestion, which was made to me by Professor Christopher Brooke, has received little attention from scholars, as has indeed the whole question of the relationship of changes in Church architecture to liturgical changes during this period. Professor Brooke provides an excellent introduction to this whole question in his *Medieval Church and Society* (London, 1971), pp. 162-82. For surviving examples of 12th-century altar screens see Christopher Brooke, *The Monastic World: 1000-1300* (New York, 1974), Plates 235, 243 and pp. 140-6.

138. On the practice of a minor elevation during the words of consecration during the 12th century see Browe, *Verehrung*, pp. 28-33; Dumoutet, *Le Désir*, pp. 46-8; Joseph Jungmann, *Missarum sollemnia*, i, 158, ii, 256-8: and Hans Bernard Meyer, 'Die Elevation im deutschen Mittelalter und bei Luther', *Zeitschrift für katholische Theologie* 85 (1963), 162-3.

139. V. L. Kennedy, 'The Date of the Parisian Decree on the Elevation of the Host', *Mediaeval Studies* 8 (1946), 87-96, suggests that this statute, attached to those of Odo along with other additional material, may

actually date from the episcopacy of Peter of Nemours, Bishop of Paris from 1208-19. The text, edited by Kennedy, 'The Moment of Consecration', p. 122 n. 4 reads: 'Praecipitur presbyteris, ut cum in canone inceperint *qui pridie* tenentes hostiam ne elevent eam statim nimis alte, ita quod possit videri a populo sed quasi ante pectus detineant donec dixerint *Hoc est corpus meum* et tunc elevent eam ita quod possit videri ab omnibus.'

140. See Browe, 'Die Elevation', pp. 24-8; *Verehrung*, pp. 28-39; Dumoutet, *Le Désir*, pp. 43-6.

141. The Cistercians had the custom of ringing the bell at the consecration from at least 1152 (Kennedy, 'The Date of the Parisian Decree', pp. 93-4). On the spread of this practice in the 12th and 13th centuries see Browe, 'Die Elevation', pp. 37-40.

142. '. . . sacerdos elevat Corpus Christi ut omnes fideles videant et petant quod prosit ad salutem.' (Ed. Dumoutet, *Le Désir*, p. 49 n. 3.)

143. On Marie's life see *Acta sanctorum*, Junii, 4, 630-84. For a short history of Marie, including an excellent bibliography, see John F. Hinnebusch, *The Historia Occidentalis of Jacques de Vitry*, p. 286.

144. Jacques' *Vita* is printed in *Acta sanctorum*, Junii, 4, 636-66. On the dating of this work see Hinnebusch, p. 9 n. 3.

145. On the eucharistic devotion of Marie and her circle, cf. Browe, *Wunder*, pp. 44-7; *Die häufige Kommunion*, pp. 126-8; Dumoutet, *Le Christ selon la chair*, pp. 129-40.

146. On the history of the Feast of Corpus Christi, cf. Browe, *Verehrung*, pp. 70-88; ibid., 'Die Ausbreitung des Fronleichnamfestes', *Jahrbuch für Liturgiewissenschaft* 8 (1928), 107-43; Dumoutet, *Le Christ selon la chair*, pp. 129-40.

147. Speaking of the elevation in particular, Browe sees the middle of the 13th century as the high point of devotion in the Middle Ages ('Elevation', p. 53). The 12th century saw not only the beginnings of eucharistic devotion, but also 'superstition' regarding the sacrament. On this point see esp. Adolf Franz, *Die Messe im deutschen Mittelalter*, pp. 73-114, but also Browe, 'Elevation', pp. 50 ff. and *Verehrung*, pp. 49-69.

148. Browe, 'Die Kommunionandacht im Altertum und Mittelalter', *Jahrbuch für Liturgiewissenschaft* 13 (1933), 45-64; idem, 'Die Kommunionvorbereitung im Mittelalter', *Zeitschrift für katholische Theologie*, 56 (1932), 408-12; *Die häufige Kommunion*, pp. 145-50. The commentary on 1 Cor. 11: 31 offered an occasion for many 12th-century theologians to insist on a proper devotional disposition for reception of the Eucharist. See, for example, the commentaries of Gilbert of La Porrée (Cambridge, Pembroke College MS 78, fol. 51^r), Peter Lombard (*PL* 191, 1648A-B), Peter the Chanter (London, British Library, Royal MS 10. C.5, fol. 324^{r}2), Hervaeus of Bourg-Dieu (*PL* 181, 937C-938A), and Stephen Langton (Cambridge, University Library MS Ii.4.23, fols. 209^{v}2-210^{v}1).

149. 'Ex hoc quod sancta eucaristia cibus est esurientium, innuitur quod cum deuotione debet sumi. Non tali consuetudine quali bos accredit ad

presepe, ut ex consuetudine proueniat fastidium, quia cibus iste fastidium fastidit, contemptum contempnat. Unde quidam religiosi non cotidie in septimana conficiunt ut ex nimia consuetudine proueniens fastidii tollatur occasio et eis in sumptione eucharistie augeatur deuotio.' William de Montibus, *Commentarium in psalmo* 21: 27 (Oxford, Bodleian Library, Bodley MS 860, fol. 35ᵛ1). The passage is repeated in his *Sententie* (idem, fol. 101ᵛ). See also Jacques de Vitry, *Historia occidentalis*: 'Quidam autem ex frequenti usu, irreuerenter et minus deuote accedunt' (Hinnebusch, p. 244).

150. For a discussion of this practice and the general attitude discouraging frequent reception see the works cited in n. 148.

151. Browe, *Die häufige Kommunion*, pp. 119-30 discusses the insistence on more frequent reception by pious women from the 12th century onwards. His discussion of Marie and her circle occurs pp. 126-8.

152. Marie of Oignies, and two of her followers, Alpais and Jutta, received miraculously from Christ himself to satisfy their longing for reception. Browe, *Wunder*, p. 22. A similar story was told by Caesarius of Heisterbach about Uda, a holy woman of Brabant (perhaps the same as Jutta?). Christ administered the sacrament to her when her confessor refused her permission to receive. *Dialogus miraculorum, dist.* 9, c. 35 (Joseph Strange (ed.), p. 191).

153. On the social role of the Eucharist see Ch. 4, pp. 118-21, 206-9.

154. Browe, 'Elevation', p. 21 and *Verehrung*, pp. 28-9, and Hans Bernard Meyer, 'Die Elevation', pp. 173-4 give a review of the defenders of this theory. Pierre Le Brun, *Explication littérale, historique et dogmatique des prières et des cérémonies de la Messe* . . . , 2nd edn. (Paris, 1726, repr. Paris, 1949), pp. 427-8 is the earliest witness I have found. Browe himself rejects this theory as an explanation for the elevation, but adopts a modified form of it to explain the whole development of eucharistic devotion during this period (*Verehrung*, p. 29). Megivern, *Communion and Concomitance*, p. 44 appears to accept this stance, as does Henri du Lubac, *Corpus mysticum*, pp. 273-4, and A. J. MacDonald, *Berengar and the Reform of Sacramental Doctrine*, pp. 221-3.

155. See Ch. 1, pp. 41-2, 150-1.

156. See n. 139 above.

157. Browe, *Wunder*, pp. 178-80 discusses the role of miracles as a means of instructing the faithful. For an excellent example of this form of polemic see the text of Gerald of Wales, *Gemma ecclesiastica* referred to in n. 130 above.

158. Jungmann, *Missarum sollemnia* i, 157-8 also sees the rise of eucharistic devotion as connected with the opposition to popular heresy, as does Grant, 'Elevation'.

159. Albert Mirgeler, *Mutations of Western Christianity*, pp. 55-6, 61-5.

160. See pp. 86-8, 186-7 above. According to the same statutes of Paris in which the elevation was first mentioned, even vestments upon which the consecrated species had been spilled were to be treated as relics (Mansi, 22, 682). The admonition also occurs in Jacques de Vitry, *Historia occidentalis* (Hinnebusch, p. 245).

161. There had been a custom in the Church dating from at least the 9th century of using a consecrated Host as a relic in an altar stone, see Dumoutet, *Corpus Domini*, pp. 61-2.

162. This is, for instance what was done at Fécamp in 1171; see Browe, *Wunder*, pp. 151-2.

163. The theme is repeated throughout his books, e.g.: 'c'est qu'un effet, au moment même où la pitié pour les humaines faiblesses du Saveur tend à devenir prépondérante dans les âmes spirituelles, on assiste à l'ascension progressive d'une dévotion qui n'était pas destinée à un moindre succès: la dévotion envers l'Eucharistie.' (*Le Christ selon la chair*, p. 113.)

164. *Le Désir*, pp. 16-82; *Le Christ selon la chair*, pp. 113-80; *Corpus Domini*, pp. 103-38.

165. This is the basic argument of *Le Christ selon la chair*, Chs. 4-6.

166. 'Mouetur igitur magis ad presentem quam ad absentem, mouetur magis ad uisum quam ad auditum Christum, mouetur ad admirandum, mouetur ad amandum . . . Non est superfluum, quia non tantum per id quod Deus est, sed etiam per id quod homo est, nobiscum est usque ad consummationem seculi. Non est superfluum, quia qui per corpus suum redemit nos, per idem corpus suum reficit nos, ut redempti per corpus eius et refecti corpore eius nutriamur et pascamur humanitate eius, donec satiemur deitate et gloria eius.' (*Contra Petrobrusianos* (Fearns, pp. 119-20).)

167. On the whole movement towards a greater interest in the individual see R. W. Southern, *The Making of the Middle Ages*, esp. pp. 219-57, and Colin Morris, *The Discovery of the Individual 1050-1200*. Particularly useful in defining and limiting the 12th-century understanding of 'individual' or 'self' and for placing this understanding into a larger context is the excellent exchange between Caroline Walker Bynum, 'Did the Twelfth Century Discover the Individual?', *Journal of Ecclesiastical History* 31 (1980), 1-17 and Colin Morris, 'Individualism in Twelfth-Century Religion. Some Further Reflections', ibid., pp. 195-206.

168. John Beleth, *Summa de ecclesiasticis officiis* (Heribert Douteil (ed.), Corpus christianorum, continuatio mediaevalis, 41A (Turnhout, 1976), p. 85).

169. e.g. 'Sumendi reverenter haec est, ut sacerdos qui sacrificavit non ante suscipiat quam pax in invicem offeratur, si tempus est offerendi, . . .' (Gerald of Wales, *Gemma ecclesiastica*, d. 1, c. 11 (Brewer, p. 29)). See also Browe, *Pflichtkommunion*, pp. 185-6; Jungmann, *Missarum sollemnia* ii, 401-7.

170. This teaching occurs, for instance, in the 8th-century *Canones Theodori* (Browe, *Die häufige Kommunion*, p. 8 n. 31). Honorius Augustodunensis, *Gemma animae*, also warned against communion without the sign of peace: 'Qui non tali pacis osculo foederati corpus Christi comedunt, ut Judas, judicium sibi per falsam pacem sumant'. l. 2, c. 62 (*PL* 172, 563B).

171. Browe, *Pflichtkommunion*, p. 185 and Jungmann, *Missarum sollemnia* i,

404 n 22 refer to the writers who speak of the kiss of peace as a substitute for communion. To these should be added a passage included in a
12th-century commentary on 1 Corinthians 11: 20 contained in
Hague, Museum Meer-manno-westreenianum MS 10 B 33, fol. 99ᵛ:
'Inde est quod cum universa ecclesia non participet ipsum sacramentum, propter eius dignitatem ut dictum est, aluid tamen sacramentum
quod eiusdem rei est significatum participare debet, scilicet osculum
pacis. Et sic istud sacramentum, si indigne participetur, *in iudicium
sumit*, quia qui hec percipit testatur se esse de unitate ecclesie pacis,
cum non sunt.' The text has been edited by P. C. Boeren, 'Un traité
eucharistique inédit du XIIᵉ siècle', *Archives d'histoire doctrinale et littéraire
du moyen âge* 45 (1978), 202.

172. 'Statutum est ut panis post missam benediceretur, et populo pro
benedictione communionis partiretur: hoc est eulogia dicebatur. Sed
quia hoc in quadragesima fieri non licuit, orationem super populum
dici Ecclesia instituit, ut per hanc particeps communionis sit.'
(Honorius Augustodunensis, *Gemma animae*, l. 1, c. 67 (*PL* 172,
565A).) Browe, *Pflichtkommunion*, p. 185 gives the references to these
writers, but see also Adolf Franz, *Die kirchlichen Benediktionen im Mittelalter* i, 256-9, and Jungman, *Missarum sollemnia* ii, 532.

173. Browe, *Pflichtkommunion*, pp. 187-200; Jungmann, *Missarum sollemnia*
ii, 562-4.

174. Browe, *Pflichtkommunion*, p. 192. Robert Pullen specifically referred to
the practice of substituting blessed bread for the Eucharist (see below,
n. 233). The School of Gilbert of La Porrée, Stephen Langton, the
Notule, and William of Auxerre all discuss the reception of *panis purus* or
panis simplex as a substitute, but may indeed be referring to blessed
bread as opposed to the consecrated species. Cf., for instance, the use
of the term *panis benedictus* by Langton in the passage quoted in Ch. 4,
n. 149.

175. 'In all diesen Fällen ist ihre Verwendung als Kommunionersatz sehr
klar und eindeutig; ebenso wenn wir aus dem altfranzösischen Hel-
denepos ersehen, dass man sie auch mit in die Schlacht nahm und im
Falle einer todlichen Verwendun als Viaticum genoss.' (Browe, *Pflichtkommunion*, p. 192.)

176. Browe, 'Elevation', pp. 56-62; *Verehrung*, pp. 55-69; Franz, *Die Messe*,
pp. 101-5.

177. 'Tertio capitulo queritur vtrum peccent mortaliter aspiciendo corpus
christi vel tangendo illi qui sunt in mortali peccato.' (*Summa aurea*, l. 4
(ed. Paris, 1500?, fol. 206ᵛ2).)

178. 'Utrum uero mortaliter peccent qui sunt in suburbio et choro ecclesie
qui tamen cum ministris altaris per deuotionem et consensum debent
corpus christi conficere, et spiritualiter et si non sacramentaliter
sumere, non diffinio.' (*Verbum abbreviatum* (Cambridge, St. John's
College, MS B.8, fol. 48ʳ2 = *PL* 205, 108D).)

179. Browe discusses spiritual communion and its importance from the 12th
century onwards in his article, 'Die Kommunionandacht', pp. 58-64.

180. See Ch. 5, pp. 135, 217. Hildegard of Bingen, the famous Rhineland
mystic, recorded just such a case of spiritual communion: 'Quicumque ex

infirmitate corporis sui vomitum patitur, et corpus Christi tota devotione desiderat, huic presbyter idem sacramentum dare non praesumat, propter honorem ejusdem corporis Christi, quod in specie panis latet. Sed corpus Domini super caput ejusdem hominis ponat, ac Deuim qui animam in corpus misit, invocet, ut corpore et sanguine animam illius sanctificare dignetur . . . Unde invisibilis anima, invisibilem sanctitatem statim in se trahit; quia spiritus hominis illum qui eum misit, mox sentit, et nunquam ab eo recedit, qui in fide eum suscipit.' (*Epistola ad praelatos Moguntinenses* (*PL* 197, 227B-C).) For a recent estimation of Hildegard's life and works see Marianna Schrader, 'Hildegarde de Bingen', *DSAM* 7 (1969), 505-21.

181. The 'School of Laon' appears to be the first advocate of spiritual communion; see Heinz Robert Schlette, *Die Lehre von der geistliche Kommunion bei Bonaventura, Albert dem Grossem und Thomas von Aquin,* p. 6. The first description of the actual practice would be a sentence of that school comparing spiritual and corporeal eating; see n. 41 above.

182. 'Sacerdos quidam luxuriosus feminam procabatur. Et cum illius non posset habere consensum, dicta missa corpus Domini mundissimum in ore tenuit, sperans si sic illam deoscularetur, quod vi sacramenti voluntas eius ad suos libitus inclineratur.' (Caesarius of Heisterbach, *Dialogus*, dist. 9, c. 6 (Strange, 2, 171).)

183. Osbert, who witnessed the death of Hugh, recounted in a letter how Hugh received spiritual communion: (*PL* 175, clxi B-C).

184. The standard work on William's life and work is J.-M. Déchanet, *Guillaume de Saint Thierry*, updated in the same author's 'Guillaume de Saint Thierry', *DS* 6 (1967), 1241-5, which includes a complete bibliography.

185. On Rupert's work see Ch. 2, pp. 65-7, 170-2.

186. On the meeting of Bernard and William see Déchanet, 'Guillaume', col. 1242; for the dedication of the *De corpore*, see *PL* 180, 343-4.

187. André Wilmart, 'Le série et la date des ouvrages de Guillaume de Saint-Thierry', *Revue Mabillon* 14 (1924), 164, dated the *De corpore* c.1128. This is due to a faulty dating of Rupert's *De officiis* to 1126, when Rupert re-dedicated his work to Abbot Cuno, then Bishop of Ratisbon. For details of the dating of Rupert's work see the introduction to R. Haack's edition of the *De divinis officiis.*

188. 'Oportebat autem, ut sicut cum necessaria nobis fuit visibilis ejus praesentia, invisibile in suis, visibile factum est in nostris Verbum caro factum; sic cum res exigit salutis nostrae, ut manducetur caro ejus, quod non est ipsa caro in natura sua, fiat in aliena, manducabilis scilicet' (*PL* 180, 349B).

189. '. . . sed corpus nostrum in suam vertit naturam; et futurae resurrectioni et perpetuae incorruptioni illud praeparans et coaptans, et in nobis est, et ubi erat, scilicet in dextera Patris' (ibid., 355B).

190. See cc. 5-7 (ibid., 351B-354C). e.g. 'Tunc autem communicamus cum fide ardente quae per dilectionem operatur, reponimus in mensa Domini qualia inde sumpsimus, . . . sic nos totos fidei ejus et charitati exhibeamus necessitate salutis nostrae' (ibid., 352D).

191. C. 5 (ibid., 351B-353B).

192. Ibid., 352D.
193. Ibid., 353A. Cf. also n. 190 and c. 7 (ibid., 354C).
194. C. 7 (ibid., 354C-355A). e.g. 'Licet enim illa sufficiat, si sic inevitabile cogat necessarium, tamen et haec non est omittenda' (ibid., 354D).
195. C. 3 (ibid., 349B-350A).
196. C. 12 (ibid., 361C-362C); c. 8 (ibid., 354D).
197. C. 9 (ibid., 365C).
198. C. 10 (ibid., 358A).
199. C. 12 (ibid., 361C-362C).
200. Peter Lombard, *Sententie*, l. 4, dist. 12, c. 1 (Collegium S. Bonaventurae, p. 808). For a representative 13th-century discussion of the existence of the accidents see Thomas Aquinas, *Summa theologiae, pars tertia*, c. 77, art. 1 (Leonine edn., vol. xii, pp. 193-4). See, for instance, the discussion of this question by Raoul Ardens, *Speculum universale*, l. 1, c. 31: 'Pane uerso in corpus christi ubi remanent illa accidentia, scilicet albedo, rotunditas, sapor et huiusmodi? Dicunt quidam quia sine subiecto sunt et tamen uere sunt, sed miraculose. Alii uero dicunt quod in circumfuso aere fundantur; sicut odor pomi, pomo remoto, remanet in archa et in aera. Alii uero dicunt quod in corpore christi sunt; sicut enim in monte thabor in carne mortali christi apparuit immortalitas, ita et in mortali apparet panis forma. Qua sentencia uera sit deus nouit' (Vatican City, Biblioteca Vaticana, MS Ottoboniana 880, fol. 10ᵛ2). On Raoul and the *Speculum universale*, written *c*. 1191-1215, see Ch. 4, pp. 111-12, 201.
201. For a recent estimation of Peter's life and works see Giles Constable (ed.), *The Letters of Peter the Venerable*, ii, 257-69. Important recent studies on Peter's career are also contained in *Petrus Venerabilis, 1156-1956*, ed. Giles Constable and James Kritzeck (Rome, 1956), vol. ii of Constable's edition of Peter's letters, and *Pierre Abélard-Pierre le Vénérable*, pp. 99-203.
202. On this work and its dating see Constable, the *Letters*, ii, 285-8, and Jean Châtillon, 'Pierre le Vénérable et les petrobrusiens', *Pierre Abélard-Pierre le Vénérable*, pp. 165-76, esp. p. 168.
203. Fearns, p. 87, see Ch. 2, n. 127.
204. Fearns, p. 117.
205. Ibid., pp. 117-18.
206. Ibid., p. 119.
207. Ibid., p. 124.
208. Ibid., p. 125.
209. 'Que memoria amorem excitans de animi recessibus mala omnia effugaret, uirtutibus universa repleret, sicque cotidie per hoc sacramentum innouans redemptionem cotidianam penitentibus peccatorum gigneret remissionem' (Fearns, p. 119). Cf. n. 205.
210. On the life and works of Baldwin see Jean Leclercq's introduction to the critical edition of the *De sacramento altaris*, by J. Morson, pp. 7-11.
211. Morson, pp. 230, 248, 292.
212. Morson, pp. 270, 214-16.
213. 'Dans autem fidem quae per dilectionem operatur, dat ut in ipsum

(Christum) credatur, ut ipse diligatur, ut ipsi sicut vero Deo serviatur. Denique seipsum dat manducandum.' (John 6: 27 (Morson, p. 246).) 'Quicumque vero fide incarnationis et passionis Christi vivificatur ut juste vivat, id est ut non sibi sed Christo et in Christo vivat, hic carnem Christi ore fidei manducat et sanguinem Christi bibit.' (John 6: 56 (Morson, p. 274).) Cf. the commentaries on Matthew 26 (Morson, p. 220), Luke 22: 19 (Morson, p. 226), John 6: 47 (Morson, p. 262), John 6: 56 (Morson, pp. 268, 272, 274), 1 Cor. 10: 11 (Morson, pp. 364, 366-8), and Ex. 12: 1-11 (Morson, p. 432).

214. Morson, pp. 450-2.

215. Morson, p. 526. Cf. also pp. 334, 338.

216. 'Spiritualem itaque potum biberunt, non solum qui haustu dominici sanguinis in ipsius sacramenti perceptione potati sunt; sed et omnes justi qui a diebus antiquis fidem passionis Christi habuerunt, et in ea fide spiritualiter vixerunt, . . .' (1 Cor. 10: 4 (Morson, p. 344)). Cf. the commentary on John 6: 53-5 (Morson, p. 266).

217. 'Nam qui corpus Christi et calicem solo ore percipiunt, et Christum in corde non suscipiunt, ut de ipso et in ipso vivant, sicut a fide qua justus vivit extranei sunt, ita a societate justorum alieni sunt, . . .' (1 Cor. 10: 17 (Morson, p. 368)). Cf. the commentary on 1 Cor. 10: 20 (Morson, p. 382).

218. For the texts and a complete discussion of Zachary's borrowing see Damien Van den Eyne, 'Les ''Magistri'' du commentaire ''Unum ex quatuor'' de Zacharius Chrystopolitanus', *Antonianum* 23 (1948), 181-5.

219. Cf. Adam, *De tripartito tabernaculo* (*PL* 198, 705A-C) and Hugh, *De sacramentis* l. 2, *pars* 8, c. 7 and 11 (*PL* 177, 466C-467B, 469B). For a recent estimation of Adam's life and works see M. J. Hamilton, 'Adam Scotus (Adam of Dryburgh)', *NCE* 1, 118.

220. '. . . in spirituali sumptione corporis christi comedens iocundatur in christo, scilicet in bonis operibus et cibo spirituali unitur, . . . Imitatur etiam cibum spiritualiter comedens corpus christi, id est imitatur christum in gestis et factis eius.' (Commentary on Ps. 21: 27 (Oxford, Bodleian Library, Bodley MS 860, fol. 35^{r}a-b).) On William's career see Richard W. Hunt, 'English learning in the Late Twelfth Century', *Transactions of the Royal Historical Society*, 4th ser., 19 (1936), 21-2, and H. MacKinnon, 'William de Montibus: A Medieval Teacher', *Essays in Medieval History Presented to Bertie Wilkinson*, pp. 32-45.

221. On Peter's life and works see John W. Baldwin, *Masters, Princes and Merchants*, i, 3-16. On the Chanter's eucharistic theology see Édouard Dumoutet, 'La théologie de l'eucharistie à la fin du XIIe siècle: Le témoignage de Pierre le Chantre d'après la ''Summa de sacramentis''', *Archives d'histoire doctrinale et littéraire du moyen âge*, 18-20 (1943-5), 181-262.

222. See, for instance, Peter's treatment of the sacrament in his *Summa de sacramentis et animae consiliis*, *pars* 1, cc. 55-71 (Jean-Albert Dugauquier, i, 133-82). Peter's interests in general seemed to lie in practical rather than theoretical theology, see Baldwin, esp., i, 53-4.

223. *Summa de sacramentis, pars* 1, c. 55 (Dugauquier, i, 135).
224. Ibid. (ibid., p. 136).
225. 'Si membris Christi, habentibus caritatem non licuit interesse confectioni corporis domini, maxime timendum est membris diaboli et non habentibus caritatem tantum sacramentum conficere uel sumere.' (*Verbum abbreviatum*, c. 30 (St. John's MS B.8, fol. 48^{r}2 = *PL* 205, 108D).)
226. 'Qui uero spiritualiter quod respondere potest etiam sine sacramento ut ille qui est in unitate pacis; esse ille uitam sibi sumit.' (Commentary on 1 Cor. 11: 29 (British Library, Royal MS 10. C.5, fol. 324^{r}2).)
227. See Ch. 4, pp. 114-18, 203-6.
228. '. . . manducare eius carnem nichil est alium quam ipsum habere in se manentem, id est in eum credere, de qua manducationem ait augustinus ut quod paras dentem et uentrem, crede et manducasti.' (Commentary on John 6: 57 (Rome, Biblioteca Vallicelliana, MS B. 47, fol. 188^{v}2).)
229. 'Spiritualiter sumunt soli boni: spiritualiter sumere est fructum provenientem ex carne Domini sumere; id est esse de unitate Ecclesiae, sive sumatur corpus Christi sive non.' (*Sententie* (*PL* 211, 1252D).)
230. 'Non manducans manducat, et manducans non manducat, id est non manducans sacramentaliter manducat spiritualiter, et manducans sacramentaliter non manducat spiritualiter.' *Speculum universale*, l. 1, c. 33 (Vat. Ottobon, MS 880, fol. 11^{r}2).
231. 'Item queritur de illo, qui laborat in extremis nec habet tempus suscipiendi eucharistiam, sed loco illius sumit panem vel herbam vel aliquid tale, utrum tantum valeat illi illa sumptio, quantum, si sumeret eucharistiam.' (The *sententia* is contained in Cod. Bamberg, Patr. 136, fol. 68 and is edited by Artur Landgraf, 'Studien zur Theologie des zwölften Jahrhunderts. II. Literarhistorische Bemerkungen zu den Sentenzen des Robertus Pullus', *Traditio* 1 (1943), 221-2. The practice of receiving grass as a substitute for viaticum continued to be practised into the 15th century; see Walter Sylvester, 'The Communing with Three Blades of Grass, of the Knights-Errant', *Dublin Review* 121 (1897), 80-98.
232. 'Sed numquid approbanda est illa sumptio? Nec laudo nec vitupero, nisi quoniam qualecumque signum est sumptionis spiritualis et devotionis interioris. Sed numquid ista sumptio meritoria est vite eterne, cum sit informata caritate? Ita utique, sed ipsum sumptum nichil ei prodest, cum non sit aliquid spirituale vel spirituali adnexum' (Landgraf, p. 222).
233. 'Ergone vulgi decretum hujus rei consideratione confirmatur, scilicet panem benedictum die Dominica libantibus; vel praeoccupatis herbam saltem quasi eucharistiam sumentibus, idem valere et pro eucharistia esse? Quis hoc absque auctoritate inducere audeat?' (*Sententie* (*PL* 186, 960D-961A).)
234. The standard study of Peter of Poitiers' life and works remains that of Philip S. More, *The Works of Peter of Poitiers, Master of Theology and Chancellor of Paris (1193-1205)*. For corrections and additions to this

initial study see *Sententiae Petri Pictaviensis*, vol. ii, ed. Philip S. More, Joseph N. Garvin, and Marthe Dulong, pp. v-xliii, and Joseph Garvin, 'Magister Udo, a Source of Peter of Poitiers' Sentences', *The New Scholasticism* 38 (1954), 286-98.

235. On the approximate dating of the work see L. Hödl, *Die Geschichte der scholastischen Literatur und der Theologie der Schlüsselgewalt*, p. 241.

236. See n. 229 above.

236. *PL* 211, 1255C. On Guibert see pp. 80-2, 180-2.

238. 'Dicendum est quia peccat quando panem purum porrexit, nec ille minus peccat qui sumit putans se sumere corpus Domini: quando vero corpus sumit, solus ille peccat qui manducat' (ibid.).

239. The standard work on the life of Stephen Langton is F. M. Powicke, *Stephen Langton*. For an updating of this work see John F. Veal, *The Sacramental Theology of Stephen Langton and the Influence Upon Him of Peter the Chanter*, pp. 13-16, and Phyllis Barzillay Roberts, *Stephanus de linguatonante*, pp. 1-5. On the dating of Langton's *Questiones* see L. Hödl, *Schlüsselgewalt*, pp. 343-4. Veal, p. 33 discusses Langton's position on the use of blessed bread, but appears to miss the point that Langton did see this form of reception as salvific.

240. Cambridge, St. John's College MS C.7, fols. 204ʳ1-204ᵛ2, *Qualis danda uel deneganda sit eucharistia* and fols. 255ᵛ1-256ʳ2, *De dispensatione eucharistie*.

241. 'Hic duplex opinio. Dicunt enim quidam quod ex quo uoluntas progressiua est ad opus, tantum est peccatum faciendo ex errore aliud opus, ac si faceret illud quod facere intendebat. . . . Secundum istos tantum peccat ille qui est in mortale et accipit simplicem panem pro eucharistia ac si sumeret eucharistiam et ita non est ei dandus simplex panis pro eucharistia' (St. John's MS C.7, fol. 204ᵛ1).

242. 'Alii dicunt de quorum opinione fuit corboliensis quod non tantum peccat quis cognoscendo suam pro aliena quantum si cognosceret aliena . . . Unde secundum istos ille qui est in mortali non tantum peccat sumendo simplicem panem pro eucharistia quantum si sumeret eucharistiam' (ibid.). On Paganus of Corbeil see A. Landgraf, 'Paganus v. Corbeil', *LThK* 7 (1962), 1348-9. For a list of his teachings and examples of similar references to him see A. Landgraf, 'Untersuchungen zur Gelehrtengeschichte des 12. Jahrhunderts', *Miscellanea Giovanni Mercati*, ii, 260-75, esp. p. 267, where the author gives another reference to Paganus found in Langton's *Questiones*.

243. 'Dicimus quod non est ei dandus pro eucharistia simplex panis quia demonstrando simplicem panem quando auderet sacerdos infirmo dicere: "Et credis hoc esse corpus christi." Et si detur ei in tali casu pro eucharistia simplex panis non tantum ualet ei quantum eucharistia quia eucharistia ex ui sua ualet ad cumulum uirtutum et pene remissionem et quod non simplex panis' (St. John's MS C.7, fol. 204ᵛ1).

244. 'Ad hoc dicimus non tamen ualet purus panis ad cumulum gratis sed tamen ualet ad uitam eternam' (ibid., fol. 256ʳ1).

245. Cf. n. 232 above.

246. On the eucharistic theology of William of Auxerre see Ch. 5, pp. 133-5, 217-18.

247. For modern theologians who adopt much the same basic theology, allowing for differences in metaphysical categories, see Edward Schillebeeckx, *Christ, the Sacrament of the Encounter with God* (London and New York, 1963), idem, *The Eucharist* (New York, 1967), and Joseph Powers, *Spirit and Sacrament: The Humanizing Experience* (New York, 1973).

248. References to the works of Augustine have been noted with the relevant works. Hugh of St. Victor's theology first appeared with his commentary on the *Celestial Heirarchy*. (See p. 83.) On Ratramnus's theology see p. 28-9, 47, and on Berengar's concern for spiritual reception see pp. 39-40, 149-50 above.

CHAPTER IV

1. On Gilbert's career and works see H. C. van Elswijk, *Gilbert Porreta*, pp. 9-31, 45-8, 54-8.

2. On the importance of Gilbert's commentary see Smalley, *The Study of the Bible in the Middle Ages*, p. 64 and the references given to the history of *Glossa ordinaria* in n. 2 of Ch. 3.

3. N. Häring, 'Die Sententie magistri gisleberti pictavensis episcopi', *Archives d'histoire doctrinale et littéraire du moyen âge* 45 (1978), 83-183 and 46 (1979), 45-105. The *sententie* appear in two recensions, that of Cod. Tortosa, Dombibl. 218, fols. 1-32^v, and that of Biblioteca Medicea Laurenziana, Plut. xxix, cod. cccic, fols. 41-60^v. The Tortosa MS contains a more complete version of Gilbert's teaching, and it is to Häring's edition of this MS that reference will be made.

4. '. . . *dedit eis*. Christus est panis qui de celo descendit, qui est cibus angelorum: nomine cuius significati uocat etiam figuram dicens, *Panem angelorum manducauit homo*. Sic et significatum panem factum lac manducat homo, uerbum quod factum est caro.' (Ps. 77: 24-25 (Vatican City, Biblioteca Vaticana, Vaticana lat. MS 89, fol. 66^{r}2; ibid., Vaticana lat. MS 4228, fol. 86^{v}2).) Cf. the commentaries on Ps. 110: 5 (Vat. lat. 89, fol. 93^{v}2; Vat. lat. 4228, fol. 124^{v}2), Ps. 131: 15 (Vat. lat. 89, fol. 111^{v}1; Vat. lat. 4228, fol. 146^{v}1); Ps. 147: 3 (Vat. lat. 89, fol. 122^{v}2; Vat. lat. 4228, fol. 159^{r}2) and 1 Cor. 10: 4 (Cambridge, Pembroke College, MS 78, fol. 48^r).

5. 'Similiter enim non per substantiam sed per significationem manna erat christus. Ipse enim est panis qui de celo descendit, de quo in euangelio: Si quis ex ipso manducauerit non morietur. Quod non quantum ad uisibile sacramentum sed quantum ad uirtutem sacramenti intelligendum est, id est qui manducat intus non foris; qui manducat corde, non premit dente . . .' (1 Cor. 10: 4 (Pembroke 78, fol. 48^r).) Gilbert's source here is Augustine, *tractatus* 26, c. 12, *In Iohannis evangelium* (Corpus christianorum 36, p. 266). Cf. the commentary on 1 Cor. 10: 5 (Pembroke 78, fol. 48^r).

6. Pembroke 78, fol. 49^r.

7. 'Hanc siue communcationem (*recte*: communicationem) siue participationem que in euangelio cibus et potus, societatem siue unitatem

quandam uult intelligi capitis et membrorum quod est ecclesia sancta in predestinatis et glorificandis quarum uocatio atque iustificatio processu temporis secundum diuersos et facta est et fit et fiet' (Pembroke 78, fol. 49^r). Gilbert's commentary on 1 Cor. 10: 16-17 depends heavily on Augustine, *In Iohannis evangelium, tract.* 26, cc. 15-18 (Corpus christianorum 36, pp. 265-6). Cf. *Sententie*, c. 9: 'Sacrum secretum est illa coniunctio que est capitis Christi et membrorum fidelium.' (Häring, 45 (1978), 134.) Cf. also cc. 10, 13, 14 (ibid., p. 134), c. 15 (ibid., p. 135), c. 50 (ibid., p. 141).

8. 'Et dominus duos modos esse manducandi: unum quo sacramentaliter manducant tam boni quam mali, alterum quo spiritualiter soli boni; spiritualiter enim manducare est in ea quam ipsum sacramentum significat christi et ecclesie unitate manere.' (1 Cor. 11: 29 (Pembroke 78, fol. 51^r).)

9. *Sententie*, c. 11 (Häring, p. 134).

10. 'Illi, qui comedunt spiritualiter uel utroque modo, saluantur, in unitate Christi et ecclesie manentes, alii uero non.' (*Sententie*, c. 15 (Häring, p. 135). Cf. n. 8 above.)

11. '. . . fideles in me manere per fidem et bona opera et me manere in eis per gratiam est carnem meam et sanguinem spiritualiter comedere. Comedunt etiam hoc sacramentum spiritualiter pueri et plures martires qui quamuis non parent uentrem et dentes, fide etiam percipiunt.' (*Sententie*, c. 12 (Häring, p. 134). Cf. c. 14 (ibid., p. 135), c. 50 (ibid., p. 142), 1 Cor. 11: 29 (ibid., fol. 51^r), 1 Cor. 11: 27 (ibid.).)

12. 'Prouecti enim et recte credentes nec criminalibus irriti sanctorumque spiritu confirmati debent communicare.' (*Sententie*, c. 61 (Häring, p. 144).) Cf. c. 13 (ibid., p. 134). 'Qui uero sic accipit mysterium (unitatis), ut pacis teneat uinculum, manet in corpore christi semper uiuens de corpore christi.' (1 Cor. 10: 16-17 (Pembroke 78, fol. 49^r). 1 Cor. 10: 31 (ibid., fols. 49$^{v \cdot r}$), 1 Cor. 11: 26 (ibid., fol. 50^v) and Hebrews 10: 19-22 (ibid., fol. 128^r).)

13. 'Et ideo, quamvis, sciamus aliquem in aliquo criminali manentem, non debemus ei denegare corpus Christi si querat nisi sit extra communionem ecclesie positus et publicatus.' (*Sententie*, c. 49 (Häring, p. 141).)

14. '. . . sicut baculus positus in aqua uidetur esse fractus nec tamen est, sic et corpus Christi, cum uidetur frangi, non frangitur.' (*Sententie*, c. 25 (Häring, p. 137).) Cf. also Ch. 2, n. 227.

15. 'Ad quod dicimus quod quamdiu uisibilis species panis et uini apparet et quamdiu retinet saporem panis et uini tantum manet nobiscum corporaliter. Ex quo uero saporem panis et uini amittit, manet nobiscum spiritualiter, non corporaliter. Dicere uero quod sequatur uiam aliorum ciborum hereticum est.' (*Sententie*, c. 46 (Häring, p. 141).)

16. *Commentarius porretanus in primam epistolam ad Corinthios*, pp. xii-xv.

17. I can detect no direct borrowing from William in this work. It would appear that the author's approach is original.

18. '. . . spiritualis gratia, qua omnes predestinati inter se et capiti Christo

corporaliter uniuntur, ut unum corpus sint ipsi et Christus' (Landgraf, p. 183). Cf. Landgraf, pp. 177-8.

19. '. . . unione spiritualis vivificationis, qua fideles uniti Christo eodem spiritu vivificantur, ut quasi unus spiritus sint ipsi et Christi' (Landgraf, p. 184).

20. 'Sed, quoniam caro et sanguis Christi sacramentum est illius unionis, illius gratie spiritualis, que nullius momenti esset, nisi eius comes esset spiritualis vivificatio, . . .' (Landgraf, p. 181). Cf. Landgraf, pp. 158, 173, 199.

21. 'Quasi, illis, qui sicut sacramento, ita re et agendi obedientia manent in unitate Ecclesiae, que est corpus Christi (Landgraf, p. 199). Cf. also Landgraf, p. 200.

22. 'Sicut enim ab omni habente annos rationis exigitur, ut omne preceptum observetur, sic et ab eo exigitur, ut statim post baptismum communicet nec aliter salvabitur vel salvandus ab Ecclesia iudicio pronuntiabitur' (Landgraf, pp. 200-1). Cf. Landgraf, p. 158.

23. Landgraf, p. 183.

24. See Landgraf, pp. 166-70; 174-6, for instance, for a treatment of the metaphysical problems concerning the real presence.

25. See Häring, *Die Zwettler Summe. Einleitung und Texte* (Münster, 1977), pp. 1-20.

26. Cc. 188, 119, 121, 130, 142, 184, 186, 202, 204, 210, 211, 215, 222 (Häring, pp. 160-1, 163, 166, 174, 177, 178, 179, 181).

27. '. . . dicimus Christum uere . . . in manibus sacerdotis in sua propria humani corporis forma et glorioso splendore inuisibiliter esse . . .' (c. 183 (Häring, p. 174)). Cf. cc. 164, 262, 269, 270, 276 (Häring, pp. 170, 188, 189, 191).

28. Cc. 120, 122, 126, 127 (Häring, pp. 161-2).

29. 'Si enim sacramentali carnis Christi manducatione uel sacramentali sanguinis ipsius potatione Christo incorporaremur—cum hec sint tam malis quam bonis communia sacramenta—fieret ut tam heretici quam scismatici essent de unitate ecclesie caritate non habent, Christi membra minime esse queunt.' (c. 127 (Häring, p. 162).)

30. Cf. cc. 117, 118, 119, 121, 202 (Häring, pp. 160, 161, 177).

31. 'Quoniam autem hec omnia ecclesia membra inuicem et cum capite unita sunt indissolubili habitu caritatis quicumque infra hanc caritatis unitatem non manserit is utique non est a iam glorificato capite assumendus in gloriam capitis iam glorificati. Nemo enim nisi qui per caritatem manserit in corpore membrum assumendus est in gloriam future resurrectionis.' (c. 159 (Häring, p. 169).) Cf. cc. 122, 133, 161, 224, 225, 236 (Häring, pp. 161, 163-4, 170, 181, 183).

32. 'Sunt denique alii qui rebus sacramenti qualitercumque communicant dum a rectitudine fidei minime exorbitant et pacis unitatem ecclesiastice utcumque conseruant qui, quoniam uite honestatem aliquibus corrumpentes enormitatibus metuunt conscientiam, sacramentis communicare uerentur.' (c. 225 (Häring, p. 181).) Cf. cc. 221, 230, 237 (Häring, pp. 180-1, 182, 183-4).

33. Cc. 233-6 (Häring, p. 183).

34.   Cc. 171-4, 179, 182, 216, 276 (Häring, pp. 172, 173, 174, 179-80, 191).
35.   '. . . species autem panis atque uini in mysticas ymagines quibus tam caro Christi et sanguis quam perfecti et imperfecti in ecclesia fideliter significantur in quibus etiam totus Christus et integer et indiuisus uidetur et tangitur et presens adoratur . . .' (c. 276 (Häring, p. 191)).
36.   'In hac enim communione sacramentorum dum species uisibiliter dissoluuntur conuertuntur quocumque modo consumuntur Christus impassibiliter inconsumptus manet.' (c. 216 (Häring, p. 180).) Cf. cc. 120, 122, 126, 127 (Häring, pp. 161, 162).
37.   Neither work can be dated with accuracy, although the *Summa 'Nostre iustitie et salutis'* was a source for the *Sententie divinitatis* and hence predates it. The *Sententie divinitatis* in its present form appears to be an interpolated and expanded copy of the work from the School of Gilbert condemned at the Council of Reims in 1148. The section on the Eucharist contains material from the *Summa sententiarum*, the *De sacramentis* of Magister Simon, and the *Summa 'Nostre iustitie'*. On the question of the milieu from which these works arose, cf. the introduction to the edition of the *Sententie divinitatis* by Bernard Geyer; Bernard Geyer, 'Neues und Altes zu den *Sententiae divinitatis*', *Mélanges Joseph de Ghellinck*, pp. 617-30, and Ludwig Hödl, 'Der Transsubstantiationsbegriff in der scholastischen Theologie des 12. Jahrhunderts', *RThAM* 31 (1964), 241-8.
38.   'Unde datur intelligi quod illi tantum digne participant corpore et sanguine domini qui in unitate ecclesie catholice uinculo caritatis et pacis conueniunt et perseuerant.' (*Summa 'Nostre iustitie'* (Vatican City, Bibliotheca Vaticana, Barberini lat. MS 484, fol. 35ᵛ2).) Cf. *Sententie divinitatis*, tract. 5 (Geyer, p. 136).
39.   '. . . spiritualiter manducat non tantum dente sed corde, id est fide et operum perfectione et uirtutum imitatione opera que gessit in corpore et uirtutes quas habuit in anima, . . .' (Vat. lat. Barb. 484, fol. 36ᵛ1-2). See also n. 38 above.
40.   'Nam quos articulus necessitatis et non contemptus religionis a participatione corporis et sanguinis christi excludit, accipiunt rem sacramenti sed non sacramentum, . . .' (*Summa 'Nostre iustitie'* (Vat. lat. Barb. 484, fol. 36ᵛ1)). Cf. *Sententie divinitatis*, tract. 5 (Geyer, p. 136).
41.   Geyer, pp. 136-7.
42.   Tract. 5 (Geyer, pp. 136-7). 'Illi qui nec digne nec indigne accedunt, sunt illi qui de suis criminibus confessi nec tamen adhuc per satisfactionem mundati. . . . Si vero in spe miserentis Dei accipere volunt, . . . poterit eis esse ad salutem' (Geyer, p. 137).
43.   Cf. Landgraf, *Introduction*, pp. 113-24; N. M. Häring, 'Simon of Tournai and Gilbert of Poitiers', *Mediaeval Studies* 27 (1965), 225-330.
44.   On the career of Simon see Joseph Warichez's introduction to his edition of the *Disputationes*; Hödl, *Schlusselgewalt*, pp. 222-5, and Richard Heinzmann, *Die 'Institutiones in sacram paginam' des Simon von Tournai*, pp. 7-23. See also N. M. Häring, 'Simon of Tournai', pp. 325-30, where the dependence of Simon on Gilbert is discussed.

45. 'Duo sunt corpora Christi. Unum materiale, quod sumpsit de virgine; et spirituale collegium, collegium ecclesiasticum. Sed spirituale adeo coherens est Christo vinculo caritatis, ut confectio materialis corporis fiat propter salutem spiritualis.' (*Disputatio* 71 (Warichez, p. 203).)

46. Cf. Marie-Thérèse d'Alverny, *Alain de Lille*, pp. 13-14, 71, and P. Glorieux, 'Alan of Lille', *NCE* 1, 239-40. On Alan's career see d'Alverny, *Alain de Lille*, pp. 11-29.

47. *PL* 210, 720A-B.

48. Ibid., 848C.

49. A long-unresolved scholarly debate has been carried on over the authorship of this work. G. F. Rossi argues in favour of the attribution to Alan of Lille, while O. Lottin and U. Betti have raised severe doubts about such an attribution. On the whole question and for a bibliography of the debate see Landgraf, *Introduction*, p. 118 n. 337; M.-T. d'Alverny, *Alain de Lille*, pp. 64-5, and Lottin, *Psychologie et morale* vi, 107-17.

50. *De eucharistia*, c. 7 (Umberto Betti (ed.), p. 41). Cf. c. 10 (Betti, p. 44).

51. 'Suscipiunt reprobi tantum sacramentum, idest corpus Christi, et non rem, idest non unitatem Christi et ecclesiae idest non sunt de unitate illa. . . . Item illi qui sacramentum, idest corpus Christi, et rem sacramenti suscipiunt sunt fideles: fideles enim tantum sunt *de unitate Christi et ecclesiae.*' (Ibid., c. 11 (Betti, p. 44).)

52. On Raoul's career see Landgraf, *Introduction,* pp. 115-16; Johannes Gründel, *Das 'Speculum Universale' des Radulphus Ardens*, and Baldwin, *Masters, Princes and Merchants*, pp. 39-41.

53. 'Res uero tantum et non sacramentum est unitas christi et ecclesie' (Vatican City, Biblioteca Vaticana, Ottoboniana MS 880, fol. 11ʳ1).

54. 'Quoniam ut corpus christi ex multis membris purissimis conpaginatus; ita societas ecclesiastica ex multis fidelibus a crimine puris congregatur' (ibid.).

55. For Raoul's teaching see n. 231 of Ch. 3. The *Summa 'Totus homo'* argued that a thief about to be hanged ought not to be given viaticum out of reverence for the sacrament. The *Summa* concluded: 'Si ergo bene credat, spiritualiter, non sacramentaliter communicat.' (*De eucharistia*, c. 34 (Betti, p. 70).) The question of giving viaticum under such circumstances was also discussed by Gilbert of La Porrée, *Epistola ad Matthaeum abbatem* (*PL* 188, 125B); *Sententie*, c. 50 (Häring, p. 141) and Peter the Chanter, *Summa Abel* (Vat. lat. 1003, fol. 14ʳ1).

56. On Gerhoh's life, cf. Peter Classen, *Gerhoh von Reichersberg*, and the article on Gerhoh by the same author in *DS* 6 (1967), 303-8.

57. On Gerhoh's stand against Anacletus, and his disagreement with Bernard, see Classen, *Gerhoh von Reichersberg*, pp. 78-9. On the uniqueness of Gerhoh's stand in this regard see Artur Landgraf, *Dogmengeschichte der Frühscholastik*, part 3, vol. ii, pp. 240-3.

58. Gerhoh had earlier referred to the ineffectual consecration of the sacraments by those outside the Church in his *Epistola ad Innocentium papam*, written in 1131 (*MGH*, Libelli de lite, iii, 203-39). For the dating of the works of Gerhoh and the editions of his works, I have used the list of works given by Classen, *Gerhoh*, pp. 407 ff., unless otherwise stated.

59.   However, as Damien Van den Eynde points out in his article, 'The Theory of the Composition of the Sacraments in Early Scholasticism', *Franciscan Studies* 11 (1951), 7-9, Gerhoh based his general sacramental theory mainly on baptism and the Eucharist.

60.   *MGH*, Libelli de lite, iii, 258.

61.   Ibid.

62.   Ibid., p. 261.

63.   'Nam in eo quod consecratur nec ipsum individuum corpus Domini significat, sed est corpus Domini transfuso in se Dei verbo per fidem passionis, resurrectionis, et ascensionis . . . Nam est corpus Domini, significat autem unam ecclesiam, quae licet et ipsa sit corpus Domini: aliud tamen est corpus Domini redimens, aliud corpus Domini redemptum' (ibid.).

64.   'Signum ergo vel sacramentum unitatis etiam extra unitatem potest esse; sed ipsa unitas ut dixi extra semetipsam non potest esse, nec potest quisquam indivisibilem unitatem dividere' (ibid., pp. 261-2).

65.   Ibid., p. 262.

66.   'Unitas enim ecclesie nequaquam potest intus et extra esse; sed in una ecclesia est unitas indivisa' (ibid., p. 261). Cf. n. 63.

67.   '. . . fideles digne sacramentis participantes et in unitate perseverantes per ea . . .' (ibid., p. 262).

68.   Cf. Classen, *Gerhoh*, pp. 121-8, 248-72; idem, 'Aus der Werkstatt Gerhohs von Reichersberg: Studien zur Entstehung und Überlieferung von Briefen, Briefsammlungen und Widmungen', *Deutsches Archiv für Erforschung des Mittelalters namens der Monumenta Germaniae Historica* 23 (1967), 80-3. For a discussion of Gerhoh's theology of the Eucharist in the *Liber contra duas haereses* see Classen, *Gerhoh*, pp. 126-7 and Henri du Lubac, 'La *res sacramenti* chez Gerhoh de Reichersberg', *Études de critique et d'histoire religieuses*, pp. 35-42.

69.   The letter was written by Hugh in 1127 and discovered by Gerhoh possibly in 1146. For a discussion of the literature on this letter see Classen, *Gerhoh*, p. 126 and n. 30. On the eucharistic theology of Hugh see Ch. 3, pp. 79-80, 180.

70.   *PL* 149, 1179B.

71.   Ibid., 1179D-1180B.

72.   Ibid., 1180D-1181A.

73.   Ibid., 1181A.

74.   Ibid., 1181B-C.

75.   'Est quidem etiam peccatoribus, et indigne sumentibus intra Ecclesiam vera Christi caro, verusque sanguis, sed specie sacramentali, et carnis, quae non prodest quidquam, vera essentia non re, aut rei efficientia' (ibid., 1180B). '. . . *caro* per essentiam *non prodest quidquam* communicantibus, vel ministrantibus intra Ecclesiam nisi ubi Spiritus per rem, et effectum vivificat eum qui digne ministrat, vel communicat' (ibid., 1181C).

76.   'Qui enim in hoc sacramento remissionem peccatorum percipit, effectu ejus potietur, dum transit ipse in corpus Christi, et fit membrum corpus Christi, . . .' (ibid., 1180C).

77.   Classen, *Gerhoh*, pp. 412-16, dates this work *c*.1144-67/8.

78. Gerhoh referred to his dependence on these works in his commentary on Ps. 33 (Damien Van den Eynde, Odulf Van den Eynde, and Angelinus Rymersdael (eds.), *Opera inedita*, p. 209). Gerhoh quoted extensively from Hugh, *De sacramentis* and Rupert, *De divinis officiis* (Van den Eynde *et al.*, pp. 181-9, 209-21).

79. Ps. 33: 2 (ibid., p. 165). Cf. the commentary on Ps. 17: 37 (*PL* 193, 883A-B) and l. 2, c. 76 of Gerhoh's *De investigatione antichristi* (Friedrich Scheibelberger, *Opera inedita*, i. 337).

80. Ps. 33: 2 (Van den Eynde *et al.*, pp. 178-9). Gerhoh mentioned this teaching several times in commenting on this psalm (ibid., pp. 176, 190-1, 221). The essential unity of which Gerhoh spoke was that of the Church with Christ: 'Vultus autem eiusdem regis David in evangelio sacrificio essentialiter et praesentialiter exhibitus, eos pleniter satiat quos mystica virtute sibimetipsi sic incorporat ut sint duo in carne una, sponsus et sponsa, Christus et Ecclesia, caput et membra.' (Ps. 33: 2 (ibid., p. 173).)

81. 'Haec *esca* est et sacramentum et res atque virtus unitatis membrorum et capitis in corpore Christi, quod est Ecclesia.' (Ps. 68: 22 (*PL* 194, 254D).)

82. The basic study of Abelard's career is still J. G. Sikes, *Peter Abailard*, but several important studies have appeared since that work. See, for instance, A. Victor Murray, *Abaelard and St. Bernard*, pp. 8-16, 32-46; D. W. Robertson, Jr., *Abelard and Heloise*; E. M. Buytaert (ed.), *Peter Abelard*; *Pierre Abélard-Pierre le Vénérable*, esp. pp. 271-520, and the works cited in Landgraf, *Introduction*, pp. 78-84.

83. On Abelard's condemnations at Soissons and at Sens see the works mentioned in n. 82 and Raymond Oursel, *La Dispute et la grace: Essai sur la rédemption d'Abélard*, and David E. Luscombe, *The School of Peter Abelard*, pp. 103-42.

84. Richard E. Weingart, *The Logic of Divine Love*, pp. 193-5, discusses the few references to the Eucharist which appear in Abelard's *Problemata Heloissae*. See also Robert Hermanns, *Petri Abaelardi ejusque primae scholae doctrina de sacramentis*, pp. 71-9 for a discussion of the eucharistic theology of Abelard and his school.

85. William wrote his *Disputatio* in 1138 or 1139 (see Luscombe, *The School of Peter Abelard*, p. 106). The 9th *capitulum* treats of this subject: 'Dicit etiam magister Petrus de sacramento altaris, substantia panis et vini mutata in substantiam corporis et sanguinis Domini ad peragendum sacramenti mysterium, accidentia prioris substantiae remanere in aera' (*PL* 180, 280C).

86. 'Legitur et alium, quem dicunt Sententiarum ejus, . . . quod sentiat . . . de Sacramenti altaris.' (*Epistola* 199 (*PL* 182, 353B-C).) Cf. also Bernard, *Epistola* 332 (ibid., 537D) and William of St. Thierry, *Epistola* (ibid., 532B).

87. William's source for this teaching may also have been the lost *Liber sententiarum*, since this book formed one of the sources for William's knowledge of Abelard's teachings. On the existence of such a work, and Bernard's and William's use of it, see Heinrich Ostlender, 'Die

Sentenzenbücher der Schule Abaelards', *Theologische Quartalschrift* 117 (1936), 208-52.

88. Luscombe, *The School of Peter Abelard*, p. 143.
89. On the *Sententie Florianenses* see the introduction to H. Ostlender's edition of this work; Ermenegildo Bertola, 'Le ''Sententiae Florianenses'' della scuola di Abelardo', *Sophia* 18 (1950), 368-78, and Luscombe, *The School of Peter Abelard*, pp. 153-8.
90. On the *Sententie Parisienses I* see the introduction to the edition of this work by Artur Landgraf, *Écrits théologiques de l'école d'Abélard*, pp. xiii-xl, and Luscombe, *The School of Peter Abelard*, pp. 158-64. On the *Sententie Hermanni* see Ostlender, 'Die Sentenzenbücher', pp. 210-15; and Luscombe, *The School of Peter Abelard*, pp. 158-64.
91. See Ostlender, 'Die Sentenzenbücher', pp. 210-13.
92. Ibid., pp. 230-42.
93. 'Quaeritur, cuius sit signum illud corpus quod est in altari. Dicimus, quod alterius corporis quod est ecclesia.' (*Sententie Florianenses* (*SF*), c. 66 (Ostlender, p. 30).) Cf. *Sententie Parisienses I* (*SPI*) (Landgraf, p. 41), and *Sententie Hermanni* (*SH*), c. 29 (*PL* 178, 1741A).
94. *SF*, c. 67 (Ostlender, pp. 30-1); *SPI* (Landgraf, p. 41) and *SH* (*PL* 178, 1741C).
95. 'Nam multos videmus salvos, qui non comederunt carnem filii hominis sicut parvulos et etiam multos adultos.' (*SF*, c. 67 (Ostlender, p. 30).) '. . . *Qui manducat carnem meam et bibit sanguinem meum in me manet* (John 6: 57). Non de sacramento dixit, quia multi de corpore suo sunt, qui hoc sacramentum non accipiunt et multi accipiunt, qui ejus membra non sunt.' (*SH* (*PL* 178, 1741C).)
96. Cf. *SF*, c. 71 (Ostlender, p. 31); *SPI* (Landgraf, p. 40) and *SH* (*PL* 178, 1741A).
97. 'Quaeritur, an forma illa sit in aliquo subiecto. Dicimus quod non. Queritur ubi sit. Potest esse in aere.' (*SF*, c. 70 (Ostlender, p. 31).) 'Si enim nolumus dicere quod illius corporis sit haec forma, possumus satis dicere quod in aere sit illa forma ad occultationem propter praedictam causam carnis et sanguinis reservata, sicut forma humana in aere est, quando angelus in homine apparet.' (*SH* (*PL* 178, 1743D).) The *Sententie Parisienses I* gives two answers to this question, that of the other tracts, and that of Guitmund of Aversa (see Landgraf, p. 43 and Ch. 2, pp. 48-9, 154.
98. 'Frangi etiam videtur nec frangitur quod saporem habet panis. Hoc fit propter nostram salutem.' (*SF*, c. 71 (Ostlender, p. 31).) Cf. *SH* (*PL* 178, 1742B).
99. Cf. *SF*, c. 70 (Ostlender, p. 31) and *SPI* (Landgraf, p. 43).
100. Cf. *SPI* (Landgraf, p. 43), *SH* (*PL* 178, 1743A-B).
101. Cf. *SF*, c. 72 (Ostlender, p. 32); *SPI* (Landgraf, pp. 43-4), and *SH* (*PL* 178, 1744A).
102. On the history of the commentary see Luscombe, *The School of Peter Abelard*, pp. 145-53.
103. '. . . ''nonne est participatio corporis'', id est nonne ostendit nos esse participes alterius corporis Christi, quod videlicet est ecclesia.' (1 Cor. 10: 16 (Artur Landgraf (ed.), pp. 257-8).)

104. 1 Cor. 11: 20-3 (ibid., p. 265).
105. This opinion continued to be recorded throughout the 12th and into the 13th century. For a partial list of works which refer to this teaching see Artur Landgraf (ed.), *Commentarius porretanus in primam epistolam ad Corinthios*, p. 174 n. 173 and Joseph Geiselmann, 'Zur Eucharistielehre der Frühscholastik', *Theologische Revue* 29 (1930), 5. Thomas Aquinas mentioned, but rejected, this teaching in his *Summa theologiae, tertia pars*, q. 77, art. 1, *respondeo* (Leonine edn. 12, 193).
106. On Roland and Omnebene, their careers, and relationship to the School of Abelard, see Luscombe, *The School of Peter Abelard*, pp. 224-59.
107. The identification of Magister Roland of Bologna with Roland Bandinelli has been seriously questioned by John Noonan, who discusses the arguments for and against the attribution in his article, 'Who was Roland?', *Law, Church, and Society. Essays in Honor of Stephen Kuttner* (Philadelphia, 1977), pp. 21-48.
108. *Sententie* (ed. Ambrose Gietl (Freiburg, 1891), p. 216).
109. Ibid. (Gietl, p. 229).
110. Ibid. (Gietl, pp. 229-30).
111. 'Sed queritur de corpore Domini, quodmodo sit visible signum invisiblis gratie. Dicimus, quod illud quod videtur corpus Domini, est signum unionis et fidei, qua fideles uniti sunt, . . .' (ed. Holböck, *Der mystische Leib*, p. 132 n. 25).
112. 'Duplex enim assumptio est, corporalis et spiritualis. Corporalis est re assumere, spiritualis unio corporis Christi, i.e. unitas Ecclesie.' (Ibid., p. 132 n. 26.)
113. On the influence of Abelard on Robert see Luscombe, *The School of Peter Abelard*, pp. 281-98.
114. According to R. Martin, *Œuvres de Robert de Melun* iii, vi-x, the 3rd part of Robert's *Sententie*, which dealt with the sacraments, is not known to have survived in any MS.
115. 'Significat autem corpus Christi quod specie panis et vini sumitur, que ex diversis vel granis vel acinis conficiuntur, corpus Ecclesie quod ex diversis colligitur. Corpus vero Ecclesie ibi tantum significatur.' (1 Cor. 10: 3 (Raymond Martin (ed.), *Œuvres de Robert de Melun* ii, 207-8).)
116. 'Et non mirum, si hec sumptio signum sit unius unionis, cum omnia quecumque fuerint in Ecclesia presenti signa sint eorum que erunt in futuro. . . . Et hoc est rerum veritate sumere, id est non figurative.' (Questio 38 (ibid., 1, 23). On the dating of these two works (*c.*1145-57), see Luscombe, *The School of Peter Abelard*, p. 281 n. 4.
117. The commentary and the influence upon it by Abelard and Robert of Melun has recently been discussed by Rolf Peppermüller, 'Zum Fortwirken von Abaelards Römerbriefkommentar in der mittelalterlichen Exegese', *Pierre Abélard-Pierre le Vénérable*, pp. 557-67. The *Notule in epistolas Pauli*, 1. 6-8 (*PL* 175, 879-924) is an abridgement of this gloss, and carries the same eucharistic theology (cf. *PL* 175, 916A-B). On the *Notule* see Peppermüller, ibid., pp. 565-7 and Ch. 3, n. 122 above.
118. 'Item corpus christi quod ibi sumitur corpus significat ecclesie, sanguis

uero karitatem, . . . Significata tamen sunt corpus christi quod est ecclesia et karitas per quam unitur capiti suo quod est christus et in qua tamquam in sanguine uita est huius corpus.' (1 Cor. 11: 20 (Vatican City, Biblioteca Vaticana, Ottoboniana lat. MS 445, fol. 116ᵛ2).)

119. 'Ideo enim dicit eum qui a christo discordat, christi carnem non manducare, quia per hanc manducationem christo non incorporatur. Causam habet sed effectus non sequitur.' (1 Cor. 11: 28 (ibid., fol. 118ᵛ1).)

120. 'Efficationem enim hanc non uirtuti sacramentorum attribuit, sed fidei. Ex fide siquidem erat quod huius erant efficatie.' (1 Cor. 10: 3 (ibid., fols. 112ᵛ2-113ʳ1).)

121. 'Si uero in mortale peccato se esse non inuenit, quia sine cotidianis non est, peniteat de ipsius et communicet . . .' (1 Cor. 11: 28 (ibid., fol. 118ᵛ1)).

122. 'Uidetur itaque sufficens nobis ad salutem, si panem (celestis) hunc spiritualiter tantum manducemus, et non sacramentaliter, corde et non ore. Sed hoc propter eos dictum est qui in articulo necessitatis positi ad sacramentum accedere non possunt. Non solum corporis christi, sed et baptismatis, quibus idem est, uelle quod accipere et deuotio reputatur pro opere.' (1 Cor. 10: 4 (ibid., fol. 113ʳ2).)

123. For 2 excellent studies on excommunication in the Middle Ages see F. Donald Logan, *Excommunication and the Secular Arm in Medieval England*, Pontifical Institute of Medieval Studies, Studies and Texts, No. 15 (Toronto, 1968) and Elizabeth Vodola, 'The Status of the Individual Within the Community According to Ecclesiastical Doctrine in the High Middle Ages' (University of Cambridge, Ph.D Thesis, 1975). A study of the important question of the relationship between the social practice of excommunication and the Eucharist falls outside the scope of this study, but deserves serious consideration.

124. The practice adopted in the 12th century depended on the Council of Agde for legitimization: 'Saeculares, qui natale domini, pascha, & pentecostem non communicaverint, catholici non credantur, nec inter catholicos habeantur.' (c. 18 (Mansi 8, 327D).) This passage was copied often in the 12th century. On the history of receiving communion 3 times a year see Browe, *Pflichtkommunion*, pp. 34-40. The practice did differ somewhat according to local custom. On the whole question of lay reception in this period see Browe, *Pflichtkommunion*, pp. 27-44, and *Die häufige Kommunion*, pp. 19-32.

125. Browe, *Pflichtkommunion*, pp. 40-2. See also Walter Dürig, 'Die Scholastiker und die communio sub una specie', *Kyriakon. Festschrift Johannes Quasten*, ii, 867-8.

126. Mansi 22, 1007E-1010A. For a discussion of the importance of this decree see Browe, *Pflichtkommunion*, pp. 42-4.

127. The custom of receiving the sacrament on special occasions is discussed at length by Browe, 'Zum Kommunionempfang des Mittelalters', *Jahrbuch für Liturgiewissenschaft* 12 (1932), 161-77.

128. In 1235-7, Gregory IX required monthly communion for the Benedictines among the decress of his reform Bull (Browe, *Die häufige*

Kommunion, p. 69). The Cistercian general chapter of 1134 also required monthly communion (ibid., 74-5).

129. In addition to the works of Browe mentioned above, Joseph Duhr, 'Communion fréquente', *DSAM* 2 (1953), 1234-92 also offers a discussion of infrequency of reception in the Middle Ages.

130. Browe, *Die häufige Kommunion*, pp. 134-8.

131. The decree forbids both simony and attacks on the custom of giving offerings for the sacrament: 'Quapropter & pravas exactiones super his fieri prohibemus, & pias consuetudines praecipimus observari: statuentes, ut libere conferantur ecclesiastica sacramenta, sed per episcopum loci, veritate cognita, compescantur qui malitiose nituntur laudabilem consuetudinem immutare.' (c. 66 (Mansi 22, 1054D-E).)

132. This is the interpretation, for example, of the Synod of Tours held in 1239: 'Item innovamus, ut sacramento ecclesiastica gratis exhibeantur: inhibentes, ne pro eis antequam fiant, aliquid petatur, seu etiam exigatur. Quibus gratis exhibitis, poterit peti quod de pia consuetudine exigi consuevit: subditos ad hoc per praelatos censura ecclesiastica compellendo.' (C. 4 (Mansi 23, 498E).)

133. Browe, 'Die Kommunion in der Pfarrkirche', *Zeitschrift für katholische Theologie* 53 (1929), 477-516; *Pflichtkommunion*, pp. 47-63.

134. Browe, 'Die Nuechternheit vor der Messe und Kommunion im Mittelalter', *Ephemerides liturgicae* 45 (1931), 279-87; idem, 'Die Kommunionvorbereitung in Mittelalter', *Zeitschrift für katholische Theologie* 56 (1932), 408-12.

135. Browe, 'Die Kommunionvorbereitung', p. 376.

136. Ibid., pp. 376-405; Browe, *Pflichtkommunion*, pp. 3-26. See also Louis Braeckmans, *Confession et communion au moyen âge et concile de Trent*, Recherches et syntheses, section de morale, 6 (Gembloux, 1971).

137. 'Confessores, nomina confitentium scribant, & ad episcopum ad synodum deferant.' The injunction is included in c. 7 (Mansi 22, 767C) of an appendix to the Constitutions of Cardinal Guala for Paris, *c.*1208. Entitled *Additiones Willelmi Parisiensis episcopi*, they were promulgated, it seems, either by some William, bishop for a short time between the episcopacies of Maurice of Sully, 1196-1208 and that of Peter of Nemours, 1208-19; or by Peter's successor, William of Seignelay, bishop from 1219-23. Both Mansi 22, 765-6, and John W. Baldwin, *Masters, Princes and Merchants*, i, 69, ii, 136 adopt the first view. See also Browe, *Pflichtkommunion*, pp. 114-18.

138. A good example of this combination of motives occurred in c. 10 of the decrees of the Council of Paris in 1212: 'Similiter prohibemus, ne excommunicatum aliquem, vel interdictum, vel penitus ignotum, vel alienum parochianum laicum, in praejudicium primi sacerdotis, vel ad sepulturam, vel ad communionem eucharistiae scienter aliquis sacerdos admittat, praecipue in solennitate (recte: solemnitate) paschali' (Mansi 22, 822A). See also Browe, *Pfarrkirche*, p. 58; *Pflichtkommunion*, p. 59.

139. 'Sed, si eum publica fama vel crimen accusat, nullo modo accedat, nec sacerdos ei det. Si enim tali det, seu gratia seu pecunia, Christum,

quantum in se est, occidit.' (Commentary on 1 Cor. 11: 28 (Raymond M. Martin (ed.), *Œuvres de Robert de Melun*, vol. ii, *Questiones theologice de epistolis Pauli*, p. 214).)

140. Browe, *Pflichtkommunion*, p. 114. See, for instance, c. 13 of the Council of Toulouse, 1229: 'Nam si quis a communione, nisi de consilio proprii sacerdotis, abstinuerit, suspectus de haeresi habeatur' (Mansi 23, 197C).

141. 'Sed et validiorem ponamus casum. Iste fecit furtum, et confessus est sacerdoti, nec tamen satisfacit; sacerdos excommunicat quotidie eum qui fecit furtum, illum compellente civi (ecclesiae), cui est furtum. Prohibebit-ne sacerdos talem si petat (eucharistiam)? Non, ne si neget ei, videntibus omnibus, accuset scelus fratris sui. Est enim adhuc civis, non hostis. Sed si nominatim excommunicatus esset, tunc prohibendus esset, videntibus etiam omnibus.' (*Questio* 329 of *Questiones magistri Odonis Suessionensis* (Jean-Baptiste Pitra (ed.), *Analecta novissima spicilegii Solesmensis alter continuatio*, vol. ii, *Tusculana*, p. 174)). The same teaching appears in a summarized form in a commentary on Gilbert of La Porrée's commentary on the Psalms found in Vatican City, Biblioteca Vaticana, Ottoboniana lat. MS 863, fol. 33ᵛ1. Friedrich Stegmüller, *Repertorium biblicum medii aevi*, No. 5669 attributes this work to Nicholas of Amiens, a student of Gilbert, who died some time after 1203.

142. 'Sacerdos debet dare eucharistiam ei quem scit esse in mortale si petat in publico. Dummodo non sit notorium crimen eius, sed in occulto debet denegare et nulla ratione dare, sed in publico petenti debet dare. Non solum propter scandalum, sed praecipue ne publicet crimen.' (*Questiones* (Cambridge, St. John's College, MS C.7 [57], fol. 204ʳ1). See also the *Notule super IIII librum sententiarum*: 'Occulto peccatori instanter exigenti corpus christi tempore assignato in ecclesia conferendum est corpus christi ne si forte negaretur sacramentum, ita publicaretur eius peccatum' (Vatican City, Biblioteca Vaticana, Reginensis lat. MS 411, fol. 71ʳ). The *Notule*, an early 13th-century commentary on Peter Lombard's *Sentences*, cites Langton among other theologians. On the dating and sources of the *Notule* see Artur Landgraf, 'Sentenzenglossen des beginnenden 13. Jahrhunderts', *RThAM* 10 (1938), 36-46.

143. 'Nam si forte cum populo in quo habitant, ad audiendum missas, sive etiam ad percepiendam Eucharistiam accedunt, omnino hoc simulatorie faciunt, ne infidelitas eorum possit notari.' (Eckbert of Schönau, *Sermones contra catharos, sermo* 2 (*PL* 195, 15C); cf. *sermo* 11, c. 10 (ibid., 90A-B).) Eckbert, the brother and biographer of the famous Elisabeth of Schönau, wrote his sermons against the Cathars in 1163. On his writings see Arno Borst, *Die Katharer*, pp. 6-7. See also Baldwin of Canterbury, *Tractatus de sacramento altaris* (J. Morrison (ed.), p. 456) and Peter of Blois, *De disciplina claustrali* (*PL* 202, 1339B-C). Peter the Chanter may also be referring to this kind of reception in his *Summa Abel*: 'Alii causa simulationis recipiunt de quibus dicit apostolus qui man. car.' (Vatican City, Biblioteca Vaticana, Vaticana lat. MS 1003, fol. 14ʳ1.)

144. Browe, *Die häufige Kommunion*, pp. 139-43.
145. This is the thesis of James Megivern, *Concomitance and Communion*. He holds that the theological doctrine of concomitance developed only after the practice of reception under one species. Cf. W. Dürig, 'Communio sub una specie', p. 867, who agrees with Megivern's thesis and offers corroborative evidence.
146. Browe, 'Wann fing man an, die Kommunion asserhalt der Messe auszuteilen', *Theologie und Glaube* 23 (1931), 755-62.
147. Most medieval authors follow the *Glossa ordinaria* on Ps. 21: 30: '*Manducauerit*. Augustinus. Non prohibeat dispensator manducare: sed exactorem moneat timere' (*Textus biblie cum Glossa Ordinaria* ... , vol. iii, fol. 115^v). I have been unable to locate this passage in Augustine. Other authors who follow the *Glossa* on this point include Gilbert of La Porrée, *Commentaria in psalmis* 21, 30 (Vatican City, Biblioteca Vaticana, Vaticana lat. MS 89, fol. 18^{r}1), *Sententie*, c. 49 (Häring, p. 141); Peter Lombard, *Commentaria in psalmis* 21: 30 (ibid., Vaticana lat. MS 90, fol. 64^{v}2); Peter the Chanter, *Summa Abel* (ibid., Vaticana lat. MS 1003, fol. 14^{r}2); Stephen Langton, *Questiones* (St. John MS C.7, fol. 204^{r}1); Peter of Capua, *Summa 'Uetustissima ueterum'* (Vatican City, Biblioteca Vaticana lat. MS 4304, fol. 66^{r}2); *Sententie divinitatis* (Bernhard Geyer (ed.), p. 137); *Notule super IIII librum sententiarum* (Vat. Reg. lat. MS 411, fol. 71^r). This sentence of 'Augustine' is also included in *Gratian, Decretum, De cons.*, dist. 2, c. 67 (Emil Friedberg (ed.), *Corpus Iuris Canonici* 1. 1338).
148. 'Queritur etiam utrum proxerio suo debeat sacerdos a damnatione eterna quantumcumque potest cauere quod uerbum esse patet ex eo quod proximum suum tamquam si ipsum debet diligere. ... Ergo corpus domini debet ei negare quia si ille suscepit, ei ad dampnationem erit.' (*Commentarius in Gilberti psalmos*, Ps. 21: 30 (Vat. Ottob. lat. MS 863, fol. 33^{v}2).) Cf. also Stephen Langton, *Questiones* (St. John MS C.7, fol. 204^{r}1-2); Peter of Capua, *Summa* (Vat. lat. MS 4304, fol. 66^{v}1); and *Notule* (Vat. Reg. lat. MS 411, fols. 71^v-72^r).
149. e.g. 'Item aliquis existens in mortale quod non uult deserere in pascha petit panem benedictum ut uitet scandalum, sed sacerdos deceptus, dat ei eucharistia (*recte*: eucharistiam) pro pane benedicto. Queritur utrum peccet mortaliter sumendo.' (Stephen Langton, *Questiones* (St. John MS C.7, fol. 204^{v}1).) The practice appears to continue into the 14th century as it is banned by the Council of Pisa in 1320 (Browe, *Die häufige Kommunion*, p. 135 n. 4).
150. Ch. 3, pp. 101-2, 196; Ch. 5, pp. 135, 217.
151. On the Lombard's life and works see the excellent introduction to the 1971 edition of his *Sententie* by the Collegium S. Bonaventurae, pp. 8-148.
152. 'Res autem significata, et non contenta est unitas Ecclesiae in praedestinatis, vocatis, justificatis et glorificatis.' (1 Cor. 11: 23-4 (*PL* 191, 1642A) = *Sententie*, l. 4, d. 8, cc. 6-7 (Collegium S. Bonaventurae, p. 791).)
153. Commentary on 1 Cor. 10: 1-4 (*PL* 191, 1618C-1620A).
154. 1 Cor. 10: 17 (ibid., 1624B). Cf. 1 Cor. 11: 18 (ibid., 1637B); 1 Cor.

11: 23-4 (ibid., 1642C-D) = *Sententie*, l. 4, dist. 8, cc. 6-7 (Collegium S. Bonaventurae, p. 792).

155. 1 Cor. 10: 16-18 (*PL* 191, 1624C). Cf. 1 Cor. 11: 23-4 (ibid., 1643C-D).

156. The Lombard quotes Fulgentius of Ruspe on this teaching in his commentary on 1 Cor. 10: 16-18 (ibid., 1624C-D) = *Sententie*, l. 4, dist. 9, c. 1 (Collegium S. Bonaventurae, 794). For the text of Fulgentius see Ch. 2, n. 30.

157. 'Spiritualiter enim manducat, qui in unitate Christi et Ecclesiae quam ipsum sacramentum significat manet. . . . De hac spirituali manducatione ait Augustinus: Utquid paras dentem et ventrem? crede et manducasti.' (1 Cor. 11: 26-9 (*PL* 191, 1647C-D) = *Sententie*, l. 4, dist. 9, c. 1 (Collegium S. Bonaventurae, p. 793).) Cf. 1 Cor. 11: 23-4 (*PL* 191, 1643C-D).

158. *PL* 192, 1095B. On Bandinus and his *Abbrevatio* see E. Dhanis, 'Bandinus', *DHGE* 6 (1932), 488-9 and L. Hödl, *Schlüsselgewalt*, p. 197.

159. On Udo and his work see A. Landgraf, 'Udo und Magister Martinus', *RThAM* 11 (1939), 62-4; Lottin, *Psychologie* vi, 9-18; Joseph N. Garvin, 'Magister Udo, a Source of Peter of Poitiers' *Sentences*', *New Scholasticism* 28 (1954), 286-8; idem, 'The Manuscripts of Udo's *Summa super sententias Petri Lombardi*', *Scriptorium* 16 (1962), 376, and Johnnes Gründel, *Die Lehre von den Umstanden der menschlichen Handlung in Mittelalter*, pp. 139-46.

160. 'Est ibi sacramentum et res sacramenti ut corpus christi materiale, quod significatum est a predicta specie et significant unitatem ecclesie predicta similitudine est, etiam ibi quiddam quod tantum est res et non sacramentum, ut corporis christi quod est ecclesia' (Vatican City, Biblioteca Vaticana, Palatina lat. MS 328, fol. 59^{v}1).

161. '. . . omnes fideles qui ex deuocione accedunt ad percipiendum inde sacramentum, qui suscipunt rem sacramenti, scilicet unitatem ecclesie que est uero caro christi spiritualis . . .' (Vat. Pal. lat. 328, fol. 59^{v}2).

162. 'Quidam uero suscipiunt rem sacramenti et non sacramentum ut fideles qui habent ecclesiasticam unitatem et non habent tempus accedendi ad sacramentum qui uere tamen corpus christi, sicut dicit Augustinus: Ut quid paras dentem et uentrem? Crede et manducasti' (ibid.).

163. 'Sed sucipere (*recte*: suscipere) corpus domini prohibitum est omni existenti in mortale peccato, . . .' (ibid., fol. 60^{r}1).

164. On the identification and dating of Gandulphus's work see the introduction to the edition of his *Sententie* by John de Walter, and A. Landgraf, 'Drei Trabanten des Magisters Gandulphus von Bologna', *Collectanea franciscana* 7 (1937), 357-73.

165. L. 4, c. 101 (de Walter, pp. 442-3). Cf. l. 4, c. 106 (ibid., p. 444).

166. '. . . nisi tantae fuerint voluntates malae, ut pro operibus earum, vel nisi tanta fuerint opera mala, ut pro operibus illis sit dignus excommunicari, "non se debet a medicina corporis" domini "separare", qualia omnia mortalia peccata intelligenda videntur.' (l. 4, c. 134 (ibid., p. 458).)

167. L. 4, c. 134 (de Walter, p. 457). Gandulphus quoted the *Decretum* of Gratian, de cons., d. 2, c. 16.
168. On the life and writings of Arnold see Guy Oury, 'Recherches sur Ernaud, Abbé de Bonneval, historien de Saint Bernard', *Revue Mabillon* 268 (1977), 97-127, and Jean Leclercq, 'Les méditations eucharistiques d'Arnaud de Bonneval', *RThAM* 13 (1946), 40-56. Dom Leclercq has edited in this article additional devotional material on the Eucharist attributed to Arnold, and corrected the faulty editions of the eucharistic passage of the *Liber de cardinalibus operibus Christi*.
169. I have used the edition of John Fell, *Arnoldi Carnotensis abbatis Bonaevallis opera* included in his 3rd edition of the works of St. Cyprian, *S. Caecilii Cypriani opera recognita & illustrata* . . . (Amsterdam, 1700). Leclercq recommends Fell's text as better than that of Nicolai Rigalti (Paris, 1648) printed in *PL* 189, 1609A-1678A. I have also used the corrected passage suggested by Leclerq, pp. 53-4.
170. Cf. Fell, p. 57, note to *prologus*.
171. 'Panis est esca, sanguis vita, caro substantia, corpus Ecclesia. Corpus, propter membrorum in unum convenientiam; panis propter nutrimenti congruentiam; sanguis, propter vivificationis efficientiam; caro, propter assumtae humanitatis proprietatem . . . & non tam corporali, quam spirituali transitione Christo nos uniri. Ipse enim & panis, & caro, & sanguis, idem cibus & substantia, & vita factus est Ecclesiae suae; quam corpus suum appellat, dans ei participationem Spiritus' (Fell, p. 74b). 'Corpus suum se et ecclesiam suam, cuius caput ipse est, intelligi uoluit, quam carnis et sanguis sui communione uniuit' (corrected text by Leclercq, p. 53).
172. 'Panis iste quem Dominus discipulis porrigebat non effigie sed natura mutatus, omnipotentia Verbi factus est caro, et sicut in persona Christi humanitas uidebatur et latebat diuinitas, ita sacramento uisibili ineffabiliter diuina se infudit essentia, ut esset religioni circa sacramenta deuotio, . . .' (Leclercq, p. 53).
173. '. . . et ad ueritatem cuius corpus sacramenta sunt sincerior pateret accessus, usque ad participationem spiritus, non quidem usque ad consubstantialitatem Christi, sed ad societatem germanissimam eius haec unitas peruenisset' (ibid.).
174. 'Solus quippe Filius Patri consubstantialis est, nec diuisibilis est, nec partibilis substantia Trinitatis' (ibid.).
175. '. . . nostra uero et ipsius coniunctio nec miscet personas, nec unit substantias, sed affectus consociat et confoederat uoluntates. Ita ecclesia corpus Christ effecta obsequitur capiti suo . . .' (ibid.). Cf. n. 135.
176. 'Ita ecclesia corpus Christi effecta obsequitur capiti suo et superius lumen in inferiora diffusum claritatis suae plenitudine *a fine usque ad finem attingens*, totum apud se manens, totum se omnibus commodat, et caloris illius identitas ita corpori assidet ut a corpore non recedat' (ibid.).
177. '. . . animalis vitae peccata, quasi sanguinem impurum horrentes & fatentes nos per peccati gustum à beatitudine privatos & damnatos, nisi

nos Christi clementia ad societatem vitae aeternae suo sanguine reduxisset' (Fell, p. 75b).

178. 'Esus igitur carnis hujus quaedam aviditas est, & quoddam desiderium manendi in ipso, per quod sic imprimimus & eliquamus in nobis dulcedinem caritatis, ut haereat palato nostro & visceribus sapor dilectionis infusus, penetrans & imbuens omnes animae corporisque recessus' (Fell, p. 76a).

179. 'Verum hi qui verbo tenus corde sicci & mente aridi sacris intersunt, vel etiam participant donis; lambunt quidem petram, sed inde nec mel sugunt, nec oleum: qui nec aliqua caritatis dulcedine, nec Spiritus sancti pinguedine vegetantur, . . .' (Fell, p. 77a).

180. See Ch. 5, pp. 133-6, 217-18.

181. For what little information is known about Simon see the introduction by his editor, Henri Weisweiler, *Simon et son groupe. De sacramentis*, and Hödl, *Schlüsselgewalt*, pp. 102-3. See also Häring, 'Die Sententie magistri gisleberti', *Archives d'histoire doctrinale et littéraire du moyen âge*, 45 (1978), 95-7.

182. Weisweiler, p. 25.

183. 'Dici potest, quod in sacramentum altaris duo sunt, id est corpus Christi verum, et quod per illud significatur: corpus eius misticum, quod est Ecclesia' (ibid., p. 27).

184. Weisweiler, p. 34.

185. '. . . (malus) rem sacramenti non accipit, quia communicando Ecclesie Christi non unitur' (ibid.).

186. 'Bonus utrumque accipit, quia et corpus Domini manducat, et manducans in corpore eius, quod est Ecclesia, esse laborat' (ibid.).

187. 'Sepe enim, qui in sacramento aliqua necessitate prepeditus corpus Domini non suscipit, in unitate Ecclesie mente et voluntate perseverat, et sic quasi non manducans manducat, dum ab esu veri corporis Christi se abstinet et tamen ab unione mistici corporis, quod est Ecclesia, se non removet' (ibid., p. 51).

188. Weisweiler, p. 35.

189. For a more detailed discussion of Simon's theology of the Eucharist see Weisweiler, *Magister Simon*, pp. cxxix-clxv.

190. On the life and works of Peter Comestor see the introduction to the critical edition of his *De sacramentis* by Raymond M. Martin, *Pierre Mangeur. De sacramentis*; R. M. Martin, 'Notes sur l'œuvre littéraire de Pierre le Mangeur', *RThAM* 3 (1931), 54-66; A. Landgraf, 'Recherches sur les écrits de Pierre le Mangeur', *RThAM* 3 (1931), 292-306, 341-72; Saralyn R. Daly, 'Peter Comestor: Master of Histories', *Speculum* 32 (1957), 62-73, and esp. the critical estimation of the Comestor's career by Ignatius Brady, 'Peter Manducator and the Oral Teachings of Peter Lombard', *Antonianum* 41 (1966), 483-90. On the Comestor's work as a biblical commentator see Beryl Smalley, *The Study of the Bible in the Middle Ages*, esp. Ch. 5, and idem, 'Peter Comestor on the Gospels and His Sources', *RThAM* 46 (1979), 84-129.

191. 'Tria enim sunt in illo sacramento: unum quia est sacramentum et non res, ut forma panis; secundum quod est res et sacramentum, ut caro

christi materialis; tercium quod est res et non sacramentum, ut caro christi spiritualis. . . . Nomine carnis et sanguinis uel cibi et potus intelligitur unitas capitis et membrorum in patria que uere tollit famem et prestat eternam satietatem.' (John 6: 57 (Rome, Biblioteca Vallicelliana, MS B.47, fol. 188ᵛ2).) Cf. *De sacramentis* (Martin, p. 35). On the Comestor's use of the Lombard's theology see Landgraf, 'Pierre le Mangeur', esp. pp. 343-50.

192. '. . . *est ecclesia in predestinatis*, quibusdam in eis, scilicet que iam glorificati sunt et bene ait in predestinatis, et si enim quidam reprobi boni sunt secundum presentem iusticiam et si sunt de unione ecclesie, in uia numquam tamen erunt de unione patrie. . . . Ecce exponit quando factum sit in uocatis et iustificatis, scilicet in spe *huius rei sacramentum* id est corpus christi materiale, quod sacramentum est collectionis fidelium in illam unionem.' (John 6: 57, commentary on Augustine, *Tractatus 26 in Iohannis* (Corpus christianorum 35, p. 267) (Vallicelliana, B.47, fol. 189ʳ1).)

193. '. . . manducare eius carnem nichil est alium quam ipsum habere in se manentem, id est in eum credere. De qua manducatione ait augustinus: Ut quid paras dentem et uentrem, crede et manducasti.' (John 6: 57 (Vallicelliana B.47, fol. 188ᵛ2).) Cf. John 6: 52 (ibid., fol. 188ᵛ1) and John 6: 49 (ibid.).

194. '. . . de unione hoc corporis (spiritualis) non est aliquis nisi per fidem, uel ab ipso christo accepitur ecclesia per fidem.' (Mark 14: 24 (Vallicelliana B.47, fol. 94ʳ1).) '. . . que spiritualiter manducata panis uiuus est, et hoc distat inter manducationem carnis christi et alteris cibi. Quia cum alius cibus, ab homine comederitur ipsi homini incorporatur, sed cum caro christo ab homine manducatur, ipse homo carni dominice incorporatur. Hoc autem non intelligendum de manducatione sacramentali, que fit ad cornu altaris, sed de spiritualis que est per fidem. Per quam, scilicet corporalem manducationem, homo peccato mortuus incorporatur, id est corpori eius, scilicet ecclesie unitur et statim spiritu christ manus quamdum est de compage corporis uiuificatur.' (John 6: 52 (ibid., fol. 188ᵛ1-2).)

195. On Robert Pullen's life and works see Francis Courtney, *Cardinal Robert Pullen. An English Theologian of the Twelfth Century.* Robert wrote his *Sententie c.*1142-4.

196. L. 8, c. 4 (*PL* 186, 965C).

197. L. 8, c. 2 (ibid., 961D).

198. See Ch. 3, pp. 101, 195.

199. L. 8, c. 7 (*PL* 186, 968D-969A).

200. 'Sic confici ex multis et purissimis granis conveniens est sacramentum corporis, quod est compactum ex mundissimis membris. Ex qua etiam similtudine, et speciem illam et corpus Domini dicimus esse sacramentum unitatis Ecclesiae, quae solummodo sacrum et secretum et non sacrum signum.' (*Questiones, pars* 2, q. 266 (Jean-Baptiste Pitra (ed.), *Analecta novissima Spicilegii Solesmensis*, vol. ii, p. 92).) For a recent criticism of the authenticity of these questions see Ignatius Brady, 'Peter Manducator', pp. 454-90. The *questiones* cited in the thesis come

from a group of questions which Brady appears to accept as genuine (pp. 461-5). On Odo's teaching career see L. Hödl, *Schlüsselgewalt*, pp. 116-30.

201. '. . . ita per hanc communionem multi fideles in unum corpus Ecclesiae conveniant, ex quibus quasi electis granis corpus unum Ecclesiae conficiatur, propter quod corpus redimendum Dominus uenit, et suum corpus quod in altari sumimus, in passionem mortis tradidit.' (*Pars* 2, q. 38 (Pitra, pp. 37-8).)

202. Dom Lottin, 'Questiones inédites de Hugues de Saint-Victor', *RThAM* 27 (1960), 47, has suggested that this *questio* represents an early stage in the teaching of Hugh of St. Victor on the Eucharist and that this *questio* was the source for the *Summa sententiarum*. Particularly on the important questions of the *res sacramenti* and the practice of spiritual communion, this work differs from either Hugh's *De sacramentis* or the *Summa sententiarum* (see Ch. 3, pp. 82-6, 182-6).

203. '. . . sacramentum que signat et efficit capitis et membrorum unionem, cum qua talem habet similitudinem, quod sicut multa membra sibi corpus unit, ita et illa unio spiritualis multos fideles in unum iungit, . . . Res uero tantum est illa unio spiritualis qua soli predestinati participant.' (Lottin, 'Questiones inédites', p. 44.)

204. Lottin, pp. 45-6, e.g. 'Corpus Christi sumendum est a fidelibus, non tantum invisibiliter, id est spiritualiter, scilicet fide operante creditur, sed etiam sacramentaliter, id est sensualiter, ut unitas conseruetur ecclesie et ut sit viaticum nobis ne deficiamus in hac peregrinationis uia. In presenti enim dignos promouet ad Christum in futuro associabit; hunc panem cotidie fides comedere debet' (ibid., p. 46).

205. Sacramentaliter etiam comestio, saltem semel in anno, necessaria est, quia unit ecclesie, remittit peccatum, munit contra peccatum' (ibid., p. 47).

206. 'Ipsa ecclesiastica unitas, res est et non sacramentum signatum et non significans.' (*Sententie*, l. 5, c. 10 (*PL* 211, 1242A).) On other aspects of Peter's theology of the Eucharist see Ch. 3, pp. 101, 195-6.

207. 'Unitas uero ecclesie est tantum res.' (*Questiones* (St. John's MS C.7, fol. 207r1).) '. . . uniusquisque debet tollere quia quicumque catholicus communicare debet condigne corpore et sanguine domini.' (Commentary on Ex. 12: 3 (Cambridge, Trinity College MS B.3.7, fol. 146r2).) On other aspects of Langton's thought on the Eucharist see Ch. 3, pp. 101-2, 196.

208. 'Et res tantum et non sacramentum, scilicet unitas ecclesie.' (*Notule* (Vat. Reg. lat. 411, fol. 70v).) On the *Notule* see n. 142 above. The *Summa* exists in Hague, Museum Meer-Manno-Westreenianum MS 10.B 33, fols. 160r-197v. On the identification of this author with the later chancellor to Baldwin of Flanders see Boeren, 'Traité eucharistique', *Archives d'histoire doctrinale et littéraire du moyen âge* 45 (1978), 184-8. The *Summa* copies Peter of Poitiers on the Eucharist (Hague MS 10 B 3, fols. 193v-195r = *PL* 211, 1241C-1257A).

209. On the life and works of Praepositinus see Georges Lacombe, *Praepositini cancellarii Parisiensis (1206-1210) opera omnia*, vol. i, *La Vie et les œuvres de Prevostin*. For a recent updating of this work see Daniel

Edward Pilarczyk, *Praepostini cancellarii De sacramentis et de novissimis* (*Summae theologicae pars quarta*), pp. 1-11, and James A. Corbett, *Praepositini Cremonensis Tractatus de officiis*, Publications in Mediaeval Studies, 21 (Notre Dame, Indiana, and London, 1969), pp. xi-xvi.

210. 'Item dicitur quod in illo sacramento tria sunt, unum quod est tantum sacramentum, sc., species panis et vini; unum quod est sacramentum et res, corpus Christi quod traxit de virgine et sanguis; aliud quod est tantum res, corpus Christi quod est ecclesia.' (*Summa* (Pilarczyk, p. 84).)

211. 'Possunt ergo predicta verba sic exponi. *Iube hec perferri*, etc., idest iube per hoc corpus tuum quod est ecclesia in sublime altare tuum perferri, idest corpori tuo in conspectu divine maiestatis tue consociari.' Ibid. (ibid., p. 92).)

212. On the relatively few facts known about this master see Damien Van den Eynde, 'Notices sur quelques "Magistri" du XIIe siècle', *Antonianum* 29 (1954), 136-41; Hödl, *Schlüsselgewalt*, pp. 250-3 and Richard Heinzmann, *Die 'Compilatio quaestionum theologiae secundum Magistrum Martinum'*, pp. 3-5.

213. Cambridge, St. John's College MS C.7 (57), fols. 1^{r}1-8^{v}2. The title is very faded and I give here the transcription by M. R. James, *A Descriptive Catalogue of the Manuscripts in the Library of St. John's College, Cambridge* (Cambridge, 1913), p. 74. Perhaps the rubric refers to a period spent by Magister Martinus at Canterbury, thus giving a new clue to his identity.

214. 'Similiter et sacramentum eucharistie est sacramentum necessitatis in adultis' (St. John's MS C.7, fol. 8^{v}1-2).

215. 'Item dicit augustinus in libro de remedio penitentie anime: Ut quid paras dentem et uentrem. Credere et manudcasti. Ergo si habeat quis fidem huius articuli et aliorum qui necessarii sunt ad salutem, fidem dico uirtutem sufficit ei ad salutem etsi numquam sumat sacramentaliter carnem Christi. Ergo semper possumus non sumere hoc sacramentum sine detrimento uirtutis' (ibid., fol. 123^{v}1).

216. 'Econtra dicit decretum. Etsi non frequentius saltem ter in anno homines communicent: in pascha, uidelicet, et penecostes et natali domini' (ibid.).

217. 'R. Hoc uerbum ut quid paras dentem et uentrem male intelligentes quidam dixerunt quod posset quis abstinere a perceptione eucharistie. Sed non est ita. Immo talis est sensus huius auctoritatis, ut quid paras dentem et cetera, necessitate instante non obest alicui si non accipit sacramentum altaris ex quo per eum stat' (ibid.).

218. 'Et nota quod in sacramentis tria considerantur, scilicet forma, potestas et unio ... Cum enim sacramentum corporis Christi sacramentum sit unitatis, extra unitatem et ab unitatis impugnatoribus confici non potest' (ibid., fol. 123^{v}2). The source of this division is the canonical tract, the *Summa Monacensis*, which offered the triad: *potestas, forma, ecclesiae unitas*. On this point see Van den Eynde, 'Notices sur quelque "Magistri"', p. 137.

219. *Tractatus de sacramentis*, c. 79 (Damien and Odulf Van den Eynde (eds.),

p. 80). On Guy's life and works see the introduction by his editors, pp. ix-xviii. P. C. Boeren, *La Vie et les œuvres de Guiard de Laon* (1170 env.-1248) (The Hague, 1956), pp. 3-4 has corrected the dating of the *Tractatus* by the Van den Eyndes. Cf. D. Van den Eynde, 'Notices sur quelque "Magistri"', pp. 141-2.

220. *Tractatus*, c. 74 (Van den Eynde, p. 76).

221. 'Manere in Christo et habere Christum in se manentem non est divinam habere in se caritatem, sed potius contritum esse de peccatis, et habere propositum non peccandi: . . .' (ibid., c. 73 (ibid., p. 74).).

222. Ibid., c. 92 (ibid., p. 94).

223. 'Ad hoc dici potest quod tantum valet bona voluntas quantum voluntas et opus si desit facultas; sed quod augetur caritas ex susceptione, non est ex merito sed ex virtute sacramenti.' (Ibid., c. 99 (ibid., p. 100).) Cf. ibid., c. 75 (ibid., p. 76).

224. Commentary on the Canticle of Canticles, Cant. 3: 7 (*PL* 195, 1134C-D). On Wolbero and his commentary see F. Ohly, *Hohelied-Studien*, pp. 271-6.

225. 'Uel ita materialis caro christi est sacramentum carnis spiritualis ipsius, id est ecclesie et sanguis materialis est sacramentum spiritualis sanguinis. Carne eius materiali et sanguine etiam utroque inuisibili istud patet, uel secundum hanc lectionem, significatur corpus christi uisibile et passibile uel palpabile, id est ecclesia.' (*Summa 'Uetustissima ueterum'* (Vatican City, Biblioteca Vaticana, Vaticana lat. MS 4296, fol. 70ʳ1).) On Peter of Capua and his work see Grabmann, *Scholastischen Methode* ii, 532-4 and Artur Landgraf, 'A Study of the Academic Latitude of Peter of Capua', *New Scholasticism* 14 (1940), 57-74.

226. 'Et notandum quod species panis et uini est hoc sacramentum tantum, quia forma panis et uini que ibi uidetur est sacramentum, id est sacre rei signum. Significat enim corpus christi quod sumpsit de uirgine quod est res predicti sacramenti et sacramentum unitatis et pacis uel caritatis ecclesiastice que est res tantum et non sacramentum.' (*Summa* (Vatican City, Biblioteca Vaticana, Vaticana lat. MS 10754, fol. 36ᵛ1).) On Gerard and his work see Artur Landgraf, 'Die Quellen der anonymen *Summe* des Cod. Vat. *lat.* 10754', *Mediaeval Studies* 9 (1947), 296-400; Thomas Kaeppeli, 'Gerardus Novariensis auteur de la Somme "Ne transgrediaris"', *RThAM* 29 (1962), 294-7, and Landgraf, *Introduction*, p. 157.

227. '. . . aliquid res et non sacramentum, ut corpus Christi spirituale quod est ecclesia, scilicet congregatio fidelium seu unitas congregatorum; . . .' (*Historia occidentalis* (Hinnebusch, p. 211).) On Jacques, his career, and his writings, see the introduction to J. F. Hinnebusch's edition of the *Historia*, pp. 1-30.

228. For an example of the use of this basic notion as a 'model' for understanding the Church see Avery Dulles, *Models of the Church* (New York, 1978), pp. 50-66. This particular approach to the Eucharist is important for modern theologians; see, for instance, Tad Guzie, *Jesus and the Eucharist* (New York, 1974), Monika Hellwig, *The Eucharist and the Hunger of the World* (New York, 1976), and Tissa Balasuriya, *The Eucharist and Human Liberation* (Maryknoll, New York, 1979).

229. See Ch. 2, pp. 59, 162.
230. See Ch. 2, pp. 56-7, 159-60.

CHAPTER V

1. On William of Auxerre's life and works see Walter Principe, *William of Auxerre's Theology of the Hypostatic Union*, pp. 14-16; Hödl, *Schlüsselgewalt*, pp. 365-6; Jules St. Pierre, 'The Theological Thought of William of Auxerre. An Introductory Bibliography', *RThAM* 33 (1966), 147-55, and Jean Ribailler, 'Guillaume d'Auxerre', *DS* 6 (1967), 1192-9.
2. *Psychologie et morale* iv, 846-7.
3. St. Pierre, 'The Theological Thought of William of Auxerre', p. 147.
4. *Summa aurea*, 1. 4 (edn. of Paris, 1500 [?]), fol. 257ᵛ1).
5. Ibid. (ibid., fol. 257ᵛ2).
6. Ibid. (ibid., fol. 258ᵛ1).
7. Ibid. (ibid.)
8. '. . . spiritualiter sumitur quando per fidem incorporamur christo. De quo modo dicit Augustinus: Crede et manducasti.' (Ibid. (ibid.).
9. Ibid. (ibid., fol. 258ᵛ1-258ᵛ2). William compared the stages of spiritual eating to those of corporeal eating. A similar comparison exists in a *sententia* from the 'School of Laon', see Ch. 3, n. 41.
10. Ibid. (ibid., fols. 258ᵛ2-259ᵛ1).
11. Ibid. (ibid., fol. 258ᵛ2). The opening statements use a *sed, ergo* construction, and are followed by arguments *contra*. The whole section is resolved by a *solutio*.
12. 'Qui enim de unitate ecclesie est, uiuit de eodem spiritu de quo et christus uiuit, secundum hoc manducare corpus christi spiritualititer (*recte*: spiritualiter) est ecclesie incorporari, id est, esse de unitate ecclesie uel incipere esse membrum christi; uel magis ac magis ei uniri, . . .' (ibid., fol. 259ᵛ2).
13. 'Secundo modo spiritualiter manducare corpus christi est per fidem incarnationis eius ei unire et assimilari, . . .' (Ibid. (ibid.)).
14. '. . . accipit simplicem hostiam et credit se accipere corpus christi non minus peccat quam si acciperet corpus christi: . . .' (Ibid. (ibid., fol. 261ʳ2)).
15. 'Quantum ergo ad meritum uite eterne equaliter merentur illi duo: qui equales caritates habent; et unus accipit simplicem hostiam; alius hostiam consecratam. Sed non equaliter merentur quantum ad dimissionem uenialium uel dimissionem pene, uel augmentum gratie: quia ille qui accipit simplicem hostiam non manducat corpus christi nisi spiritualiter; sed alius et spiritualiter et sacramentaliter et sacramentalis modus comedendi quando est cum spirituali multum prodest.' (Ibid., fol. 261ᵛ1.)
16. '. . . unde simulatio et mendacium ibi non debet habere locum; sed debet ei dicere, "Crede et manducasti".' (Ibid. (ibid.).)
17. Ibid. (ibid., fols. 260ᵛ2-261ʳ1).
18. See Ch. 3, p. 89 and n. 142.
19. '. . . dicimus quod aspicere corpus christi non est, . . . peccatum, imo

bonum est, . . . aspicere corpus christi prouocatiuum est ad dilectionem dei. Unde per huiusmodi aspicere exercitat et preparat se ad dilectionem et multorum petitiones exaudiuntur in ipsa uisione corporis christi.' (*Summa aurea*, l. 4 (Paris, 1500 [?], fols. 260ᵛ2-261ʳ1).)

20.   For the dating of William's work see Joseph Kramp, 'Des Wilhelm von Auvergne "Magisterium divinale"', *Gregorianum* 1 (1920), 538-84, 2 (1921), 42-78, 174-87.

21.   *Guilielmi alverni episcopi parisiensis . . . Opera omnia*, printed by B. Leferon (Paris, 1674), fol. 449bA-D.

22.   'Nulli enim dubium est, quod absque cordiali unitione Dei, quae verus, ac sanctus amor est, nulli umquam fuit, vel est, vel erit vitae (*recte*: vita) aeterna' (ibid., fol. 430bH).

23.   Ibid., fols. 449bD ff.

24.   'Communio ergo in patre spirituali, qui est Christus Dominus omnium regeneratorum, & communio victus spiritualis, quae est causa maximè conservans esse spirituale, id est vitam gratiarum communicatio domus spiritualis, idest Ecclesiae, . . .' (ibid., fol. 448bF).

25.   On the dating of William's work see the introduction by Caelestinus Piana, one of the editors of his *Questiones de Sacramentis*, pp. 24-8.

26.   'Si autem velimus extendere nomen boni, ita quod sub magno sive summe bono comprehendatur corpus Christi, dicemus quod tunc dicitur haberi, quando fide operante per dilectionem habetur; non enim dicitur haberi cum habetur in pyxide vel in ore, sicut nec virtutes dicuntur haberi cum habentur in cognitione vel intellectu, sed solum cum informant animam.' (Q. 43, n. 9 (ed. C. Piana and Gedeon Gal, vol. ii, pp. 691-2).)

27.   '. . . non sumentes sacramentaliter, sed tamen credentes virtutem et veritatem sacramenti, spiritualiter tantum, secundum quod dicit Augustinus: "Crede et manducasti"; et haec manducatio unit corpore mystico.' (Q. 44, n. 8 (ibid., ii, 695-6).)

28.   On the dating of this work see Franz-Joseph Nocke, *Sakrament und personaler Vollzug bei Albertus Magnus*, BGPTM 41/4 (Münster, 1967), p. 9.

29.   'Unde sicut in aliis sacramentis est, ita est his, quod spirituale non est sine sacramentali, sed sacramentale potest esse sine spirituali propter obstaculum, quod invenit in suscipiente sacramentum.' (*Tractatus* 5, *pars* 2, q. 2 (Albert Ohlmeyer (ed.), p. 66).)

30.   I have used the dates for this work given by Martin Grabmann, *Die Werke des hl. Thomas von Aquin. Eine literahistorische Untersuchung und Einführung*, BGPTMA 22/1-2 (Münster, 1949).

31.   '. . . ita etiam aliqui manducant spiritualiter hoc sacramentum antequam sacramentaliter sumant. . . . propter desiderium sumendi ipsum sacramentum, et hoc modo dicuntur baptizari et manducare spiritualiter et non sacramentaliter, illi qui desiderant sumere haec sacramenta . . .' (*Summa theologiae*, 3a, 80, 1, *ad* 3 (Leonine edn., vol. xii, p. 229).

32.   'Frustra autem esset votum nisi impleretur quando opportunitas adesset. Et ideo manifestum est quod homo tenetur hoc sacramentum

sumere, non solum ex statuo Ecclesiae, sed ex mandato Domini . . .'
(ibid., 3a, 80, 11, *respondeo* (ibid., 12, 243)).

33. Mansi 22, 981-2.

34. Most modern writers still refer to the Council in these terms. For two
recent examples see *The Oxford Dictionary of the Christian Church* (2nd
edn., London, 1974), s.v. Eucharist (p. 476) and s.v. Lateran Councils
(p. 802); Pelikan, *The Growth of Medieval Theology*, p. 203.

35. Stone, *A History of the Doctrine of the Holy Eucharist*, vol. i, p. 313; Joris-
son, *Die Entfaltung*, e.g. pp. 54-64; James McCue, 'The Doctrine of
Transubstantiation from Berengar through the Council of Trent',
Lutherans and Catholics in Dialogue. III. The Eucharist (New York and
Washington, 1967), pp. 89-124.

36. McCue, pp. 94-102.

BIBLIOGRAPHY

Works written before 1500

Abbaudus. *De fractione corporis Christi*. Edited by Jean Mabillon. *Vetera analecta*. 2nd rev. edn. Paris, 1723, pp. 52-5. Reprinted *PL* 166, 1341-1348.

Peter Abelard. *Theologia christiana*. Edited by Eligius Buytaert. *Petri Abaelardi opera theologica*. Corpus christianorum, continuatio mediaeualis, 12. Turnhout, 1969.

Adam of Dryburgh. *De tripartito tabernaculo*. Edited by Godfried Ghiselbrecht. *Eximii d. magistri Adami praemonstratensis Opera* . . . Antwerp, 1659, pp. 328-449. Reprinted *PL* 198, 609-792.

Alan of Lille. *Contra haereticos*. Edited by Karl de Visch. *Alani magni de Insulis* . . . *Opera* . . . Antwerp, 1654, pp. 201-278. Reprinted *PL 210, 306-430*.

—— *Liber in distincionibus dictionum theologicalium*. Edited anonymously Deventer, 1477?, Strasbourg, 1474? Reprinted *PL* 210, 685-1612.

Albert the Great. *De sacramentis*. Edited by Albert Ohlmeyer. *Alberti magni ordinis fratrum praedictorum Opera omnia*. Vol. xxvi. *De sacramentis*. Aschendorff, 1958.

Alger of Liège. *De sacramentis corporis et sanguinis Dominici*. Edited by J.B. Malou. Louvain, 1847. Reprinted *PL* 180, 749-854.

Anselm of Alexandria. *Tractatus de hereticis*. Edited by Antoine Dondaine. 'La hiérarchie cathare en Italie. II. Le Tractatus de hereticis d'Anselme d'Alexandrie, O.P.', *Archivum fratrum praedicatorum* 20 (1950), 234-329.

Arnold of Bonneval. *Liber de cardinalibus operibus Christi*. Edited by John Fell. *S. Caecilii Cypriani Opera recognita & illustrata* . . . *Opuscula vulgo adscripta* . . . , pp. 56-92. 3rd edn. Amsterdam, 1700.

Augustine. *Ennarratio in psalmos*. Edited by the monks of St. Peter's, Steenbrugge, *Sancti Aurelii Augustini Enarrationes in psalmos*. Corpus christianorum. Series latina, 38-40. Turnhout, 1956.

Augustine. *Tractatus XXVI in evangelium Ioannis*. Edited by the monks of St. Peter's, Steenbrugge. *Sancti Aurelii Augustini in Iohannis evangelium tractatus CXIV*. Corpus christianorum. Series latina, 36. Turnhout, 1954, pp. 323-32.

Baldwin of Canterbury. *De sacramento altaris*. Edited by J. Morson. *Baudouin de Ford. Le sacrement de l'autel*. Introduction by Jean Leclercq. Sources ehrétiennes, 93-4. Paris, 1963.

Magister Bandinus. *Sententie*. Edited anonymously Louvain, 1555. Reprinted *PL* 192, 971-1112.

Berengar of Tours. *De sacra coena adversus Lanfrancum.* Edited by W.H. Beekenkamp. Kerkhisorische Studien behoorende bij het nederlandsch Archief voor Kerkgeschiedenis, 2. The Hague, 1941.

Bruno the Carthusian. *Expositio in psalmos.* Edited by Theodor Petrae. Cologne, 1611. Reprinted *PL* 152, 637-1420.

Bruno the Carthusian (?). *Expositio in epistolas Pauli.* Edited by Theodor Petrae. Cologne, 1611. Reprinted *PL* 152, 11-566.

Caesarius of Heisterbach. *Dialogus miraculorum.* Edited by Joseph Strange. *Caesarii Heisterbacensis . . . Dialogus miraculorum.* 2 vols. Cologne, Bonn and Brussels, 1851. Reprinted Ridgeway, New Jersey, 1966.

Commentarius Cantabrigiensis in epistolas Pauli. Edited by Artur Landgraf. *Commentarius Cantabrigiensis in epistolas Pauli.* Publications in Mediaeval Studies, the University of Notre Dame, 2. 4 parts. Notre Dame, Indiana, 1937-45.

Commentarius in evangelium Iohannis. Edited by the Canons of St. Victor. *M. Hugonis de S. Victore . . . Opera omnia . . .* Vol. i. Rouen, 1648. Reprinted *PL* 175, 827-880.

Commentarius in Gilberti psalmos. Vatican City, Biblioteca Apostolica Vaticana, Ottoboniana lat. MS 863, fols. 1-55.

Commentarius in primam epistolam ad Corinthios. Vatican City, Biblioteca Apostolica Vaticana, Ottoboniana lat. MS 445, fols. 94-123.

Commentarius porretanus in primam epistolam ad Corinthios. Edited by Artur Landgraf. *Commentarius Porretanus in primam epistolam ad Corinthios.* Studi e Testi, 117 Vatican City, 1945.

Contra amaurianos. Edited by Clemens Baeumker. *Contra amaurianos. Ein anonymer, warscheinlich dem Garnerius von Rochefort zugehörigen Traktat gegen die Amalrikaner aus dem Anfang des XIII. Jahrhunderts.* BGPTMA, 24/5-6. Münster, 1929.

Durand of Huesca. *Liber antiheresis.* Edited by Kurt-Victor Selge. *Die ersten Waldenser.* 2 vols. Arbeiten zur Kirchengeschichte, 37/2. Berlin, 1967.

Durand of Troarn. *De corpore et sanguine domini.* Edited by Andria Galland. *Bibliotheca veterum patrum.* Vol. xiv, pp. 245-65. Venice, 1786. Reprinted *PL* 149, 1375-1424.

Ébrard of Béthune. *Liber contra waldenes uel antihaeresis.* Edited by Jacob Gretser. *Trias scriptorum aduersus Waldensium sectam.* Ingoldstadt, 1614. Reprinted by M. La Bigne. *Maxima bibliotheca veterum patrum . . .* Vol. xxiv, pp. 1525-84. Lyon, 1677.

Eckbert of Schonau. *Sermones contra catharos.* Edited anonymously, *Adversus pestiferos . . . Catharorum . . . damnatos errores . . .* (?, 1530). Reprinted *PL* 195, 11-98.

Elmer of Canterbury. *Compilationes Ailmeri (Sententie magistri A.).* Cambridge, University Library, MS Ii. 4. 19, fols. 31ʳ-7ʳ. Vatican

City, Biblioteca Apostolica Vaticana, Vaticana lat. MS 4361, fols. 1ʳ1-146ʳ2.

Epistola de sacramentis haereticorum. Edited by Emil Sackur. *MGH*, Libelli de lite, 3, 12-20. Hanover, 1897.

Ermengaud of Béziers. *Contra haereticos.* Edited by Jacob Gretser. *Trias scriptorum aduersus Waldensium sectam.* Ingoldstadt, 1614. Reprinted *PL* 204, 1235-1272.

Magister Gandulphus. *Sententie.* Edited by John de Walter. *Magistri Gandulphi Bononiensis Sententiarum libri quatour.* Vienna and Breslau, 1924.

Georgius. *Disputatio inter catholicum et paterinum haereticum.* Edited by Edmond Martène and Ursin Durand. *Thesaurus novus anecdotorum.* vol. v, pp. 1703-58. Paris, 1717.

Gerald of Wales. *Gemma ecclesiastica.* Edited by J.S. Brewer. *Giraldis Cambrensis opera.* Vol. ii. Rerum britannicarum medii aevi scriptores, 21/2. London, 1862.

Gerard of Novara. *Summa.* Vatican City, Biblioteca Apostolica Vaticana, Vaticana lat. MS 10754, fols. 1ʳ1-82ʳ1.

Gerhoh of Reichersberg. *De gloria et honore filii hominis.* Edited by Bernard Pez. *Thesaurus anecdotorum novissimus.* Augsburg, 1721-9. Vol. i, cols. 163-280. Reprinted *PL* 194, 1073-1160.

—— *De investigatione Antichristi.* Edited by Friedrich Scheibelberger. *Gerhohi Reichersbergensis praepositi opera hactenus inedita.* Vol. i. Linz, 1875.

—— *Epistola ad Innocentium papam.* Edited by Emil Sackur. *MGH*, Libelli de lite, 3, 203-39. Hanover, 1879.

—— *Expositionis psalmorum. Libri* 1-2, 4-8, 10 edited by Bernard Pez F.-M. Wirtenberger. *Magni Gerhohi . . . Commentarius aureus in Psalmos . . .* Augsburg and Graz, 1728. Reprinted *PL* 193, 619-1814, *PL* 194, 117-484, 729-998. *Libri* 3 and 9 edited by Damien and Odulf Van den Eynde and Angelinus Rymerdael, *Gerhohi praepositi Reichersbergensis opera omnia inedita.* 1 vol. in 2. Spicilegium pontificii athenaei, 9-10. Rome, 1956.

—— *Libellus de eo quod princeps huius mundi iam iudicatus sit (Liber de simoniacis).* Edited by Emil Sackur. *MGH*, Libelli de lite, 3, 239-72. Hanover, 1879.

—— *Liber contra duas haereses.* Edited by Bernard Pez. *Thesaurus anecdotorum novissimus . . .* Augsburg, 1721-9. Vol. i, cols. 281-314. Reprinted *PL* 194, 1161-1184.

Gezo of Tortona. *Liber de corpore et sanguine Domini.* Edited by Lodovico Antonia Muratori. *Anecdota quae ex Ambrosianae bibliothecae codibus nunc primum eruit.* Vol. iii, pp. 239 ff. Milan, 1712. Reprinted *PL* 137, 371-406.

Gilbert of La Porrée. *Commentarius in primam epistolam ad Corinthios.* Cambridge, Pembroke College MS 78.

—— *Commentarius in psalmos.* Vatican City, Biblioteca Apostolica Vaticana, Vaticana lat. MS 89, fols. 1^{r}1-225^{r}1; Vatican City, Biblioteca Apostolica Vaticana, Vaticana lat. MS 4228, fols. 1^{r}1-161^{v}2.

Glossa ordinaria. Edited anonymously, *Textus biblie cum glossa ordinaria* . . . Basel, 1506-8. (For the text of the *Glossa* on the Pauline epistles, I have used Cambridge, Pembroke College, MS 214 (12th c.) and Cambridge, University Library, MS Ff. 4. 40 (13th c.).

'Gratiadei'. *Super primam epistolam ad Corinthios.* Oxford, Bodleian Library, Theo. lat. MS c. 28, fols. 1^{r}1-150^{v}2. Partial edition by Anselme Stoelen. 'Bruno le Chartreux, Jean Gratiadei et la 'Lettre de S. Anselme sur l'eucharistie' ', *RThAM* 24 (1967), 22-65.

Gratian. *Concordantia discordantium canonum (Decretum).* Edited by Emil Friedberg. *Corpus iuris canonici.* Vol. i. Leipzig, 1879.

Gregory of Bergamo. *Tractatus de veritate corporis Christi.* Edited by H. Hurter. *Scriptorum veterum de eucharistia opuscula selecta*, pp. 1-123. Sanctorum patrum opuscula selecta, 39. Leipzig, 1879.

Guibert of Nogent. *De pignoribus sanctorum.* Edited by Jean Luc d'Achéry. *Venerabilis Guiberti . . . Opera omnia . . .* Paris, 1651. Reprinted *PL* 156, 607-680.

—— *De vita sua, sive monodiarum libri XIII.* Edited by Georges Bourgin. *Guibert de Nogent. Histoire de sa vie (1053-1124).* Paris, 1907.

Guitmund of Aversa. *De corporis et sanguinis Christi veritate in eucharistia.* Edited by M. La Bigne. *Maxima bibliotheca veterum patrum . . .* Lyons, 1677. Vol. x, pp. 440-65. Reprinted *PL* 149, 1427-1494.

Guy of Orchelles. *Tractatus de sacramentis.* Edited by Damien and Odulf Van den Eynde. *Guidonis de Orchelles. Tractatus de sacramentis et officiis ecclesiae.* Franciscan Institute Publications. Text series, 4. St. Bonaventure, New York, Louvain, and Paderborn, 1953.

Heriger of Lobbes. *Libellus de corpore et sanguine Domini.* Edited by Bernard Pez. *Thesaurus anecdotorum novissimus.* Augsburg, 1721-9. Vol. i, pp. 131-46. Reprinted *PL* 139, 179-188.

Hermann. *Sententie.* Edited by R.H. Rheinwald. *Petri Abaelardi Epitome theologiae christianae.* Berlin, 1835. Reprinted *PL* 178, 1695-1758.

Hervaeus of Bourg-Dieu. *Commentarius in epistolas Pauli.* Edited by René de Chasteigner. *Divi Anselmi Cantuariensis . . . Opera . . .* Paris, 1533. Reprinted *PL* 181, 591-1692.

Hilary of Poitiers. *De Trinitate.* Edited by F.S. Maffei. Verona, 1730. Reprinted *PL* 10, 25-472.

Honorius Augustodunensis. *Elucidarium.* Edited by Yves Lefèvre. *L'Elucidarium et les lucidaires. Contribution par l'histoire d'un texte, à l'histoire des croyances religieuses en France au moyen âge*. Bibliothèque des écoles francaises d'Athènes et de Rome, 124. Paris, 1954, pp. 359-477.

—— *Eucharisticon*. Edited by Bernard Pez. *Thesaurus anecdotorum novissimus* . . . Augsburg, 1721-9. Vol. ii, cols. 347-62. Reprinted *PL* 172, 1249-1258.

—— *Gemma animae*. Edited by Andreas Scottus in M. La Bigne. *Maxima bibliotheca veterum patrum* . . . Vol. xx, pp. 1046-1128. Lyon, 1676. Reprinted *PL* 172, 541-738.

—— *Sacramentarium*. Edited by Bernard Pez. *Thesaurus anecdotorum novissimus* . . . Augsburg, 1721-9. Vol. ii, cols. 247-346. Reprinted *PL* 172, 737-806.

Hugh of Amiens. *Dialogorum seu questionum theologicarum libri septem*. Edited by E. Marténe and U. Durand. *Thesaurus novus anecdotorum*. Paris, 1717. Vol. v, cols. 859-1000. Reprinted *PL* 192, 1141-1248.

Hugh of Langres. *Tractatus de corpore et sanguine Christi*. Edited by Jean Luc d'Achéry. *Beati Lanfranci . . . Opera omnia . . . Appendicem adiecit* . . . Paris, 1648. Appendix, pp. 68-71. Reprinted *PL* 142, 1325-1334.

Hugh Metel. *Epistolae* 26, 33. Edited by Charles Louis Hugo. *Sacrae antiquitatis monumenta historica, dogmatica, diplomatica*. Estival, 1725-31. Vol. ii, pp. 361-3, 372-4. *Epistola* 33 is also printed *PL* 188, 1273-1276.

Hugh of St. Victor. *De sacramentis Christianae fidei*. Edited by the Canons of St. Victor. *M. Hugonis de S. Victore . . . Opera omnia . . .* 3 vols., Rouen, 1648. Vol. iii, pp. 482-712. Reprinted *PL* 176, 173-618.

—— *In hierarchiam eoelestem*. Edited by the Canons of St. Victor. *M. Hugonis de S. Victore . . . Opera omnia . . .* 3 vols., Rouen, 1648. Vol. i, pp. 469-587. Reprinted *PL* 175, 925-1154.

Ioannis et apostoli et evangelistae interrogatio in coena sancta regni coelorum de ordinatione mundi, et de principe et de Adam (The Secret Supper). Edited by Johann von Döllinger. *Beiträge zur Sektengeschichte des Mittelalters*. 2 vols., Munich, 1890. Reprinted New York, n.d. Vol. ii, pp. 85-92.

Jacques de Vitry. *Historia occidentalis*. Edited by John Fredrick Hinnebusch. *The Historia Occidentalis of Jacques de Vitry. A Critical Edition*. Spicilegium Friburgense. Texts Concerning the History of Christian Life, 17. Fribourg, 1972.

—— *Vita B. Mariae Ogniacensis*. Edited in *Acta sanctorum, Junii* 4, pp. 636-66. Antwerp. 1707.

John of Mantua. *Tractatus in cantica canticorum*. Partial edition by Bernard Bischoff. 'Der Canticumkommentar des Johannes von Mantua für die Markgräfin Mathilde', *Lebenskräfte in der abendländischen Geistesgeschichte*, Dank-und Erinnerungsgabe an Walter Goetz zum 80. Geburtstage am 11. November 1947 . . . Marburg, 1948, pp. 37-48.

John of Noyon. *Summa*. The Hague, Hague Museum Meer-Manno-Westreenianum MS 10 B 33, fols. 160ʳ-197ᵛ.

Lanfranc. *Commentarius in Pauli epistolas*. Edited by Jean Luc d'Achéry. *Beati Lanfranci . . . Opera omnia . . . Appendicem adiecti . . .* Paris, 1648. pp. 7-229. Reprinted *PL* 150, 105-406.

—— *De corpore et sanguine domini*. Edited by Jean Luc d'Achéry. *Beati Lanfranci . . . Opera omnia . . . Appendicem adiecit . . .* Paris, 1648, pp. 231-51. Reprinted *PL* 150, 407-42.

—— *Epistola 33*. Edited by Jean Luc d'Achéry. *Beati Lanfranci . . . Opera omnia . . . Appendicem adiecit . . .* Paris, 1648, pp. 316-317. Reprinted *PL* 150, 532-533.

Lanfranc (?). *Sermo sive sententiae*. Edited by Jean Luc d'Achéry. *Spicilegium*. Vol. iv, pp. 227-8. Paris, 1661. Reprinted *PL* 150, 637-640.

Stephen Langton. *Glossa in glossam Petri Lombardi super epistolas Pauli*. Cambridge, University Library MS Ii. 4. 23, fols. 161ʳ1-253ᵛ2.

—— *Questiones*. Cambridge, St. John's College MS C. 7. (57), fols. 171ʳ1-345ᵛ2.

Libellus adversus errores Alberonis. Edited by Edmond Martène and Ursin Durand. *Amplissima collectio . . .* Vol. ix, pp. 1251-70. Paris, 1733.

Magister Martinus. *Questiones*. Cambridge, St. John's College MS C. 7. (57), fols. 1ʳ1-8ᵛ2.

—— *Summa questionum theologie*. Cambridge, St. John's College MS C. 7. (57), fols. 9ʳ1-144ʳ1.

Moneta of Cremona. *Adversus catharos et valdenses*. Edited by Tommaso Augostino Ricchini. *Venerabilis patris Monetae cremonensis ordinis praedicatorum . . . aduersis Catharos et Valdenses libri quinque*. Rome, 1743.

Notule in epistolas Pauli. Edited by the Canons of St. Victor. *M. Hugonis de S. Victore . . . Opera omnia . . .* 3 vols., Rouen, 1648. Vol. i. Reprinted *PL* 175, 879-924.

Notule super IIII sententiarum. Vatican City, Biblioteca Apostolica Vaticana, Reginensis lat. MS 411, fols. 60ᵛ-97ᵛ.

Odo of Ourscamp. *Questiones*. Edited by Jean-Baptiste Pitra. *Analecta novissima Spicilegii Solesmensis. Altera continuatio*. Vol. ii, Tusculum, 1888. Reprinted Farnborough, Hants, 1967, pp. 3-187.

Paschasius Radbertus. *De corpore et sanguine domini*. Edited by Bede Paulus. Corpus Christianorum, continuatio medievalis, 16. Turnhout, 1969.

Peter of Capua. *Summa 'Vetustissima veterum'*. Vatican City, Biblioteca Apostolica Vaticana, Vaticana lat. MS 4296, fols. 1ʳ1-74ʳ2. Vatican City, Biblioteca Apostolica Vaticana, Vaticana lat. MS 4304, fols. 1ʳ1-69v2.

Peter the Chanter. *Commentarius in epistolas Pauli.* London, British Library, Royal MS 10. C. 5., fols. 296ʳ1-380ᵛ2.

—— *Commentarius in psalmos.* London, British Library, Royal MS 10. C. 5., fols. 4ʳ1-170ᵛ2.

—— *Summa Abel.* Vatican City, Biblioteca Apostolica Vaticana, Vaticana lat. MS 1003, fols. 2-70.

—— *Summa de sacramentis et animae consiliis.* Edited by J.-A. Dugauquier. *Summa de sacramentis et animae consiliis* ..., 3 vols. in 5. Analecta mediaevalia Namurcensia, 4,7,11,16,21. Lille, 1954-67.

—— *Verbum abbreviatum.* Cambridge, St. John's College MS B. 8., fols. 28 ff. Edited by George Galopin. *Venerabilis Petri Cantoris ... Verbum abbreviatum* ... Montibus sub Bibliis, 1639. Reprinted *PL* 205, 23-307.

Peter Comestor. *De sacramentis.* Edited by Raymond M. Martin. *Pierre le Mangeur. De sacramentis.* Appendix to Henri Weisweiler. *Maître Simon et son groupe. De sacramentis.* Louvain, 1937.

—— *Commentarius in evangelium Marci.* Rome, Biblioteca Vallicelliana MS B. 47, fols. 55-103.

—— *Commentarius in evangelium Iohannis.* Rome, Biblioteca Vallicelliana MS B. 47, fols. 171-206.

Peter Lombard. *Collectanea in Pauli epistolas. Petri Longobardi ... In omnes D. Pauli apost. epistolas collectanea* ... (Paris) 1535. Reprinted *PL* 191, 1297-1696, *PL* 192, 9-520.

—— *Sententie.* Edited by the Collegium S. Bonaventurae. *Magistri Petri Lombardi Parisiensis episcopi Sententiae in IV libris distinctae.* For Books 1 and 2, 3rd. edn., Spicilegium Bonaventurianum cura PP. Collegii S. Bonaventuriae ad Claras Aquas, 4. Rome, 1971. For Books 3 and 4, ibid., 2nd edn. Rome, 1916.

Peter Martyr of Verona. *Summa contra hereticos.* Edited by Thomas Kaeppeli. 'Une somme contre les hérétiques de s. Pierre Martyr (?)', *Archivum fratrum praedicatorum* 17 (1947), 295-335.

Peter of Poitiers. *Sententie.* Edited by Hugo Mathoud. *Roberti Pvlli S.R.E. ... Sententiarum libri VIII. Item Petri Pictaviensis ... Sententiarum libri V.* Paris, 1655. Reprinted *PL* 211, 790-1280.

Peter the Venerable. *Contra petrobrusianos hereticos.* Edited by James Fearns. *Petri Venerabilis Contra petrobrusianos hereticos.* Corpus christianorum, continuatio mediaevalis, 10. Turnhout, 1967.

Peter of Vienna. *Summa.* Edited by N. Häring. *Die Zwettler Summe, Einleitung und Texte.* BGPTMA, Neue Folge, 15. Münster, 1977.

Praepositinus of Cremona. *Summa.* Partially edited by Daniel E. Pilarczyk. *Praepositini cancellarii de sacramentis et de novissimis* ... Rome, 1964.

Robert Pullen. *Sententie.* Edited by Hugo Mathoud. *Roberti Pvlli S.R.E. ... Sententiarum libri VIII. Item Petri Pictaviensis ... Sententiarum libri V.* Paris, 1655. Reprinted *PL* 186, 639-1010.

Questiones super epistolam primam ad Corinthios. Edited by the Canons of St. Victor. *M. Hugonis de S. Victore . . . Opera omnia . . .* 3 vols., Rouen, 1648. Vol. i, pp. 416-30. Reprinted *PL* 175, 513-544.

Raoul Ardent. *Speculum universale.* Vatican City, Biblioteca Apostolica Vaticana, Ottoboniana lat. MS 880.

Ratramnus. *De corpore et sanguine domini.* Edited by J. N. Bakhuizen van den Brink. *Ratramnus. De corpore et sanguine domini. Texte original et notice bibliographie.* Verhandelingen der koninklijke Nederlandse Akademie Wetenshappen, afd. Letterkunde. Nieuwe Reeks, 87. Amsterdam, 1974.

Pseudo-Remigius. *Ennarrationes in psalmos.* Edited by Eucarius Hirtzhorn. *Remigii episcopi Antissiodorensis . . . Ennarationum in psalmos liber unus, . . .* Cologne, 1536. Reprinted *PL* 131, 149-844.

Responsio cujusdam. Edited by Jean Luc d'Archéry. *Spicilegium.* Vol. i, pp. 149-50. Paris, 1661.

Robert of Bridlington. *Compilationes in epistolas Pauli.* Cambridge, University Library MS Dd. 8. 14, fols. 1-294.

Robert of Melun. *Questiones de divina pagina.* Edited by Raymond. M. Martin. *OEuvres de Robert de Melun,* vol. i *Questiones de divina pagina.* Spicilegium sacrum Lovaniense. Etudes et documents, 13. Louvain, 1932.

—— *Questiones (theologice) de epistolis Pauli.* Edited Raymond M. Martin. *OEuvres de Robert de Melun,* vol. ii, *Questiones (theologice) de epistolas Pauli.* Spicilegium sacrum Lovaniense. Études et documents, 18. Louvain 1938.

Magister Rolandus. *Sententie.* Edited by Ambrose M. Gietl. *Die Sententzen Rolands nachmals Paptes Alexander III.* Freiburg im Breisgau, 1891.

Rupert of Deutz. *Commentaria in evangelium sancti Iohannis.* Edited by Raban Haacke. *Ruperti Tuitiensis Commentaria in evangelium sancti Iohannis.* Corpus christianorum, continuatio mediaevalis, 9. Turnhout, 1969.

—— *De divinis officiis.* Edited by Raban Haacke. *Ruperti Tuitiensis Liber de divinis officiis.* Corpus christianorum. Continuatio mediaevalis, 7. Turnhout, 1967.

—— *De sancta Trinitate et operibus eius.* Edited by Raban Haacke. *Ruperti Tuitiensis De sancta Trinitate et operibus eius.* Corpus christianorum, continuatio mediaevalis, 21-4. Turnhout, 1971-2.

Raynier Sacconi. *Summa de catharis et pauperibus de Lugduno.* Edited by Antoine Dondaine. *Un traité néo-manichéen du XIIIe siècle, le Liber de duobus principiis suivi d'un fragment de rituel cathare.* Institutum historicum FF. Praedicatorum Romae ad S. Sabina. Rome, 1939, pp. 64-78.

Sententie Anselmi. Edited by Franz Bliemetzrieder. *Anselms von Laon systematische Sentenzen.* BGPTMA, 19/2-3. Münster, 1919, pp. 47-153.

Sententie Atrebatenses. Edited by Odon Lottin. *Psychologie et morale aux XIIe et XIIIe siècles.* Vol. v. Louvain and Gembloux, 1959, pp. 400-40.

Sententie 'Augustinus. Semel immolatus est Christus'. Edited by Heinrich Weisweiler. *Das Schrifttum der Schule Anselms von Laon und Wilhelms von Champeaux in deutschen Bibliotheken.* BGPTMA, 33/1-2. Münster, 1936, pp. 281-311.

Sententie 'Deus de cuius principio et fine tacetur'. Edited by Heinrich Weisweiler. 'Le recueil des sentences 'Deus de cuius principio et fine tacetur', *RThAM* 5 (1933), 252-74.

Sententie divine pagina. Edited by Franz Bliemetzrieder. *Anselms von Laon systematische Sentenzen.* BGPTMA, 18/2-3. Münster, 1919, pp. 3-46.

Sententie divinitatis. Edited by Bernard Geyer. *Die Sententiae divinitatis, ein Sentenzenbuch der Gilbertschen Schule.* BGPTMA, 7/2-3. Münster, 1909.

Sententie 'Dubitatur a quibusdam'. Edited by Heinrich Weisweiler. *Das Schrifttum der Schule Anselms von Laon und Wilhelms von Champeaux in deutschen Bibliotheken.* BGPTMA, 33/1-2. Münster, 1936, pp. 314-58.

Sententie Florianenses. Edited by Heinrich Ostlender. *Sententiae Florianenses.* Florilegium patristicum, 19. Bonn, 1929.

Sententie Parisienses I. Edited by Artur Landgraf. *Écrits théologiques de l'école d'Abélard. Textes inédits.* Spicilegium sacrum Lovaniense, 14. Louvain, 1934, pp. 1-60.

Sententie 'Potest queri, quid sit peccatum'. Edited by Heinrich Weisweiler. *Das Schrifttum der Schule Anselms von Laon und Wilhelms von Champeaux in deutschen Bibliotheken.* BGPTMA, 33/1-2. Münster, 1936. pp. 259-69.

Sententie 'Tribus ex causis'. Edited by Heinrich Weisweiler. *Das Schrifttum der Schule Anselms von Laon und Wilhelms von Champeaux in deutschen Bibliotheken.* BGPTMA, 33/1-2. Münster, 1936, pp. 312-14.

Sententie 'Voluntas Dei'. Edited by Odon Lottin. *Psychologie et morale aux XIIe et XIIIe siècles.* Vol. v. Louvain and Gembloux, 1959, pp. 342-52.

Magister Simon. *De sacramentis.* Edited by Heinrich Weisweiler. *Maître Simon et son groupe. De sacramentis.* Spicilegium sacrum Lovaniense. Études et documents, 17. Louvain, 1937.

Simon of Tournai. *Disputationes.* Edited by Joseph Warichez. *Les Disputationes de Simon de Tournai.* Spicilegium sacrum Lovaniense. Études et documents, 12. Louvain, 1932.

Speculum de mysteriis ecclesiae. Edited by the Canons of St. Victor. *M. Hugonis de S. Victore . . . Opera omnia . . .* 3 vols., Rouen, 1648. Vol. iii, pp. 335-6. Reprinted *PL* 176, 335-380.

Summa de sacramentis 'Cum multa sint sacramenta nove legis'. Vatican City, Biblioteca Apostolica Vaticana, Palatino MS 619, fols. 1ᵛ-17ᵛ.

Summa de sacramentis 'Totus homo'. Edited by Umberto Betti. *Summa de sacramentis 'Totus homo'.* Spicilegium pontificii athenaei antoniani, 7. Rome, 1955.

Summa 'Inter cetera alicuius scientie'. Vatican City, Biblioteca Apostolica Vaticana, Vaticana lat. MS 1345, fols. 4ʳ-211ᵛ.

Summa 'Nostre iustitie et salutis causa fides esse'. Vatican City, Biblioteca Apostolica Vaticana, Barberini lat. MS 484, fols. 1ʳ1-46ᵛ2.

Summa sententiarum. Edited by the Canons of St. Victor. *M. Hugonis de S. Victor . . . Opera omnia . . .* 3 vols., Rouen, 1648. Vol. iii, pp. 417-81. Reprinted *PL* 176, 41-174.

Thomas Aquinas. *Summa theologiae.* Edited by the Order of Preachers. *Sancti Thomae Aquinatis doctoris angelici Opera omnia iussu impensaque Leonis XIII p.m. edita.* Vols. v-xii. Rome, 1889-1906.

Magister Udo. *Abbrevatio.* Vatican City, Biblioteca Apostolica Vaticana, Palatino lat. MS 328.

Vacarius. *Liber contra multiplices et varios errores.* Edited by Ilarino da Milano. *L'eresia di Ugo Speroni nella confutazione del maestro Vacario. Testo inedito del secolo XII con studio storico e dottrinale.* Studi e Testi, 115. Vatican City, 1945.

Walter of St. Victor. *Contra quatuor labyrinthos Franciae.* Edited by P. Glorieux. 'Le Contra quatuor labyrinthos Franciae de Gauthier de Saint-Victor. Édition critique', *Archives d'histoire et littéraire du moyen âge* 19 (1952), 187-335.

William of Auvergne. *Magisterium divinale.* Edited anonymously *Guilielmi Alverni episcopi Parisienses . . . Opera omnia.* Vol. i. Paris, 1674.

William of Auxerre. *Summa aurea.* Printed by Philip Pigouchet. *Summa aurea in quattuor libros sententiarum . . .* Paris, 1500 (?). Reprinted Frankfurt, 1964.

William of Middleton. *Questiones de sacramentis.* Edited by Caelestinus Piana and Gedeon Gal. *Guillelmi de Militona Questiones de sacramentis.* Bibliotheca franciscana scholastica medii aevi, 22-3. Florence, 1961.

William de Montibus. *Super psalmos.* Oxford, Bodleian Library, Bodley MS 860, fols. 9-94.

William of St. Thierry. *De corpore et sanguine domini.* Edited by Bertrand Tissier. *Bibliothecae patrum cisterciensium . . .* Vol. iv, pp. 132-40. Bono-fonte, 1662. Reprinted *PL* 180, 343-366.

—— *Disputatio adversus Petrum Abaelardum.* Edited by Bertrand Tissier.

230   *Bibliography*

Bibliothecae patrum cisterciensium . . . Vol. iv, pp. 112-226. Bono-fonte, 1662. Reprinted *PL* 180, 249-328.
—— *Epistola ad quemdam monachum qui de corpore et sanguine domini scrip-serat.* Edited by Bertrand Tissier. *Bibliothecae patrum cisterciensium* . . . Vol. iv, pp. 130-2. Bono-fonte, 1662. Reprinted *PL* 180, 341-344.
Wolbero of Cologne. *Commentaria in cantica canticarum.* Edited by Henricus Gravius. *Commentaria vetustissima* . . . *super Canticum canti-corum* . . . Cologne, 1630. Reprinted *PL* 195, 1005-1278.
Ysagoge in theologiam. Edited by Artur Landgraf. *Écrits théologiques de l'école d'Abélard. Textes inédits.* Spicilegium sacrum Lovaniense. Études et documents, 14. Louvain, 1934. pp. 63-285.
Zachary of Besançon. *In unum ex quatuor.* Edited by Eucharius Cer-vicornus. *In unum ex quatuor sive de concordia evangelistarum* . . . (Cologne), 1535. Reprinted *PL* 186, 11-620.

Works written after 1500

d'Alverny, Marie-Thérèse. *Alain de Lille. Textes inédits avec une introduc-tion sur sa vie et ses œuvres.* Études de philosophie médiévale, 52. Paris, 1965.
Auer, Wilhelm. *Das Sakrament der Liebe im Mittelalter. Die Entwicklung der Lehre des hl. Altarsakramentes in der Zeit von 800-1200.* Mergen-theim, 1927.
Baldwin, John W. *Masters, Princes and Merchants. The Social Views of Peter the Chanter and his Circle.* 2 vols. Princeton, 1970.
Baron, Roger. *Études sur Hugues de Saint-Victor.* (Paris), 1963.
—— Étude sur l'authenticité de l'œuvre de Hugh de Saint-Victor d'après les MSS Paris Maz. 717, BN 14506 et Douai 360-366', *Scriptorium* 10 (1956), 182-220.
—— 'Note sur l'énigmatique "Summa Sententiarum" ', *RThAM* 25 (1958), 26-41.
—— *Science et sagesse chez Hugues de Saint-Victor.* Paris, 1957.
Beinert, Wolfgang. *Die Kirche-Gottes Heil in der Welt: Die Lehre von der Kirche nach den Schriften des Rupert von Deutz, Honorius Augus-todunensis und Gerhoh von Reichersberg. Ein Beitrag zur Ekklesiologie des 12. Jahrhunderts.* BGPTMA, 13. Münster, 1973.
Bertola, Ermengildo. 'La Glossa ordinaria biblica ed i suoi prob-lemi', *RThAM* 45 (1978), 34-78.
—— 'La "Sententiae Florianenses" della scuola di Abelardo', *Sophia* 18 (1950), 368-78.
Bischoff, Bernhard. 'Der Canticumkommentar des Johannes von Mantua für die Markgräfin Mathilde', *Lebenskräfte in der abendlän-dischen Geistesgeschichte.* Dank-und Erinnerungsgabe an Walter Goetz zum 80. Geburtstage . . . . Marburg/Lahn, 1948, pp. 22-48.

Bischoff, Guntram. 'The Eucharistic Controversy Between Rupert of Deutz and His Anonymous Adversary'. Unpublished dissertation, Princeton Theological Seminary, 1965.

Bliemetzrieder, Franz. 'L'œuvre d'Anselme de Laon et la littérature théologique contemporaine. I. Honorius d'Autun', *RThAM* 5 (1933), 275-91.

—— 'L'œuvre d'Anselme de Laon et la littérature théologique contemporaine. II. Hughes de Rouen', *RThAM* 6 (1934), 261-83, 7 (1935), 28-51.

Boeren, Peter. C. *La Vie et les œuvres de Guiard de Laon (1170 env.-1248)*. The Hague, 1956.

—— 'Un traité eucharistique inédit du XIIe siècle. *Covenientibus vobis in unum* (1 Cor. 11.20)', *Archives d'histoire doctrinale et littéraire du moyen âge* 45 (1978), 181-214.

Borst, Arno. *Die Katharer.* Schriften der Monumenta Germaniae historica, 12. Stuttgart, 1953.

Bouhot, Jean-Paul. *Ratramne de Corbie. Histoire littéraire et controverses doctrinales.* Études augustiniennes. Paris, 1976.

Brady, Ignatius. 'Peter Manducator and the Oral Teaching of Peter Lombard', *Antonianum,* 41 (1966), 454-90.

Braeckmans, Louis. *Confession et communion au moyen âge et concile de Trent.* Recherches et syntheses, section de morale, 6. Gembloux, 1971.

Brigue, Louis. *Alger de Liége. Un Théologien de l'eucharistie au début du XIIᵉ siècle.* Paris, 1936.

Brilioth, Yngve. *Eucharistic Faith and Practice: Evangelical and Catholic.* Translated by A. G. Herbert. London, 1961.

Bakhuizen van den Brink, J. N. 'Ratramn's Eucharistic Doctrine and its Influence in Sixteenth-Century England', *Studies in Church History* 2 (1965), 54-77.

Brooke, Christopher N. L. *Medieval Church and Society.* London, 1971.

—— *The Monastic World, 1000-1300.* New York, 1974.

Browe, Peter. 'Die Ausbreitung des Fronleichnamfestes', *Jahrbuch für Liturgiewissenschaft* 8 (1928), 107-43.

—— 'Die Elevation in der Messe', *Jahrbuch für Liturgiewissenschaft* 9 (1929), 20-66.

—— *Die eucharistischen Wunder des Mittelalters.* Breslauer Studien zur historischen Theologie, Neue Folge, 9. Breslau, 1938.

—— *Die häufige Kommunion im Mittelalter.* Münster, 1938.

—— 'Die Kommunionandacht im Altertum und Mittelalter', *Jahrbuch für Liturgiewissenschaft,* 13 (1933), 45-64.

—— 'Die Kommunion in der Pfarrkirche', *Zeitschrift für katholische Theologie* 53 (1929), 447-516.

—— 'Die Kommunionvorbereitung im Mittelalter', *Zeitschrift für katholische Theologie* 56 (1932), 375-415.

—— 'Die Nuechternheit vor der Messe und Kommunion im Mittelalter', *Ephemerides liturgicae* 45 (1931), 279-87.

—— *Die Pflichtkommunion im Mittelalter.* Münster and Regensbeurg, 1940.

—— *Die Verehrung der Eucharistie im Mittelalter.* Munich, 1933.

—— 'Wann fing man an, die Kommunion außerhalt der Messe auszuteilen', *Theologie und Glaube*, 23 (1931), 755-62.

—— 'Zum Kommunionempfang des Mittelalters', *Jahrbuch für liturgiewissenschaft*, 12 (1932), 161-77.

Buytaert, Eloi. M. (ed.), *Peter Abelard. Proceedings of the International Conference, Louvain, May 10-12, 1971.* The Hague, 1974.

Bynum, Caroline Walker. 'Did the Twelfth Century Discover the Individual?', *Journal of Ecclesiastical History* 31 (1980), 1-17.

Cantin, André. '*Ratio et auctoritas* dans la première phase de la controverse eucharistique entre Bérengar et Lanfranc', *Revue des études augustiniennes* 20 (1974), 155-86.

Capelle, G. C. *Autour du décret de 1210: III. Amaury de Bène. Étude sur son panthéisme formel.* Bibliothèque Thomiste, 16. Paris, 1932.

Capitani, Ovidio. ' "L'affaire berengarienne" ovvero dell'utilità delle monografie', *Studi medievali*, 3rd series, 16, fasc. 1 (1975), 353-78.

Châtillon, Jean. 'Chronique. De Guillaume de Champeaux à Thomas Gallus: chronique d'histoire littéraire et doctrinale de l'école de Saint-Victor', *Revue du moyen âge latin* 8 (1952), 139-62, 247-72.

—— 'Le contenu, l'authenticité et la date du *Liber exceptionum* et des *Sermones centum* de Richard de Saint Victor', *Revue du moyen âge latin* 4 (1948), 23-51, 343-66.

—— 'Pierre le Vénérable et les pétrobrusiens', *Pierre Abélard - Pierre le Vénérable. Les Courants philosophiques, littéraires et artistiques en occident au milieu du XIIe siècle.* Paris, 1975, pp. 165-179.

Chenu, M.-D. 'Un cas de platonisme grammatical au XIIIe siècle', *Revue des sciences philosophiques et théologiques* 51 (1967), 666-8.

Classen, Peter. 'Aus der Wekstatt Gerhohs von Reichersberg: Studien zur Entstehung und Überlieferung von Briefen, Briefsammlungen und Widmungen', *Deutsches Archiv für Erforschung des Mittelalters namens der Monumenta Germaniae Historica* 23 (1967), 31-92.

—— *Gerhoh von Reichersberg. Eine Biographie mit einem Anhang über die Quellen, ihre handschriftliche Überlieferung und ihre Chronologie.* Wiesbaden, 1960.

Clemens, R. E., *et al. Eucharistic Theology Then and Now.* Theological Collections, 9. London, 1968.

Cohn, Norman. *The Pursuit of the Millennium. Revolutionary Millenarians and Mystical Anarchists of the Middle Ages.* Revised and expanded. New York, 1970.

Conciliorum oecumenicorum decreta. 3rd edn. Bologna, 1973.

Constable, Giles (ed.). *The Letters of Peter the Venerable.* 2 vols. Harvard Historical Studies, 78. Cambridge, Massachusetts, 1967.

Constable, Giles and James Kritzeck (eds.). *Petrus Venerabilis, 1156-1956. Studies and Texts Commemorating the Eighth Centenary of His Death.* Studia Anselmiana, 40. Rome, 1956.

Courtney, Francis. *Cardinal Robert Pullen. An English Theologian of the Twelfth Century.* Analecta Gregoriana, 64. Rome, 1954.

Cristiani, Marta. 'La controversia nella cultura del secolo IX', *Studi medievali,* 3rd series, 9 (1968), 167-233.

Daly, Saralyn R. 'Peter Comestor: Master of Histories', *Speculum* 32 (1957), 62-73.

Déchanet, J.-M. *Guillaume de Saint-Thierry; l'homme et son œuvre.* Bibliothèque médiévale. Spirituels préscholastiques, Vol. i. Paris, 1942.

Delhaye, Philippe. 'Un dossier eucharistique d'Anselme de Laon à l'abbaye de Fécamp au XIIe siècle', *L'abbaye bénédictine de Fécamp. Ouvrage scientifique du XIIIe centenaire, 658-1958,* 2. Fécamp, 1960. pp. 153-61.

Dix, Gregory. *The Shape of the Liturgy.* Westminster, 1945.

Dondaine, Antoine. 'Le Manuel de l'Inquisiteur (1230-1330)', *Archivum fratrum praedicatorum* 17 (1947), 85-194.

—— *Un traité néo-manichéen du XIIIe siècle, le Liber de duobus principiis suivi d'un fragment de rituel cathare.* Rome, 1939.

Dürig, Walter. 'Die Scholastiker und die communio sub una specie', *Kyriakon. Festschrift Johannes Quasten.* Edited by Patrick Granfield and Josef A. Jungmann. 2 vols., Münster, 1970.

Dugmore, C. W. *The Mass and the English Reformers.* London, 1958.

Dumoutet, Édouard. *Corpus Domini: Aux sources de la piété eucharistique médiévale.* Paris, 1942.

—— 'La théologie de l'eucharistie à la fin du XIIe siécle: Le témoignage de Pierre le Chantre d'après la "Summa de sacramentis" ', *Archives d'histoires doctrinale et littéraire du moyen âge,* 18-20 (1943-45), 181-262.

—— *Le Christ selon la chair et la vie liturgique au moyen-âge.* Paris, 1932.

—— *Le Désir de voir l'hostie et les origines de la dévotion au saint-sacrement.* Paris, 1926.

van Elswijk, H. C. *Gilbert Porreta. Sa vie, son œuvre, sa pensée.* Spicilegium sacrum Lovaniense. Études et documents, 33. Louvain, 1966.

Endres, Joseph. *Honorius Augustodunensis. Beitrag zur Geschichte des geistigen Lebens im 12. Jahrhundert.* Kempten and Munich, 1906.

Flint, Valerie I. J. 'Some Notes on the Early Twelfth Century Commentaries on the Psalms', *RThAM* 38 (1971), 80-8.

—— 'The Career of Honorius Augustodunensis: Some Fresh Evidence', *Revue bénédictine*, 82 (1972), 215-42.

—— 'The Chronology of the Works of Honorius Augustodunensis', *Revue bénédictine* 82 (1972), 215-42.

—— 'The Place and Purpose of the Works of Honorius Augustodunensis', *Revue bénédictine* 87 (1977), 97-127.

—— 'The School of Laon: A Reconsideration', *RThAM* 43 (1976), 89-100.

Fortia d'Urban, Agricola Joseph, marquis de. *Histoire et ouvrages de Hugues Metel né a Toul en 1080.* Paris, 1839.

Franz, Adolf. *Die kirchlichen Benediktionen im Mittelalter.* 2 vols. Freiburg, 1909.

—— *Die Messe im deutschen Mittelalter. Beiträge zur Geschichte der Liturgie und des religiösen Volkslebens.* Freiburg, 1902; reprinted Darmstadt, 1963.

Frédéricq, Paul. *Corpus documentorum Inquisitionis haereticae pravitatis neerlandicae*, 1. Hoogeschool van Gent. Werken van den practischen leergang van vaderlandsche geschiednis, 1. Ghent and s'Gravenhage, 1889.

Friedberg, Emil (ed.). *Quinque compilationes antique.* Leipzig, 1882.

Garrigues, Marie-Odile. 'Quelques recherches sur l'œuvre d'Honorius Augustodunensis', *Revue d'histoire ecclésiatique* 70 (1975), 388-425.

Garvin, Joseph N. 'Magister Udo, a Source of Peter of Poitiers' *Sentences'*, *New Scholasticism* 28 (1954), 286-98.

—— 'the Manuscripts of Udo's *Summa super sententias Petri Lombardi*', *Scriptorium* 16 (1962), 376.

Geiselmann, Joseph Rupert. *Die Abendmahlslehre an der Wende der christlichen Spätantike zum Frühmittelalter. Isidor von Seville und das Sakrament der Eucharistie.* Munich, 1933.

—— *Die Eucharistielehre der Vorscholastik.* Forschungen zur christlichen Literatur-und Dogmengeschichte, 15/ 1-3. Paderborn, 1926.

—— 'Die Stellung des Guibert von Nogent in der Eucharistielehre der Frühscholastik', *Theologische Quartalschrift* 110 (1929), 66-84, 279-305.

—— 'Zur Eucharistielehre der Frühscholastic', *Theologische Revue* 29 (1930), 1-12.

—— 'Zur frühmittelalterlichen Lehre vom Sakrament der Eucharistie', *Theologische Quartalschrift* 116 (1935), 323-403.

Geyer, Bernard. 'Neues und Altes zu den *Sententiae divinitatis*', *Mélanges Joseph de Ghellinck, S. J.* 2 vols. Museum Lessianum. Section historique, 13-14. Gembloux, 1951. Vol. ii, pp. 617-30.

de Ghellinck, Joseph. 'Eucharistie au XIIe siécle en occident', *DTC* 5 (1924), 1233-1302.

—— *Le Mouvement théologique du XIIe siècle. Sa préparation lointaine avant et autour de Pierre Lombard ses rapports avec les initiatives des canonistes. Études, recherches et documents.* 2nd rev. edn. Museum Lessianum. Section historique, 10. Brugge, Brussels, and Paris, 1948.

—— *L'Essor de la littérature latine au XIIe siècle.* Museum Lessianum Section historique, 4-5. 2nd edn. Brussels, Brugge, and Paris, 1955.

Gibson, Margaret. 'Lanfranc's "Commentary on the Pauline Epistles" ', *Journal of Theological Studies* 22 (1971), 86-112.

—— 'The Case of Berengar of Tours', *Councils and Assemblies: Papers read at the Eighth Summer Meeting and the Ninth Winter Meeting of the Ecclesiastical History Society.* Edited by G. J. Cuming and Derek Baker. Cambridge, 1971. pp. 61-8.

Glorieux, Palémon. 'Essaie sur les "Questiones in epistolas Pauli" du Ps-Hughes de St. Victor', *RThAM* 19 (1952), 48-59.

Grabmann, Martin. *Die Geschichte der scholastischen Methode nach den gedruckten und ungedruckten Quellen.* 2 vols. Freiburg-im-Breisgau, 1909-11. Reprinted Berlin, 1957.

Grant, Gerard G. 'The Elevation of the Host: A reaction to Twelfth Century Heresy', *Theological Studies* 1 (1940), 228-50.

Gründel, Johannes. *Das 'Speculum Universale' des Radulfus Ardens.* Mitteilungen des Gragmann-Instituts der Universität München, 5. (Munich, 1961).

—— *Die Lehre von den Umständen der menschlichen Handlung im Mittelalter.* BGPTM, 39/5, Münster, 1963.

Grundmann, Herbert. *Religiöse Bewegungen im Mittelalter. Untersuchungen über die geschichtlichen Zusammenhänge zwischen der Ketzerei, den Bettelorden und der religiösen Frauenbewegung im 12. und 13. Jahrhundert und über die geschichtlichen Grundlagen der deutschen Mystik. Anhang. Neue Beiträge zur Geschichte der religiösen Bewegungen im Mittelalter.* Darmstadt, 1961.

Guth, Klaus. *Guibert von Nogent und die hochmittelalterliche Kritik an der Reliquienverehrung.* Studien und Mitteilungen zur Geschichte des Benediktiner-Ordens und seiner Zweige, 21. Ottobeuren and Augsburg, 1970.

Guzie, Tad. *Jesus and the Eucharist.* New York, Paramus, N. J., and Toronto, 1974.

Haacke, Rhaban. 'Zur Eucharistielehre des Rupert von Deutz', *RThAM* 32 (1965), 20-42.

Häring, Nicolaus. 'A Study in the Sacramentology of Alger of Liège', *Mediaeval Studies* 20 (1958), 41-78.

—— 'Berengar's Definitions of *Sacramentum* and Their Influence on Medieval Theology', *Mediaeval Studies* 10 (1948), 109-46.

—— 'Die Sententie magistri gisleberti pictavensis episcopi', *Archives d'histoire et littéraire du moyen âge* 45 (1978), 83-183 and 46 (1979), 45-105.

—— *Die Zwettler Summe. Einleitung und Texte*. BGTPMA, Neue folge, 15. Münster, 1977.

—— 'Simon of Tournai and Gilbert of Poitiers', *Mediaeval Studies* 27 (1965), 225-30.

—— '*The Sententiae Magistri A* (Vat. *MS.* lat. 4361) and the School of Laon', *Mediaeval Studies* 17 (1955), 1-45.

Hartmann, Wilfried. 'Psalmenkommentare aus der Zeit der Reform und der Frühscholastik', *Studi gregoriani* 7 (1972), 315-66.

Hauréau, Berthelemy. *Les œuvres de Hugues de Saint-Victor. Essai critique.* 2nd edn. Paris, 1886.

Heinzmann, Richard. *Die 'Compilatio quaestionum theologiae secundum Magistrum Martinum'.* Mitteilungen des Grabmann-Instituts der Universität München, 9. (Munich, 1964).

—— *Die 'Institutiones in sacram paginam' des Simon von Tournai. Einleitung und Quaestionenverzeichnis*. Veröffentlickungen des Grabmanns-Institutes zur Erforschung der mittelalterlichen Theologie und Philosophie, neue Folge, 1. Munich, Paderborn, and Vienna, 1967.

Hermanns, Robert. *Petri Abaelardi ejusque primae scholae doctrina de sacramentis.* Pontificum Athenaeum Antonianum. Facultas s. theologiae, Theses ad Lauream, 147. Mecheln, 1965.

Heurtevent, Raoul. *Durand de Troarn et les origines de l'hérésie bérengarienne.* Études de théologie historique, 5. Paris, 1912.

Histoire littéraire de la France. 40 vols. to 1974. Paris, 1733-1974.

Hödl, Ludwig. 'Der Transsubstantiationsbegriff in der scholastischen Theologie des 12. Jahrhunderts', *RThAM* 31 (1964), 230-59.

—— *Die Geschichte der scholastichen Literatur und der Theologie der Schlüsselgewalt*, Vol. i, BGPTMA, 38/4. Münster, 1960.

—— 'Die ontologische Frage im frühscholastischen Eucharistietraktat Calix benedictionis', *Sola ratione. Anselm-Studien für Pater Dr. h. c. Franciscus Salesius Schmitt OSB zum 75. Geburtstag am 20 Dezember 1969.* Stuttgart-Bad Cannstatt, 1970, pp. 87-110.

—— 'Sacramentum et res—Zeichen und Bezeichnetes. Eine begriffsgeschichtliche Arbeit zum frühscholastischen Eucharistietraktat', *Scholastik* 38 (1963), 161-82.

Holböck, Ferdinand. *Der eucharistische und der mystische Leib Christi in ihren Beziehungen zueinander nach der Lehre der Frühscholastik.* Dissertatio ad lauream in facultate theologica pontificiae universitatis Gregorianae. Rome, 1941.

Hugo, Charles Louis. *Sacrae antiquitatis monumenta historica, dogmatica, diplomatica.* 2 vols. Estival, 1725-31.

Hunt, Richard W. 'English Learning in the Late Twelfth Century', *Transactions of the Royal Historical Society,* 4th ser. 19 (1936), 19-42.

Huygens, R. B. C. 'A propos de Berengar et son traité de l'Eucharistie', *Revue bénédictine* 66 (1966), pp. 133-39.

Jaffé, Philipp. *Regestra pontificum romanorum* . . . 2nd rev. edn., Vol. ii, Leipzig, 1888.

Jorissen, Hans. *Die Entfaltung der Transsubstantiationslehre bis zum Beginn der Hochscholastik.* Münsterische Beiträge zur Theologie, 28/1. Münster, 1965.

Jungmann, Joseph. *Missarum sollemnia; eine genetische Erklärung der römischen Messe.* 5th rev. edn. Vienna, Friedburg, and Basel, 1962.

Kaeppeli, Thomas. 'Gerardus Novariensis auteur de la Somme "Ne transgrediaris"', *RThAM* 29 (1962), 294-97.

—— 'Une somme contre les hérétiques de s. Pierre Martyre(?)', *Archivum fratrum praedicatorum* 17 (1947), 295-335.

Kelly, John N.D. *Early Christian Doctrines.* 5th edn., San Francisco, 1978.

Kennedy, Vincent L. 'The Date of the Parisian Decree on the Elevation of the Host', *Mediaeval Studies* 8 (1946), 87-96.

—— 'The Moment of Consecration and the Elevation of the Host', *Mediaeval Studies* 6 (1944), 121-50.

Kleineidam, Erich. 'Literargeschichtliche Bermerkungen zur Eucharistielehre Hugos von St. Victor', *Scholastik* 24 (1949), 564-6.

Kramp, Joseph. 'Des Wilhelm von Auvergne "Magisterium divinale"', *Gregorianum* 1 (1920), 538-84; 2 (1921), 42-78, 174-87.

Lacombe, Georges. *Prepositini, cancellarii Parisiensis (1206-1210) Opera omnia.* Vol. i. *La Vie et les œuvres de Prévostin.* Bibliothèque Thomiste, 11. Kain, 1927.

Landgraf, Artur M. 'A Study of the Academic Latitude of Peter of Capua', *New Scholasticism* 14 (1940), 57-74.

—— 'Der Paulinenkommentar des Hervaeus von Bourg-Dieu', *Biblica* 21 (1940), 113-32.

—— 'Die Quaestones super epistolas s. Pauli und die Allegoriae', *Collectanea franciscana* 16 (1946), 186-200.

—— 'Die Quellen der anonymen *Summe* des Cod. Vat. *lat.* 10754', *Mediaeval Studies* 9 (1947), 296-300.

—— 'Die Summa Sententiarum und die Summe des Cod. Vat. lat. 1345', *RThAM* 11 (1939), 260-70.

—— *Dogmengeschichte der Frühscholastik.* 4 vols. in 6. Regensburg, 1952-6.

—— 'Drei Trabanten des Magisters Gandulphus von Bologna', *Collectanea franciscana* 7 (1937), 357-73.

—— *Introduction à l'histoire de la littérature théologique de la scolastique naissante.* Translated by Albert M. Landry and Louis B. Geiger. Université de Montréal. Publications de l'Institut d'études médiévales, 32. Montreal and Paris, 1973.

—— 'Recherches sur les écrits de Pierre le Mangeur', *RThAM* 3 (1931), 292-306, 341-72.

—— 'Sentenzglossen des beginnenden 13. Jahrhunderts', *RThAM* 10 (1938), 36-55.

—— 'Studien zur Theologie des zwölften Jahrhunderts. II. Literarhistorische Bemerkungen zu den Sentenzen des Robertus Pullus', *Traditio* 1 (1943), 210-22.

—— 'Udo und Magister Martinus', *RThAM* 11 (1939), 62-4.

—— 'Untersuchungen zur Gelehrtengeschichte des 12. Jahrhunderts', *Miscellanea Giovanni Mercati*, Vol. ii. Studi e Testi 122. Vatican City, 1946, pp. 259-81.

—— 'Werke aus dem Bereich der Summa Sententiarum und Anselms von Laon', *Divus Thomas. Jahrbuch für philosophie und Spekulative Theologie*, 3rd series, 14 (1936), 209-16.

Leclercq, Jean. 'Les méditations eucharistiques d'Arnaud de Bonneval', *RThAM* 13 (1946), 40-56.

Leclerq, Jean and J. P. Bonnes. *Un maître de la vie spirituelle au XIᵉ siècle: Jean de Fécamp.* Paris, 1946.

Lottin, Odon. 'La doctrine d'Anselme de Laon sur les dons du Saint-Esprit et son influence', *RThAM* 24 (1957), 267-95.

——'Les théories du péché originel au XIIᵉ siècle. III. Tradition Augustinienne', *RThAM* 12 (1940), 236-74.

—— *Psychologie et morale aux XIIᵉ et XIIIᵉ siècles.* 6 vols. Louvain-Gembloux, 1942-60.

—— 'Questions inédites de Hugues de Saint-Victor', *RThAM* 26 (1959), 177-213; 27 (1960), 42-6.

de Lubac, Henri. *Corpus mysticum: L'Eucharistie et l'église au moyen âge. Étude historique.* 2nd rev. edn. Théologie. Études publiées sous le direction de la Faculté de Théologie S. J. de Lyon-Fourvière, 3. Paris, 1949.

—— 'La *res sacramenti* chez Gerhoh de Reichersberg', *Études de critique et d'histoire religieuses.* Bibliothèque de la faculté catholique de théologie de Lyon, 2. Lyon, 1948, pp. 35-42.

Luscombe, David E. *The School of Peter Abelard: The influence of Abelard's thought in the early scholastic period.* Cambridge studies in medieval life and thought, new series, 14. Cambridge, 1969.

Mabillon, Jean. *Vetera analecta, sive collectio veterum aliquot operum* . . . 2nd rev. edn. Paris, 1723.

MacKinnon, H. 'William de Montibus: A Medieval Teacher', *Essays in Medieval History Presented to Bertie Wilkinson.* Edited by T. A. Sandquist and M. R. Powicke. Toronto, 1969, pp. 32-45.

McCue, James F. 'The Doctrine of Transubstantiation from Berengar through the Council of Trent', *Lutherans and Catholics in Dialogue. III. The Eucharist.* New York and Washington, D. C., 1967.

MacDonald, A. J. *Berengar and the Reform of Sacramental Doctrine.* London, 1935.

McGuire, Martin R. P. and Dressler, Hermigild. *Introduction to Medieval Latin Studies. A Syllabus and Bibliographical Guide.* Washington, D. C., 1977.

Macy, Gary. 'A Bibliographical Note on Richardus Praemonstratensis', *Analecta Praemonstratensia* 52 (1976), 64-9.

—— 'The Development of the Notion of Eucharistic Change in the Writings of Thomas Aquinas.' Unpublished M.A. thesis, Marquette University, 1973.

Manselli, Raoul. 'Il monacho Enrico e la sua eresia', *Bullettino dell' Instituto storico italiano per il medio evo e archivo muratoriano* 65 (1953), 1-63.

—— *La Religion populaire au moyen âge. Problèmes de méthode et d'histoire.* Conférence Albert-le-Grand, 1973. Montreal and Paris, 1975.

—— *Studi sulle eresie del secolo XII.* 2nd rev. edn. Instituto storico italiano per il medio evo. Studi storici, 5. Rome, 1975.

Martène, Edmond and Ursin Durand. *Veterum scriptorum et monumentorum historicorum, dogmaticorum, moralium, amplissima collectio.* 9 vols. Paris, 1724-33.

Martin, Raymond M. 'Notes sur l'œvre littéraire de Pierre le Mangeur', *RThAM* 3 (1931), 54-66.

Mascall, E. L. *Corpus Christi. Essays on the Church and the Eucharist.* 2nd rev. edn. London, 1965.

McKitterick, Rosamond. *The Frankish Church and the Carolingian Reforms 789-895.* Royal Historical Society Studies in History, 1. London, 1977.

Megivern, James J. *Concomitance and Communion. A Study in Eucharistic Doctrine and Practice.* Studia Friburgensia, new series, 33. Freiburg, 1963.

Meyer, Hans Bernhard. 'Die Elevation im deutschen Mittelalter und bei Luther', *Zeitschrift für katholische Theologie* 85 (1963), 162-217.

da Milano, Ilarino. *L'eresia di Ugo Speroni nella confutazione del maestro Vacario. Testo inedito del secolo XII con studio storico e dottrinale.* Studi e Testi, 115. Vatican City, 1945.

—— 'Le eresie popolari del secolo XI nell'Europa occidentale', *Studi gregoriani* 2 (1947), 43-89.

Mirgeler, Albert. *Mutations of Western Christianity.* Translated by Edward Quinn. London, 1964.

de Montclos, Jean. *Lanfranc et Bérengar; La Controverse eucharistique du XIe siècle.* Spicilegium sacrum Lovaniense. Études et documents, 37. Louvain, 1971.

Moore, Philip S. 'The Authorship of the *Allegoriae super vetus et novum testamentum*', *New Scholasticism* 9 (1935), 209-25.

—— *The Works of Peter of Poitiers, Master of Theology and Chancellor of Paris (1193-1205).* Publications in Mediaeval Studies, 1. Notre Dame, Indiana, 1936.

Moore, Philip S., Joseph N. Garvin, and Marthe Dulong. *Sententiae Petri Pictaviensis.* Vol. ii. Publications in Medieval Studies, 11. Notre Dame, Indiana, 1950.

Moore, R. I. *The Birth of Popular Heresy.* Documents of Medieval History, 1. London, 1975.

Morin, Germain. 'Les *Dicta* d'Heriger sur l'Eucharistie', *Revue bénédictine* 24 (1908), 1-18.

Morris, Colin. *The Discovery of the Individual, 1050-1200.* Church History Outlines, 5. London, 1972.

—— 'Individualism in Twelfth-Century Religion. Some Further Reflections', *Journal of Ecclesiastical History* 31 (1980), 195-206.

Murray, Albert Victor. *Abelard and St. Bernard; a study in twelfth century 'modernism'.* Manchester and New York, 1967.

Neunheuser, Burkhard. *L'Eucharistie. II. Au moyen âge et à l'époque moderne.* Translated by A. Liefooghe. Histoire des dogme, 4/b. Paris, 1966.

Nocke, Franz-Joseph. *Sakrament und personaler Vollzug bei Albertus Magnus.* BGPTMA, 41/4. Münster, 1967.

Noonan, John T., Jr. 'Who was Roland?', *Law, Church and Society. Essays in Honor of Stephan Kuttner.* Edited by Kenneth Pennington and Robert Somerville. Philadelphia, 1977, pp. 21-48.

Ohly, Friedrich. *Hohelied-Studien. Grundzüge einer Geschichte der Hohelie-dauslegung des Abendlandes bis um 1200.* Schriften der wissenschaftlichen Gesellschaft an der Johann Wolfgang Goethe. Universität Frankfurt am Main, Geisteswissenschaftliche Reihe, 1. Wiesbaden, 1958.

Ostlender, Heinrich. 'Die Sentenzenbücher der Schule Abaelards', *Theologische Quartalschrift* 117 (1936), 208-52.

Ott, Ludwig. *Untersuchungen zur theologischen Briefliteratur der Frühscholastik; unter besonderer Berücksichtigung des Viktorinerkreises.* BGPTM, 34. Münster, 1937.

Oursel, Raymond. *La Dispute et la grâce: Essai sur la rédemption d'Abélard.* Publications de l'Université de Dijon, 19. Paris, 1959.

Oury, Guy. 'Essai sur la spiritualité d'Hervé de Bourg-Dieu', *Revue d'ascétique et de mystique* 43 (1967), 369-92.

—— 'Recherches sur Ernaud, Abbe dé Bonneval, historien de Saint Bernard', *Revue Mabillon* 268 (1977), 97-127.

Pelikan, Jaroslav. 'A First-Generation Anselmian, Guibert of Nogent', *Continuity and Discontinuity in Church History. Essays Presented to George Huntston Williams on the Occasion of his 65th Birthday.* Edited by F. Forrestor Church and Timothy George. Studies in the History of Christian Thought, 19. Leiden, 1979, pp. 92-102.

—— *The Growth of Medieval Theology (600-1300).* The Christian Tradition, vol. iii. Chicago and London, 1978.

Peppermüller, Rolf. 'Zum Fortwirken von Abaelard's Römerbrief-kommentar in der mittelalterlichen Exegese', *Pierre Abélard-Pierre le Vénérable: Les Courants philosophiques, littéraires et artistiques en occident au milieu du XIIe siècle.* Paris, 1975, pp. 557-67.

de Peregrini, Bartholomeus. *Opus divinum de sacra ac fertili Bergomensi vinea.* Brescia, 1553.

Pierre Abélard-Pierre le Vénérable. Les Courants philosophiques, litéraires et artistiques en occident au milieu du XIIe siècle. Abbaye du Cluny. 2 au 9 juillet 1972. Colloques internationaux du centre national de la recherche scientifique, 546. Paris, 1975.

Pilarczyk, Daniel Edward (ed.). *Praepositini cancellarii de sacramentis et de novissimis (Summae theologicae pars quarta). A Critical Text and Introduction.* Collectio Urbaniana. Series III. Textus et documenta, 7. Rome, 1964.

Powers, Joseph. *Eucharistic Theology.* New York, 1967.

Powicke Frederick Maurice. *Stephen Langton: Being the Ford Lectures delivered in the University of Oxford in Hilary Term 1927.* Oxford, 1928.

Principe, Walter Henry. *William of Auxerre's Theology of the Hypostatic Union.* Pontifical Institute of Mediaeval Studies. Studies and Texts 7. Toronto, 1963.

Reinhardt, Heinrich J. F. 'Die Identität der Sententiae Magistri A. mit dem Compilationes Ailmeri und die Frage nach dem Autor dieser frühscholastichen Sentenzsammlung', *Theologie und Philosophie* 50 (1975), 381-403.

—— 'Literarkritische und theologiegeschichtliche Studie zu den Sententiae magistri A. und deren Prolog (Ad iustitiam credere debemus)', *Archives d'histoire doctrinale et littéraire du moyen âge* 36 (1969), 23-56.

Roberts, Phyllis Barzillay. *Stephanus de lingua-tonante. Studies in the*

Sermons of Stephen Langton. Pontifical Institute of Mediaeval Studies. Studies and Texts, 16. Toronto, 1968.

Robertson, Durant W., Jr. *Abelard and Heloise*. Crosscurrents in World History Series. New York, 1972.

Russell, Jeffrey Burton. *Dissent and Reform in the Early Middle Ages*. Center for Medieval and Renaissance Studies, 1. Berkeley and Los Angeles, 1965.

—— 'Interpretations of the Origins of Medieval Heresy', *Mediaeval Studies* 25 (1963), 25-53.

—— *Religious Dissent in the Middle Ages*. Major Issues in History Series. New York, London, Sydney, and Toronto, 1971.

St. Pierre, Jules A. 'The Theological Thought of William of Auxerre. An Introductory Bibliography', *RThAM* 33 (1966), 147-55.

Schlette, Heinz Robert. 'Die Eucharistielehre Hugos von St. Viktor', *Zeitschrift für katholische Theologie* 81(1959), 67-100, 163-210.

—— *Die Lehre von der geistliche Kommunion bei Bonaventura, Albert dem Grossem und Thomas von Aquin*. Münchener theologische Studien. Systematische Abteilung, 17. München, 1959.

Schulte, Raphael. *Die Messe als opfer der Kirche. Die Lehre frühmittelalterlicher Autoren über das eucharistiche Opfer*. Liturgiewissenschaftliche Quellen und Forschungen, 35. Münster, 1958.

Selge, Kurt-Victor. *Die ersten Waldenser*. 2 vols. Arbeiten zur Kirchengeschichte, 37/1-2. Berlin, 1967.

Shrader, Charles R. 'The False Attribution of an Eucharistic Tract to Gerbert of Aurillac', *Mediaeval Studies* 35 (1973), 178-204.

Sikes, Jeffrey Garrett. *Peter Abailard*. Cambridge, 1932.

Silvestre, Herbert. 'A propos de la lettre d'Anselme de Laon à Héribrand de Saint Laurent', *RThAM* 28 (1961), 5-25.

—— 'Notes sur la controverse de Rupert de Saint-Laurent avec Anselme de Laon et Guillaume de Champeaux', *Saint-Laurent de Liège. Église, Abbaye et Hospital Militaire: Mille ans d'histoire*. Rita Lejeune (ed.). Liège, 1968, pp. 63-80.

Smalley, Beryl. 'Gilbertus Universalis, Bishop of London (1128-34), and the Problem of the "Glossa ordinaria" '. *RThAM* 7 (1935), 235-62, 8 (1936), 24-60.

—— 'Les commentaires bibliques de l'époque romane: glose ordinaire et glose perimées', *Cahiers de civilisation médiévale* 4 (1961), 15-22.

—— 'Peter Comestor on the Gospels and His Sources', *RThAM* 46 (1979), 84-129.

—— 'Some Gospel Commentaries of the Early Twelfth Century', *RThAM* 45 (1978), 147-180.

—— *The Study of the Bible in the Middle Ages*. Notre Dame, Indiana, 1964.

Smalley, Beryl, and Georges Lacombe. 'The Lombard's Commentary on Isaias and Other Fragments', *New Scholasticism* 5 (1931), 123-62.

Smith, Mahlon H. *And Taking Bread . . . Cerularius and the Azyme Controversy of 1054.* Théologie historique, 47. Paris, 1978.

Southern, Richard W. 'Lanfranc of Bec and Berengar of Tours', *Studies in Medieval History Presented to Frederick Maurice Powicke.* R. W. Hunt, W. A. Pantin, and R. W. Southern (eds). Oxford, 1948, pp. 27-48.

—— 'Master Vacarius and the Beginning of an English Academic Tradition', *Medieval Learning and Literature. Essays presented to Richard William Hunt.* Edited by J. J. G. Alexander and M. T. Gibson. Oxford, 1976. pp. 257-86.

—— *St. Anselm and His Biographer. A Study of Monastic Life and Thought, 1059-c.1130.* Cambridge, 1963.

—— *The Making of the Middle Ages.* London, 1953.

Spätling, Luchesius. 'Die Legation des Erzbischofs Hugh von Rouen (1134/35)', *Antonianum,* 43 (1968), 195-216.

Stegmüller, Friedrich. *Repertorium biblicum medii aevi.* 7 vols. Madrid, 1940-61.

Stein, Peter. 'Vacarius and the Civil Law', *Church and Government in the Middle Ages. Essays presented to C. R. Cheney on his 70th Birthday.* C. N. L. Brooke, D. E. Luscombe, G. H. Martin, and Dorothy Owen (eds.). Cambridge, New York, and Melbourne, 1970, pp. 119-37.

Stoelen, Anselme. 'Bruno le Chartreaux, Jean Gratiadei et la "Lettre de S. Anselme" sur l'eucharistie', *RThAM* 34 (1967), 18-83.

—— 'Les commentaires scripturaires attribués à Bruno le Chartreux', *RThAM* 25 (1958), 177-247.

Stone, Darwell. *A History of the Holy Eucharist.* 2 vols. London, 1909.

Sylvester, Walter. 'The Communing with Three Blades of Grass, of the Knights-Errant', *Dublin Review* 121 (1897), 80-98.

Thouzellier, Christine. *Catharisme et valdéisme en Languedoc à la fin du XIIᵉ et au début du XIIIᵉ siècle.* Publications de la faculté des lettres et sciences humaines de Paris. Série 'Recherches', 27. Paris, 1966.

—— *Hérésie et hérétiques. Vaudois, cathares, patarins, albigeois.* Storia e letteratura. Raccolta di studi e testi, 116. Rome, 1969.

—— 'Le "Liber antiheresis" de Durand de Huesca et le "Contra hereticos" d'Ermengaud de Béziers', *Revue d'histoire ecclésiastique* 55 (1960), 130-41.

Van den Eynde, Damien. 'Complimentary Note on the Early Scholastic *Commentarii in psalmos*', *Franciscan Studies* 17 (1957), 149-72.

Weisweiler, Heinrich. 'Die Arbeitweise der sogennanten Sententiae

Anselmi. Ein Beitrag zum Entstehen der systematischen Werke der Theologie', *Scholastik* 34 (1959), 190-232.

—— *Das Schrifttum der Schule Anselms von Laon und Wilhelms von Champeaux in deutschen Bibliotheken: Ein Beitrag zur Geschichte der Verbreitung der ältesten scholastichen Schule in deutschen Landen.* BGPTM, 33/1-2. Münster, 1936.

—— 'Hugos von St. Victor Dialogus de sacramentis legis naturalis et scriptae als frühscholastisches Quellenwerk', *Miscellanea Giovanni Mercati.* Vol. ii. Studi e testi, 122. Vatican City, 1946. pp. 179-219.

—— 'Le recueil des sentences Deus de cuius principio et fine tacetur', *RThAM* 5 (1933), 245-74.

—— 'Sakrament als Symbol und Teilhabe. Der Einfluß des Ps.-Dionysius auf die allgemeine Sakramentenlehre Hugos von St. Victor', *Scholastik* 27 (1952), 321-43.

—— 'Zur Einflusssphäre der "Vorlesungen" Hugos von St. Victor', *Mélanges Joseph de Ghellinck, S. J.* 2 vols. Museum Lessianum. Section historique, 13-14. Gembloux, 1951. Vol. ii, 527-81.

Williams, John R. 'The Twelfth Century "Questiones" of Carpentras MS. 110', *Mediaeval Studies* 28 (1966), 300-27.

Wilmart, Andre. 'Le série et la date des ouvrages de Guillaume de Saint-Thierry', *Revue Mabillon* 14 (1924), 157-67.

—— 'Un commentarie des Psaumes restitué à Anselm de Laon', *RThAM* 8 (1936), 325-44.

INDEX OF MANUSCRIPTS

GENERAL INDEX